DEMOCRACY AND DETERRENCE

Also by Philip Bobbitt

TRAGIC CHOICES
(*with Guido Calabresi*)

CONSTITUTIONAL FATE

US NUCLEAR STRATEGY: A Reader
(*editor with Lawrence Freedman and Gregory F. Treverton*)

Democracy and Deterrence

The History and Future of Nuclear Strategy

Philip Bobbitt

Professor of Law, University of Texas
Fellow of Nuffield College, Oxford

M
MACMILLAN
PRESS

First published 1988

Published by
THE MACMILLAN PRESS LTD
Houndmills, Basingstoke, Hampshire RG21 2XS
and London
Companies and representatives
throughout the world

Printed in Hong Kong

British Library Cataloguing in Publication Data
Bobbitt, Philip
Democracy and deterrence.
1. Nuclear warfare 2. United States —
Military policy
I. Title
355.4'307'0973 U263
ISBN 0–333–43537–0 (hardcover)
ISBN 0–333–43721–7 (paperback)

To Oscar Price Bobbitt

'What makes a subject hard to understand – if it's something significant and important – is not that before you can understand it you need to be specially trained in abstruse matters, but the contrast between understanding the subject and what most people *want* to see.'

— LUDWIG WITTGENSTEIN, *Vermischte Bemerkungen*

Contents

List of Tables

List of Illustrations

Acknowledgements

I am anxious to express thanks for the resources and moral encouragement of those persons and institutions on whom I have so depended during the years I wrote this book.

Foremost among these institutions are the International Institute for Strategic Studies in London, Nuffield College, Oxford, and the University of Texas at Austin, Texas. A tacit collaboration among these remarkable groups enabled my work to proceed at a pace restrained only by my understanding.

I am especially grateful to Dr Gregory F. Treverton, who brought me to the Institute as a Visiting Fellow in 1981; to Professor Michael Howard – a founding father of the IISS – who brought me to Oxford to continue my researches; to the Warden of Nuffield College, Mr Michael Brock, and the Dean of the Law School at the University of Texas, Mr Mark Yudof, who provided academic environments within which I could work and flourish.

A great many persons have read one version or another of this manuscript; many of these persons were students, either in Oxford or Austin. Diverse officials and former senior officials in the US Government read copies. I particularly wish to thank Dr Ronald Stivers, Director of the Office of Nuclear Targeting for the US Department of Defense, who convened a study group to comment on an earlier version of this book; Mr McGeorge Bundy; Mr Lloyd Cutler; Dr William V. Hyland; Mr Walter Slocombe. My colleagues in Texas, Dr Susan Chisholm, Professor Richard Markovits, Professor Steven Weinberg, and in England, Professor Lawrence Freedman and Professor Adam Roberts, have been especially supportive. I am grateful also to Dr Richard Darilek, Dr Robert Nurick and Dr John van Ondenaren, of the RAND Corporation. This is an incomplete list, partial in two senses of the word, of debts scarcely discharged by mere remembering. For Philip Williams and Hedley Bull, this acknowledgement of professional debts comes too late and there is only memory and gratitude that has no object to release it.

David Boelzner was my research assistant during the preparation of the final draft; formerly my student, he became my assistant, interrogator and friend. Miss Selden Wallace 'proofed' these pages; she is perfect.

All these, and others unnamed here, gave me valuable criticism and timely aid. While they cannot be held responsible for the views expressed herein – indeed each would doubtless disagree with some of my formulations and conclusions – this book would not have its present form but for this encouragement and selfless efforts. And this book might not exist, in any form, but for the generous and decisive support of the M.D. Anderson Foundation. Of the trustees who stoutheartedly supported my work I will mention only one: Mr Gibson Gayle whose confidence and trust I especially value.

A book belongs to no one once it is written. And yet it is somehow owed. Miss Marlise Aimone, whose patience and sublime attention made my working hours comfortable, then gave me back the hours spent alone.

Parse the word 'encouragement'. For the enfusing of courage I wish to thank Mr O. P. Bobbit. And I should like to observe that the whole point of writing a book such as this is learned from those one admires, who by example show their faith in thought.

Everbody knows how difficult it is to prepare a manuscript through many drafts, and I am grateful to Candace Howard for her friendly yet tireless work in coping with a complicated text. My editors at the publishers – Mr T. M. Farmiloe, Miss Judy Carreck, Mr Simon Winder – have guided the book to you, the reader. I thank them.

To my colleagues and small circle of readers on both sides of the Atlantic, who inspire the confidence and hope that animates this book, I offer these grateful acknowledgements.

PHILIP BOBBITT

Introduction

1 The Ideologies of Nuclear Deterrence

Nel mezzo del cammin di nostra vita mi ritrovai per una selva oscura chè la diritta via era smaritta.

(In the middle of the journey of our life I came to within a dark wood where the straight way was lost.)

Canto I, *Inferno*

The development of the ideas of nuclear deterrence has reached an impasse, one that almost replicates, intellectually, the stalemate that has been thought to persist strategically. Two views, locked in dialectic since the beginning of the thermonuclear age, appear at present as if imprisoned in amber. Neither offers independent criteria for choosing between them. Taking these two views together, we are unable to predict the future conditions of deterrence. And finally, they do not enable us to decide whether effective deterrence is eroding or simply recurring in a cyclical pattern of anxiety and reassurance.

These two views have become ideologies, clusters of opinions that are internally consistent while antithetically hostile to each other. One view stresses the sufficiency of the countervalue[1] deterrent and the benefits of such sufficiency so that we can know when we have 'enough' weapons for deterrence; it stresses the risks of threatening the enemy's capacity for retaliation and the value of stability; and it assumes the inevitability of the annihilation of the developed world if nuclear weapons should ever come to be used in war.

The opposing view focuses on the *relative* outcomes of a nuclear war, implicitly assuming that something short of complete destruction is possible both for one's own country and for one's adversary; it focuses on preparing to achieve significant strategic objectives should deterrence fail (and by such preparation, ensuring deterrence); and it aims to deny the enemy the achievement of his objectives by destroying his capability to wage war and limiting the damage he can inflict. Thus the second view relies on counterforce[2] strikes and technologies for defence.

The nuclear strategy of the United States has never been wholly given over to either of these views; neither has it ever resolved their essential tension. Recently, a leading commentator lamented,

> the absence of doctrinal consensus in the field [of nuclear strategy. It is unreasonable for the community of strategists to still be] undecided as to the *desirability* (as opposed to the technical feasibility) of civil defense, of a major hard-target kill capability, or of the posing of a credible threat to the Soviet political leadership.[3]

There can be no such consensus, however, so long as the present opposing paradigms structure the debate, for each depends upon contradictory assumptions about the fundamental nature of human conflict and collaboration; indeed each is partially defined by the rejection of the premises of the other.

This book offers, in contrast to the two classic models, a somewhat different characterization of nuclear deterrence. Those models of nuclear deterrence arose from the strategic possibilities presented by air power while this book rejects the thesis, implicit in both ideologies, that modern nuclear strategy must be a perpetuation of the strategic bombing programme that dominated the Second World War.

In Book I my description of nuclear strategy is connected to the familiar distinction between central[4] and extended[5] deterrence. It is notorious that the debate about nuclear strategy has become detached from the precise political objectives that various strategies are supposed to serve. Any real contribution to analysis must renew this connection and thereby expose the strategic commitments and assumptions made.

I will describe nuclear strategy as driven by developments in vulnerability which led to crises in extended deterrence although the relationship of central deterrence remained stable. These crises precipitated recurrent doctrinal innovations that then played back into the central relationship. Thus this book has two main parts: a history of the development of United States nuclear strategy that displays a cyclical pattern in the doctrines of central deterrence (Book I) and an assessment of the directional development of extended deterrence for the future (Book II).

The analysis applied in Book I suggests that American extended deterrence is achieved by reducing the threat to the United States. In the present period this requires making convincing plans to limit nuclear conflict to the extended theatre. Book II explores the effect of such plans on those nations with which the United States is allied and predicts that such strategies will render strategic planning within the

Alliance problematic, and will destroy the political consensus on which planning depends. Various alternatives to this unfortunate state of affairs are then examined: Perhaps public opinion can be assuaged through political initiatives. Perhaps, as before, doctrinal innovation will mend any breach in extended deterrence. Or perhaps new weapons will accomplish the 're-coupling'[6] of the United States and her allies. Or perhaps this can be done through arms control or heightened conventional defences or even ballistic missile defence. These possibilities are considered in Chapters 9, 10, 11 and 13, respectively.

If the US cannot provide nuclear deterrence for Europe or Japan save by the threat to confine nuclear war to regions that include those homelands – then it may be that these nations, or some of them, will acquire their own nuclear arsenals, on a scale and of a variety similar to that of the withdrawn, or discredited, US deterrent. Chapter 12 evaluates this possibility in terms of its effect on central deterrence, the hitherto stable deterrence relationship between the US and the Soviet Union.

It is hoped that, in the course of this discussion, some contributions to the theory of nuclear strategy are made. The strategic dynamic of extended relations is discussed. The view that central and extended deterrence are similar concepts, differing only as to geography, but originating in the same historic strategic events, is refuted. The usual separation of declaratory and employment policy[7] – which makes chaos out of attempts to understand doctrinal developments since these developments are made to appear either illusory or revolutionary – is resolved. The distinction between Assured Destruction – the nuclear strategy – and an assured destruction capability is used to clear away some of the more absurd characterizations of US policy, still widely and tenaciously held, and to enable us to identify the continuity with and evolution of this strategy from its predecessors. The puzzling failure of the US to limit Multiple Independently Retargetable Vehicle (MIRV)[8] development in the Strategic Arms Limitation Talks (SALT), the US enthusiasm for the Multilateral Force (MLF),[9] the shape of US procurement that bore little relation to Soviet weapons acquisition: these and other matters are described in terms of a strategic analysis of American doctrine.

The value of this book does not lie, however, in these interstices. Rather it is to be found, if it is to be found, in the contribution to understanding made by its general thesis and the arguments introduced in behalf of that thesis. If it is true, as I believe, that extended deterrence is the means of preserving bipolarity[10] and resisting proliferation, and if the dynamic of doctrinal innovation in central deterrence can be understood as arising from the difficult paradox of maintaining classical deterrence (in the extended theatre) within the new, *nuclear* deterrence (of the central relationship); then we shall have a means of resolving the stalemated and arid deterrence debate, of choosing among alternatives and establishing coherent priorities. The debate that will result will not bear much resemblance, however, to the current public debate. At the present time, deterrence has ceased to be an appropriate subject for analysis[11] and is merely the occasion for the expression of credulous faith and acrimonious denial. The current debate is not simply incapable of giving us definitive answers, it asks the wrong questions. The crucial relationship between deterrence and proliferation, for example, is virtually never examined. We are ignoring life-threatening issues while neglecting to develop the analytical perspectives by which these issues could be addressed. I hope the treatment of doctrine in the manner I propose will enable new perspectives on our strategic problems. But, recalling the epigraph, even if the analysis of this book should prove helpful, we are scarcely out of the woods yet.

2 Some Concepts in the Theory of Deterrence

E io a lui: 'Poeta, io ti richeggio . . . acciò ch' io fugga questo male e peggio che tu mi meni là dove' or dicesti . . .'

(And I answered him: 'Poet, I entreat thee . . . in order that I may escape this evil and worse, lead me where thou hast said. . .')

Canto I, *Inferno*

Nuclear deterrence is, we may be reminded, an extraordinarily limited theory that relies on extraordinarily broad assumptions. The theory is limited to those conflicts in which the fundamental security of the state is put at risk. Thus the theory is of limited value in international relations. It is not deterrence, much less nuclear deterrence, that prevents the US from invading Canada (or the other way around). At the same time, the theory arises from a general assumption about national behaviour, namely that, at least when national survival is at issue and the mind wonderfully concentrated thereby, decisions will be made by balancing the benefits to be achieved by a proposed course of action against the costs incurred in pursuing those benefits by those means. This assumption, in turn, arises from an even more general assumption regarding human nature: that we can imagine pain greater than that we now suffer, that we can imagine happiness greater than that in which we now delight, and that we will evaluate possible futures in terms of their mixtures of these imaginary states.

It has long been fashionable from one of the ideological perspectives mentioned in the last chapter to regard nuclear deterrence as being 'concerned only with the threat and use of punishment'.[1] This fits nicely into the ideological assumption that deterrence is divisible into deterrence by defence (conventional) and by punishment (nuclear).[2] But such a characterization generates several important paradoxes, of which the most fundamental may be: if nuclear deterrence fails, the credibility of the threat – to respond to an attack on one's homeland with an all-out strike against the aggressor's cities – actually declines as the aggression escalates since 'punishment' is then irrelevant as a deterring act. A similar paradox arises from the prevailing division between a *declaratory* and an *employment* policy for nuclear weapons.

If nuclear weapons have any purpose other than absolute deterrence then, it has been argued, the threat of nuclear strikes must be severed from planning for their actual use since the conditions for the advantageous invocation of threats are by no means co-extensive with those of actual use. Such a distinction also fits nicely into the current nuclear ideologies: it allows one camp to maintain plausible planning despite its commitment to highly disproportionate retaliation; it allows the other camp to insinuate that, whatever the politics of nuclear strategy, military considerations will prevail if deterrence fails. This severance, however, has led to quite fantastic depictions of US nuclear strategic policy such as the caricature of 'mutual assured destruction' that rules in popular circles.[3] Moreover, the division between declaratory and employment policies makes hash out of intra-war deterrence, though, as will be seen, every American nuclear strategy in the thermonuclear period has depended on such a concept.

Similarly unhelpful has been the habit of characterizing US nuclear strategies as either 'counterforce' or 'countervalue' when every United States war plan has necessarily included important elements of both these target types. I use the word 'necessarily' advisedly: by it I mean that the various strategies in the thermonuclear era have depended upon the interplay between counterforce and countervalue targets. In this book US doctrine will be seen to oscillate between 'graduated' and 'total' response policies. *Graduated* response doctrines tend to lower the nuclear threshold but, by doing so, ensure that if deterrence fails the consequences of failure need not be catastrophic; the chance for maximum harm is minimized. *Total* response doctrines raise the nuclear threshold by a promise of overwhelming retaliation; they maximize the chances that minimum harm – no war – will prevail, but they run the risk that, if they fail, the cost of failure is high.

For the purposes of this book, 'nuclear strategies will be regarded as eventuating in national war plans which spell out the range of military actions in accordance with a given philosophy of how (and sometimes why) to conduct a war'.[4]

To understand these strategies, we must understand the notion of deterrence. A satisfactory definition of nuclear deterrence, in the present context, is 'the ability through the nuclear threat to make an opponent refrain from what he might otherwise want to do'.[5] Insofar as this definition accomodates a spectrum of threats which might deter a spectrum of hostile acts, it is a good definition of *general* nuclear deterrence. From it, one could deduce that effective deterrence is a matter of convincing an opponent that certain harm to him will accompany the act one wishes to deter; and thus that deterrence amounts to the imposition of a calculus of risk and value on an opponent such that the value of the act sought to be deterred does not exceed the risk, which is an assessment of the likelihood and extent of harm. This rather featureless description allows us to determine also what factors are used in this calculus: the importance to the deterred of the political objective sought; the perceptions of the force capabilities of the deterror and the confidence in civil defence, industrial recovery, and passive defences of his opponent; the importance to the deterror of the particular interests defended. For deterrence to succeed, 'the enemy has to be persuaded that the deterror has the capacity to act';[6] 'that in acting [he] could inflict costs greater than the advantages to be won from attaining the objective, and that [he] really would act as specified in the stated contingency'.[7] Once we enrich this one-directional view by the hypothesis that each party is symmetrically placed with respect to the other, each deterring and deterred at the same time, then deterrence takes on a kinaesthetic, mutually affecting quality. Deterrence becomes the imposition of a calculus of risk and value by a deterror who himself, in assessing the certainty and extent of harm he will threaten to inflict, must also calculate the value of the objective this threat is supposed to protect versus the likelihood and extent of the retaliatory or pre-emptive harm his opponent would inflict if the deterror's threat were executed. A robust general deterrence, as such, cannot survive this mutuality. If the deterror must take the threat of retaliation into account, he can no longer deter all objectionable acts. The deterror must distinguish between those objectives of indispensable value – such as national survival, however defined by the deterror – and those objects of deterrence whose value is less.

With this simple theoretical background, we can distinguish *central* and *extended* deterrence. *Central deterrence* is the relationship between vital objectives whose very centrality guarantees them the highest value to the deterror and therefore guarantees also the willingness to run the highest risks of retaliation or pre-emption in their behalf as well as the will to inflict a level of harm commensurate with the necessity to protect those objectives. In our present world this is the relationship between the homelands of the two superpowers. It is central deterrence that protects the American homeland from attack by Russia, and also the other way around.

Extended deterrence, by contrast, projects nuclear deterrence beyond the absolutely central, into either theatres of extension (e.g., to protect Europe or Japan by means of an American nuclear guarantee) or for extensive purposes (to compel a political act, e.g., to commence peace negotiations in Korea). Given the kinaesthetic nature of superpower relations to which I have alluded, extended deterrence can function only if there is a decisive advantage to the deterror either by capability (which determines the potential extent of harm) or intensity of interest (which determines the likelihood of the harm).

Although the Bayesian calculus they employ is the same, it will be seen from this description that central and extended deterrence are very different. Research and development programmes, weapons choices, force structures, operational plans and arms control objectives,[8] among other policy choices, will differ depending on whether they are responsive to the requirements of central or extended deterrence. The very centrality of physical integrity to the nation-state (the apparatus, after all, that is making security decisions) so heightens the value of protection that highly credible threats are possible in the face of high risks. It may be that to prevent self-destruction, any risks – including the risk of destruction itself – are worth running. Thus the United States might plausibly threaten that it would virtually destroy Soviet society if even a tenth of American society were destroyed, despite the fact that such retaliation might lead to the further destruction of the American survivors, since the failure to reply would abandon their protection anyway. In such cases the nuclear arsenal required is not great, and, between the superpowers, far less than contemporary equivalence[9] would be sufficient.

The requirements of extended deterrence are more varied, more demanding, and more sensitive. Indeed the requirements of central deterrence, in the context of mutuality, may sometimes undermine extended deterrence. Thus the mutual achievement of a secure, second-strike capability by the superpowers,[10] considered by many to be crucial to the stability of central deterrence, may have eroded the credibility of the American nuclear guarantee to NATO since it casts doubt on the effectiveness of a nuclear first strike against the Soviet Union.[11] Moreover the objects of protective extension will vary, and thus command and control mechanisms must be capable of assessing the risk and benefit in greatly differing situations. Armaments capable of manipulating the calculus through damage limitation[12] will be wanted. A far greater range of procurements and deployments will certainly be required because the threats to be deterred will vary, and 'overgunning' reduces the marginal cost of an opponent's escalation thereby inviting a higher risk to the deterror. A completely shattered opponent has little to lose.

But 'central' and 'extended' deterrence are not merely terms of strategic art. They link political objectives to nuclear strategies. Carefully distinguishing between these competing concepts, enables us to address these questions: Why should we deploy nuclear weapons? What purposes do they serve? How do they serve these purposes?

We deploy nuclear weapons to achieve the political security of our own nation-state, and of our other interests which include the security of other states. Nuclear weapons accomplish these objectives by posing risks to any state that would threaten our security interests in such a way, or to such an extent, that we might use these weapons against that state. Nuclear weapons pose these risks in two ways: as a potential consequence of war, and as a retaliation when vital interests are truly jeopardized. Thus there are two forms of nuclear deterrence, precisely to the extent that there are two spheres of political purpose served by their deployment.

It may be that, in 1960, it was sensible for a leading analyst to write, 'The central theoretical problem in the field of national security policy is to classify and distinguish between the two . . . concepts of deterrence and defense. . . . [D]eterrence means discouraging the enemy from taking military action by posing for him a prospect of cost and risk outweighing his prospective gain. Defense means reducing our own prospective costs and risks in the event that deterrence fails'.[13] Such a distinction does not survive the emergence of interdependent vulnerabilities. We cannot separate deterrence and defence into post and ante, then and afterward. Rather with the kinaesthetic relationship of mutually affecting vulnerabilities, the truly important distinction is between two different kinds of deterrence: (1) deterrence as preparedness – which is a matter of manipulating the imposed calculus of risks by both limiting the damage the deterror must contemplate as a prerequisite to the credible assertion of a threat, and manipulating, in the light of this assessment, the harm to be inflicted; and (2) deterrence as stalemate – which rejects any risk/benefit analysis by the threat of overwhelming harm in support of incalculable values. This distinction allows us to link nuclear strategies to political objectives by connecting these strategies to the purposes of extended and central deterrence.

The earlier categories of deterrence by denial and deterrence by punishment were really not so new as the atomic age[14] – naval bombardment of ports and the enforcement of blockades long ago presaged the theories of strategic bombing.[15] But neither were they so fundamental that they would continue to impress their structure on the atomic age, once the mutual acquisition of the thermonuclear weapon made certain that a new sort of deterrence would make the classic categories seem assimilable into each other by contrast to it.

The shortcoming of this brief sketch of a contemporary definition of the terms of deterrence is that it is entirely formal. Fate has not followed but created these categories and only an appreciation of the historical realities of the postwar strategic environment will give their definitions more than a superficial plausibility. Indeed the purely formal characteristics of deterrence are in part responsible for prevailing misconceptions as to its nature. Thus, on little more than a semantic similarity, it is commonly assumed that central and extended deterrence are species of the same kind, that they originate in the same puzzles.[16] In fact, the objective of extended deterrence was recognized relatively late, and did not animate the original acquisition of nuclear weapons.

Initially, the United States and Europe enjoyed an identity of deterrence. The central relationship existed between them and the Soviet Union who was only able to deter Western action by targeting European cities. The United States had made clear in the legislative history of the Atlantic treaty its commitment to use its stockpile of atomic weapons to attack the Soviet Union in the event of an attack on Western Europe. Here is Article 5 of the North Atlantic Treaty:

> The Parties agree that an armed attack against one or more of them in Europe or North America shall be considered an attack against them all and consequently they agree that, if such an armed attack occurs, each of them, in exercise of the right to the individual or collective self-defence recognized by Article 51 of the Charter of the United Nations, will assist the Party or Parties so attacked by taking forthwith, individually and in concert with the other Parties, such action as it deems necessary, including the use of armed force, to restore and maintain the security of the North Atlantic area.
>
> Any such armed attack and all measures taken as a result thereof shall immediately be reported to the Security Council. Such measures shall be terminated when the Security Council has taken the measures necessary to restore and maintain international peace and security.[17]

Dean Acheson[18] has given us the construction of the crucial term in this passage: 'By [a collective force] was meant a force for the defense of Europe, complete and balanced in its components when viewed as a collectivity, rather than a collection of national forces each complete with all the necessary component arms.' That is, the United States would provide the atomic elements of such a force; other NATO members would provide the bulk of conventional forces. Each member nation was not expected to develop, indeed was specifically discouraged from developing its own atomic capability. Balanced national forces, it was argued, could not deter the Soviet Union; 'both deterrence and effective defense could be provided only through the collective force, which would include *all* the power of the United States'[19] (emphasis added).

At this time, the Soviet Union had no comparable threat to deploy against the US since not until some point in the early 1950s did she possess a long-range bomber force capable of a significant strike against the continental United States.[20] Owing to the political consequences of this fact, the classical categories of deterrence and defence were at this time sufficient.

It was the gradual development of the Soviet bomber force in the early 1950s that ended the deterrence identity between the US and her European allies. So long as the US was invulnerable, an attack on Germany could in fact be treated as an attack on the American homeland: nothing was risked thereby and much was gained. Once the US became vulnerable, however, the measure of 'centrality' had to be taken more carefully. It was at this point that extended deterrence came into being in the space evacuated by the shrinking of those interests for which the United States was willing to launch its nuclear weapons without calculation.

This event – the creation of extended deterrence – provides the initial example of an hypothesis I shall propose. I shall argue that from this time in the early 1950s the history of the nuclear period can be usefully understood as a sequence of this recurring dynamic: events related to vulnerability bring about a crisis in extended deterrence, the resolution of which is achieved through doctrinal innovation in the central relationship.[21] By 'doctrinal innovation' I mean a change in strategic policy, sometimes made possible by technology, and made convincing by the professional criticism of the previously prevailing policy. Accordingly, Part 2 will describe several historical periods whose parentheses, as it were, are provided by the dynamic of vulnerability, crisis, and innovation.

Formulating strategy is a creative act, and, at certain moments, our creative faculties are more conspicuously demanded than at others. In the area of US nuclear strategy, these moments have come when events rendered the US relatively more vulnerable to Russian nuclear attack and thereby reduced the scope of the guarantee the US could give to her allies. At these moments, the need to formulate doctrine that would rationalize our resources with our objectives became particularly compelling.

I do not use the term 'rationalize' pejoratively. On the contrary, the decisions that embody strategic doctrine make sense of the past only retroactively. Such decisions give meaning to the past by projecting the continuity of past values and decisions into the future. Questions we have all asked of US nuclear strategy: Why are we doing this? or even What are we doing? are not satisfyingly answered by the glib explanations of specialists who substitute the other modes of analysis for the *strategic* strategy forces us to find a design, even if, in a democracy, we do not discover the design but instead create it.

An older school of modern history, of which Lawrence Freedman's *Evolution of Nuclear Strategy* is a superb example, was concerned with how political events influenced strategic ideas. My own assumption is that certain intellectual patterns – I called them ideologies – determine the shape of strategic doctrine. I therefore look for connections between events and ideas, without assuming that historical reality is the mold for our strategic concepts – assuming, one might say, the reverse. For example, with respect to superpower modern competition, I do not simply see two nations in conflict; rather I see two versions of reality. And thus many of the much-debated questions about Soviet intentions or national character are irrelevant to me (and I think useless to the analyst).

This method requires caution and patience. Excessive determinism must be resisted and I should emphasize that while I have chosen to write about events in this sequence, I am not claiming that doctrinal criticism *caused* innovation or even that developments in extended deterrence alone can be said to wholly account for the changes in doctrines of central deterrence. Service rivalries and bureaucratic competition, superpower diplomacy and struggle in non-nuclear arenas, considerations of domestic politics, the personalities of the principal players and the possibilities posed by technological advance – to these and to a great many other influences I am willing to concede causal roles in events even if I am unable to assess their extent. I claim only that the sequence I have described can be used as an overlay to permit analysis. And I claim that such analysis, because it is *strategic* in the sense that it links up political commitments with particular security approaches, is indispensable to the evaluation of past and present policies. Only then can we determine whether the evolution of nuclear strategic policy is cyclical (and therefore the crises which drive innovation are perhaps manageable but are not resolvable) or whether this evolution is directional and deterrence can be said to be eroding (or perhaps strengthening). And only then will we be able to unite the questions of vulnerability and deterrence into a single issue so that we can determine when vulnerabilities require compensation and what form this compensation ought to take. The failure to do this has led to the present impasse and obscures, in our current horror at the threatening prospects we face, the truly horrible future we will bring about if we persist in this failure.

Book I

The Age of Faith

3 Prologue: The Theory of Strategic Bombing and the Coming of Nuclear Weapons

Dinanzi a me non fuor cose create
se non etterne, e io etterna duro.

(Before me nothing was created but eternal things and I endure eternally.)

Canto III, *Inferno*

'Strategic thought draws its inspiration each century, or rather at each moment in history, from the problems which events themselves pose.'[1] The decisive strategic events of the post-war nuclear age, those that determined the utterly changed strategic circumstances of that age, occurred within a few months of each other. They were the acquisition by the Soviet Union, in August 1949, of a workable fission bomb and the decision by the United States, in January 1950, to develop the hydrogen bomb. These two events, *taken together*, meant that, in time, the classical strategic paradigms of defence and punishment would be opposed by a new paradigm. Yet it would be some time before this fact was appreciated, as we shall see, and this forces a Conradian chronology on our narrative: even after these events, political and doctrinal choices were made that were responsive to the old world. To see why the context was wholly changed by these particular events, to appreciate the depth and character of this change, we must look at the period superseded.

We may date the beginning of that period with President Roosevelt's decision in October 1941 to produce the atomic bomb although in fact it is an era of considerable strategic continuity with the past. This initial period culminates in December 1953 with the decision memorandum NSC-68. The lineal ancestor of a number of Presidential strategic directives, NSC-68 was promulgated as a result of a study ordered by Acheson as part of the hydrogen bomb decision – that is, the period ends with a document confidently addressing a world that would soon cease to exist by virtue of a decision already made, a decision whose inadvertent by-product was the document itself.

To begin this sketch of background with President Roosevelt's decision is to some extent arbitrary. Hitler[2] and Stalin[3] had made similar decisions independently. All three decisions were well fitted to the prevailing theories of the strategic uses of air power in this century, and, by extension, to at least a century's consensus that to defeat the enemy one pursued the strategic goal of attacking the national basis for promoting war. Certainly since Grant and Sherman, American commanders had accepted that modern wars – which is to say, wars between modern societies capable of fielding and supporting vast modern armies – would not be won by the elegant Napoleonic manoeuvres of a Lee or Jackson, isolating, distracting and dividing armies in the field, but by the relentless destruction of a society's ability to carry on. The theory of *strategic* bombing holds that air power will accelerate this process by leapfrogging the lines of defence and directly attacking the supporting society.

We do not know whether President Roosevelt had read *Il Dominio dell' Aria*,[4] Douhet's seminal exposition of the theory of 'strategic' bombing, but it is undeniable that its principal strategic ideas were assumed in his decision to develop the atomic bomb.[5] These ideas are precisely reflected in the final directive governing the Combined Bombing Offensive undertaken against Germany which stated its objective:

> To conduct a joint United States–British air offensive to accomplish the progressive destruction and dislocation of the German military, industrial and economic system and the undermining of the morale of the German people to a point where their capacity for armed resistance is fatally weakened.[6]

The atomic bomb was developed as a weapon that, like other counter-city incendiary bombs, could be used to compel the Axis political structure to collapse. 'Deterrence' as such only entered the picture, if at all, to the extent that Roosevelt feared that Germany would acquire the weapon first. As Secretary of War Stimson later recorded,

> The possible atomic weapon was considered to be a new and tremendously powerful explosive, as legitimate as any other of the deadly explosive weapons of modern war. The entire purpose was the production of a military weapon; on no other ground could the wartime expenditure of so much time and money have been justified.[7]

On 19 September 1944, at Hyde Park, Churchill and Roosevelt concluded a secret agreement to continue excluding the Soviets from information about the mundanely named Manhattan Engineering District Project and to consider that a bomb, when ready, be used against the Japanese.[8] It is doubtful that the exclusion of the Russians reflected an appreciation of the changed strategic relationship that the mutual possession of the atomic weapon would imply; after this agreement President Roosevelt considered trading the atomic monopoly for various cooperative concessions by the USSR at the War's end.[9]

What President Truman inherited, then, was not a strategic decision that foreshadowed a wholly new era in national conflict, but rather the orderly continuation, by more effective means, of the strategic bombing campaign conducted during Roosevelt's tenure. In his last four months in the White House, FDR never discussed with anyone, so far as we know, whether the atomic bomb should be used. Stimson maintained that Roosevelt never had any doubts about using it and this attitude was perhaps communicated to his successor.[10]

This understanding of the earliest nuclear weapons provides a context in which to evaluate the Hiroshima–Nagasaki decision, otherwise obscured by the moral debate following the bombings and President Truman's characteristically robust, if misleading, account of his own role in that decision: his claim that he never doubted the rightness of the bombing decision, and so forth.[11] In fact there really was no decision as such.[12] As General Groves described it, Truman's decision 'was one of non-interference – basically, a decision not to upset the existing plans'.[13] This impression is reinforced by the events surrounding the plans to drop a third bomb. These plans were halted by an instruction from General Marshall that, '[i]t is not to be released over Japan without the express authority of the President,' an instruction scarcely necessary if Presidential release had been the rule regarding earlier bombings.[14] Viewed within the assumptions of the strategic bombing campaign, it is not hard to answer the distinguished historian of this period who asked, 'the issue is not why it was *decided* to use the bomb, but rather how policymakers came to *assume* the bomb would be used and why they never questioned this assumption'.[15] Presidents, and their advisers, perceived the new weapon through the organizing principles of the prevailing doctrine, the theory of strategic bombing. There was no 'decision' to be made: the bomb fitted the theory perfectly since its overwhelming lethality avoided the attrition problems that other bombing campaigns had faced. Its link to a political decision – the strategic inquiry that would in due course have revealed issues such as the necessity, moral impact, and postwar implications of use – was already provided by the prevailing theory. These questions simply did not arise.

The first US postwar plans for atomic weapons were prepared in late 1945 for use against the Soviet Union. The initial plan, called TOTALITY,[16] was followed by the PINCHER series of studies, initiated in December 1945 and completed in late 1947.[17] These studies called for the use of twenty or more atomic bombs against a variety of Russian targets. The Russian petroleum industry, 67 per cent of which was located in seventeen cities, presented the most available target, Russian transportation being too dispersed, and to these targets were soon added major industries such as hydroelectric power and steel manufacture. A critical June 1946 Air Staff study observed,

> It is assumed that if sufficient force were applied in a short enough period of time against the major cities of a modern nation, a morale collapse would end the war.[18]

In a single sentence, this states the essential premise of the theory of strategic bombing.

Subsequent war plans were studied – codenamed BROILER, FROLIC, GRABBER – each calling for the use of nuclear weapons as part of a strategic bombing campaign until the spring of 1948 when the Joint Chiefs of Staff (JCS) forwarded HALFMOON[19] for Presidential approval. The key element in HALFMOON was 'a powerful air offensive designed to exploit the destruction and psychological power of atomic weapons against the vital elements of the Soviet warmaking capacity',[20] the classic objective in a strategic bombing campaign. The air offensive under HALFMOON called for fifty atomic bombs to be delivered against targets in twenty cities which, it was thought, would achieve 'immediate paralysis of at least 50 percent of Soviet industry'.[21] Only one senior official appeared to have anticipated that atomic weapons might not be used in a future campaign. Upon being briefed by JCS planners about HALFMOON, President Truman on 5 May 1948 ordered the development of an alternative plan based on conventional forces without atomic weapons. The chiefs were instructed to prepare plans on the possibility that nuclear weapons would come under the international control of the United Nations. By the summer of 1948, however, as the crisis over Berlin grew more tense and it became clear that the Russians were unwilling to accept American proposals for internationalizing nuclear capabilities,[22] work on the alternative plan was halted. By 13 September Truman stated to Secretary of Defense Forrestal that 'if it became necessary' he was prepared to use atomic weapons and finally, on 16 September, he endorsed NSC-30, a Presidential memorandum authorizing reliance on atomic weapons as an appropriate means of waging a bombing campaign in the event of war.[23]

The rebuffed HALFMOON was succeeded by FLEETWOOD, DOUBLESTAR, and TROJAN, the last of these calling for strikes on seventy Russian urban targets with 133 atomic bombs within thirty days. According to David Alan Rosenberg, the principal historian of this period, the 'primary objectives [of this war plan] would be urban industrial concentrations and government control centers; secondary targets would include the petroleum industry, transportation networks, and the electric power industry'.[24] Air Force Chief of Staff Hoyt S. Vandenberg concluded that the successful execution of such a campaign could well 'lead to Soviet capitulation and in any event would destroy their overall capability for offensive operations'.[25] A summary of the later DROPSHOT plan similarly speaks in the terms of strategic bombing theory:

> In a campaign employing atomic and conventional bombs against Soviet and satellite industry, the latest available air-force intelligence studies have concluded that the greatest overall effects can be achieved by attacking the petroleum industry, the electric power system, and the iron and steel industry. Destruction of 75–85 percent of [the] petroleum industry, including storage facilities, would reduce offensive capabilities of all Soviet forces and seriously affect agriculture, industry, transportation, and shipping; destruction of 60–70 percent of the important electric-power-grid systems would paralyze the Soviet industrial economy, since modern industry requires a continuous supply of electric power, which cannot be stockpiled; elimination of 75–85 percent of [the] iron and steel-producing facilities would prevent recovery of industrial capacity for two to three years. Important by-products of attacks on these systems would be destruction of political and administrative centers and internal communication systems; in addition there would probably be an extreme psychological effect, which if exploited might induce early capitulation.[26]

So thoroughly did the atomic weapon fit within the prevailing concepts of strategic air power that subsequent war plans were even designed around an ongoing controversy over the most effective role for strategic bombing. This controversy might be stated thus: should strategic bombing be directed solely at the industrial base and political will of the enemy or should it also attack offensive operations (should, in other words, the 'deterrence' that first appears in NSC-20/4, be achieved by *punishment* or active *defence*)? Directed by the Joint Chiefs of Staff in April 1949 to prepare a war plan for the first two years of a war beginning on 1 July, the Joint Strategic Plans Committee produced OFFTACKLE. This plan simply repeated the unresolved positions by proposing alternative objectives. The central feature of OFFTACKLE is the passage:

> VII Basic Undertakings
>
> 7. In collaboration with our allies: . . . .
>
> View 'A'
>
> c. To conduct, at the earliest practicable date, a strategic air offensive against the vital elements of the Soviet war making capacity.
>
> View 'B'
>
> c. To conduct, at the earliest practicable date, a strategic air offensive against the vital elements of the Soviet war making capacity, and against other elements of the Soviet offensive military power.[27]

All this reflected an utter rejection of the conclusions of the US Strategic Bombing Survey, commissioned by the Army Air Force to review and evaluate the bombing campaign in World War 2, and published in 1946. The survey had concluded that the daylight bombing of German industrial targets resulted in such high bomber attrition that, in view of the inaccuracy of the bombing, the campaign was rendered ineffective. The report contained the startling revelation that the peak of the daylight bombing progamme in 1944 actually corresponded to the highest point of German war production. German cities had shown a surprising resilience and extraordinary ability to recover. Despite the deaths of over 65 000 people in raids on Hamburg in the late summer of 1943, and the total destruction of one third of all houses in the city, Hamburg as an economic unit was not destroyed. Within five months it had regained 80 per cent of its former productivity, despite the fact that great areas of the city lay in dust and rubble. The report concluded, '[a]s in the case of industrial plants, when it was found much easier to destroy the buildings than the machines in them, so also it is much easier to destroy the physical structure of a city than to wipe out its economic life'.[28]

The report observed that the presumed effect on enemy morale could also not be substantiated. Indeed it appeared that, after the initial shock of the bombardment of urban areas, their further bombing stiffened the will of civilians. Thus were the two principal objectives of strategic air power which, taken together, were the basis of an adversary's war-making capacity, debunked as effective goals for a bombing campaign. 'Cumulatively' one writer has observed, 'the [Strategic Bombing Survey] suggested that the only effective means of strategic bombing was to raze entire enemy cities as the atomic bombs had done in Hiroshima and Nagasaki'.[29] But while it is tempting to conclude that it was the terror, speed, and resistance to attrition of air power armed with the atomic bomb that salvaged the defunct theory of strategic bombing, in fact it may have been the other way round. Because the Joint Chiefs of Staff chose to treat the atomic bomb as a more lethal but essentially classical air weapon – because that is, the bomb seemed to fit the theory so perfectly – little thought appears to have been given to the consequences of proliferation. Thus, for example, the possibility of a test ban on the development of thermonuclear weapons seems never to have been considered. And the great lessons of World War 2 air conflict, that there would be decisive *air* battles before strategic bombing could effectively commence, and that armies in the field must be defeated by forces that can call on scarce air resources before any true collapse can be brought about, were submerged in the rising confidence that the 'bomb' would always get through. As Henry Rowen has concluded,

> the nuclear planning task was seen as an extension of strategic bombing in World War II – greatly compressed in time, magnified in effect, and reduced in cost. The task was principally the destruction of critical war-supporting industries in order to affect Soviet battlefield operations, the longer term ability of its economy to support combat, and its will to continue the conflict.[30]

While OFFTACKLE was being circulated for comment two shattering events occurred that began the age of deterrence, and ultimately closed the strategic bombing era (though its paradigms continue to structure debate about nuclear strategy). In the spring of 1949, the Soviets exploded an atomic device and, at the very end of that portentous year, the United States decided to acquire the 'super' bomb. As we shall see, these events meant that deterrence would of necessity become a diplomatic means to a military end, in a dramatic reversal of classical deterrence.

The H-Bomb, as the 'super' became known when it was proved possible to achieve a fusion of hydrogen isotopes, is a weapon of very great technological versatility. The atomic bomb, which depends on the chain reaction of fissionable material, is limited in size: detonation of such a bomb requires the rapid assembly of a mass exceeding critical size, i.e., that amount of uranium or plutonium whose releasing neutrons will cause other fissions as they are captured such that a sustaining reaction is begun. As soon as this mass is achieved, the assembly blows up in about a half a millionth of a second. Great ingenuity is needed to achieve an instantaneous result that exceeds the critical size by over a few per cent. No amount of ingenuity, thus far, has been able to design a usable fission bomb that is two or three times critical mass. There are inherently narrow limits to the size of the fission bomb: as it begins to exceed the critical mass, it explodes at once; if it is smaller, it cannot be exploded at all.[31] With a fusion bomb, however, the size of the explosion depends exactly on the amount of the reacting elements. There is no limit, in principle, on the size of the fusion bomb. Since the elements involved – excluding the fission trigger[32] – are the lightest in the periodic table, a weapon relying on their fusion could release great energy at no great variance in size. It is absurd, therefore, to say that the H-bomb is 10 or 100 times more powerful than the A-bomb. It is as powerful as we choose to make it.

The strategic importance of this fact is that the heightened upper limit effectively removes attrition as a factor in assessing the likely success of a bombing campaign. This can be shown in the simple exposure of a common fallacy. Active air defence, it has been argued, can suppress perhaps 20 per cent of the sorties flown against the defending society. Wouldn't it, it is then asked, be worthwhile to save 20 per cent of America's cities or even 20 per cent of the populations in the cities that are struck? But of course destroying 2 out of 10 planes in a mission does not imply that 2 out of 10 missions fail; destroying 9 out of 10 incoming planes armed with fusion bombs might well not save *any* cities, for one device is enough to destroy a city. Thus, Winston Churchill wrote,

> There is an immense gulf between the atomic and hydrogen bombs. The atomic bomb, with all its terrors, did not carry us outside the scope of human control or manageable events, in thought or action, in peace or war . . . [but with the coming] of the hydrogen bomb, the

entire foundation of human affairs was revolutionized, and mankind placed in a situation both measureless and laden with doom.[33]

The atomic weapon could be fitted nicely into theories of strategic bombing,[34] but did not silence critics of such theories. Attrition was still a factor. It had been calculated that it would require 400 atomic bombs to inflict damage on Germany equivalent to that of the World War 2 campaign, and there were the further questions of the cost of achieving the air supremacy necessary to such a campaign, and indeed the strategic effectiveness of the World War 2 campaign itself. When a single American submarine armed with fusion warheads could inflict such damage, the attrition issue is largely mooted.

At first this might appear to give new vitality to strategic bombing, and absolutely settle the question of its effectiveness. So it would but for the mutual acquisition of such weapons by adversaries. Then the resistance to attrition tends to reverse the strategy called for by the theory. Neither side can now employ its nuclear weapons in the coercive way required by strategic bombing.

The OFFTACKLE War Plan expressly included the assumption that 'intelligence estimates indicate that the USSR will not have atomic bombs available in fiscal year 1950' (an assumption that, though perhaps operationally true, was discredited by the Russian detonation). Not only did the Soviet acquisition of atomic weapons affect the difficulties faced by US planners; it meant, as all knew, that eventually there would be a mutual acquisition of *fusion* weapons. It was absurd to postulate a Russian intercontinental suprise attack even with atomic weapons in 1950; the range of Soviet bombers, their number and the limitations of the fission bomb made such a strike implausible, and each factor reinforced the others. By 1954, as we shall see in the first of four historical sections, this had utterly changed.

The mutual acquisition of fusion bombs meant a strategic stalemate at the level of central deterrence. In the next period, we will observe this element of stalemate as a persistent characteristic of the strategic context, an element not present heretofore – hence the title of this Chapter, 'Prologue'. Bismarck's celebrated remark that one does not commit suicide for fear of death, might well have been an ironic comment on the new age.

1949 ended much of what had gone before, and began much of what we now must live with and within. The period's culminating national security document was NSC-68, intended as a successor to NSC 20/4, the strategic basis for OFFTACKLE, and to NSC-30. NSC-68 is an elaborate effort to encompass the national security context of the Cold War. Yet it, unlike assessments of the Soviet threat prior to the Soviet atomic test, explicitly assumes that the Soviet Union might initiate a war in Europe despite the full expectation of American resistance. It is primarily a strategic rather than a military document because it comprehensively sets the political and military terms within which the security debate is to be carried on. NSC-68 contains nascent ideas that later events would bring to maturity, for even though NSC-68 was itself a document from the age of strategic bombing, it foreshadows the two doctrinal paradigms between which US nuclear policy has oscillated in the three decades of the era of deterrence. In particular it introduces the notion of appropriate response, for, ironically, the theory of 'strategic' bombing was remarkably devoid of planning connected to realistic political objectives.

> In the words of the Federalist (No. 28) 'The means to be employed must be proportioned to the extent of the mischief.' The mischief may be a global war or it may be a Soviet campaign for limited objectives. In either case we should take no avoidable initiative which would cause it to become a war of annihilation, and if we have the forces to defeat a Soviet drive for limited objectives it may well be to our interest not to let it become a global war.[35]

NSC-68 avoided, in George Kennan's words, leaving Washington with 'no better choice than to capitulate or precipitate a global war'.[36] It was imperative, accordingly, 'to increase as rapidly as possible our general air, ground and sea strength and that of our allies to a point where we are militarily not so heavily dependent on atomic weapons'.[37] This would require the capacity to counter aggression at whatever level of violence it occurred, whilst avoiding unintended escalation.

Between two pure approaches – graduated response and total response – American strategic thought has alternated since the mutual acquisition of fusion bombs, while strategic policy has always, prudently, included elements of each. 'Prudently', because the pure approaches also represent wholesome corrections of each other's shortcomings, shortcomings that become apparent when either approach is used without modification. Thus graduated response programmes emphasize counterforce threats, with an expressed lower threshold of nuclear conflict, more credible thereby but accordingly, like Wellington's troops, frightening to their commander as well as to his enemy. Total response doctrines are usually expressed in counter-value terms, require *some* proportionality to the threat to be credible, but are, nevertheless, the 'unthinkable' ones commentators speak of when I fear they sometimes mean 'unbelievable'. They make deterrence less likely to fail and more costly if it does.

For this reason it is tempting to think of the postwar period as a series of cycles, each successive doctrine replying to the flaws in its predecessor as criticism and experience make these flaws more evident.[38] Cycles, however, do not dictate, but are responsive to events. When we enlarge our view, it will appear that it is the dynamic of vulnerability within the political dilemma of central and extended deterrence that began and continued these cylical movements, and that the theory of strategic bombing, like the period in which it was absolutely dominant, was only prologue.

4 Massive Retaliation

Ruppemi l' alto sonno nella testa
un greve truono, sì ch' io mi riscossi
come persona ch' é per forza desta;

(A heavy thunder-clap broke the deep sleep in my head so that I started like one who is waked by force)

Canto IV, *Inferno*

For NSC-68, nuclear strategic policy was a continuation of the ideas of strategic bombing.[1] Despite rather confident claims by the Air Force,[2] however, this continuity caused concern in some observers. In 1949, the Secretary of Defense, James Forrestal, commissioned the Harmon Committee to evaluate US plans for an atomic campaign against the Soviet Union. The Committee estimated that the projected attack on seventy Soviet cities would result in a 30 to 40 per cent reduction in Soviet industrial capacity and perhaps 2.7 million fatalities and 4 million casualties. Even such staggering industrial losses, however, 'would not be permanent and could be alleviated by Soviet recuperative action depending on the weighted effectiveness of follow-up attacks.' Furthermore, 'the capability of Soviet armed forces to advance rapidly into selected areas of Western Europe, the Middle East and the Far East would not be seriously impaired'. The Committee concluded that planned air attacks alone would not 'destroy the roots of Communism, or critically weaken the power of Soviet leadership to dominate the people'.[3] A strategic air offensive against urban industrial targets could not promise 'victory' no matter how that crucial word might be defined.

One historian has concluded that these 'doubts over the prevailing . . . strategic concept, fears about Soviet intention in Europe, and the emergence of a Soviet nuclear threat combined to produce a shift in the US strategy for nuclear war'.[4] This chapter is devoted to that shift and to those factors precipitating it, i.e., the criticism of strategic bombing in the nuclear era, emerging US vulnerability, and doubts about the ability of the US to protect Europe. The results of the shift were the declaration of the doctrine of Massive Retaliation and the adoption of NSC-162 and 162/2 which codified that doctrine and augmented it by the endorsement of tactical nuclear deployments in Europe. By the end of the decade the new programme had run its course. Strategic events had yielded developments in the extended theatre whose consequences were revisions in the central doctrine. The first Single Integrated Operations Plan (SIOP) was brought into being by this first decade of central and extended deterrence.

A few months before the Bikini tests in July 1946, an assistant professor at the Yale Institute of International Studies edited and published *The Absolute Weapon: Atomic Power and World Order*,[5] a collection of essays to which he was the main contributor. Although Bernard Brodie's assessment of the strategic significance of atomic weapons was premature, as the Bikini tests would confirm, *The Absolute Weapon*, or rather Brodie's work in that volume, is astonishing for its anticipation of the strategic world that the mutual possession of fusion weapons would bring into being. Drawing on a paper by Jacob Viner, professor of economics at the University of Chicago and Brodie's teacher and mentor, Brodie expressed a unique notion of *nuclear* deterrence, different in kind from the strategic bombing deterrence of the earlier era.

Viner's paper contained the following passage:

> There seems to be universal agreement that under atomic-bomb warfare there would be a new and tremendous advantage in being the first to attack . . . I remain unconvinced. No country possessing atomic-bombs will be foolish enough to concentrate either its bomb-production and bomb-throwing facilities or its bomb-stockpiles at a small number of spots vulnerable to atomic bomb or other modes of attack. Let us suppose that a country has been subjected to a surprise attack by atomic bombs, and that all its large cities have been wiped out. If it has made the obvious preparations for such an eventuality, why can it not nevertheless retaliate within a few hours with as effective an atomic-bomb counter attack as if it had made the first move? What difference will it then make whether it was country A which had its cities destroyed at 9 a.m. and country B which had its cities destroyed at 12 a.m., or the other way around?[6]

In his treatment of deterrence in *The Absolute Weapon*, Brodie proceeds by inference from Viner's insight, methodically presenting the various possibilities of the new atomic situation, supported by descriptions of the weapon itself, its capabilities, means for its delivery and potential models for defence.

Having shown that the atomic weapon was cost-efficient, despite the expense of its development, when compared to the number of sorties and planes required to deliver an equivalent explosive power to a target, Brodie then demonstrated that the atomic bomb increased the range of the B-29. With a smaller payload of bombs, and more capacity for fuel, the round trip range of a B-29 could be expanded substantially. Brodie observed that,

> [t]he gross weight of the atomic bomb is secret, but even if it weighed four to six tons it would still be a light load for a B-29. It would certainly be a sufficient payload to warrant any conceivable military expenditure on a single sortie. The next step then beomes apparent. Under the callously utilitarian standards of military bookkeeping, a plane and its crew can very well be sacrificed in order to deliver an atomic bomb to an extreme distance.[7]

Having made this suggestion, Brodie drew the conclusion that,

> under the existing technology the distances separating, for example, the Soviet Union and the United States offer no direct immunity to atomic bomb attack, though it does so for all practical purposes with respect to ordinary bombs.[8]

This dramatic and ominous surmise prompted a review of the possibilities for defence, about which Brodie was pessimistic. Even assuming American air superiority, an intolerable level of destruction would result from an attack by only a small fraction of the Soviet force. In light of the cost-effectiveness of this weapon, and the relative abundance of the resources needed to produce it, Brodie predicted that the American monopoly of atomic fission could not be expected to last more than five to ten years.

Having established that both superpowers were likely to possess a weapon against which there was no defence, Brodie assayed the means to manage this mutuality. Thus Viner's insights led Brodie to the celebrated statement of the new age of deterrence.

> The first and most vital steps in any American security program for the age of the atomic bombs is to take measures to guarantee to ourselves in case of attack the possibility of retaliation in kind. The writer in making that statement is not for the moment concerned about who will win the next war in which the atomic bomb is used. *Thus far the chief purpose of our military establishment has been to win wars. From now on its chief purpose must be to avert them. It can have almost no other useful purpose.*

> Reducing vulnerability is at least one way of reducing temptation to potential aggressors. And if the technological realities make reduction of vulnerability largely synonymous with a preservation of striking power, that is a fact which must be faced.[9]

Follow the argument: there is no possible defence; therefore we must use our forces to avert war; the best way to avert war is to reduce the attractiveness of war to aggressors; so the only 'defence' is an overwhelming offense. This obviously required a complete rejection of previous habits of thought, which related the offense to war-winning. Brodie wrote that,

> [t]he most dangerous situation of all would arise from a failure not only of the political leaders but especially of the military authorities of a nation like our own to adjust to the atomic bomb in their thinking and planning.[10]

Once this change in perceptions and appreciation was accomplished, the requirements of the new deterrence were fairly clear. In an atomic war, as in earlier wars, the United States would attempt to maximise defensive facilities in order to minimize the destruction of the initial strike against it, and then to regain the offensive initiative.

To accomplish this, Brodie's model divided forces into three categories. The first was reserved to launch the retaliatory atomic attack; the second, delegated to invasion and occupation of enemy territory; the third would be devoted to the repulsion of enemy invasion and administration of war relief within the United States. The entire argument rested with the use of the first force.

> The force delegated to the retaliatory attack with atomic bombs will have to be maintained in rather sharp isolation from the national community. Its functions must not be compromised in the slightest by the demands for relief of struck areas. Whether its operations are with aircraft or rockets or both, it will have to be spread over a large number of widely dispersed reservations, each of considerable area, in which the bombs and their carriers are secreted and as far as possible protected by storage underground. These reservations should have a completely independent system of intercommunications, and the commander of the force should have sufficient autonomy of authority to be able to act as soon as he has established with certainty the fact that the country is being hit with atomic bombs.[11]

Brodie's uncanny clairvoyance was, as clairvoyance must be, somewhat premature. The two atomic weapons detonated in July 1946, one in the lagoon of Bikini atoll where World War 2 surplus ships were moored for the experiment, one in the atmosphere above Bikini, were widely observed. The existence of the atomic weapon was no longer a closely held national secret, and a number of civilian and military analysts were present. US Naval Institute Proceedings and one remarkable book by the *New York Times* military correspondent Hanson Baldwin record an unusual agreement between Brodie's pre-Bikini tactical analyses and the results of the tests. The divergence, however, is equally striking. Nowhere in Baldwin's book, *The Price of Power*, and nowhere in the Naval analysis, is the notion of nuclear deterrence discussed. Instead, the shortcomings of strategic bombing theories (and the results analyzed in the *US Strategic Bombing Survey*) are belaboured, and quite properly so, for the world that Brodie described had not yet come into being. Bikini showed that atomic weapons, in Baldwin's words, were 'probably not the "absolute weapon"' and the tests were observed in the confidence that only one power possessed such weapons.[12] The developments that Brodie claimed for 1946 did not come to pass until the early nineteen-fifties, almost concurrently with the election of a new American President.

It was the development of thermonuclear (fusion) weapons by both the US and the USSR that truly had immeasurable consequences for the vulnerability of nations. 'Even with fission weapons numbering in the hundreds there was a real – difficult – analytical problem in choosing targets that would make the campaign decisive rather than merely hurtful' Brodie acknowledged in his masterpiece, *Strategy in the Missile Age*, published at the end of the period.[13] With the acquisition of hydrogen bombs, however, plus the knowledge that their possession would soon be mutual, the atomic bombing campaigns of NSC-68 were utterly discredited, and the need for a theory of absolute deterrence became inescapable.

For the theory of strategic bombing, deterrence was derivative from its war-fighting function. It was because these concepts of denial and punishment had utility in war that they might act as a deterrent in peacetime. Nuclear deterrence – the relationship that eventuated from mutual fusion capabilities between adversaries – put the avoidance of war-fighting (as distinguished simply from the avoidance of the commencement of war) as its principal rather than derivative objective. Its concepts, preparedness and stalemate, depended upon husbanding (or wholly avoiding) violence so as not to trigger retaliatory violence.

NSC-68 had promised absolute security by countering, politically and militarily, every Soviet threat. Atomic bombs were simply part of the arsenal to be used in a large-scale war. This commitment to respond to every encroachment or threat was 'containment'. But the Truman administration had never devised a strategy for deriving coercive political results from simply the threat posed by the American nuclear arsenal; its strategy was responsive only. Certainly that administration was at no point willing deliberately and publicly to threaten the use of nuclear weapons.[14] The incoming Eisenhower administration, however, faced an imperative its predecessor had been able to avoid. For there had now arisen a US vulnerability precisely to the extent that the US sought to involve itself in the defence of non-homeland theatres. The effect of this vulnerability was to require the exploitation of Russian vulnerability in disproportionate but credible terms if any political use of the threat of nuclear weapons, other than the stalemate of simple homeland (central) deterrence, was to be gained and the fruits of war in Europe denied to the Russians without war itself having to be fought. Since US vulnerability had brought into being the problem of 'extended deterrence', the new American administration immediately turned to this extension, that is, it turned to the difficult problem of getting political results out of nuclear threats at the very time the US homeland was becoming vulnerable to threats against it.

In 'Operation Solarium'[15] the new President convened three study groups, each charged with presenting the case for its assigned option. The options were: a continuation of containment; adoption of a new doctrine of deterrence that involved the threat of overwhelming nuclear retaliation to Soviet aggression in protected theatres;[16] liberation, the rollback of existing Soviet hegemony in Eastern Europe and Asia. It was to be assumed that the US had two years before the Soviet Union gained the nuclear capacity to counterbalance American nuclear superiority. The result was the Administration's strategic policy, the 'New Look', which has often been thought to reflect a decision in favour of the first option,[17] perhaps tempered by the second. It is now clear however that, at least from the perspective of nuclear weapons policy, the New Look opted for nuclear deterrence based on total response, that is, the Administration rejected the proportionate replies of containment that treated nuclear weapons as an appropriate resort in war, and chose instead the terrific threat of nuclear attack whenever the Soviet Union jeopardized the fundamental security of the European state system. So on 12 January 1954, Secretary of State John Foster Dulles went before the Council on

Foreign Relations to announce that the US planned to rely on the 'deterrent of massive retaliatory power' to dissuade aggressors from hostile acts. Rather than containment, which was tailored to every provocation and demanded large, expensive[18] conventional deployments in many parts of the world, and which was reactive and therefore conceded the initiative, President Eisenhower opted for the threat of total response limited to the protection of US vital interests. It would exploit Soviet vulnerability, since a thermonuclear attack was highly credible despite US conventional inferiority; it would protect the political status quo (despite eventual US vulnerability) by the very magnitude of its threat if the essential international equilibrium were disrupted. Thus, as was not clear to many at the time, it was a strategic doctrine completely incompatible with rollback or liberation plans. 'Basic National Security Policy', NSC-5501, summed up the position early in 1955: 'So long as the Soviets are uncertain of their ability to neutralize the US nuclear air retaliatory power, there is little reason to expect them to initiate general war or actions which they believe would . . . endanger the regime and the security of the USSR'.[19]

Although Brodie was critical of the expansiveness of the massive retaliation idea – in 1955 Eisenhower authorized an extension of this approach to limited wars as well[20] – it represented the adoption of Brodie's fundamental approach with respect to central deterrence. Acknowledging this, in the idiom of a general but actually quite personal disclaimer, Brodie wrote:

> No one has ever questioned the appropriateness of massive retaliation as a response to a direct attack upon ourselves. Let us also be clear that in the next most important and critical area of the world as far as our defense obligations are concerned, namely Europe, there has thus far been little alternative to massive retaliation as the basic organizing principle of our security system. The NATO powers were induced to make the precedent-shattering commitments of that alliance only upon our promise that the United States SAC [Strategic Air Command – the U.S. bomber force armed with nuclear weapons] stood ready at all times to implement it. The NATO alliance was the means by which our partners could avail themselves of that kind of support, and it was the only way to defend themselves vigorously and in combination.[21]

Indeed he recognized, as few critics did, that the crisis of US vulnerability had been felt in *extended* deterrence and that it was the maintenance of massive retaliation that prevented war in Europe despite the inability of the Allies to even approach the Lisbon goals[22] thought necessary to halt a Soviet invasion. While massive retaliation *simpliciter* was not enough for all contingencies of extended deterrence, it was indispensable in Brodie's view.

> What gives a modest number of NATO divisions the chance of coping with the Soviet Army is not their capacity to use nuclear weapons, which the Soviet Army also enjoys, but the fact that massive intervention of Soviet ground forces is unlikely except with a Soviet decision to wage total war. So long as the United States seems to be committed to retaliate massively to such intervention, the Soviets would have to anticipate our reaction by a strategic bombardment of the United States.[23]

Brodie saw that the mutual possession of overwhelming force cast both defence and punishment in a new light. He saw the new world, with its new look, but he was unsure of the next step; Brodie was most insightful when trying simply to perpetuate the terrible paradox he had portrayed.

The Eisenhower administration recognized the difficult puzzle of extended deterrence that Brodie depicted. It was apparent that the new doctrine, responding to this problem, would be a successful link only so long as American superiority existed, and only with respect to those threats against which this superiority might usefully be brought to bear. While it has been recognized that the policy of massive retaliation was 'keyed for both its credibility and operative efficiency to American air superiority',[24] this fact and the policy's very label have partially obscured the correlative fact that strategic superiority was not, in itself, sufficient. As Dulles himself acknowledged in the *Foreign Affairs* article that was the public expression of the doctrine, 'massive atomic and thermonuclear retaliation is not the kind of power which could most usefully be invoked under all circumstances'.[25] It wasn't that massive retaliation was simply inappropriate to some provocations – too big, the way a screwdriver is too big for some screws – after all, disproportion was what gave the strategy its character and decisiveness. It was that the *credibility* of such use in strategically inappropriate circumstances was subject to doubt. Accordingly, the US decided to build and deploy tactical nuclear weapons (TNW) to supplement the strategic, long-range arsenal. The administration believed that once the central deterrent had been established on total response grounds, for that very reason TNW became indispensable. This belief arose from a recognition of the ambivalent character of the central deterrent and thus US reliance on TNW built into NATO policy a fundamental ambiguity because that reliance was responsive to a fundamental dilemma in the use of central threats to maintain an extended protection. The European members of the Alliance sought tactical nuclear weapons as a fuse for the central nuclear deterrent. Americans tended to stress their capability as weapons that could contain the conflict at the lowest levels of nuclear capability. When, in 1956, a military exercise, 'Operation Carte Blanche', simulated a Soviet attack without Soviet TNW and resulted in enormous casualties, especially among West Germans from NATO TNW, the issue was dramatically underscored. A carefully managed ambiguity was preserved, however, so long as the central doctrine was healthy.[26] It is not obvious that the Eisenhower administration was wrong in choosing the lower costs – political and fiscal – of TNW over an enhanced conventional presence in Europe. If it was shortsighted – Brodie, again, was ahead of his time: the Soviet TNW deployment he predicted only became significant at the end of the decade – it was acute enough within its field of vision.

The period ended with the central relationship changed. The strategic bombing paradigms of NSC-68 had been replaced. During the late forties, the operational US stockpile had been composed of 80–120 weapons of doubtful reliability. Since the US also lacked the capability of all-weather, accurate delivery and combat-ready bomber forces, 'the only US strike option then would have been to strike at the major Soviet cities, and the outcome would have been highly uncertain because of the inability to predict the results in terms of damage to the USSR'.[27] This was the legacy of the Second World War and the theories of strategic airpower.

By contrast, massive retaliation also embodied a counterforce posture.[28] It depended upon enormous power: between 1954 and 1960, although the number of US bombers remained largely unchanged, the total megatonnage in the US strategic offensive and defensive forces increased over twenty times. In fact, 'the [historical] peak in [US] megatonnage – and in "effective megatonnage", another index of damage potential – [came] in 1960'.[29] The new doctrine accepted the fundamental assumption of Brodie's work, that nuclear deterrence in central systems would produce a stalemate, and sought to overcome this assumption and its implications for extended deterrence by the concentration of force in defence of solely vital interests.

> By the late fifties it would appear that the United States was well situated to devastate the Russian economy, disrupt Red Army

operations and disable the budding Soviet nuclear force. Whether planned strikes could actually have prevented Soviet nuclear attacks on the US and its allies would have depended a great deal on unpredictable operational factors such as warning time, alert rates, political willingness to launch a preemptive strike and so on.[30]

Yet already events were taking place that would re-assert the primacy of nuclear deterrence and undo the administration's doctrinal mending of the rupture of deterrence identity between the US and Europe.

5 Controlled Response

Ed elli a me: 'Ritorna a tua scienza,
che vuol, quanto la cosa é più perfetta,
pin senta il bene, e cosï' la doglienza'.

(And he answered me: 'go back to thy science, which requires that in the measure of a creature's perfection it feels more both of pleasure and of pain.')

Canto VI, *Inferno*

US nuclear strategy in the 1950s culminated in the first Single Integrated Operations Plan (SIOP),[1] promulgated in 1960. Massive Retaliation logically required the unification of nuclear targeting among the services, the reconciliation of their missions and the co-ordination of launches, if necessary, to enable a single spasm. This co-ordination was the purpose of the SIOP, which replaced the various separate plans generated by the services. Targeting was unified in the Optimum Target Mix (OTM), a single target set composed of high priority military, industrial and political targets. NATO doctrine was similarly brought into line: MC 14/2 called for a nuclear response to any, even local, Soviet intrusion if it continued.[2]

Eisenhower seems to have shared Brodie's perception of the centrality, if you will, of central deterrence and of the crucial but finite requirement of the necessary minimum of forces required by total response to maintain that deterrence. Like Brodie, Eisenhower followed Clausewitz in the view that military means had to be subordinated to political ends lest those means be expended purposelessly, and he stressed this view regarding nuclear matters. Perhaps this conviction enabled him to hold opinions that were remarkably sophisticated, *vis-à-vis* those of many of his contemporaries, regarding the utility of nuclear weapons and the exaggerated promise of strategic bombing. At a time when most US military personnel were strongly opposed to any intermingling of political and military considerations – a separation that reinforced the view that the consequence of nuclear weapons was simply to make strategic bombing more effective – Eisenhower was a more profound observer. Speaking to a group of senior officers in 1954, he said:

> No matter how well prepared for war we may be, no matter how certain we are that within 24 hours we could destroy Kuibyshev and Moscow and Leningrad and Baku and all the other places that would allow the Soviets to carry on wars, I want you to carry this question home with you: gain such a victory, and what do you do with it? Here would be a great area from the Elbe to Vladivostok and down through Southeast Asia torn up and destroyed, without government, without its communications, just an area of starvation and disaster. I ask you what would the civilized world do about it? I repeat there is no victory in any war except through our imagination, through our dedication and through our work to avoid it.[3]

Moreover, the political objectives of military policy must also include domestic stability and the well-being of the society and it is interesting to observe that Brodie eventually came around to accept Eisenhower's concerns about the effect on the national economy and the national psyche of ambitious military preparations beyond those required to maintain central deterrence.[4] Central deterrence required a relatively modest nuclear capability; and it was open to doubt just what uses, beyond maintaining central deterrence, a larger more flexible nuclear threat might serve. Both men asserted that:

> If we assume reasonably secure retaliatory forces, unrestricted thermonuclear war seems to be at once much too destructive and too unpredictable to be invoked in any but the most dire straits. It is unpredictable because not only industrial superiority but even superiority in mobilized forces will probably count for less than in the past, being much overshadowed by questions like who strikes first, and in what way. . . . The advent of the thermonuclear bomb seems to have had a decisive influence in this respect by making it highly probable that even a relatively small amount of retaliation would do a very large amount of damage.[5]

Yet it was apparent by the end of the decade that the very events that brought this system into being also would undermine it. In the same paragraph quoted above, Brodie acknowledged,

> This stabilizing factor is, however, at least partly offset by the fact that an extremely destructive surprise attack upon the opponent's retaliatory force is more feasible with thermonuclear weapons than with the ordinary fission variety.[6]

By the time he wrote this passage, Brodie had left Yale to go to the RAND Corporation. It was there that, during the 1950s, the doctrinal criticism had been developed that would be used to renovate strategic doctrine in its next brief period of crisis.

The Eisenhower administration assumed that an attack upon the United States by the Soviet Union would be deterred by the possession of large stockpiles of nuclear weapons and sufficient bomber-capacity to deliver them. A team of analysts at RAND, led by Albert Wohlstetter, had begun in the mid-1950s a series of studies on the siting of overseas US strategic air bases.[7] Their initial conclusions were in harmony with the prevailing strategy: since the United States and Soviet deterrents were predicated on aircraft based in highly vulnerable modes, there was a significant advantage to the party striking first; and any counterforce strike intended to limit damage to the US and its allies would have to be quick and massive. As this analysis proceeded, however, in a series of classified studies, briefings and reports culminating in Wohlstetter's widely read article in the January 1959 issue of *Foreign Affairs*,[8] its logic took it further away from the prevailing approach. In contrast to Brodie's assumption that deterrence was largely automatic once a minimum of capability was achieved, Wohlstetter argued that, in the famous title of his article, the balance of terror was 'delicate'. Deterrence capabilities were 'both relative and dynamic'.

Wohlstetter assumed that the objective of a particular level of capabilities could not be an absolute, *a priori* matter nor even a mere question of numerical equality. In accordance with the conclusion of the earlier study, it appeared that the deterrent forces themselves presented the most tempting target, for *both* sides. What was decisive was the residual force: that deterrent remaining that could still threaten retaliation after suffering an initial strike. A deterrent force of numbers insufficient to survive such an attack was actually a provocation to a surprise first attack by an adversary. It was Wohlstetter who thus introduced the terms *first strike* and *second strike* into the vocabulary of the Age.

The criticism of the stable balance went further. It was claimed that if the logic of the prevailing doctrine was accepted, and both sides sought and eventually possessed the crucial second strike capacity to retaliate, then Massive Retaliation as a doctrine must fail because the United States could no longer deter any aggression except a disarming first strike against itself. The US dare not retaliate *massively*, since this would at once fail to destroy the enemy's retaliation *it* triggered and at the same time insure that *that* retaliation would be equally massive. From this rejection of total response doctrine, the search for relevant uses of nuclear force led almost necessarily to a programme of graduated response.

> Rather than engage in either hyperdestructive but militarily pointless attacks on cities, or formalized exchanges for bargaining purposes, the preference ought to be for nuclear strikes that had some utility for the hard-pressed military commanders attempting to hold back the Soviet advance. Nuclear strikes would gain their effect through a combination of the impression of determination created by their actual use, and the military value of the targets attacked, which, by holding up the enemy advance, would facilitate a satisfactory settlement.

> These concepts are linked to the notion of flexible options, the desire for a choice of actions according to operational circumstances. In a scenario in which a localized conflict is expanding in scope and intensity, the preferred targets might be enemy military forces being employed, or about to be employed, in and around the original combat zone, or forces threatening key ports or airfields as well as those threatening civilians. The presumption is that a future war could well be a complicated affair, in which one particular engagement would not necessarily be decisive. In fact, because it is expected that both sides would make every effort to protect their strategic forces, they would not necessarily appear as attractive targets at all. Thus the objective is not a disarming first strike but objectives geared to a type of conflict which excluded the mutual destruction of cities.[9]

Eisenhower was scarcely sympathetic to this analysis. Commenting on a similar view expressed in a 'very provocative book'[10] he had been reading, he observed that it called for 'undoubtedly . . . a more expensive operation than we are carrying on at this time'.[11] Eisenhower's objections went deeper. 'Remember this', he told a USIA staff, 'when you resort to force as the arbiter of human difficulty, you don't know where you are going; . . . if you get deeper and deeper, there is just no limit except what is imposed by the limitations of force itself'.[12] Taken seriously, this terrible uncertainty ought to have maintained Massive Retaliation as an adequate doctrine: if escalation is uncertain, its potential consequences ought to deter effectively the very initiation of aggression. Two events in the relationship of central deterrence, however, occurred that cast doubt on the ineluctability of escalation and these drove the disillusionment with and finally abandonment of Massive Retaliation.

In the late 1950s the United States relied on only about forty Strategic Air Command bases for its nuclear deterrent. This small force presented a small target set for an adversary hoping to wipe out the American nuclear deterrent; there were no nuclear submarines and no intercontinental ballistic missiles. But this fact cut both ways: there was, symmetrically, no secure Soviet deterrent and the mission times and range of Soviet bombers permitted at least the illusion of relative security to US bases and to the US homeland. Thus when in October 1957 the launch of Sputnik shattered the public sense of well-being in the United States, it also had consequences for more serious analysts. As the 'bomber gap' hearings in the mid-1950s had shown, the Soviets had not put a high priority on the development of a long-range bomber force, choosing instead to push an ICBM programme. The successful completion of that programme – of which the Sputnik launch was a signal – meant that, given contrasting US priorities, there would be some period in which the Russians would enjoy superiority in ballistic missile technology. Monitoring Soviet ICBM tests earlier that year, the US Air Force had postulated a 'missile gap' during which the Soviet Union would soon deploy ICBMs in superior numbers to the US.[13] These projections were reinforced by other intelligence forecasts, including those of the CIA.

This strategic inferiority never materialized because the Soviet Union did not proceed with the full-scale production of her first generation ICBM as predicted by American analysts in 1958–9 (as indeed the Soviets had not greatly expanded their long-range bomber force as had been predicted in 1956). The 200 to 250 Soviet ICBMs that were forecast for 1961 actually numbered only fifteen to twenty. The impact of the unmaterialized 'missile gap' was, however, altogether real and it reinforced analytical fears that also tended to press for an expanded US force.

Because the strategic forces of both sides were vulnerable to attack, even forces capable of delivering a massive attack on an opponent would be too small to execute a significant retaliatory strike. Analytically, therefore, such strategic forces could not deter attack, but only provoke it. For deterrence to function the launch force itself had to be greatly increased. Moreover, the expected American vulnerability had two additional effects on perceptions of the central relationship.

First, the consequences of the changed US perception of the threat it faced were felt in Europe where, additionally, Soviet deployment of a significant number of their own TNW had begun to take place. The Soviet central threat, it was thought in some quarters, forced the US into a situation that 'would be equivalent to disowning our alliance obligation by [tacitly agreeing to] what would amount to a non-aggression treaty with the Soviets – a non-aggression treaty with almost 200 million American hostages to guarantee performance'.[14] Thus the 'tripwire' in Europe of Massive Retaliation amounted to no more than a commitment to replay Operation Carte Blanche, this time with *both* sides devastating European territory with TNW. Brodie recognized the problem posed by the vulnerability of US strategic forces.

> Suppose, for example, the enemy attacked our retaliatory forces with great power but took scrupulous care to avoid major injury to our cities. . . . He might indeed understand that, in a thermonuclear war, the mere ability to destroy cities may well confer more military advantage than the actual destruction of them. If his attack is successful to any serious degree, we should be left with a severely truncated retaliatory force while his remained relatively intact. These hardly seem propitious circumstances for us to initiate an exchange of city destruction, which would quickly use up our remaining power, otherwise useful for bargaining, in an act of suicidal vindictiveness. Our hitting at enemy cities would simply force the destruction of our own, and in substantially greater degree.
>
> We may be quite certain that we will hit back if hit directly ourselves, regardless of the state of our civil defenses, but will we do so if the United Kingdom is hit? Or if it is threatened with being hit? Of course we are legally committed to respond with all our power, and our leaders may presently be convinced that if the occasion arose they would honor that commitment. But surely they would on such an occasion be much affected by the consideration – assuming no radical change from the present situation – that our people are hopelessly exposed to enemy counter-attack.[15]

His solution – civil defence – might have been taken but for the second effect of the crisis in American confidence.

This effect was to stimulate American central deployments and American investment in intelligence gathering such that when more accurate intelligence assessments of the Soviet threat were made by satellite in 1961,[16] it became apparent that *Soviet* vulnerability had been greatly underestimated. The United States had:

> increased its relative strength in the late 1950s . . . This, and the relative vulnerability of the Soviet strategic forces at this time, had the effect of moving the US towards a true counterforce capability. During the Cuban missile crisis the US had approximately 1500 B-47s and 500 B-52s, and had already deployed over 200 of its first generation of ICBMs. In marked contrast, the Soviet strategic missile threat consisted of a few token ICBM deployments whose unreliability was so great that it was uncertain exactly whom they threatened. Soviet long-range bomber forces consisted only of 100 Tu-20 Bears and 35 May Bison, whose range and flight characteristics forced them to fly at medium and high altitudes, and which made them extremely vulnerable to US fighters and surface-to-air missiles.[17]

This lop-sided ratio now permitted the introduction of graduated response that the perceived lapse in extended deterrence demanded.

RAND had developed a graduated response doctrine and, in President Kennedy and his Secretary of Defense, Robert McNamara, there were American leaders anxious to master and adopt the new ideas.[18] McNamara viewed several plausible contingencies as inappropriate for Massive Retaliation: a Soviet nuclear strike limited to the US strategic forces; a limited nuclear strike against US or allied troops in Europe or in other non-homeland theatres (a contingency to which the Eisenhower administration had explicitly committed a nuclear response); an accidental or unauthorized launch. In light of the changed context of central deterrence as it was thought to be in 1961, each of these contingencies was an inappropriate occasion for the vast response of the SIOP. As a candidate during the 1960 campaign, the President had sharply criticized not only the rigidity of American strategy but the insufficiency of American deployments. These assertions of declining American strength were by no means disingenuous or merely partisan; toward the end of 1950s even the Eisenhower Administration had acknowledged similar estimates and had begun a build up that was to be accelerated by Kennedy.

President Kennedy felt – the perhaps characteristic response of a former lieutenant j.g. to the planning of a five-star staff general – that earlier planning had been both unrealistic and overdrawn. Seemingly unaware of the revolution in systems analysis,[19] the previous administration represented for Kennedy much of what his own administration would define itself against: complacency, anti-intellectualism, exaggerated bombast in service of a diffident international policy. In the view of McNamara and the President, SIOP plans for the use of nuclear weapons were too destructive, too inflexible, too 'massive'. The SIOP, if executed, would not limit damage against the US, and whether or not executed actually put a premium on the Russians' maximizing the initial damage of their strikes, as the threat of spasm prompts spasm. Because SIOP plans were themselves threats of all-out war, they were responsive only to such threats and hence did nothing to deter aggression short of such war. In brief, they were plans that were largely useless to political authority. To the analyst's complaints that the SIOP did nothing to remedy US force vulnerability had to be added the criticism that such planning ignored US civilian vulnerability.

The new President and his Secretary of Defense were men willing to accept the doctrinal innovations of the analysts – innovations bred in concern over American vulnerability – and were at the same time also anxious to seize the geopolitical initiative and craft a more threatening and versatile deterrent. In this context the recommendations of the analysts and the surprising if pleasurable discovery that the Soviets were indeed vulnerable were not in conflict. American superiority merely reinforced a doctrinal initiative derived from analyses that had originated in concerns over American vulnerability. For in the new world of ICBMs, a nation might be both very vulnerable and vastly superior at the same time; the RAND doctrines showed how to integrate these two values. Indeed one might conclude that, but for American superiority, the RAND innovations would not have provided a satisfactory remedy for vulnerability.

The increasing vulnerability of the US bomber force was a development in central deterrence as described by Wohlstetter. But this development affected extended deterrence in two ways: since the US was committed to a first strike in behalf of NATO, the value of this commitment was undercut by the possibility that Soviet retaliation might simply erase the remaining US deterrent and, second, were the Soviets to strike first, the US deterrent might be destroyed on the ground. Contemplating these eventualities, the Americans concluded that European confidence would be dramatically diminished: either *only* the spasm was possible in such a situation (and in whose behalf was it likely to be launched if the Soviet reply was the destruction of American cities?) or the American deterrent was so vulnerable as to be a target and little more.

The proposal to redress this vulnerability took two compensatory forms. Targeting would be directed against the Soviet nuclear forces, since by suppressing Soviet counterforce capabilities and thereby limiting the damage to itself, the US rehabilitated the credibility of a US first strike in behalf of NATO. And a secure second strike capability – through the acquisition of SLBMs and ICBMs – would be sought. This capability would permit the termination of war even if the Soviets struck first while enhancing the deterrent (since it reduced the gain to the Soviets of a first strike). This, it was thought, ought to ease the self-deterrence[20] problem which stood at the centre of the extended deterrence dilemma. (This was true only so long as the US alone had this second-strike capability, but as we shall see, this point was not immediately appreciated.) Controlled Response was the doctrine that embodied these views. It was a counterforce, city-avoiding targeting strategy.

In early 1961, a review of the SIOP had begun; initial work on revision was completed by summer – largely by analysts from RAND[21] – JCS approval was quickly forthcoming and the new strategy was formally adopted in January 1962. In a series of speeches that year, McNamara outlined the new programme of 'Controlled Response'. In February McNamara claimed that

> our forces can be used in several different ways. We may have to retaliate with a single massive attack. Or, we may be able to use our retaliatory forces to limit damage done to ourselves and our allies, by knocking out the enemy's bases before he has had time to launch his second salvos. We may seek to terminate a war on favorable terms by using our forces as a bargaining weapon – by threatening further attack. In any case, our large reserve of protected firepower would give an enemy an incentive to avoid our cities and to stop a war.[22]

Then, in an historic speech at Ann Arbor, Michigan in June 1962,[23] McNamara offered a complete view of the revised strategy, in which he addressed civilian vulnerability.

In a general war, he argued, destruction should not be unconfined. Deterrence should continue, *intra-war* as it were, discrimination among targets should be attempted, and some options ought to exist that would enable ending the war by some means other than utter destruction. Cities were not simply strategic targets whose immediate destruction would so weaken the enemy that its war effort would fail for lack of support. For this purpose, nuclear warfare was too fast, too total, beyond the calculation of Douhet. Instead, cities were to be preserved as hostages: to destroy them at the outset was to sacrifice their principal value as objects of leverage against the enemy.[24]

If war came the United States would destroy 'the enemy's military forces, not . . . his civilian population,' while retaining 'even in the face of a massive surprise attack, sufficient reserve striking power to destroy an enemy society if driven to it'. This configuration of US forces and options would, in McNamara's words, give 'a possible opponent the strongest imaginable incentive to refrain from striking our own cities'. As one historian has concluded,

> The reasoning behind US war plans was thus clear and direct. In the event of war the primary US objective would have been to strip away Soviet strategic nuclear power while minimizing civilian casualties and holding Russian cities hostage. Residual US forces would have been used to extract a satisfactory political settlement from the Soviet leadership.[25]

The new strategy was in some respects a humanitarian effort to mitigate the consequences of nuclear war. It also created a force structure and options that provided NATO with the capability for a first strike. The new SIOP held some pre-emptive counterforce options as part of its graduated response list.

The new doctrine was an instance of the general phenomenon that events in central deterrence precipitate a crisis in extended deterrence with which innovative doctrine must cope. The Ann Arbor speech is usually taken simply as a statement of the new central strategy.[26] In fact this revision of policy was an effort to rehabilitate *extended* deterrence by demonstrating how the US might be credibly expected to use its strategic superiority to enforce that deterrence. It is useful to recall precisely what McNamara said in that famous address.

> It has been argued that the increasing vulnerability of the US to nuclear attack makes us less willing as a partner in the defense of Europe, and hence less effective in deterring such an attack.
>
> It has been argued that nuclear capabilities are alone relevant in the face of the growing nuclear threat, and that independent national nuclear forces are sufficient to protect the nations of Europe.
>
> I believe that all of these arguments are mistaken. I think it is worthwhile to expose the US views on these issues as we have presented them to our allies. In our view, the effect of the new factors in the situation, both economic and military, has been to increase the interdependence of national security interests on both sides of the Atlantic and to enhance the need for the closest coordination of our efforts.

A central military issue facing NATO today is the role of nuclear strategy. Four facts seem to us to dominate consideration of that role. All of them point in the direction of increased integration to achieve our common defense. First, the alliance has over-all nuclear strength adequate to any challenge confronting it. Second, this strength not only minimizes the likelihood of major nuclear war, but makes possible a strategy designed to preserve the fabric of our societies if war should occur. Third, damage to the civil societies of the Alliance resulting from nuclear war could be very grave. Fourth, improved non-nuclear forces, well within Alliance resources, could enhance deterrence of any aggressive moves short of direct, all-out attack on Western Europe.

The very strength and nature of the Alliance forces make it possible for us to retain, even in the face of a massive surprise attack, sufficient reserve striking power to destroy an enemy society if driven to it. In other words, we are giving a possible opponent the strongest imaginable incentive to refrain from striking our own cities. . . .

We know that the same forces which are targeted on ourselves are also targeted on our allies. Our own strategic retaliatory forces are prepared to respond against these forces, wherever they are and whatever their targets. This mission is assigned not only in fulfillment of our treaty commitments but also because the character of nuclear war compels it. More specifically, the US is as much concerned with that portion of Soviet nuclear striking power that can reach Western Europe as with that portion that also can reach the United States. In short, we have undertaken the nuclear defense of NATO on a global basis. This will continue to be our objective. In the execution of this mission, the weapons in the European theatre are only one resource among many. . . .

We accept our share of this responsibility within the Alliance. And we believe that the combination of our nuclear strength and a strategy of controlled response gives us some hope of minimizing damage in the event that we have to fulfill our pledge.[27]

I have quoted at some length from this often-cited address to emphasize that Controlled Response was actuated by a desire to remedy problems of extended deterrence. The new SIOP – a counterforce, city-withholding plan with several target sets, shifting away from the single Optimum Target Mix but still involving thousands of weapons – did not seek to enhance central deterrence by its changes. Indeed, the threat to carry out large-scale nuclear operations, including particularly strikes against urban-industrial targets, remained. To be sure the acceleration of the Polaris and Minuteman programmes, and the increase in the number of bombers on ready-alert, were decisions initially taken with the objective of strengthening central deterrence by making the second strike capability secure. But it was the desire to free up the President on behalf of Europe by means of damage limitation (the counterforce option) and the possibility of civilian survival (the cities-withholding option) that shaped Controlled Response. As will become apparent, however, the very security of the American central deterrent makes city-withholding by the Russians (and therefore by the Americans) unlikely; and, as we shall encounter again, efforts to reduce the President's reluctance to enter nuclear war by reducing the US's risks stimulate fears of the detachment of the European theatre and its designation as a nuclear battleground. As a result, the new policy was highly controversial in Europe even though its purpose, as the title of the Ann Arbor speech discloses, had been to address European concerns.

After the Ann Arbor address, Leonard Beaton wrote,

> Almost every aspect of the doctrine shows the same characteristics: sound internal analysis and largely unanticipated difficulties in the alliance . . . The Americans are unlikely to convince themselves that Massive Retaliation is no strategy without having the same effect on their allies[28] . . . [while] the Ann Arbor doctrine could, however, be looked at in [several] ways. One is that the United States has in effect offered to limit its strikes to Soviet forces if the Soviet Union will limit itself to Western Europe. . . .
>
> The best estimates of their force levels [provide] only for use against medium range targets. The idea of Europe as a hostage is strongly implanted in Soviet military doctrine. It could be argued that the Americans are saying that a limitation of conflict to Europe would be met by a restriction of American strikes to Soviet forces.[29]

As a result of perceptions of this kind, and an internal weakness in the doctrine discussed at the end of this chapter, Controlled Response was superseded in only two years by yet another major innovation, Assured Destruction. In the interim, promulgation of Controlled Response was accompanied by an unusual proposal for nuclear weapons deployment, the Multilateral Nuclear Force (MLF) scheme. Precisely because the Ann Arbor speech, and the doctrine it announced, were efforts to reinforce extended deterrence, they were at the same time efforts to dampen enthusiasm in Europe for independent nuclear deterrents, an enthusiasm arising from the same crisis in the US guarantee.[30] That the Ann Arbor doctrine alone was unsuccessful at accomplishing these goals can be observed from the resurgence in American policy of the MLF scheme, which President Kennedy had earlier decided to shelve.

The idea of creating a multilaterally owned and operated force of nuclear weapons within NATO originated in studies conducted at the Supreme Headquarters Allied Powers Europe (SHAPE) in the late 1950s. In light of the then unresolved technological question of whether and when the United States could find a dependable long-range missile to match apparent Soviet ICBM superiority, it was suggested that a force of mobile medium range missiles in Western Europe be assembled, mounted on trucks, railway cars or barges. Since a missile made relatively invulnerable by its mobility could not, by virtue of the very ability to move from country to country, be operated under the bilateral agreements covering tactical nuclear weapons, and since the suggestion had originated in doubts about the credibility of US extended deterrence in behalf of Europe, the study recommended that a mix-manned allied force ought to be detailed to run the new system.[31] Mooted by events in ICBM development, this bizarre proposal never attracted the enthusiasm of either American planners or their European counterparts. Doubtless the proposal would have been interred by the Acheson study President Kennedy commissioned for that purpose but for the dismay of the West German government at realizing that the strategy of Massive Retaliation had been abandoned. In Alastair Buchan's view, 'this development revived doubts about the credibility of the American response and began to increase German enthusiasm for a multilaterally controlled NATO force'.[32]

The United States was determined to prevent the proliferation of independent European nuclear deterrents[33] – an altogether plausible outcome of any genuine doubt about the US guarantee of extended deterrence. George Ball was dispatched to Europe to make the following, quite diffident offer:

> From a strictly military standpoint, we do not feel that the Alliance has an urgent need for a European nuclear contribution. But should other NATO nations so desire, we are ready to give serious consideration to the creation of a genuine multilateral medium-range ballistic missile force fully co-ordinated with the other deterrent forces of the North Atlantic Treaty Organization. It is not

> for us – indeed, it would be out of keeping with the spirit of the Atlantic partnership – to dictate how such a force should be manned, financed or organized. But it is a proper responsibility of the United States which has had so much experience in the nuclear field, to make available to others our information and ideas with respect to the characteristics and capabilities of a multilateral force. And we are now in the process of doing so.[34]

Buchan has concluded that

> in reality, Mr Ball was being somewhat modest and disingenuous: the United States had by then a plan for a multilateral force which she was about to insist that her allies consider. . . . The assumption behind Mr Dean Rusk's exposition of this proposed force was that if it materialized the British and French forces would become part of it, but that its employment would remain subject to an overriding American veto for the time being.[35]

MLF was a legacy of Controlled Response: not only of the centralized planning required by the new doctrine and the unanticipated European reaction to the US rejection of Massive Retaliation, but, more importantly, of the effort (bound up in the doctrine) to discourage an independent European nuclear force.[36] MLF would linger on into the next period; it was dispatched when it became apparent that European support for a scheme sought to cure European concerns was based largely on American pressure.

Controlled Response, despite the initial advantage it derived from exploiting American superiority, was but a temporary success.[37] Once implemented, however, it completed the cycle I have described by altering the central relationship, although it did so in ways perhaps not intended by the American Administration. The total response plans of Brodie and Eisenhower were decisively replaced by a graduated response strategy. But this strategy could not be permanent because it depended on Soviet vulnerabilities that were vanishing even as the MLF corollary was being worked out. Failing to appreciate this aspect of a second strike, counterforce strategy, Secretary McNamara believed that:

> because we have a sure second-strike capability, there is no pressure on us whatsoever to preempt. I assure you that we really never think in those terms. Under any circumstances, even if we had the military advantage of striking first, the price of any nuclear war would be terribly high. One point I was making in the Ann Arbor speech is that our second strike capability is so sure that there would be no

> rational basis on which to launch a preemptive strike. I believe myself that a counterforce strategy is most likely to apply in circumstances in which both sides have the capability of surviving a first strike and retaliating selectively. This is a highly unpredictable business, of course. But today, following a surprise attack on us, we would still have the power to respond with overwhelming force, and they would not then have the capability of a further strike. In this situation, given the highly irrational act of an attempted first strike against us, such a strike seems most likely to take the form of an all-out attack on both military targets and population centers. This is why a nuclear exchange confined to military targets seems more possible, not less, when both sides have a sure second-strike capability. Then you might have a more stable 'balance of terror'.[38]

The distinction between these two ideas – that a secure, second strike capability ensures crisis stability (because the secure party is not pressured into striking first) and that such a secure capability ensures intra-war stability (because it permits city-withholding bargaining since an all-target attack is no longer necessary) – is perhaps easy to overlook, but in that distinction lay the necessary lifespan of Controlled Response. For, contrary to McNamara's intuition, both sides could not achieve a secure second strike, counterforce capability. Once one side appeared to have it, the other side lost its second strike counterforce targets. Controlled Response was unworkable in the context of mutual invulnerability. In the meantime, for the Russians,

> to fight such a war against the United States, targets would have to exist which could be destroyed at an acceptable cost to the forces of the Soviet Union. It may be doubted whether either the Polaris or Minuteman forces fall into this category. There would be no alternative to strikes against cities or other targets of value if all American strategic retaliatory forces were so hardened as to make attacks on them impossible or disproportionately costly.[39]

This acute observation by Beaton is followed by the absurd conclusion that,

> [t]he logic of the McNamara doctrine therefore appears to dictate an actual requirement for vulnerable forces (such as the B-52 bomber fleet) which will provide a less destructive alternative while the bargaining process takes place. American cities would also, presumably, have to meet the traditional requirement for an 'open cities' doctrine – that they should not be used for military activities.[40]

In fact it is not that the Russians will attack cities simply because they must have something to strike at, and so by giving them counterforce targets the US could spare its cities. Rather the Russians are forced by the US secure retaliatory force to attack US cities since no amount of Russian counterforce attacks can jeopardize the US force; that is what 'secure' means. The Russians must attack cities because that is the only politically coercive choice available.

Facing an even-partially disarming first-strike from a largely invulnerable adversary, Soviet retaliation would have to encompass counterforce and countervalue strikes simultaneously.[41] For the period before Soviet acquisition of a nuclear force sufficiently numerous, dispersed and protected to be secure, an even more ominous prospect arose. It had earlier been observed that a *first strike* counterforce strategy was highly destabilizing in a crisis and this was perhaps one reason why Secretary McNamara was at such pains to persuade his interviewer that the US counterforce strategy, regardless of appearances, was a second strike strategy. For the Russians, facing such a force without great faith in American expressions of benign intent, and for the Americans who, despite their professions of good faith, had to be cognizant of the precariousness of the Russian position, a horrible possibility emerged. Thomas Schelling described it:

> If surprise carries an advantage, it is worth while to avert it by striking first. Fear that the other may be about to strike in the mistaken belief that we are about to strike gives us a motive for striking, and so justifies the other's motive. But, if the gains from even successful surprise are less desired than no war at all, there is no 'fundamental' basis for an attack by either side. Nevertheless, it looks as though a modest temptation on each side to sneak in a first blow – a temptation too small by itself to motivate an attack – [changes] expectations, with [an] additional motive for attack being produced by successive cycles of 'He thinks we think he thinks we think . . . he thinks we think he'll attack; so he thinks we shall; so he will; so we must'.[42]

These fears were soon to be tested in the next round of events in the relationship of central deterrence: the Cuban missile crisis and the acquisition by the Russians of a secure second strike capability.

6 Assured Destruction and Strategic Sufficiency

Cred' io ch' ei credette ch' io credesse
(I think he thought I thought. . .)

Canto XIII, *Inferno*

Before these crises were upon him, McNamara was driven by the considerations outlined above, and others, from the position of the Ann Arbor speech to a modification of Controlled Response. Controlled Response had two elements, city withholding and damage limitation. The new doctrine, Damage Limitation, modified the 'second strike counterforce option' of the old doctrine standing alone. It was an attempt to serve the purposes of the city-withholding feature of Controlled Response which had been rendered implausible by the coupling of this feature with damage limitation, first-strike threats, and to preserve the counterforce elements of Controlled Response without its intensely destabilizing effects. The modifications embodied in Damage Limitation responded to concerns that the Russians were forced to fire for fear of losing their arsenal to a US first strike *and* were not deterred from attacking US cities by the US threat to destroy Russian cities. With Damage Limitation the US tried to protect US cities by means other than simply threatening Russian cities and sought the goals of counterforce targeting while loudly abjuring first strike intentions.

This strategy proved to be the worst of both worlds. Soon Soviet deployment of ICBMs in hardened silos and the increasing number and dispersal of Soviet strategic forces made significant damage limitation both technically unfeasible and cost-ineffective. Moreover, declarations denying first strike intentions are open to doubt by an adversary since the counterforce capability required for a 'second strike counterforce option' is indistinguishable from that necessary for a first strike. As a policy it has all the destabilizing features of a first strike declaration compounded by a delay in execution. Finally, while Controlled Response was fundamentally a therapy for problems in extended deterrence, the isolation of its damage limitation feature and the movement to a second-strike mode actually exacerbated these problems. This insight, and other criticisms of the strategy, are illuminated by a discussion of the work of the gifted microeconomist Thomas Schelling.

Schelling's analysis proved to be both substantively acute, and also indicative of the sort of approach that replaced Controlled Response and its modifications, an approach that dominated the period we are about to discuss. In Schelling and other bargaining-oriented economists,[1] analysis had found not only strategic thinkers who understood and fully endorsed the deterrence assumptions of Brodie, but also persons who had ideas about how to make the assumptions work for political goals other than deterrence, in other words, how to create a system of incentives that were responsive to the new world of mutual, overwhelmingly destructive power. Virtually all historians of the subject assume that McNamara wholly rejected the counterforce/no-cities approach announced in the Ann Arbor address when he ultimately turned to the doctrine of Assured Destruction[2] and if these doctrines are understood as alternatives deriving from graduated and total response paradigms, respectively, there is a sense in which this is so. Schelling's analysis of the Controlled Response (counterforce/no-cities) approach, however, will show how Assured Destruction derives easily from the earlier doctrine. This in turn will help explain the continuity of targeting throughout the two doctrinal periods and enable a fresh explication of the latter doctrine.

Schelling's views were expressed in a paper, *Controlled Response and Strategic Warfare*,[3] published in 1965, therefore after 'Controlled Response' *per se* had been repudiated and after the new doctrine of 'Assured Destruction' had been announced.

Schelling began by claiming that the 'no-cities' component of Controlled Response, (the city avoidance element of the doctrine that is coupled with a counterforce, damage limitation component to form the strategy) can actually be a 'cities' strategy. Schelling would transform McNamara's humane gradualism into a sharply defined threat using the extension of deterrence into the period of war itself as a means of war termination. 'Cities' he wrote,

> are not merely targets to be destroyed as quickly as possible to weaken the enemy's war effort, to cause anguish to surviving enemy leaders, or to satisfy a desire for vengeance after all efforts at deterrence had failed.
>
> Instead live cities [are] to be appreciated as assets, as hostages, as a means of influence over the enemy himself. If enemy cities could

be destroyed twelve or forty-eight hours later, and if their instant destruction would not make a decisive difference to the enemy's momentary capabilities, destroying all of them at once would be to abandon the principal threat by which the enemy might be brought to terms.

We usually think of deterrence as having failed if a major war ever occurs. And so it has; but it could fail worse if no effort were made to extend deterrence into war itself.[4]

Having foreshadowed this dialectical move in an overture, as it were, Schelling then reviewed the doctrine of Controlled Response and began the transformation to a new doctrine by isolating the feature of the old doctrine that the US would abandon.

> There were two components of the strategy that Secretary McNamara sketched [at Ann Arbor]. . . . '[C]ounterforce' describes one of them; 'cities' (or 'no-cities') describes the other.
>
> The reason for going after the enemy's military forces is to destroy them before they can destroy our own cities (or our own military forces). The reason for not destroying the cities is to keep them at our mercy. The two notions are not so complementary that one implies the other: they are separate notions to be judged on their separate merits.[5]

As will be seen, this set the stage for severing the counterforce aspect of Controlled Response and thus for the movement to a new doctrine for, while there may be no necessary logical connection between the two aspects of the policy as interlocking pieces in a paradigm of graduated response, each was fitted to the other. It was because the US could destroy Soviet retaliatory forces that it was, mistakenly, thought feasible to offer the tacit withholding of a counter-cities strike. This mistake had hidden a serious weakness in the doctrine as discussed above and had led some thinkers to believe that Controlled Response would induce a counterforce strategy from the Russians. Schelling was sceptical.

> The question is often raised whether a [Controlled Response] is not self contradicting: it depends on a decisive military superiority over the enemy, and yet to succeed it must appeal equally to the enemy, to whom it cannot appeal because he must then have a decisive inferiority. This widespread argument involves a switch between the two meanings, 'counterforce' and 'cities'. A decisive capability to disarm the enemy and still have weapons left over, in a campaign

that both sides wage simultaneously, is not something that both sides can exploit. Both may aspire to it; both may think that they have it; but it is not possible for both to come out ahead in this contest.[6]

Having identified a fundamental flaw in a 'retaliatory' counterforce programme, Schelling then proceeded to rehabilitate the 'cities' component of the doctrine. In contrast to counterforce ambitions, he argued, it does

make sense for both sides to take seriously a 'cities' strategy that recognized cities as hostages, that exploits the bargaining power of an undischarged capacity for violence, threatening damage but only inflicting it to the extent necessary to make the threat a lively one. In fact, this 'cities' aspect of the [Controlled Response] strategy should appeal at least as much to the side with inferior strategic forces. If the inferior side cannot hope to disarm its enemy, it can only survive by sufferance. It can only induce such sufferance by using its capacity for violence in an influential way. This almost surely means not exhausting a capacity for violence in a spendthrift orgy of massacre, but preserving the threat of worse damage yet to come.[7]

Of course if this were intended to be a defence of *Controlled Response*, it would have been analytically flawed because in its separate discussion of the two aspects of the doctrine, Schelling neglects the degree to which one aspect might undermine the other. Facing a successful counterforce launch, it *is* implausible to think that the Russians would withhold attacks on American cities, not because they have to shoot at 'something', but because they have to shoot at something *now* and it is impossible to completely pre-empt American nuclear assets. The city-avoidance strategy makes sense to the Soviets only if they can either halt or avoid US counterforce strikes and this can't be done simply allowing their weapons to be successively destroyed. Schelling is far too penetrating an analyst not to have seen this; why then does he separate the two strategic elements of the policy – counterforce and cities – if this separation can bring about, at best, a lame defence? Because Schelling was not really interested in defending the policy, but rather in questioning the counterforce element, which he has now neatly detached. This is made quite clear by the following passage:

Separating the two components of this strategy is also necessary in dealing with whether a 'counter-force' strategy is of transient or enduring interest. There has been a genuine argument whether the

> United States can reliably expect a capability to disarm the Soviet Union by an offensive campaign, bolstered by defense of the home land. By 'genuine', I mean an argument that either side could win, depending on the facts, and that neither can win by sheer logic or casuistry. The outcome is going to depend on technology, costs, and the sizes of budgets; the actual facts may never be reliably clear. . . . But if we distinguish the 'counterforce' from the 'city-threatening' components of the strategy, it is evident that one part of the strategy does, and the other does not depend on the outcome of this argument. If as a result of technology, budgets, and weapon choices, it is going to turn out that we do not have a capability to disarm the enemy forcibly, then of course a strategy that depends on doing so becomes obsolete – at least until some later time when that capability is available. But there is no reason why that makes the 'cities' strategy obsolete. In fact, it virtually yields front rank to the 'cities' strategy.[8]

These 'facts' (amounting to the inability to execute the damage limitation mission) were precisely the ones that the Defense Department was forced to concede in the early to middle 1960s.

Moreover, the one supreme event in central deterrence that shattered confidence in Controlled Response appeared to verify Schelling's criticism of the doctrine. This was the Cuban Missile crisis.[9] In this crisis, American declaratory policy went immediately to total response threats and American actions set up a trip-wire, the blockade and quarantine. Thus in his address to the American people on 22 October 1962 informing them of the crisis underway, President Kennedy implicitly repudiated Controlled Response. In a carefully drafted statement he said, 'It shall be the policy of this nation to regard any nuclear missile launched from Cuba against any nation in the Western hemisphere as an attack by the Soviet Union on the United States requiring a full retaliatory response upon the Soviet Union.' As Schelling observed,

> coming less than six months after Secretary McNamara's official elucidation of the strategy of controlled. . . . response, the reaction implied in the President's statement would have been not only irrational but probably . . . inconsistent with the foundation that was laid as early as his first defense budget message of 1961, which stressed the importance of proportioning the response to the provocation, even in war itself. Nevertheless, it was not entirely incredible; and, [quite possible] the President meant it.[10]

This was a dramatic event in the US–USSR central relationship, perhaps the most dramatic in the turbulent history of that relationship. It demonstrated that the chess-like moves of the RAND doctrine were too subtle for the simple messages that nations send to each other when the stakes are very high. This crisis did not create the facts that undermined the old doctrine, however, and the new doctrine that emerged was every bit as counter-intuitive and maddeningly rational as welfare economics could make it.

Controlled Response, the city-avoidance/counterforce strategy, depended upon a US pre-emptive (or retaliatory) attack that would have disabled Soviet long-range nuclear forces while holding Russian cities hostage. This mission could not be executed with confidence by the middle of the decade. Again the critical development in central deterrence arose from a change in vulnerability – it was the Soviets' acquisition of more delivery vehicles, more weapons, and their dispersal that undermined the necessary context for Controlled Response.

By late 1963, the Soviets had solved most of the development problems that had initially kept their ICBM deployments so far below American expectations.[11] In the mid-1960s the Soviet Union began a rapid build-up and dispersal of nuclear forces. Despite the fact that these weapons were soft targets, were unsheltered and, being liquid fueled, required lengthy preparation for launch, confidence in US counterforce targeting greatly slackened. US forces had reliability problems that were exacerbated by the proliferation of targets. Its missiles were not very accurate and carried only one RV,[12] thus necessitating a net launcher loss[13] for a counterforce strike that targeted two missiles for each site. The US confronted the fact that the Soviets could increase their ICBM force faster and more cheaply than the United States could expand its ability to target them with a high degree of confidence.

As before, the effect was felt in Europe. Since, as Walter Slocombe noted,

> it was in an effort to increase the credibility of its declarations of readiness to use nuclear weapons in the defense of Western Europe by employing a more sophisticated doctrine than 'massive retaliation' that the United States made its most extensive public exposition of the possible role of massive counter-force attacks in American nuclear strategy, the end of the technical feasibility of such attacks could be expected to be significant, if anywhere, in connection with deterrence in Europe.[14]

This impact was accentuated by the fact that the Soviet ICBM buildups had been accompanied by a dramatic increase in Soviet IRBM and MRBMs whose ranges extended to Europe only.[15] 'These shifts . . . put pressure on the link between US strategic forces and the long-range NATO theatre systems based in Europe',[16] Anthony Cordesman has concluded. By 1963, the US had phased out its unreliable Thor and Jupiter missiles and in an effort to reduce the vulnerability of its bomber force whose range had been increased by in-flight refuelling, the US withdrew its B-47 command as well. This left only a highly vulnerable force of British V-bombers and NATO strike fighters whose vulnerability was further enhanced by the Russian deployment of SS-4s and SS-5s, such that any fighters which were not on Quick Reaction Alert (QRA) would probably be lost.

Of this period, Cordesman observes that, in practical terms, NATO's growing vulnerability forced the Supreme Allied Command in Europe, SACEUR, to plan on the basis of a pre-emptive strike using all nuclear alert forces under attack warning conditions. This gave NATO's nuclear forces a 'hair trigger' character and, although no one used the term at the time, it was clear that they could only survive if NATO 'launched on warning'. At the same time, such NATO plans meant that the SIOP had to be based on the assumption that *any* major NATO nuclear conflict would involve the initial release of over 1000 long- and medium-range theatre nuclear strikes. These had to suppress and interdict Warsaw Pact conventional and theatre nuclear forces as effectively as possible in the first day of conflict, and gave NATO little or no ability to avoid massive collateral damage to Warsaw Pact civilians or economic facilities.[17] This effectively made restraint impossible, since both sides had to launch strikes of such magnitude that escalation would be made inevitable.

Thus deployment against Europe of IRBMs and MRBMs in survivable modes and greatly increased numbers eroded the usefulness of Controlled Response as an instrument of extended deterrence in the new, central strategic context. Now, even if the Soviet Union was deterred from striking American cities, they would certainly strike European ones, while retaining in reserve an anti-US central force.

The US reaction to this crisis in extended deterrence brought about by the increasing invulnerability of Soviet forces to a US counterforce attack (and the fact that US forces were themselves becoming vulnerable) was to adopt the policy of 'Assured Destruction', and to force NATO to enhance its conventional options as part of a new NATO doctrine, 'flexible response'.[18] This amounted to a 'cities' strategy without the damage limitation component. The new policy was adopted when the strategic context made damage limitation an unattainably ambitious goal. Of the brief hiatus that preceded Assured Destruction, John Newhouse has written that,

> Damage Limitation was a straddle policy intended by McNamara to extract the maximum political and military premium for America's waning strategic superiority. To the extent that it temporarily underwrote extended deterrence, it posited that the ability to detract from your opponent's assured destruction capability was essential. But as Soviet nuclear forces became larger, more diversified, and less vulnerable, the probability receded that the US could limit damage to acceptable levels by striking first in support of extended deterrence or by retaliation in a second strike. Under these changing circumstances, a threatened countervalue response to every provocation gradually replaced Damage Limitation as the central plank of US nuclear deterrence.[19]

On 18 February 1965, Secretary McNamara announced that the US would henceforth rely on a policy of 'Assured Destruction' to deter Soviet aggression. The US intended to dissuade the Soviets from an attack on the US by promising that such an attack would be returned with a devastation that could not be eliminated by Soviet counterforce pre-emption; and that an attack on Europe would, in light of a greatly increased conventional force there, lead to a process of escalation whereby the assured destruction capability[20] would be engaged. Unlike Controlled Response and Damage Limitation, which were open-ended with respect to procurement and force-sizing because they were graduated responses, Assured Destruction promised the finite appropriations possible with total response programmes. If we trace McNamara's Congressional testimony during this decade, we can see, thanatrope-like, the movement to a policy of Assured Destruction by looking at the purpose assigned the secure, second strike capability and the pre-emptive first strike force.

Explaining the planned Defense Program for Fiscal Years 1964 to 1968, McNamara repeated his assertion that the United States should have a secure second strike force able to

1) Strike back decisively at the entire Soviet target system simultaneously or
2) Strike back first at the Soviet bomber bases, missile sites and other military installations associated with their long-range

> nuclear forces to reduce the power of any follow-on attack – and then if necessary, strike back at the Soviet urban and industrial complex in a controlled and deliberate way. . . .
>
> In planning our second strike force, we have provided, throughout the period under consideration, a capability to destroy virtually all of the 'soft' and 'semi-hard' military targets in the Soviet Union and a large number of their fully hardened missile sites, with an additional capability in the form of a protected force to be employed or held in reserve for use against urban and industrial areas.[21]

It was in this testimony that McNamara first voiced doubts about a strategy that relied on a large-scale counterforce attack. He pointed to the continuing growth of Soviet strategic forces, conceding that a

> very large increase in the number of fully hardened Soviet ICBMs and nuclear powered ballistic missile launching submarines would considerably detract from our ability to destroy completely the Soviet strategic nuclear forces.[22]

In 1964 McNamara moved the analysis further by differentiating between the two missions which the strategic forces programme was designed to perform. The first purpose of these forces was to deter deliberate nuclear attack against the United States and its allies by maintaining a highly reliable ability to inflict an unacceptable degree of damage upon any aggressor, even after absorbing a surprise first strike. This McNamara termed the 'assured destruction' mission. The second purpose (termed 'damage limitation' by McNamara) called for US forces 'in the event . . . [of] war . . . to limit damage to our population and industrial capacity'.[23] Then in early 1965 McNamara, while repeating the distinction between the two missions, went on to stress that 'assured destruction' was the more important. The Secretary suggested a rough quota of targets (and capabilities) such that 'the destruction of, say one-quarter to one-third of [the aggressor's] population and about two-thirds of its industrial capacity would be achieved, [meaning] the elimination of the aggressor as a major power for many years'.[24]

By January 1967 McNamara disclosed that his thoughts had gone further.

> Damage limiting programs, no matter how much we spend on them, can never substitute for an Assured Destruction capability in the deterrent role. It is our ability to destroy an attacker as a viable 20th

> Century nation that provides the deterrent, not our ability to partially limit damage to ourselves.[25]

Conceding a point often made by critics of the counterforce elements of Controlled Response and Damage Limitation, McNamara pointed out that

> If the general nuclear war policy of the Soviet Union also has as its objective the deterrence of a US first strike (which I believe to be the case), then we must assume that any attempt on our part to reduce damage to ourselves (to what they would estimate we might consider an 'acceptable level') would put pressure on them to strive for an offsetting improvement in their deterrent forces.[26]

Finally, in 1968, McNamara admitted that:

> For a 'Damage Limiting' posture to contribute significantly to the deterrent . . . it would have to be extremely effective, i.e., capable of reducing damage to truly nominal levels . . . We now have no way to accomplish this.[27]

This odyssey ended with McNamara's return to the 'cities' strategy. 'If . . . we do not have a capability to disarm the enemy forcibly,' Schelling had written, 'then of course a strategy that depends on doing so becomes obsolete . . . [T]here is no reason why that makes the "cities" strategy obsolete. In fact, it virtually yields front rank to the "cities" strategy'.[28]

The Assured Destruction doctrine is composed of much more, *necessarily*, than as assured destruction capability and plans. Schelling had explained why emphasizing the massive retaliation/countervalue aspects of Assured Destruction ought not to imply that the strategy implementing such a policy be limited to those aspects. Indeed, Schelling went so far as to dispute any conflict between such a policy and its wider, richer field of implementing options.

> One might pretend, in order to make war as fearsome as possible, that the obvious way to fight a war if we cannot successfully destroy military forces is to destroy the enemy's cities, while he does the same to us with the weapons that we are powerless to stop. But, once the war started, that would be a witless way to behave, about as astute as a head-on collision to preserve the right of way. And general nuclear war is probably fearsome enough anyway to deter any but a most desperate enemy in an intense crisis; making it somewhat less fearsome would hardly invite efforts to test just how

> bad the war would be. And in the intense crisis, belief that the war could be controlled if it broke out, and stopped short of cataclysm, might actually help to deter a desperate gamble on pre-emption. So the alleged hard choice between keeping deterrence as harsh as possible and making war, if it should occur, less harsh, may not be the dilemma it pretends to be.[29]

In the earlier strategy, a disarming counterforce exchange provided the lead-up to the bargaining of a cities approach. Now it was to be conventional and then tactical and if necessary theatre nuclear war in Europe. Thus the US 'sought to shift NATO from reliance on a thin screen of conventional forces designed only to defend against incursions and other local hostile actions' and an attempt at forcing the Soviet Union into making an attack sufficiently large to trigger a NATO nuclear response (the 'sword and the shield' concept of MC 14/2) to an emphasis on 'major NATO conventional defence options supported by existing short-range theatre nuclear systems and backed by US strategic superiority'.[30] The new policy was named Flexible Response, and without it, Assured Destruction would have been as 'witless' as it is routinely described by politicians and journalists. Among the important elements in Flexible Response were doctrinal answers to the developments that had undone Controlled Response: there was to be less reliance on the vulnerable nuclear strike aircraft, secure SLBMs were dedicated instead to SACEUR and there would be greater emphasis on conventional power.

Thus was completed the shift in doctrine away from Controlled Response. This shift was initiated owing to developments in the central deterrence relationship; ultimately, the shift in policy itself played back into that relationship. The new *relationship* (not a doctrine)[31] was one of mutual assured destruction. In the event of war, this relation would dissolve into exchanges according to doctrinal protocols far richer than simply a demand for the engagement of each side's assured destruction capability. Mutual assured destruction made the 'world safe for no-cities strikes' . . . but', Schelling put it, 'if I waylaid your children after school, and you kidnap mine, and each of us intends to use his hostages to guarantee the safety of his own children and possibly to settle some other disputes as well, there is no straight forward analysis that tells us what form the bargaining takes, which children in our respective possessions get hurt, who expects the other to yield – and how it all comes out'.[32]

This modest and disarming remark is characteristic of Schelling's insight; it is reminiscent of Calabresi for it is the 'form of bargaining' aspect that previous commentators had overlooked and that made economic analysis so powerful during this era.

Even granting the assumption of nuclear deterrence – that the mutual possession of thermonuclear weapons brought forth into the world a new type of deterrence by means of threats whose utility existed solely in their not having to be carried out – previous policy makers had found no guidance in deciding how to make this sort of deterrence work for US international security, how to avoid, for example, having to carry out the threat and to obtain some political benefit – principally the protection of Europe – beyond the mere maintenance of stalemate. Neither the systems analysts of the late 1950s nor the social scientists of a similar period could provide such a framework. Systems analysts could create a doctrine or criticize an existing doctrine in light of its own objectives, but systems analysis yielded no criteria for establishing or evaluating the objectives themselves.

Systems analysis – like its sister discipline, operations research – was essentially instrumental in its methods. Given a set of objectives that were clearly defined, it could tell the decision-maker whether or not particular programmes served those objectives efficiently. The basic objectives of national military preparedness were well understood and thus the systems analysts at RAND and elsewhere could bring powerful mathematical and computer-assisted tools to bear on the problem of optimizing American resources in the service of American objectives.

The context of mutual assured destruction, however, forcibly brought to the minds of thoughtful diplomats and politicians the need for analysis that went beyond efficient service to the national defence posture. What was needed was an analysis that took account of (1) the disagreement as to objectives when more than one nation's interest had to be taken into account, and (2) the symmetry of objectives among adversaries. Rather than simply assuming priorities, which in the international context were the subject of hot debate and conflict, analysts had to create systems that would tell politicians how to rank priorities, and this ranking had to be accomplished with an eye to the priorities of the adversary.

Modern welfare economics was developing these tools. In contrast to its classical models, in which there were no negotiations, no coalitions, and only atomistic competition, the microeconomist of the 1960s and 1970s tried to take into account the imperfections in the marketplace that made co-operation and bargaining crucial. The phrase of the period – 'It takes two to tango' – was just as true of maintaining national security, in the new context of mutual vulnerability, as it was of firms functioning in a market environment where co-operation was required to reduce transaction costs and externalities.

Schelling's first book, *The Strategy of Conflict*,[33] appeared in 1960;[34] it aimed to describe the system of incentives that the era of deterrence demanded. Politicians and planners needed more than advice on how to maintain a closed, delicate system: they had to learn where they were going so they could decide how much to spend in getting there. They had to learn how to explain their objectives to their adherents and defend them against detractors. By providing what Lawrence Freedman has called 'the strategy of stable conflict',[35] Schelling and others had served an objective rather similar to that of the Pareto standards: they sought a world in which neither of the parties to the bipolar arrangement – an island very much like those in Coase's parables – would be made better off unless the other's position were also bettered, or at least remained unchanged. This commitment in part explained the American fury over the Russian deployments in Cuba (an effort to gain a unilateral advantage at the cost of American security) as well as the Kennedy–Johnson enthusiasm for arms control. (Indeed Schelling's second book was devoted to the latter subject.)[36]

Fair arms control, proceeding by negotiation, would presumably arrive only at those arrangements that met the Pareto standards, as it were. The negotiation process was virtually an illustration of Coase's bribes and counter-bribes. Given this and the clear analysis of force-sizing that Schelling's theory made possible (enabling a quantitative answer to the question of what constituted a secure, second-strike retaliatory force) American security could be enhanced and would not be diminished by such negotiations. The Test Ban treaty, anathema to those Pentagon research and development chiefs who hoped to steal a technological march on the Soviets, followed quickly on the heels of the Cuban missile crisis. Impelled by the emotional relief and remembered anxiety of that crisis, the treaty was made possible by theory.

The theory, however, is susceptible to criticism of the basic underlying approach. We shall treat six objections.[37]

First, the approach depends on rational decision making, that is, a responsiveness to incentives. As such, Schelling is the direct descendant of Clausewitz whose work argues that the initiation and continuation of war must be measured against its political objectives. Yet Clausewitz also repeatedly reminds us of the unpredictability of war, and one is inclined to suspect that the axiomatic rationality of microeconomic man – that he maximizes his utility by his acts since by his acts we know his utility curves – has an awkward place in the strategic decisions of nuclear conflict. Survival, it is true, appears to be a value as universally held as the desire to maximize happiness. Yet bureaucratic and social decisions are not made on the basis of a single paramount value, or ordering of values. This is not to say they are not rational; rather that the incentives do not have the axiomatic validity they are otherwise accorded by the microeconomic approach. Moreover, there remain erroneous rational decisions entirely apart from those that can be put off to mistaken facts, inept judgements, or fanaticism, that arise from the structure and history of how a decision is presented.

Second, the approach, because it is so very generalized, tends to be apolitical (this is not to say non-ideological, because it is conservative in a profound sense). This is hardly surprising since so much of the approach depends on Pareto assumptions that were devised as a means of achieving consensus in an ideologically riven society (or, here, between ideological foes). The difficulty arises from treating parties as though they are similarly ideologically hollow and stand in a neutrally charged position with respect to the planner. In torts, there is culpability and shame, revenge and spite, regardless of a legislature's adoption of a no-fault programme. In world politics, there is aggressive and threatening behaviour that takes place precisely because it is de-stabilizing and 'wrong', i.e., inimical to our values. Indeed the apolitical quality of the analysis only projects the American tendency to treat foreign societies as replicas of our own, driven by our manic desires for prosperity, largely heedless of sectarian differences, easy-going with respect to other peoples' habits. In this regard one is tempted to recall President Johnson's repeated offers of economic aid to North Vietnam in exchange for a pledge to 'leave South Vietnam alone'. This was an apolitical approach from an otherwise politically sensitive President. Moreover, it is worth noting that if McNamara was captivated by systems analysis, strategic approaches like Schelling's were repeatedly endorsed by President Johnson. With their emphasis on bargaining these approaches must have appealed to the President's hostility to fatalism but, as the Vietnam experience demonstrates, these approaches are limited by some very limiting assumptions. Indeed it can be argued that it was President Johnson's personal attentiveness to the incentives presented to the other side for the wider war he so much wished to avoid – his concern not to present North Vietnam with the prospect of imminent destruction that would make Chinese intervention, otherwise abhorrent to the Vietnamese, a desperate alternative – that brought about a paradox in cost-benefit analysis that is particularly cruel. Measured at the outset, and at any moment, the benefits of successful continuation of the war must have seemed enough to justify the American presence while the likelihood of that success diminished as domestic sensitivity increased, a by-product of the very careful measuring of risks itself. The public would not support a lengthy engagement in Southeast Asia, but a lengthy counterinsurgency campaign was the only kind that matched the incentives Washington sought to give Hanoi. The very bargaining process undermined the credibility of the American commitment by eroding domestic consensus. Thus the magnitude of miscalculation could only appear gradually.

Third, the approach assumes mutually agreed-upon goals for the two participants. In theory these need not be the same goals so long as they are not inconsistent, but as a practical matter they are almost always assumed to be the same because a contrary assumption immensely complicates the analysis. In fact, it may not be that the American goal of stable, stalemated competition was ever shared by the Soviets. At any rate, there was surprise in the American community when dramatically large Soviet defence budgets followed SALT 1 and SALT 2. Indeed, in the period 1963 to 1973, the US consistently underestimated the size and the velocity of the Soviet arms programme.[38] And in the following decade it has been estimated that the Soviet Union outspent the United States by approximately $100 billion in strategic weapons expenditures.[39] The Soviet deployment of countersilo weapons, the war fighting doctrines of their military strategists, and various geopolitical moves (e.g., the Arab attack on Israel in 1973) would suggest, from very different quarters, that a 'strategy of stable conflict' has had thus far only one committed adherent. The difficulty this poses – quite apart from the political difficulties of retaining a domestic consensus in favour of arms control, for example, and reassuring allies who require confidence in the American assessment of international reality – is analytical. Without a shared, or at least compatible, set of goals, the maximizing Pareto strategies are inoperable. Agreements tend to become a source of self-doubt (were we *taken*?) and the force-sizing advantages provided by the analysis are replaced by a competitive effort not to fall behind.

Fourth, the analysis exaggerates the perception of the interdependence of commitments. It made sense for President Johnson to say that American troops were in Vietnam, in part, so that the US might maintain the stability of the US–Soviet relationship by demonstrating the reliability of our threats. This declaration had nothing to do with the view of monolithic Communism that it was so often caricatured to be; indeed the message that the painful validation of commitment sends is just as importantly received by one's allies as by one's adversaries. The difficulty is that, as President Eisenhower appears to have appreciated regarding the nuclear competition, the linkage of commitments surrenders the initiative to one's adversary and thereby subjects the public to Korean-style conflicts for which it has no taste, and in which, by virtue of the very abstractness of the doctrine, it has no belief. Indeed one might question whether a recent history of great sacrifice does strengthen the credibility of one's commitments. This was not the case in France in 1940. If it is true, as Hemingway writes, that life breaks us, that we heal and that some are strong in the broken places, it is equally true that some are weakened in the broken places, that we may be so reluctant to repeat the experience that we are unable to judge our own interests when a similar threat arises.

Fifth, the implementation of a strategy based on this approach depends on the easy communication between parties; hence the 'hot-line', formerly a teletype machine of dubious integrity that came into place in an office in the White House in 1962. Bargaining, it need hardly be said, depends on the communicability of incentives; Assured Destruction – particularly if it is properly understood as a 'cities approach' dependent on Flexible Response – absolutely depends on it. War itself, however, tends to degrade the communications apparatus: the signal sent by satellite to order a launch, which must be neutralized, might have been the signal recalling an order to launch, and so forth.

This shortcoming is related to the sixth objection, that the United States may not possess command and control facilities necessary to permit the strategy to function. Indeed the principal force relied upon by Assured Destruction – the secure, second strike SLBMs – presents control problems that unsuit them for intra-war bargaining.[40] It is obvious, perhaps, that a strategy based on welfare economics – the theory of rational expectations – depends upon the ability to *execute* rational commands. Doubt about this ability in the midst of a protracted conflict is important to the extent that the theory demands high confidence in such ability.

'In recent years economists have become very bold', Schelling recently wrote. 'Once primarily concerned with such mundane matters as how consumers allocate their budgets between food and clothing and whether a person should be charged to cross a bridge, they are now invading territories formerly regarded as outside the realm of their discipline – suicide, religion and ethics, marriage and family planning.'[41] To this list ought to be added nuclear strategy. By contrast, it is interesting to note that Vietnam, and not the nuclear balance, preoccupied Brodie in his last years, and that he was particularly intrigued by the psychological (which is to say non-economic) imperfections of military and political leaders.[42] For in the Vietnamese war, analysts confronted a conflict in which the US's failure to demonstrate the reliability of its threats was mainly due to misconceptions of the Vietnam situation in general and of the peculiar assets of Vietnamese communism in particular.

Undoubtedly, microeconomic doctrinal innovation made a powerful contribution to strategic policy. It dictated Flexible Response in the European theatre, for which President Johnson strove mightily (and successfully) to achieve an allied consensus. At the same time, it reimposed a version of total response on the central relationship. As Schelling put it,

> deterrence, particularly deterrence of anything less than mortal assault on the United States, often depends on getting into a position where the initiative is up to the enemy and it is he who has to make the awful decision to proceed to a clash. . . .
>
> The commitment process on which all American [extended] deterrence depends – and on which all confidence within the alliance depends – is a process of surrendering and destroying options that we might have been expected to find too attractive in an emergency. We not only give them up in exchange for commitments to us by our allies; we give them up on our own account to make our intentions clear to potential enemies. In fact, we do it not just to display our intentions but to adopt those intentions. If deterrence fails it is usually because someone thought he saw an 'option' that the American government had failed to dispose of, a loophole that it hadn't closed against itself.[43]

This description of a total response regimen bears little resemblance to the mindless, orgastic countervalue retaliation that is the usual misunderstanding of Assured Destruction. Once we have corrected the common misimpression that Assured Destruction, the doctrine, is to be equated with the assured destruction mission alone, however, we must then avoid adopting an equally distorted and misleading view that Assured Destruction was never more than a *declaratory* rather than a *employment* policy. It is understandable how even very thoughtful analysts might succumb to this, in frustration at the widespread and impervious nature of the Assured Destruction myth.

The evidence for such a view is found in the fact that, between 1962 and 1974, the SIOP remained essentially unchanged. It is true that the targets required by Controlled Response were never removed from the SIOP after the US adopted Assured Destruction; but this is only misleading if one holds the view that Assured Destruction consisted solely in plans to destroy Soviet population and industrial assets. The contradictory implications arising from retaining targets sets once the doctrine had changed were resolved 'either by changing the targeting (by changing the targeting priorities accorded the given target elements) or by simply increasing the number and variety of particular target elements covered in US nuclear war plans.'[44] In a SIOP that contains many more targets that there are warheads (by a factor of 4 to 1 at present and as much as 10 to 1 in the early war plans) a change in priorities amounts to a change in employment. If one understands Assured Destruction in the way described in this chapter, then it will be clear why the target sets of Controlled Response need not have been removed from the SIOP after 1962.

David Schwartz, a valuable commentator, writes,

> US declaratory policy did gradually move away from counterforce options towards a posture of assured destruction. But on the level of war plans, the [employment] policy of the United States, the SIOP was never revised to reflect this shift in declaratory policy. McNamara never had counterforce options removed from US strategic war plans, and as new counterforce targets appeared, new US weapons were allocated to these targets. Operationally, McNamara and his successors never incorporated assured destruction as an [employment] policy.[45]

This conclusion depends, however, on making the usual error of identifying assured destruction, the mission, with Assured Destruction, the policy. The former was part of the superseded doctrine of Controlled Response (and therefore it was not necessary to add targets to the SIOP). The latter did not require that counterforce options be removed from the SIOP.

Despite subsequent, more extreme declarations which encouraged the belief that only urban areas would be hit in an all-out war, in fact the targeting of military facilities continued throughout the sixties and into the seventies. Henry Rowen notes that, 'the priority in the assignment of weapons was first, to the urban-industrial targets, and then to nuclear threat and other military forces'. But he goes on to explain:

> A high 'priority' in this context means 'most important.' It does not mean first in time. Presumably the most time urgent targets would be military forces, especially nuclear threat ones. Highest priority also does not mean that the greatest weight of effort would have to be allocated against urban-industrial targets; rather that the confidence of being able to destroy these targets should be high.[46]

There had been then a substantial change in doctrine, as indicated by the subordination of counterforce targets. Massive damage limitation had been superseded by the 'run-up' of Flexible Response, and the abandonment of a strategy that depended upon the complete destruction of the Soviet nuclear arsenal.

Assured Destruction, the careful, well-advertised process of foregoing some options, then played back into the central relationship. Protecting it, for example, from ABM deployment, brought us MIRV; propounding it brought us parity (which would have arrived anyway); relying on it in conjunction with its corollary, Flexible Response, ultimately induced both ICBM vulnerability (a development that was not fatal to the Assured Destruction doctrine) and the collapse of NATO escalation dominance (which was). These were events, however, still to come when President Nixon was inaugurated in 1968.

7 Essential Equivalence and the Countervailing Strategy

Io fei giubbetto a me de le mie case.

(I made a gibbet for myself of my house.)

Canto XIII, *Inferno*

The period between 1968 and 1974 may fairly be characterized as one of continuity in strategic doctrine. President Nixon renamed the doctrine he inherited, calling it 'Strategic Sufficiency',[1] doubtless appreciating its positive contributions to fiscal restraint. Relying on the unchanged substance of the doctrine, he used it as the basis for strategic arms limitation talks, originated by Johnson but uncommenced owing to the Russian invasion of Czechoslovakia.[2] Strategic doctrine of this period, as we have seen, included an important role for arms control and that doctrine also structured the treaties that then and have since emerged from the SALT process.

In 1968 the US enjoyed a lead in anti-ballistic (ABM) technology that promised to enable a new damage limiting capability by some time in the early 1980s. At the same time, the US had taken a significant lead in the developing technology of multiple, independently targetable re-entry vehicles (MIRV). The interaction of these two phenomena, and the result of this interplay in the SALT 1 negotiations are easily understood if one fully appreciates the Assured Destruction approach and understands that SALT was an effort to preserve the vitality of the doctrine. Thus the new administration, gratified and to some extent intrigued by US ABM development, clearly foresaw that such damage limiting technology would inevitably become mutual and that the relatively austere force-sizing requirements of Assured Destruction would then be replaced by a very expensive, largely open-ended competition with the defensive system, ultimately frustrated by the introduction of MIRVs that could more cheaply swamp any ground based ABM system than the capabilities of that system could be multiplied. The result would be ABM systems that would *only* be effective against an opponent weakened by a first strike and thus create an inevitable pull in the direction of damage limitation and away from Assured Destruction. Foreseeing these developments, the US used its lead in MIRV technology to deploy large numbers of SLBM warheads with high survivability but relatively low lethality, i.e., relatively limited damage limitation capability.[3] Then the Administration convened SALT negotiations to exploit these favourable trends in the direction of enhanced stability, according to the received doctrine.

In retrospect, it would appear that the US lead in ABM and MIRV technology was, if not overestimated, at least given an illusory significance. The US failed to appreciate the speed with which the Soviet Union could develop and deploy MIRVs and, while the US did in fact possess a significant advantage in ABM technology, this fact was of marginal, perhaps solely, negotiating consequence beside the US inability to develop an effective ABM defence system against Soviet MIRV deployment. The result of these misperceptions was that the Nixon Administration failed to develop a strategic doctrine that could have served as the basis for MIRV limitation in SALT 1. One practical side effect of this was that targeting planners had to assign the increased number of warheads made available by MIRVing to roughly the same number of SIOP target sets. When, on 15 March 1971 Secretary of Defense Laird defined the 'new' doctrine of 'Strategic Sufficiency', the actual targeting options were more massive than those of Assured Destruction even though the doctrine – maintaining a secure second strike that 'assured no incentive for a first strike' and the capability to ensure vast Soviet economic and civil damage – was unchanged.[4] When events in the central relationship cast doubt on the intermediate strategic options that a 'cities' approach required – the run-up of Flexible Response – the very massiveness of the 'sufficiency' options wold appear an unappealing drawback.

Three developments in the central relationship precipitated the crisis in extended deterrence that yielded a doctrinal replacement for Assured Destruction/Strategic Sufficiency. These were (1) the arrival of parity in central systems, (2) the increasing vulnerability of US land-based missile forces, and (3) the collapse of escalation dominance beneath the central level.

These events did not occur simultaneously but the trends culminating in them can now be seen to have emerged in the late 1960s and early 1970s. Between 1966 and 1970 the size of the Soviet land based missile force grew by 1007, from 292 to 1299 ICBM launchers while the US force remained unchanged in number. During the same period, the Soviet Union deployed twenty new ballistic missile submarines, increasing their SLBM force from 107 to 304.[5] Once MIRVing began – which the US deployed on its SLBM force, strictly according to doctrine[6] – the USSR acquired a significant counterforce capability against US ICBMs by deploying its multiple warhead technology on now vastly increased land based ICBMs, evidently governed by wholly different doctrinal considerations. Also, in 1966, the Soviets had begun to deploy their ICBMs in hardened underground silos. 'Increases in the number, hardness and mobility of Soviet long-range nuclear forces . . . resulted in a decline in damage expectancies for this class of targets'.[7] While the Soviet offensive arsenal was thus becoming larger and less vulnerable, the number of US ballistic missile launchers deployed had levelled off and was becoming more vulnerable.[8] Again in accordance with the prevailing US strategic doctrine, large numbers of warheads specifically designed to destroy hardened Soviet military installations were not procured.[9] As a consequence, the capabilities of US forces against the Soviet nuclear threat targets began to decline.

By 1970 the attack options available to a US President had been significantly narrowed. In February, in his Foreign Policy Message to the Congress, President Nixon asked:

> Should a President, in the event of a nuclear attack, be left with the single option of ordering the mass destruction of enemy civilians, in the face of the certainty that it would be followed by the mass slaughter of Americans? Should the concept of assured destruction be narrowly defined and should it be the only measure of our ability to deter the variety of threats we may face?[10]

Although the President and his National Security Adviser certainly knew that existing plans did not contain only a single, countervalue urban–industrial option, the President's statement, repeated in a subsequent message,[11] underscored an important fact. The caricature of Assured Destruction as being no more than the threat to employ an assured destruction capability was becoming a grotesque reality. Events were casting doubt on the ability to advantageously execute non-urban attacks. A President contemplating ordering a nuclear attack would then be faced with three basic options: (1) to authorize strikes, pre-emptive or retaliatory, against Soviet forces (strikes that would probably weaken the United States more than the USSR because they would cost more US missiles than they would kill Russian ones and, in any event, the Soviet Union would still retain, after these attacks, a significant force); (2) to order the massive assured destruction strike on all targets, military and urban/industrial; or (3) do nothing.[12]

After 1970, the strategic impact of the events mentioned above in the central relationship began to be felt. In 1972, the Department of Defense began to study revisions of the SIOP and in the ensuing two years a full scale inter-agency review was undertaken resulting in the announcement of a new strategic doctrine by the Secretary of Defense, James Schlesinger. Why had these particular events precipitated the rejection of a doctrine so recently embraced, and why did they call forth the particular new doctrine that resulted?

Parity in central systems had been achieved by the Soviets. The coming of parity in the central systems of the superpowers should not be confused, however, with their mutual acquisition of a secure, second-strike assured destruction capability. This acquisition had come much earlier and was in part responsible, as has been argued, for the abandonment of Controlled Response, just as the even earlier end of the American nuclear monopoly had undermined previous doctrine. But whatever may have been the doctrinal effect of the loss of a credible US first strike deterrent,[13] those effects pre-date the successful Soviet effort to build a missile force roughly equal to the US force in terms of the numbers of central system launchers (ICBMs and SLBMs).[14] Writing on the political consequences of parity, Walter Slocombe observed,

> The technical capabilities of equal-sized assured-destruction forces do not differ greatly from those of unequal ones. Even if it is much smaller than the force it faces, an assured-destruction force, by definition, denies the stronger side the possibility of a true first strike. . . . The only place where the technical changes in capabilities brought about by parity require a fundamental re-examination of doctrine is in connection with the virtual elimination of whatever plausibility there may have been to the idea that even after the United States lost first-strike superiority, it retained in the option of a massive attack on Soviet strategic nuclear forces a potentially decisive ultimate instrument of policy.[15]

It was, however, precisely the possibility of escalating *counterforce* strikes (which, it must be conceded, did not destroy so much of the Soviet force as to disable significant retaliation), that with city withholding amounted to the Assured Destruction/cities doctrine. Granted that the other side had an invulnerable ability to destroy US cities, the US relied on its margin above assured destruction forces to implement its 'cities' strategy: cities could be threatened so long as that threat could be maintained largely intact, while the US could attack other targets, for example in response to an advancing invasion of Europe. These attacks were not the wholly disarming strikes against central strategic weapons planned by Controlled Response – such strikes were admittedly too difficult to be made with confidence and in any event, would only tempt a cities-strike by the Soviets should their assured destruction capability appear jeopardized. Rather, such strikes were counterforce strikes against military targets, such as medium range bombers and Soviet IRBMs and MRBMs targeted on Europe, conventional forces, command centres, SSBNs[16] in port, and so forth. These strikes had the goal of reducing Soviet options to two: either she must desist or initiate a suicidal countervalue exchange, for there could be no marginal gain in using her own counterforce capability. In other words, even once a mutual, invulnerable assured destruction capability existed, the wide margin on mere numbers preserved the political utility of US assured destruction forces. It made a 'cities' strategy possible.[17] When Soviet forces grew to those needed for an assured destruction capability – about half the US force in the mid-1960s – many analysts mistakenly assumed that the buildup was over, overlooking, perhaps, the significance of parity.[18] In fact, it continued until the Soviets surpassed the US in some measures in 1970 and by 1971, Slocombe could give the following wary summary:

> [T]here are important senses in which the strategic forces on the two sides are in balance. Each has an assured-destruction capability against the other and neither has a potential for destroying by a first strike enough of the other's offensive forces seriously to restrict its choices of response. The present parity of numbers of launchers and the absence of any near-term threat to a major element in the forces of either side are likely to prevail for at least the next few years.[19]

In fact, the arrival of parity made possible the development of a threat to a major element of the US force structure. For second in the events occurring within the central relationship was the development of MIRV technology by the Soviets and the increasing vulnerability of the US land based ICBM force.

During 1975–8 it steadily became clear that the USSR would create a major counterforce capability against the Minuteman force by the early 1980s. Virtually every three months during this period the US discovered yet another significant improvement in Soviet ICBM design and deployment, missile accuracy, missile reliability and fractionation capability. . . . [B]y the time [Defense] Secretary Rumsfeld wrote his FY 1978 *Annual Report*, the US was projecting inferiority in several key measures of the balance and therefore a major risk that the USSR could 'win' a counterforce exchange.[20]

It will be easily understood that something like Soviet parity – and certainly not merely a secure assured destruction force significantly inferior in numbers – is a precondition for Soviet attacks on US ICBMs. Otherwise such attacks actually worsen the ratio of opposing forces from the Soviet point of view. For the same reason, another condition, once parity is achieved, is the availability of multiple independently targetable warheads. Even assuming very high counter-military potential (CMP), a Soviet single-warhead ICBM attack on US ICBMs would also at best amount to a mere trade and, as a practical matter, leave the Soviets worse off than before the attack since it must require 1 + Soviet missiles to eliminate 1 US missile. In other words, there can be no incentive for a pre-emptive, countersilo attack if the ratio of missiles is made worse off by the attack, from the attacker's point of view, and this will be the case so long as the attacker must use at least one missile to attack one silo. But what is not so easily seen is why the US would permit these two preconditions to take place. Why, in other words, didn't the US take the opportunity provided by the SALT negotiation, which ultimately codified parity, to insist on a MIRV prohibition especially considering that, at the time of negotiations, the US held what must have appeared to be a formidable lead in MIRV technology while the USSR did not even test its first MIRVs until 1973? Doctrine is the answer; it was the way we thought.

As parity approached, the 'cities' doctrine shrank increasingly to deterrence assumptions *simpliciter*, that is, to a role within central but not extended deterrence. This narrowing emphasized the stabilizing goals of the doctrine but, as we shall see, eroded the basis for its political role in achieving US security objectives. From the point of view of stability there appeared two technological challenges: MIRVs and ABMs. MIRVs threatened stability because they could enable *first* strikes that decisively altered the exchange ratios in favour of the attacker, and hence rendered insecure an important leg of the triad; ABM, because they eroded the confidence of a *second* strike, robbing it of its 'assured' destructiveness by preventing its warheads from getting through. Both these technologies threatened stability, but one – the ABM system – was considerably more threatening since it applied to any missile while the threat posed by MIRVs applied only to the ICBM (and not the SLBM, the principal carrier of countervalue destruction). Moreover, Russian possession of an effective ABM system, even assuming the US acquired an equally effective system, would amount to a net gain for the Soviet Union in Europe where their preponderance in conventional arms was checked by US threats of nuclear first use. The effect of MIRVing Soviet missiles, on the other hand, might be no more significant than the consequences of parity, threatening perhaps the counterforce, time-responsive US capability that underlay a 'cities' strategy, but keeping the assured destruction component intact (just as, as Slocombe had argued, the effect of parity might be no more than that we had accepted with the mutual acquisition of a secure, second strike capability). Finally, the decisive factor was that ABM and MIRV issues were intertwined, since the most compelling argument to the Russians against ABM – given their professed uninterest in merely maintaining the stability of the system of deterrence – was that it was technically infeasible in light of MIRVing. SALT 1 emerged, therefore, as a finite force-sizing agreement accompanied by an ABM treaty and without a MIRV prohibition. Given the relative reliance by the Russians on a land based force, this must have seemed, at the time, a US triumph. What was perhaps unanticipated was the rapid gain in accuracy[21] that both sides would make and that, with the deployment of a new generation of Soviet missiles of high throw-weight (the SS17/18/19) in the early 1970s, the Soviets could exploit to render US ICBMs vulnerable.[22]

This improvement in guidance has been a mutual affair: indeed it is doubtful that either side could have halted it since it was a laboratory development,[23] independent of official doctrine. In any event, neither side would be likely to acquiesce for long in being the sole subject of an advantageous[24] hard target, countersilo capability. (Although it was predicted that, in the early 1980s, the Soviet Union possessed the capability to destroy 90 per cent of all US ICBMs in a first strike, using only a slight fraction of her own ICBMs,[25] while the US has not acquired a similar capability *vis-à-vis* the Soviets, having postponed the deployment of the MX in the mid-1980s.)

The effects of the 'window of vulnerability', as the period between these two events (i.e., the Soviet acquisition of this threat and the US parrying of the threat) has been named, would have weakened extended deterrence even if the US were to close the window and acquire a similar capability. Table 7.1, derived from Payne offers a pessimistic calculus of US ICBM vulnerability to a Soviet first strike.

Table 7.1 US ICBM vulnerability to a Soviet first strike

	55–19	*55–18*
Deployed on-launcher ICBMs	300	308
SS-19/SS/18 operational (.9)	270	277
Warheads available assigned to targets	1620	2770
		1052
Assigned warheads on ICBMs reliable through boost (.9)		947
Warheads reliable through MIRV separation (.95)		899
Warheads reliable on target (.95)		854
Single Shot Kill Probability against 2000 psi hardened target (.84)		
Silos destroyed: First wave		718
Residual available warheads		1718
assigned to targets		1052
Warheads on ICBMs:		
reliable through boost		947
reliable through impact		854
Silos destroyed: Second wave		227
US silos destroyed:	945	
Surviving US on-launcher ICBMs:	107	
Surviving US on-launcher ICBM warheads:	215	
All Remaining Soviet on-launcher ICBMs:	1186	
All Remaining Soviet on-launcher ICBM warheads:	4120	

Source: K. Payne, *Nuclear Deterrence in US–Soviet Relations* (Boulder, Colorado, Westview, 1982), p. 173.

US ICBM vulnerability – unless we assume that in arms control negotiations MX deployment can be traded off for a teardown of Soviet heavy missiles – is doctrinally significant regardless of its mutuality. As Gregory Treverton has observed, 'American (ICBM) vulnerability is essentially a problem for deterrence in Europe'[26] and this would persist even if the US had rendered Soviet ICBMs vulnerable at an earlier date. While it may be true that *mutual* ICBM vulnerability to advantageous pre-emption enhances stability by reducing the possibility of a post-exchange advantage to the attacker,[27] the stabilizing effect of this mutual acquisition is likely to be felt in the central relationship. The US ICBM force, one may conclude, is unlikely to be wiped out or attacked en masse in such a context. But those elements in the US force that previously were an invulnerable, indispensable factor in protecting the extended theatre have suffered by the change whether or not it is parried. By eroding confidence in a leg of the triad essential to those missions required by the Assured Destruction doctrine that are beyond the assured destruction mission, ICBM vulnerability crucially weakened the doctrine so far as extended deterrence was concerned.

The third important event in the 1970s was the reversal of US escalation dominance when the Soviets deployed highly accurate, mobile and largely invulnerable IRBMs (the SS-20s), a new medium range bomber (the Backfire), and a new generation of short range theatre weapons. A number of features of the SS-20s combined to make NATO forces highly vulnerable to pre-emption:[28] the accuracy of the SS-20s (with a CEP (see p. 301 n. 3 *infra*) of .26 nm compared to CEPs of over 1.0 nm for the SS-4s and 5s); their multiple warhead packaging (3 RVs); their survivability and capability for surprise (they were, unlike the SS-4 and SS-5, both solid-fuel and mobile). Such pre-emption was particularly likely since NATO nuclear assets (with the exception of the strategic missiles of the Poseidons dedicated to SACEUR) were in soft basing modes. Moreover, the SS-20s could be used in limited attacks, thwarting the NATO strategy of reserving to itself the options of escalation. As Edward Luttwak has noted:

> The difference between the new SS-20 and the old SS-4s and SS-5s is not merely greatly increased accuracy but also greatly diminished vulnerability. Because of their vulnerability, SS-4s and SS-5s could scarcely be used in a selective, discrete fashion: all would be immediate candidates for destruction if any were used. SS-20s, by contrast, are mobile and easily concealed, so that selective attacks by them are a true option.[29]

The doctrine of Assured Destruction demanded the corollary of Flexible Response, which in turn depended on escalation dominance. It makes no sense to bargain while holding cities hostage – when one's own cities are similarly held hostage – unless there is the potential for ever-escalating strikes that do not engage, and do not diminish, the countervalue assured destruction capability. 'Assured Destruction' was a doctrine of war termination, a threat that could be used to end hostilities. If these were to be ended on terms that favoured NATO, then dominance, if not at the conventional level, at least at the tactical and theatre levels, would have to be maintained. During the early 1970s this dominance was lost and with the deployment of the new Soviet SS-20, -21, -22 and the new planned deployments of the SS-23 series, escalation dominance passed to the Soviet side. From the *Military Balance*:

> The SS-21 will be deployed in large quantities by the mid-1980s and will be the first nuclear missile stationed in Eastern Europe in over ten years. The SS-23 will replace a part of the SCUD-A force and will probably have a range of up to 350km with either a nuclear or conventional warhead. The SS-22 missile will replace the SCALE-BOARD or SS-12 and will have a maximum range of 1000km with yields of up to 500kt. It will be in mass production by the end of 1981 at the latest. The SS-22 is comparable to the SS-20 in size, tactical deployment, range, and prospective targets in Central Europe from remote areas of the Soviet Union. Some analysts have postulated that for this reason a rule of thumb for defense policy could be: three SS-22s equal one SS-20 with three RVs, at least with respect to NATO's heartland.[30]

This was a bitter reversal for the United States since she had relied on superiority in nuclear weapons to redress the conventional imbalance in Europe. It is also significant that the Warsaw Pact's aircraft appear to be better able to survive and penetrate to their targets than NATO's, as shown by the judgement that 29 per cent of Warsaw Pact air-delivered warheads are expected to survive and arrive at their targets, against 23 per cent for NATO. Soviet aircraft are generally newer than NATO's while the IISS estimates that Warsaw Pact air defences are denser and more effective.

If Poseidon is excluded,[31] the Warsaw Pact's overall advantage in arriving warheads is about 2.37 : 1; with Poseidon that advantage falls to about 1.57 : 1. Nevertheless, the IISS concludes that 'even with the inclusion of Poseidon on the Western side and continued exclusion of Soviet strategic systems, the balance is distinctly unfavourable to NATO and is becoming more so. The Soviet SS-20 programme . . . is complete, [and at the same time] nothing has yet been done to reduce substantially the vulnerability of NATO's existing nuclear delivery systems or to increase their ability to penetrate Pact defenses'.[32] All this has occurred during a period in which the conventional balance has not yet improved for NATO.

> The numerical [conventional] balance over the last 20 years has slowly but steadily moved in favor of the East. At the same time the West has largely lost the technological edge which allowed NATO to believe that quality could substitute for numbers. One cannot necessarily conclude from this that NATO would suffer defeat in war, but one can conclude that there has been sufficient danger in the trend to require urgent remedies.[33]

This unfavourable conventional posture was once thought to be compensated for by tactical nuclear weapons. Gregory Treverton, however, has accurately captured the political realities of this doctrine in the current climate.

> [To] put it starkly, what would ensue if NATO were actually losing a conventional war, and its leaders decided that the time had come to face the great abyss of nuclear use? First, there would be no automatic decision, and great emphasis would be given to those nuclear systems which are most controllable. The US President would certainly want to approve every release of a nuclear weapon and every single target; he could hardly do less. Yet that suggests that he would be extremely reluctant to release short-range weapons for battlefield use at the subsequent discretion of commanders on the scene.[34]

NATO consensus – or German acquiescence if consensus is not possible – regarding a decision to launch a nuclear strike would doubtless require American commitments not to use nuclear weapons in Germany (East or West) and, Treverton speculates, also a pledge not to launch at least the initial strikes from German territory. These requirements – plus that of sparing the Soviet Union in the early stages – suggest that only Poseidon strikes against Eastern Europe are likely to be negotiable. Thus, early in a nuclear war, precisely because it is early, NATO would be forced to commit the sort of central system that doctrine had reserved for late in the conflict, in pursuit of targets of marginal advantage, in fear of a Soviet reply that would be likely to worsen the NATO position in any case. The escalatory pattern of play and trump on which NATO depended had yielded to new Soviet deployments while these in turn were likely to skew Western decision making away from its doctrine in a crisis. It was no longer possible for the US to redress any losing conflict by confidently raising the level of exchange, nor to confine that exchange to a particular level through Soviet awareness that ever higher levels of escalation mean ever worsening relative Soviet positions. The effect was to make 'Assured Destruction' (the doctrine) into simple 'assured destruction' (the mission), that is, to transform the 'cities' doctrine, with its careful run-up and emphasis on bargaining and termination into the senseless doctrine of a mutually suicidal alternative to capitulation, enforced only by an unwillingness to test a threat premised on such vast irrationality. Lynn Davis has concluded that,

> [g]iven the projected developments in Soviet strategic nuclear forces, the United States in the 1980s/1990s will not be able to re-establish superiority over the Soviet Union. The balance of US and Soviet strategic nuclear warheads is projected to be approximately equal assuming SALT II limits and to the Soviet advantage without SALT constraints. The Soviet Union will maintain superiority in equivalent megatons and time-urgent hard-target kill capability. . . . The United States cannot expect as a result of a limited nuclear exchange to achieve superiority, or what is sometimes called 'escalation dominance'.[35]

These three events – the arrival of parity, the prospect of ICBM vulnerability and the collapse of flexible response – operated synergistically, and their interrelated impact was, as before, felt with respect to extended deterrence. One may doubt whether US ICBM vulnerability really affects the central relationship for much the same reason that one doubted that Controlled Response was analytically sound: no political leadership could be expected to witness the destruction of its land-based nuclear strategic forces and the attendant casualties (estimated, in the US at 12 to 20 million)[36] with the *sangfroid* necessary to resist retaliation. Parity does not change the structure of central deterrence beyond that which was brought about by both sides achieving an assured destruction capability. Flexible Response is not even a doctrine of central deterrence. Yet, as with earlier periods, these developments had profound effects on the extension of US deterrence to other theatres, principally Europe.

Put most simply: parity is a necessary condition for self-deterrence in central systems because parity erases the US margin above assured destruction capabilities that enables the threat of assured destruction to be successful as a threat, in other words, without its actual engagement; once parity is achieved, US ICBM vulnerability negates the US option of a counterforce strike against the USSR on behalf of

European objectives (since retaliation would leave the US with an increasingly unfavourable position with respect to her own national security). Such a negation therefore permitted the Soviets the option of launching a nuclear attack on Europe without attacking the US; this option, in turn augmented by an invulnerable Soviet counterforce capability against European based NATO nuclear weapons, would be sufficient to permit a Soviet conventional or conventional/tactical nuclear assault to proceed on its own terms. Interacting, these events ensure decoupling, the detachment of the US strategic deterrent from the European theatre.

Even this scenario hardly captures the scope of the problem (indeed, as will be argued in Chapter 8, seeing the problem as one of 'decoupling' virtually dictates a paradoxical and problematical solution). Taken together, these developments were fatal to the prevailing doctrine. Assured Destruction targeting – consisting entirely of options for large-scale counterforce and combined counterforce–countervalue options – had to be wholly restructured to avoid reducing the ambit of a total response threat to the assumption of central deterrence itself. That assumption holds that the destructiveness of nuclear weapons (and the survivability of launchers) is such that initiation of a large-scale nuclear attack on a super-power is tantamount to the suicide of the attacking nation-state, and therefore that large-scale nuclear attacks can rationally be used only to deter such attacks by the other side and not for any other less ultimate or more active purposes. Although, as has been argued, such a position is stable for *central* deterrence, it is unstable for *extended* deterrence. If American doctrine were reduced to such terms in actuality then, regardless of US declarations of support for Europe, a new strategic doctrine was required. The Russians and the Americans, in 1974, appeared to approach a fast-arriving day when they would stand again in the position of adversaries in the assured destruction doctrinal context, only with their roles reversed. The Russians knew, even if we hadn't taken their fears seriously, how potent a genuine Assured Destruction doctrine could be. (And we should not confuse their current interest in such doctrines with a new found commitment to stability.) Soviet superiority in the European theatre and her qualitative ability to exploit US strategic launcher vulnerability were roughly analogous to the conditions that had permitted the US doctrine to operate. Accordingly, the new US doctrine proclaimed the objective of 'Essential Equivalence' and sought a strategic means to open up usable nuclear options within the possibilities and constraints of that equivalence. A doctrine for central deterrence, it took its name from a feature of the central relationship, but its most significant innovations were the design and incorporation in the SIOP of limited nuclear options, since these were conceived as the means of curing the crisis in *extended* deterrence. As Laurence Martin observed at the time,

> [O]nly some form of limited nuclear option can plausibly sustain any strategic guarantee to allies . . . From now on only more subtle and limited doctrines, ranging from the virtually symbolic strike to the discriminating, damage minimizing attack, can be planned in aid of extended deterrence for allies.[37]

That such options did not directly affect US ICBM vulnerability, or promise to achieve damage limitation to any meaningful extent, simply underscored the perception – whatever the rhetoric – of the prevailing stability of central deterrence and the deep concern over the European theatre. To emphasize this point, and to repeat again the important but universally obscured distinction between 'assured destruction' (the doctrine) and 'assured destruction' (the mission within but not co-extensive with that doctrine), it remained US policy to preserve, unaltered, the assured destruction capability and plans within the new doctrine.

As a heuristic device,[38] this depiction of role-reversal has much to recommend it, because one can observe, in the American search for a new doctrine and a SIOP revision, precisely those concerns that the Soviets had faced earlier. Thus Lynn Davis wrote,

> In the light of the build-up of Soviet strategic forces, American analysts were worried that in a crisis the Soviet Union might fire, or threaten to fire, a limited number of nuclear weapons, selectively against significant military targets, while at the same time holding American cities hostage to future destruction. If the United States' only choice lay between responding massively against enemy cities or doing nothing, the enemy might threaten or carry out a limited use of nuclear weapons on the assumption that she would do nothing.[39]

The new Secretary of Defense, James Schlesinger, prepared the political basis for change by repeatedly posing the problem, to Congress and in press conferences, as if the US really were in the previous Soviet position and faced dominance at lower levels, vulnerability and a lack of options and self-deterrence at the central level. But this obscures the analysis behind the new doctrine of Limited Nuclear

Options (LNOs) and its source in concern about extended deterrence. Such concern is clear in Kissinger's account of the initial efforts by the Administration to replace the Assured Destruction doctrine. 'It was all very well to threaten mutual suicide for purposes of deterrence, particularly in case of a direct threat to national survival . . . [but how] could the US hold its allies together as the credibility of its strategy eroded?'[40]

Desmond Ball has chronicled the bureaucratic development of the drafting process:

> In mid-1972, without public announcement, President Nixon directed Kissinger to head a top-level inter-departmental group tasked with the development of additional strategic nuclear war options, including some involving selective attacks on certain military targets, so that the President might have more flexibility in the event of a strategic nuclear exchange. . . . The work of these groups led directly to National Security Study Memorandum (*NSSM*)-169, approved by President Nixon in late 1973.
>
> *NSSM*-169 led directly to the promulgation of National Security Decision Memorandum (*NSDM*)-242, signed by President Nixon on 17 January 1974.[41]

The descriptions we have of the policymaking process make clear that extended deterrence was the animating force behind the decision.

> When [the study group] focused on real world cases they were initially worried about the possibility of mounting tension in a crisis provoking Soviet use of nuclear weapons in western Europe. However, given their general ideas about deterrence, flexibility would also be potentially helpful elsewhere to deter limited nuclear attacks, particularly in such areas of possible major power confrontation as the Middle East, the Sino–Soviet border, etc.[42]

NSDM-242 directed that plans for limited employment options be developed and incorporated into the SIOP; it also authorized the Secretary of Defense to promulgate the Nuclear Weapons Employment Policy (NUWEP), a policy guidance document spelling out the targeting implications of the new strategy. NSDM 242 established the policy programmes that govern the present SIOP and the current NUWEP. In substantive terms also, NSDM 242 indicated the direction the US government was to follow in the ensuing decade. The new strategy was a return to the graduated response paradigm. This was to be achieved by using limited nuclear options in a variety of pre-packaged, relatively selective forms (1) to halt the immediate aggression and (2) thereby threaten, and if necessary execute, those remaining options necessary to change perceptions about the possibility of victory such that no rational objective could be achieved while (3) the ultimate assured destruction capability remained in reserve to enforce rationality, that is, to prevent a re-calculation of objectives and costs that might justify continuing the aggression. In March 1974 Schlesinger announced the adoption of the new American strategy, and began a public campaign to explain it.

In a broadcast interview[43] Schlesinger reiterated the basis for the new doctrine.

> Q: This means, if I understand it, that you are saying [that], even if only in limited ways, the American strategic nuclear deterrent is still available in dire circumstances to be used as a first strike, on behalf, even though a limited strike, of Western Europe and therefore, as the jargon goes, is still 'coupled' with the integrity of Western Europe?
>
> Schlesinger replied:
>
> It is certainly still coupled to the security of Western Europe; that is a major reason behind the change in our targeting doctrine during this last year. I would not use the phrases about first strike, initiating and what not. I would stress that we are prepared to take the means necessary in the event of aggression that we do not anticipate, but for which we should be prepared.[44]

And still later,

> Our allies have good grounds for asking how we would respond to threats against them from intermediate and variable range nuclear systems . . .[45]
>
> I think the only way a nuclear war is likely to get started is by miscalculation when the other side believes that the US might be self-deterred and that it is worth running the risk. Principally I think the risk would be in Europe . . . To the extent that we have changed our targeting doctrine, we have recoupled US strategic forces to the security of W. Europe and as long as we have that coupling action, I think we have strengthened deterrence – reduced the risk of nuclear war.[46]

Limited nuclear options, though inspired by extended deterrence, were the centrepiece of the new central doctrine. In addition to these options, Essential Equivalence still embraced an assured destruction capability. In his Fiscal Year 1975 Report to Congress, Schlesinger explained:

> If, for whatever reason, deterrence should fail, we want to have the planning flexibility to be able to respond selectively to the attack in such a way as to (1) limit the chances of uncontrolled escalation, and (2) hit meaningful targets with a sufficient accuracy – yield combination to destroy only the intended target and to avoid widespread collateral damage. If a nuclear clash should occur – and we fervently believe that it will not – in order to protect American cities and the cities of our allies, we shall rely into the wartime period upon reserving our 'assured destruction' force and persuading, through intrawar deterrence, any potential foe not to attack cities. It is through these means that we hope to prevent massive destruction even in the cataclysmic circumstances of nuclear war.[47]

This strategy has continued until the present time. The first SIOP prepared under the new strategy was SIOP-5, formally approved in December 1975.[48] It took effect on 1 January 1976. Schlesinger's successor, Donald Rumsfeld, modified the McNamara calculation for assured destruction force planning by directing attention away from destruction *per se* to the retardation of recovery.

> The effectiveness of the retaliation would be measured in two ways: – by the size and composition of the enemy military capability surviving for postwar use; – by his ability to recover politically and economically from the exchange.[49]

Notwithstanding this technical variation in the assured destruction component of the strategy, Essential Equivalence remained the United States nuclear doctrine throughout the Ford period and the 'Countervailing Strategy' unveiled by President Carter's Secretary of Defense Harold Brown in 1980 merely represented a conscientious step in the difficult task of implementing NSDM 242.

Shortly after taking office, President Carter ordered Presidential Review Memorandum (PRM) 10, the Comprehensive Net Assessment and Military Force Posture Review[50] which was to contain an examination of NSDM 242. This analysis, a study entitled The Military Strategy and Force Posture Review, resulted in Presidential Directive (PD) 18 (US National Strategy) which in fact reaffirmed NSDM 242 and NUWEP-1 and directed that a Nuclear Targeting Policy Review (NTPR) be undertaken.[51] The NTPR, in turn, focused on the operational elements still remaining to be brought into being before the goals of NSDM 242 could be realized. Specifically, the NTPR directed attention to the command, control, communications and intelligence (C^3I) functions required by Essential Equivalence; and it called for more options in the SIOP, particularly for the development of counter-political options, i.e., the targeting of Soviet leadership, exploiting Russian vulnerability to China, effecting post-strike regional dismemberment, and other issues thought to be of supreme political significance to the Soviet regime.[52] The NTPR eventually resulted in PD 59, a codification of the NTPR recommendations and a endorsement of the prevailing strategic concept.

In his Newport, Rhode Island speech on 20 August 1980, a speech chosen to present a public account of PD 59 after reports of the endorsement by the President of a dramatic, 'new' nuclear doctrine had appeared in the press, Defense Secretary Brown was clear on the point of continuity with the Schlesinger doctrine:

> At the outset [Brown said] let me emphasize that PD 59 is *not* a new strategic doctrine; it is *not* a radical departure from US strategic policy over the past decade or so. It *is*, in fact, a refinement, a codification of previous statements of our strategic policy. PD 59 takes the same essential strategic doctrine, and restates it more clearly, more cogently, in the light of current conditions and current capabilities.
>
> This doctrine, as I emphasized earlier, is *not* a new departure. The US has never had a doctrine based simply and solely on reflexive, massive attacks on Soviet cities. Instead, we have always planned both more selectively (options limiting urban-industrial damage) and more comprehensively (a range of military targets). Previous Administrations, going back into the 1960s, recognized the inadequacy of a strategic doctrine that would give us too narrow a range of options. The fundamental premises of our countervailing strategy are a natural evolution of the conceptual foundations built over the course of generations, by, for example, Secretaries McNamara and Schlesinger, to name only two of my predecessors who have been most identified with development of our nuclear doctrine.[53]

Secretary Brown stated his operational objectives in a way that virtually assimilated them into past doctrine.

> Operationally, our countervailing strategy requires that our plans and capabilities be structured to put more stress on being able to employ strategic nuclear forces selectively, as well as by all-out retaliation in response to massive attacks on the United States. It is our policy – and we have increasingly the means and the detailed plans to carry out this policy – to ensure that the Soviet leadership knows that if they chose some intermediate level of aggression, we could by selective, large (but still less than maximum) nuclear attacks, exact an unacceptably high price in the things the Soviet leaders appear to value most – political and military control, military force both nuclear and conventional, and the industrial capability to sustain a war. . . . And, of course, we have, and we will keep, a survivable and enduring capability to attack the full range of targets, including the Soviet economic base, if that is the appropriate response to a Soviet strike.[54]

It is well to remember, however, that a strategy of LNOs was forced on the US by events and was not simply the product of rather more creative planning staffs than had hitherto designed American strategy. We can partly appreciate that fact by grasping the enormous difficulty of executing LNOs.

> The United States would need to tailor a response which by demonstrating restraint, gave the enemy time to reconsider, but at the same time left open the possibility of future larger destruction. In theory, nuclear options would have to be designed: (1) to prevent the enemy from achieving his immediate military objective, while holding other high-value enemy targets hostage; (2) to convince the enemy that the attack was limited and that its purpose was to end hostilities immediately; (3) to gain control of the future conduct of the war until the enemy agreed to negotiate; and (4) to foreclose opportunities for future low-cost, low-risk initiatives by the enemy. In the end, success would depend on the real objectives of the enemy and the associated risks and losses he was prepared to take.[55]

The chief task of the Carter Administration was (and of the Reagan Administration remains) the implementation of NSDM 242. Thus the US promulgated PD 53, PD 57 and PD 58, presidential directives signed by President Carter in the last year of the Administration that attempt to ensure the endurance of the command authority essential to a protracted, LNO strategy.[56] PD 59 and NUWEP-2, which followed shortly thereafter, should be seen as a part of that task. This task requires considerable new procurement, a wholesale review and redesign of command and control functions (whose roles are greatly taxed by LNOs), and the supplementation in Europe by a modernized long-range theatre nuclear force (LRTNF) just as Assured Destruction had required Flexible Response, Massive Retaliation had required the deployment of tactical nuclear weapons, and so on. When concerns arising in extended deterrence changed central deterrence doctrine, supplementary theatre doctrines have changed accordingly.

The procurement issue entailed by LNOs has tended to focus on the MX,[57] a highly accurate, potentially mobile (though so heavy as not to be all-that-mobile) countersilo weapon. While it is clear that LNOs do require a time-urgent, highly responsive[58] (and hence, at this time, land-based) weapon, it is not necessarily so that either survivability or hard-target capability is absolutely essential. As to survivability, it is usually argued that the United States would hesitate to use her ICBM force on behalf of Europe lest a Soviet retaliatory strike so degrade the remaining force that none were left for central purposes. This is referred to as a 'competition' for ICBM warheads between central and extended uses. It is open to doubt, however, whether a competition for warheads in fact pits extended and central deterrence options against one another in the SIOP[59] since target sets that might be said to serve these separate goals are in fact inclusive.[60] As to hard-target capability, countersilo potential might actually undercut the LNO mission in Essential Equivalence (by threatening Russian assured destruction capabilities in light of their reliance on land based ICBMs), although such a potential capability does present some interesting, if paradoxical effects on the stability of the central relationship that will be discussed in Chapter 11. It is of course true that the credibility and flexibility of the LNO mission are doubtless enhanced by the appropriate incorporation of features that promote survivability and lethality with the overall strategy in mind.

The truly crucial procurement decisions, however, have to do with command and control programmes. Assured Destruction was designed around large scale exchanges. It is hardly surprising, therefore, that the US warning system did not have the ability to identify the origin and precise character of Soviet attacks. Communication systems had been designed on the basis of 16–48 hour periods for re-targeting and there was virtually no ability to provide the National Command Authorities with information that would have allowed an intelligent decision (and consultation with allies) on re-targeting, even if this were possible. Moreover, the US did not have a system for reprogramming

SLBMs that made them suitable for LNOs.[61] Indeed the entire complex infrastructure of reporting, decision and execution required by LNOs was so vastly more extensive than that required by Assured Destruction that even an optimistic assessment of US ability to implement the new nuclear strategy when announced was a qualified 'maybe'.[62] Some of the most significant Reagan strategic decisions[63] – including the controversial MX procurement without secure basing – are inexplicable without an attentiveness to the LNO procurement requirement still to be satisfied (and indeed there is some doubt whether these requirements *can* be satisfied).

Finally, the requirement of the new doctrine that proved most politically complex was the deployment of a Long Range Theatre Nuclear Force.[64] The intricacies of Alliance decision-making have clouded the basis for LRTNF force-sizing while the ambiguities that are the very foundation of extended deterrence have tended to proliferate employment schemes. Nevertheless, it ought to be clear that precisely the developments that brought an LNO strategy to central systems, including the vulnerability of allied aircraft on deep strike missions, the inappropriateness of the early use of Poseidon SLBMs dedicated to NATO, and the scepticism regarding time-urgent, controllable ICBMs based in the US, require relatively secure, highly accurate systems capable of limited strikes against the Soviet Union and Eastern Europe. This perception was the source of Helmut Schmidt's celebrated reference to LRTNF in his 1977 address to the IISS.[65] He stated that NATO must

> succeed in removing the disparities of military power in Europe parallel to the SALT negotiations. So long as this is not the case, we must maintain the balance of the full range of deterrence strategy. The Alliance must, therefore, be ready to make available the means to support its present strategy, which is still the right one, and to prevent any development that could undermine the basis of this strategy.[66]

Indeed one could say that the Countervailing Strategy scarcely makes sense without survivable, accurate and responsive LRTNF. It may be that ground-based forces are not the most suitable forces for this purpose – because not the most survivable – but there ought to be little doubt that target denial and greatly enhanced SACEUR ability for theatre-wide strikes independent of the SIOP are the theatre correlatives of the Countervailing Strategy. Thus the December 1979 NATO decision to deploy GLCMs and Pershing 2s in the European theatre must be seen as another step in the implementation of NSDM 242.

In concluding a review of this period, we return to the SIOP. I have argued that events in the central relationship, related to vulnerability, have created crises in extended deterrence, crises that were resolved by innovations in strategic doctrine that, in turn, played back into the central relationship. SIOP-5, signed in December 1975, and SIOP-5a, its successor, provide evidence of this sequence in the most recent period. Each codifies, with minor variation, the ideas of NSDM 242, ideas that, as will be seen in the next section, have profoundly affected the bipolar relationship. And a new period is beginning in which new vulnerabilities are already arising that cast doubt on NSDM 242's ability to provide a strategy that will insure extended deterrence.

Book II

The Age of Anxiety

8 Introduction of the Theorem

Godi, Fiorenza, poi che se' sì grande,
che per mare e per terra batti l'ali,
e per lo 'nferno tuo nome si spande!

(Rejoice, Florence, since thou art so great that
over land and sea thou beatest thy wings and
through Hell thy name is spread abroad!)

Canto XXVI, *Inferno*

It was the conviction of Western statesmen that neither of the world wars fought in this century need have occurred if German leaders had known at the outset of each of those wars that the United States would ultimately intervene in decisive numbers on behalf of England and France. Therefore it was a paramount objective of post-World War 2 diplomacy to commit the United States, unmistakably and unambiguously, to any future European conflict and, *thereby*, so alter the calculus of costs and benefits to an aggressor that war would become unthinkable. It is perhaps a coincidence that NATO was formed in 1949, the same portentous year in which the events occurred that began the era of deterrence, but it is an agreeable one. For the deterrence of war, not its ambitious prosecution, was the goal of the Western allies at the same time that fate brought into being the events that culminated in the mutual deterrence of the thermonuclear era.

The deterrent objective of US nuclear strategy has been the protection of both the United States and its European and Asian allies. The vulnerability of the US homeland forced the US to recognize a distinction between central and extended deterrence, but the US has never distinguished, in its strategic targeting policy, the deterrent response that protects Europe from that which protects the US.

The United States has recognized conceptually the difference between deterrence of an attack against the United States and Europe but has not defined these as separate strategic objectives. The primary goal of deterrence encompassed both the United States and its European allies. Targets threatening to the United States are

> not differentiated from those threatening Europe. The current US Single Integrated Operational Plan (SIOP-5D) includes approximately 40 000 installations and divides these into four classes of targets: the Soviet nuclear forces, the general purpose forces, the Soviet military and political leadership centers, and the Soviet economic and industrial base. With fewer weapons than potential targets, the United States assigns priority to the various types of targets.
>
> Neither US nor SACEUR targeting plans provide a basis for establishing a unique set of targets which must be put at a risk for European defense.[1]

Thus two strategic paradigms have coexisted within US targeting plans: the paradigm of central deterrence whose stability depended upon the assumptions of mutual deterrence, and the paradigm of extended deterrence whose stability rose and fell with the American commitment to the extended theatres, such as the European and Japanese ones. This latter commitment, in turn, was essentially determined by US interests versus risks, which effectively meant (since those interests did not greatly vary during this period), by US vulnerability. This vulnerability was a function of the relationship between US–Soviet capabilities in the central and extended theatres: thus the conjunction of parity in central systems (and the loss of meaningful US superiority) with the collapse of NATO escalation dominance in Europe rendered the extended commitment doubtful, while leaving the central stalemate essentially untouched. So we may say that both these commentators who observed that nothing had changed and those who claimed the situation was deteriorating were to a certain extent correct. The failure to distinguish extended from central deterrence has led to much unnecessary confusion.

Concern over the vitality of this extended commitment was labelled a fear of 'decoupling' – a mechanical rather than sensual metaphor that seeks to convey the idea of a disengagement of the American central, strategic deterrent from its role in protecting Europe and hence from the overall effort to deter another war by the unmistakable commitment of overwhelming resources to defensive purposes. As we have seen, the Countervailing Strategy/Essential Equivalence doctrine was a means of overcoming this fear. The commitment was made less costly (in terms of vulnerability) and thereby its vitality sought to be restored. The Countervailing Strategy accomplished this by moving central, strategic weapons (of lower yield and higher accuracy) and longer range theatre weapons into the vacuum created beneath central deterrence by the collapse of escalation dominance. It is worth reviewing this strategy to understand the crisis it has precipitated.

We have seen how the arrival of parity in central systems, and the collapse of Flexible Response in subcentral systems, fatally undermined the Assured Destruction/Sufficiency doctrines. As Pierre Lellouche put it,

> (1) [NATO's] continued inferiority in conventional means will make them . . . become increasingly dependent on first and early use of nuclear weapons by NATO; (2) yet, at the same time, the newly acquired Soviet superiority in theater systems, as well as parity at the strategic level, will in effect neutralize any attempt by NATO to escalate the conflict to nuclear weapons.[2]

In central systems, these doctrines required a substantial cushion of superiority – over and above the assured destruction capability that both sides possessed by the mid-sixties – to execute the large non-countervalue target packages that were the enforcement elements of the 'cities' approach. In the event of conflict, American cities would be spared by the continuing threat to Russian cities; the war would be ended by the destruction of Soviet military assets by central systems if necessary, or by means lower on the escalatory ladder if possible. True, it was not necessary for the West to have conventional superiority, since this was the lowest rung on the ladder. But only superiority in the upper rungs would confine the conflict *and* permit NATO to coerce a solution at the level of intensity that it chose. Assured Destruction, as a doctrine, required Flexible Response.[3]

By contrast, the Essential Equivalence/Countervailing Strategy does not depend on even sectoral superiority; it cannot, however, succeed in conditions of substantial inferiority, as will be seen. This strategy is a cost-imposing dissuasion strategy, not an escalation-dominance, coercion-to-termination programme.[4] It is perhaps best explained by way of an analogy to non-military strategic alternatives.

These alternatives – economic sanctions, embargoes, boycotts, asset and currency freezes, covert action, and the like – are often misunderstood because their aims and hence their appropriateness as means to those aims are not appreciated. It is commonly said, for example, that economic sanctions 'don't work', by which is meant that they don't amount to a successful coercive tactic. The US-led Olympic boycott was not going to compel the Russians to leave Afghanistan. But as I have endeavoured to show elsewhere,[5] non-military alternatives are valuable *precisely* because they do not work in this way. If the grain embargo, for example, could have starved Russia into famine, it would not have starved that country into submission regarding Afghanistan but rather into war. Sanctions and the like are useful when conventional war is against one's own interests and therefore the relative costs of going to war, which are usually very high, must be kept high. Sanctions so powerful that they gravely weakened the opposing state would just as greatly lower the relative costs of war. It may be that this is what happened to the Japanese as a result of the US petroleum embargo in 1941: the sneak attack on Pearl Harbor (a counterforce first strike, if you will) moved from being a clever theoretical possibility to a daring course of action acceptable to Japanese political authorities when the relative costs of war plummeted owing to imposition of a stringent oil embargo.[6]

Non-military alternatives are means of imposing costs on an adversary such that continuation of a particular policy becomes less attractive. So, also, is the countervailing nuclear strategy. It promises to impose costs on any Soviet aggression such that no political objective of that aggression could, by any calculation, be worthy of further pursuit. Thus it does not depend on superiority or even absolute equivalence any more than a small boy needs to be as large as a playground bully to dissuade the latter from a fistfight: he simply needs to be big enough to hurt the larger boy enough. The Countervailing Strategy can't force an end to the conflict; indeed, it requires highly accurate weapons to avoid an attempt at such coercion since that might lower the relative cost to the other side of expanding the war. Instead it imposes mounting costs, always leaving the adversary the option of withdrawal to a point which is more favourable to it than continued conflict.

The principal shortcoming of such a strategy, as with non-military strategic alternatives, arises from the fact that it costs to impose costs. Indeed it often costs the cost-imposer more than the party on whom the strategic cost is to be imposed. A decision to pursue such a course is not necessarily irrational for the imposing party, since the alternative outcome may otherwise be a steadily degraded and even more costly situation, but it is an extremely difficult policy for which to build political support. In the first place, there is a natural reluctance to accept policies that cost one more than they cost one's adversary. The national political leadership begins to appear as the nation's own worst enemy. Second, such costs are usually borne by groups unaccustomed to bearing them. A non-military strategy often imposes costs on civilians (as the grain embargo initially imposed substantial costs on wheat farmers) and these groups may be highly motivated thereby to oppose the strategy which may depend on their consent (as to some extent the Olympic boycott depended on the consent of US Olympic athletes). With respect to the Countervailing Strategy, the group singled out to run the greatest risks is the European nations who will bear the brunt of destruction if US–USSR homelands become sanctuaries for the purpose of containing the conflict, that is, for allowing 'countervailing' rather than coercive pressure to be brought against a Russian aggressor.

The positions of attacker and defender are not symmetrical: the Russian attack itself will no doubt greatly reduce the relative costs to NATO of going forward with its cost-imposing strategy. In such a context, the Soviet Union must have a war-winning strategy while it is necessary for NATO only to have a countervailing strategy. The missing element in the Essential Equivalence/Countervailing Strategy is the means of gauging the costs to the West of carrying it out.

Soviet deployment of its new generation of longer-range, highly accurate and mobile missile systems meant that NATO airbases in every European country were more vulnerable to weapons that were themselves now invulnerable. New, shorter-range Soviet systems had a simple trumping effect on NATO frontal deployments.

Accordingly, the new Countervailing Strategy required the deployment of LRTNF (long range theatre nuclear force) systems, not to match Soviet SS-20 deployments, but to repair the rupture in alliance deterrence caused both by the SS-20 – a weapon capable both of executing limited threats and of suppressing any correspondingly limited response – and by the coincidence of Soviet modernization and NATO obsolescence in shorter range, once parallel systems. Once again we observed a vulnerability making itself felt in the extended theatre, whose cure was fashioned from a revised strategic concept. The Countervailing Strategy might perhaps be described as 'flexible response in central systems', but it is dissuasive and reactive rather than coercive. It has no plan for war termination other than the enemy simply quitting.

The 1979 NATO LRTNF modernization decision was a cure for decoupling; this is indisputable.

> Fear that Western Europe might become the target of selective threats was an inevitable consequence of strategic parity, and so too was concern that the credibility of NATO's strategy of a flexible

response would be eroded once the Alliance's capability and determination to contemplate the escalation of a conflict to the nuclear level could no longer be taken for granted. NATO's reaction to this uncomfortable truth was the 'dual track' decision of December 1979.[7]

Chancellor Schmidt's 1977 IISS speech, spurred by reports from Geneva that the Americans were about to conclude a restriction on cruise missiles as part of a SALT 2 agreement,[8] had gestured obliquely to the alternatives of LTRNF modernization and theatre arms control (the 'dual' track). The High Level Group decided at its first meeting that LRTNF required modernization, after urging by the European members.[9] When the new deployments were agreed upon, the US was asked to provide weapons systems. By early 1979, a consensus was achieved on a mix of ballistic and cruise missiles; in the summer of that year the number 572 (108 Pershing 2, 464 GLCM) was agreed upon.

> Alliance officials present the rationale for LRTNF modernization as resulting from the coincidence of three separate but related developments: strategic parity, existing NATO LRTNF obsolescence and Soviet LRTNF modernization. It is argued that the development of strategic parity as codified by the SALT process has raised questions concerning the credibility of the American strategic nuclear forces to defend Europe. The credibility of the American nuclear deterrent vis-à-vis Europe has been further diminished by the declining effectiveness of existing NATO long-range nuclear assets in Europe, notably American F-111 and British Vulcan aircraft, whose penetration capability has been put in doubt by improvements to Soviet air defences and by their own obsolescence. It is also argued that because the 400 Poseidon warheads allocated to NATO are part of America's strategic forces, they are not sufficiently identified with, or linked to, the defence of Europe. Neither do their characteristics facilitate their use for the selective response that NATO strategy requires. These deficiencies in NATO's forces contrast with the very substantial improvements in Soviet LRTNF capabilities targeted on Europe, notably the introduction of the SS-20 and the Backfire bomber.[10]

At the same time, NATO was trying to formulate an arms control position that would serve as a parallel track to that of deployment.

In the evolution of the LRTNF decision, NATO saw each approach

– deployment and negotiation – as complementary. The NATO Communiqué states that:

> A modernization decision including commitments to deployments is necessary to meet NATO's deterrence and defence needs, to provide a credible response to unilateral Soviet deployments and to provide the foundation for the pursuit of serious negotiations on TNF . . . NATO's TNF requirements will be examined in the light of concrete results reached through negotiations.[11]

This course – preparing for deployments while pressing for arms limitation that could, if successful, reduce the need for new deployments – has its logic. What is striking, however, is the awkward position in which this course places the US. For it must at the same time urge that its deterrent is no longer credible in order to build support for modernization whilst pressing for fresh deployments and treaties. Earlier examples of this uncomfortable posture can be seen in Secretary of Defense McNamara's efforts to persuade the US's European allies to accept Controlled Response, an enterprise that required him to deprecate the credibility of the prevailing US deterrent in his Athens speech to the Allies while underscoring the US commitment to Europe in the public version of that speech given at Ann Arbor.

In much the same genre was former Secretary Kissinger's treatment of the LRTNF/decoupling issue. First, he was required to deprecate American willingness to indefinitely continue to couple its nuclear deterrent to Europe. We can hear this in the following 'confession' made as part of the persuasive effort to convince European sceptics that a change in the deployments of weapons systems was needed for re-coupling.

> I have sat around the NATO Council table in Brusssels and elsewhere and have uttered the magic words which had a profoundly reassuring effect, and which permitted the ministers to return home with a rationale for not increasing defense expenditures. And my successors have uttered the same reassurances. And yet if my analysis is correct, these words cannot be true indefinitely; and if my analysis is correct we must face the fact that it is absurd in the 1980s to base the strategy of the West on the credibility of the threat of mutual suicide.
>
> And therefore I would say – what I might not say in office – that our European allies should not keep asking us to multiply strategic

> assurances that we cannot possibly mean or if we do mean, we should not want to execute because if we execute, we risk the destruction of civilization.[12]

Then, second, he offered a prescription:

> Our strategic dilemma is not solved be verbal reassurances; it requires redesigning our forces and doctrine. Given the diminishing credibility of the threat of strategic war initiated from the United States, the argument is plausible that the Soviet Union might be tempted to exploit its preponderance of intermediate-range missiles for blackmail against Europe – reasoning that no American responses with strategic weapons could alter the outcome.
>
> The Soviet Union could not risk attacking Europe with conventional weapons without destroying our intermediate range missiles also, lest they devastate Soviet command centers in a retaliatory blow. And it could not seek to destroy the missiles in Europe while leaving our strategic arsenal in America unimpaired for a possible strike against Soviet ICBM. . . . [I]ntermediate-range missiles in Europe indissolubly link the two theatres.[13]

This is an example of the sort of doctrinally inspired refurbishing we observed repeatedly in the cycles described in Book I. It now operates, however, in a changed strategic environment, and I will endeavour to show why it cannot wholly succeed and why, therefore, the cyclical pattern we observed in the thermonuclear period has also a direction, the tendency of which is erosion. The relationship of extended to central theatres has been described. So long as the cost of the extension of deterrence could be somehow separated from the stability of the assumptions of central deterrence, strategic innovation (and its consequent deployments) could compensate for the risks posed by new vulnerabilities. Once this ceased to be so – when either the deterrence assumption had to be modified and the possibility of homeland strikes accepted or alternatively, deterrence extended in spite of the disengagement of the central deterrent–extended deterrence entered a crisis from which it has yet to emerge. This argument will be developed as, metaphorically, a 'theorem' and its ramifications explored in the remainder of Book II.

Any American nuclear effort to bridge the gap between the assured destruction mission and a conventional holding action in Europe – that is, any effort to *re-couple* the American nuclear guarantee that may have become decoupled owing to the Soviet threat of retaliation –

seeks to lower the threshold of nuclear use. The very purpose of providing the President with intermediate options is to make his resolve more credible by making it more likely that he will order an attack – by making it less likely that American cities will be destroyed in response to his decisions. In the current strategic context, this necessarily, if inadvertently, means a heightening of the probability of a war confined to the European theatre. This invites, as we shall see, a kind of *uncoupling*.

The deployment of cruise missiles and Pershing 2s in Europe is an effort to use weapons to re-establish the link between Europe's security and that of the United States. If an American President faced the choice of responding to a threat in Europe either by (a) launching an attack on the Soviet Union using a significant (non-demonstrative) portion of US central systems – whether a full-scale nuclear attack or otherwise – which would trigger equally significant retaliation against the United States or (b) doing nothing, it is perhaps doubtful that a President would risk American destruction for any political goal other than the survival of the American homeland. 'Decoupling' is a term that captures this doubt. The means of removing this doubt through weapons deployment is to present the President with an alternative less daunting than one that is certain to imply the destruction of the American homeland owing to Russian retaliation.

This is the goal of the Countervailing Strategy. Yet that strategy carries within it a substantial array of risks for the West. Seeking to deter an attack on Europe by the Soviet Union, for example, the Countervailing Strategy poses four possibilities. (1) The options available to the US President may endanger vital Russian interests (contrary to US intentions) and the President will act, collapsing central deterrence; or (2) he will refrain, effectively ending extended nuclear deterrence; or (3) the options provided by the strategic plan will sanctuarize Russian vital interests and the President will abstain (reneging on the extended deterrence commitment) or (4) he will act, within the constraints of the sanctuary, imposing the risks of action on the local theatre. Thus if American policy succeeds, and central and extended deterrence hold, this can only be because the Russians expect (1) or (4) – either suicidal action against their vital interests or countervailing, non-vital costs permitting retaliation against US allies. Such a policy is quite credible and ought to be effective but cannot, I think, long be acquiesced in by allied publics.

Thus the theorem may be stated: Any effort to cure decoupling will either (1) fail because it does not provide the President with both a lower threshold of choice and some kind of a firebreak to stop retaliation against the United States (or does not persuade him that he has such choices), or (2) it will 'succeed' by confining risks to the theatre, and thus it *uncouples* the two theatres of war, making war in the theatre more or less likely at the discretion of an American President precisely to the degree that US nuclear protection is extended. This possibility is clearly perceived by the Europeans and accounts for their considerable reluctance to affect the cure for decoupling that they themselves originally proposed, as well as making manifest the otherwise inexplicable positive correlation between SALT and LRTNF. One would hardly expect that US acceptance of SALT 2 would be a crucial precondition for European acquiescence in LRTNF modernization since SALT (and the parity it acknowledges) are partly responsible for the latest decoupling crisis. Yet this is indeed the case because the collapse of superpower collaboration in SALT would so cast a shadow on US–Russian co-operation in strategic stability that Europeans would have to contemplate American war plans with a sceptical lucidity that those plans have until now been spared.

Because extended deterrence depends on denying the Soviet Union the possibility of replying with its own limited nuclear option (or beginning with one) the operation of this theorem has important implications for the Countervailing Strategy and extended deterrence. Either it must lead to US disengagement (decoupling), since it will fail to provide a deterring limited option, or it will sever the theatres (uncoupling) in which case it invites a Soviet limited reply (or initiation). If the latter, then European publics and their leaders will doubtless wish to govern the manipulation of the stakes of deterrence. Of course, US deterrence of the Soviet Union can always be extended to any theatre without the consent of the populations involved. The Carter Doctrine that threatened to employ nuclear weapons against a Soviet invasion of Iran did not rest on the consent of the Iranian public. But the relationship of the Atlantic Alliance (and the US relationship with Japan) is one between democracies and allies and thus it is unlikely that any European-based US deployment could take place in the face of the perception that it was coerced by the US. Either Europe would develop its own 'polar' arsenal – for such a threat guided by sophisticated control, command, communications, and intelligence (C^3I), beyond any of the present independent deterrents, would be required to prevent Soviet limited attacks, or it would seek political accommodations to reduce the Soviet threat.

In light of the theorem, one would expect that the US President will discount the use of US controlled weapons whenever they are likely to trigger retaliation against the US homeland, regardless of their basing. If he is not seen to do so by the American public, we can expect increased domestic pressures for the United States to distance herself from European security guarantees. At the same time, Europeans will increasingly come to see US war preparations as the principal threat to their survival. And this reaction in turn will irritate the Americans, who are running great risks and substantial expenses simply to protect their allies.

To recapitulate: concern over *decoupling* (the detachment of the US nuclear threat from the protection of Europe, and elsewhere, for fear of retaliation) has led to various efforts at *re-coupling* (restoring the credibility of the US commitment to attack the Soviet Union if she attacks Europe, for example) that henceforth can only be validated by strategies that depend on *uncoupling* (detaching the US and Soviet theatres by confining retaliation by either side to the European or other extended theatre).

In the following chapters of Book II we shall take up various implications of the analysis suggested by the theorem. First, the 'next vulnerability' predicted by Book I will be discussed. Then various possible innovations in US strategic doctrines will be explored. Although these are the subject of an intense debate at present, it is seldom shown that these alternatives differ principally with respect to extended deterrence. This is, of course, to be expected from the analysis in Book I. Following this review, alternative weapons systems are evaluated in light of their potential contribution to extended deterrence.

Finally, two alternatives to extended deterrence are discussed: the multiplication of central deterrents and various means of reducing the threat to be deterred (arms control, enhanced conventional force postures, and defensive systems).

9 The Social Dimension of Nuclear Strategy

'O frati,' dissi 'che per cento milia
perigli siete giunti a l'occidente. . . .
Considerate la vostra semenza:
fatti non foste a viver come bruit,
ma per seguir virtute e canoscenza.'

('O brothers,' I said, 'who through a thousand perils have reached the West. . . .
Take thought of the seed from which you spring.
You were not born to live as brutes, but to follow virtue and knowledge.')

Canto XXVI, *Inferno*

In the preceding chapter I introduced a theorem, *viz*, that any present effort to cure decoupling through the deployment of weapons must either fail (in that, despite deployment, the threshold of US nuclear commitment is not reduced) or 'succeed' and thereby uncouple the central and extended theatres. The Countervailing Strategy, I argued, would provoke political division between the United States and her allies, threatening the long-term viability of the strategy, and casting doubt on the vitality of the strategy itself. One requirement of a deterrent strategy must be to render that strategy convincingly executable in crises or when deterrence fails.

In this chapter I shall argue that the next cyclical vulnerability in the central relationship to be manifested in the extended theatre, as were the various vulnerabilities that propelled events in Book I, arises from public alienation from deterrence itself, and that this alienation also threatens to render the American nuclear strategy inexecutable. I shall examine five recent proposed strategic responses to this alienation: the campaign for a nuclear freeze, the zero option INF proposal, the deep cuts START proposals, the call for a no-first-use pledge by NATO, and the dramatic call for a 'Star Wars' defence system shared between the superpowers. I shall show that each of these responses is incompatible with present US strategy. Whatever their strategic merits, these various proposals share the characteristic that they are public relations attempts to stimulate support from a public alienated from the system of nuclear deterrence that the partisans of each programme claim to be deteriorating (although there is little consensus on precisely why this deterioration is taking place). That these proposals are incompatible with prevailing strategy, indeed with some aspects of all previous nuclear strategy, is therefore to be expected since they reject the premises of that strategy. What is perhaps more troubling, however, is that each promises unfortunate consequences for international stability in light of the 'theorem' introduced in Chapter Eight.

The *deterrence assumption* is a term I shall use in this book for the consequence of the fact that nuclear weapons render credible the threat to destroy another nation such that *that* nation will be wholly dissuaded from destroying the threatening nation. This assumption was mutually realized upon the acquisition of thermonuclear weapons by the United States and the Soviet Union. This assumption has been shared by all the strategies, of total or graduated response, contrived by the United States in the last thirty years. It is one feature in the present context of mutual assured destruction, but it should not be confused with this context. As we shall see in Chapter 12, the deterrence assumption does not necessarily accompany the context of mutual assured destruction, for example it might be eroded even though the context remained.

Public alienation from the deterrence assumption may have been unwittingly hastened by President Johnson's and President Nixon's descriptions of the Assured Destruction/Sufficiency doctrine. In their anxiety to build a constituency for arms control, President Johnson and Secretary McNamara made the American position appear more absurd than it in fact was,[1] sometimes depicting the American strategy as a kind of suicide pact, with only one devastating option available to fend off a Russian attack that, logically, the threat would all but ensure if it had to be carried out. For other purposes, which involved a desire to overcome Congressional opposition to defence spending that had for fifteen years prevented the procurement of any new strategic weapon, President Nixon and his Secretary of Defense exploited this misperception of the Assured Destruction doctrine, repeated it and ridiculed it.[2] After fifteen years of this, it is hardly surprising that members of Congress[3] and the American public[4] came to accept it as dogma and ultimately recoil from it precisely because it only made sense dogmatically. *Certum est quia impossibile est.* Like the thirteenth stroke of a clock, it was not only absurd in itself, but cast doubt on all that had gone before. When superpower tensions heightened, it was perhaps predictable that public opinion would react with a disenchantment with nuclear policy so complete that the public would become alienated from the deterrence assumption itself.

This alienation is shared not only by long time disarmament organizations such as SANE and the Union of Concerned Scientists in the United States and CND in Great Britain, but has picked up a momentum that has brought forth new organizations: Physicians for Social Responsibility, International Physicians for the Prevention of Nuclear War (who were recently awarded the Nobel Prize), The Lawyers Alliance for Nuclear Arms Control, the Business Alert to Nuclear War, Artists for Survival. Some forty new books on nuclear issues were scheduled to be published in the last six months of 1982 alone.[5] A publisher printed 100 000 copies of Roger Molander's *Nuclear War: What's In It For You?*[6] But at once the most influential and the most expensive of the new tracts was Jonathan's Schell's *The Fate of the Earth*,[7] originally serialized in *The New Yorker* magazine and then a nationwide best seller in the United States.

With a prose style that would be the envy of any of the wooden writers on nuclear subjects, Schell provides a *tour d'horizon* of the issue of nuclear conflict. He devotes most of the pages of his essay to descriptions of the effects of nuclear war, but these descriptions are embedded in the argument of the book, an argument that is a direct attack on the deterrence assumption. The argument and organization of the essay follows this pattern: assume a Soviet attack; these are the results of that attack, on the atmosphere, on life in the United States, on the suffering of individuals, and so on; given these results, we cannot assume a United States reply or, if we did, it would destroy all life on earth for these are the results of such a reply on the atmosphere, on life in the Soviet Union and elsewhere, and so on; the present threat is therefore either incredible and will destroy us, or universally murderous since if carried out, it will destroy all mankind.

The first portion of the essay begins with a fleeting reference to the deterrence assumption.

> [T]he fundamental logic of the strategy of both sides is, in McNamara's words, to hold not just the military forces of the other side hostage but also its 'society as a whole'. Just how the strategists on both sides achieve this is unknown, but it seems unwarranted to suppose that there will be much relief for either population in the merciful sentiments of targeters.[8]

Schell dismisses the graduated response of current US strategy by observing that, since the US faces a conventional imbalance in various secondary theatres, these theatres are necessarily unstable and will lead to the use of tactical nuclear weapons which will, in turn, necessarily lead up the escalatory ladder. (There is little use, one supposes, in pointing out that this is true, on Schell's assumptions, only if every stage of escalation reiterates the first two with respect to stability, in other words, one side gains or expects to gain by raising the level of conflict, since Schell has ample official sources, Soviet and American, to quote to the effect that any use of nuclear weapons is unlikely to remain limited.) Schell then assumes a Soviet attack distributed across all targets – military, industrial and population – sufficient to destroy all these targets (and tacitly assumes that none of these several thousand launches will tempt an effort to suppress necessarily later launches by pre-empting them.) There are many ludicrous aspects to the actual assumptions made in order to permit this literary mixture of one-tenth analysis and nine-tenths description: the total megatonnage of Soviet weapons is estimated and then simply distributed according to population (having subtracted 2000 megatons for military targets) so that Schell may describe the effects of a particular megatonnage on the population.

> In the first moments of a ten-thousand-megaton attack on the United States, I learned from Dr Kendall and from other sources, flashes of white light would suddenly illumine large areas of the country as thousands of suns, each one brighter than the sun itself, blossomed over cities, suburbs, and towns. In those same moments, when the first wave of missiles arrived, the vast majority of the people in the regions first targeted would be irradiated, crushed, or burned to death. The thermal pulses could subject more than six hundred thousand square miles, or one-sixth of the total land mass of the nation, to a minimum level of forty calories per centimetre squared – a level of heat that chars human beings (at Hiroshima, charred remains in the rough shape of human beings were a common sight.)[9]

But Schell's point is well taken regardless of the unlikely and erroneous factual assumptions used ('Without serious distortion we can begin by imagining that we would be dealing with 10 000 weapons of one megaton each')[10] since the fundamental point is indisputable: the Soviet Union, in an all-out attack using 90 per cent of its strategic warheads, could destroy the United States.

This simple point, if augmented by the risk to the species of destroying the Soviet Union in a similarly massive strike, sets up the argument that there can be no motive for retaliation against the Soviet Union. Schell carefully, and repeatedly, emphasizes that it is the deterrence assumption of the nuclear era, an assumption that abandons the war-winning objectives of pre-nuclear deterrence, that he is attacking.

> The logical fault line in the doctrine runs straight through the center of its main strategic tenet – the proposition that safety is achieved by assuring that any nuclear aggressor will be annihilated in a retaliatory strike. For while the doctrine relies for its success on a nuclear-armed victim's resolve to launch the annihilating second strike, it can offer no sensible or sane justification for launching it in the event. In pre-nuclear military strategy, the deterrent effect of force was a useful by-product of the ability and willingness to wage and win wars. . . . Nuclear deterrence, however, supposedly aims solely at forestalling any use of force by either side, and has given up at the outset on a favorable decision by arms. . . . [S]ince in nuclear-deterrence theory the whole purpose of having a retaliatory capacity is to deter a first strike, one must ask what reason would remain to launch the retaliation once the first strike had actually arrived. Nuclear deterrence requires one to prepare for armed conflict not in order to 'win' it if it breaks out but in order to prevent it from breaking out in the first place. [T]he logic of the deterrence strategy is dissolved by the very event – the first strike – that it is meant to prevent. Once the action begins, the whole doctrine is self-cancelling. In sum, the doctrine is based on a monumental logical mistake: one cannot credibly deter a first strike with a second strike whose *raison d'etre* dissolves the moment the first strike arrives. It follows that, as far as deterrence theory is concerned, there is no reason for either side not to launch a first strike.[11]

This argument ignores the option of a less-than-total US response that, because of America's very great capabilities, can nevertheless destroy the Soviet military and political structure by using a slender fraction of the megatonnage in the US arsenal. Since it is not difficult to imagine – indeed it is hard not to imagine – both a motive and justification for such a strike that would be consistent with the interests even of a fatally wounded US, that strike ought to be expected by the Soviet leadership. It is simply inconceivable that the US leadership would refuse any limited retaliation whatsoever on the grounds that, deterrence having failed, there could be no worthwhile political goals for a dying society. Preventing the domination of the postwar world by one's attacker is motive enough I should think. Nor is it persuasive to conclude that the President's hand would be stayed because all-out retaliation would, when taken together with the effects of the attack, doom the ecosystem. There is more than this one button on the console. Schell's argument depends upon the caricature of 'Assured Destruction' that I have endeavoured to discredit, but which I must acknowledge is widely accepted. The claim by which he earlier in the essay dismissed a consideration of less-than-total options – that they will inevitably lead to total war as war escalates – hardly applies to a nation struck with the ferocity of the Schell hypothetical.

I shall not try to account for the popular and critical reception of *The Fate of the Earth*, a reception that the *New York Review of Books*[12] called 'rapturously favorable', but it is useful to point out that for Schell it is extended deterrence that ultimately undermines deterrence strategy. Strategic doctrine is based on a contradiction of 'two irreconcilable purposes'.

> The first purpose is to permit the survival of the species, and this is expressed in the doctrine's aim of frightening everybody into holding back from using nuclear weapons at all; the second purpose is to serve national ends, and this is expressed in the doctrine's permitting the defense of one's nation and its interests by threatening to use nuclear weapons.[13]

Put in a somewhat more technical framework, Schell perceives a contradiction in using the threat of nuclear weapons simply to survive – a matter of central deterrence – and in exploiting that threat for political purposes – for the extension of deterrence – since the success of the latter depends upon making nuclear threats when in fact no political purpose other than national survival (if that) can render those threats credible. As Schell's readers come to realize this, we may find that a development in central deterrence, public alienation from the deterrence assumption, will once again precipitate a crisis in extended deterrence. (For Schell himself the solution to the contradiction is the perfectly logical one of world government.)

Public alienation from the deterrence assumption is widespread across the Western democracies, although only in the US does it appear to arise from a reaction to the erroneous Assured Destruction policy while in Europe the implications of the actual US policy seem to be a source of anxiety, as predicted by the 'theorem' in Chapter 8.[14] In recent polls, substantial percentages of NATO European publics: (1) don't know whether the US or the USSR is more likely to initiate a nuclear war in Europe (35 per cent in West Germany, 24 per cent in the UK, 49 per cent in the Netherlands, 40 per cent in France) or think the US is more likely to do so (20 per cent in West Germany, 20 per cent in the Netherlands, 28 per cent in UK); and (2) oppose LRTNF deployment if the INF talks fail (31 per cent U.S.; 35 per cent FRG; 51 per cent Netherlands; 34 per cent UK).[15]

In Europe, LRTNF has provided a focal point for political demonstrations. On 25 October 1981, a demonstration in Brussels brought out 200 000 persons for the goal 'Refuse nuclear missiles in Europe – one step towards disarmament'.[16] That month, on 10 October 1981, one of the largest public demonstrations seen in Germany since the war was organized in Bonn. 250 000 rallied under the slogan, 'Against nuclear threat'.[17] In Rome, on 24 October 1981, a protest 'Against all weapons systems in Europe, in the West and in the East' drew between 200 000 and 300 000 marchers in a column that took six hours to pass.[18] A mass rally in Amsterdam on 21 November 1981 took place in which between 300 000 and 400 000 people took part. The purpose of the rally was to urge the Dutch government and NATO to rescind LRTNF plans.[19]

Many commentators and public officials believe that the crisis triggered by LRTNF deployment will simply disappear once the deployments are completed. These critics see the LRTNF issue as another in the many topical events that, from time to time, perturb the US–European relationship. If the theorem is correct, however, this conclusion is wrong. As long as the deployments persist, Europeans will be forcefully reminded of the deadly ambivalence of the American position. And there are some critics who have noted this.

> Surveys of European opinion taken during the Intermediate-range Nuclear Forces (INF) years reveal that the Euromissile debate has left a more fragile public consensus in its wake. Fundamental long-term changes in the perception of threats to European security emerged and will not disappear with the deployments. Renewed nuclear anxieties are a reflection of a long-term decline in a confidence in US policy and of a fundamental divergence between European and American assessments of the Soviet threat. These trends are most pronounced and significant among the younger, better educated sections of the public, and have especially important implications for the Federal Republic of Germany.

INF is likely to be viewed retrospectively as a watershed rather than as another of the cyclical crises which have plagued the US–European relationship.[20]

I would dissent from this summary only to this extent: renewed nuclear anxieties are not merely a reflection, but are a powerful cause of the European perception of a divergence of interests from the US.

Surveys of public opinion in Europe show that the LRTNF crisis did not change European views of the Soviet Union, nor were views changed about the sufficiency of American conventional and nuclear forces. What changed was that 'an American dimension has been added to European threat perceptions', according to a recent analysis of European public opinion polls. This appears to be particularly true in West Germany.

The issue of nuclear weapons in the FRG raises broader concerns about national autonomy and control. Non-nuclear West Germany relies totally upon the American nuclear guarantee and remains the site of a large concentration of nuclear warheads, all under foreign control. Concerns about nuclear weapons, while the product in part of an anti-technological pessimism embodied by the Green Party, is largely a function of broader concerns about the direction of American policy as well as a manifestation of a new assertiveness by a new generation of West Germans.[21]

Public opinion surveys do not indicate a shift in public attitudes towards nuclear weapons *per se* (in important contrast to US opinion). What has changed is the attitude of Europeans toward American-controlled nuclear weapons. Increasingly, European publics are 'equi-distancing' themselves from the superpowers and this 'is a major change in post-war attitudes. The significant alteration in European attitudes over the past decade has not been in regard to the USSR but rather in relation to the changing image of the US. . . . A subtle shift in threat perception has been occurring, from one concerned with a threat from the East to one more concerned with the dynamics of super-power conflict'.[22]

The most thoughtful writer to draw attention to the strategic importance of public morale, indeed almost the only one, is the historian Sir Michael Howard. Sir Michael notes the paradox that nuclear strategists have altogether ignored the social element of strategy, even though this dimension has assumed far greater importance in the last hundred years.[23] It was society at large that provided the logistical support that proved decisive in the three great wars of the nineteenth century and that was assumed by recent theorists of strategic bombing and insurgency alike to present the most crucial and most vulnerable element in war. Nevertheless,

> [w]orks about nuclear war and deterrence normally treat their topic as an activity taking place almost entirely in the technological dimension. . . . The technological capabilities of nuclear arsenals are treated as being decisive in themselves, involving a calculation of risk and outcome so complete and discrete that neither the political motivation for the conflict nor the social factors involved in its conduct – nor indeed the military activity of fighting – are taken into account at all. In their models, governments are treated as being as absolute in their capacity to take and implement decisions, and the reaction of their societies are taken as little into account as were those of the subjects of the princes who conducted warfare in Europe in the eighteenth century. . . . But the question insistently obtrudes itself: in the terrible eventuality of deterrence failing and hostilities breaking out between states armed with nuclear weapons, how will the peoples concerned react, and how will their reactions affect the will and the capacity of their governments to make decisions? And what form will military operations take? What, in short, will be the social and the operational dimensions of a nuclear war?[24]

Sir Michael appreciates the impact of the stages of conflict preceding a nuclear war on the actuality of that war – the crucial relevance of who initiates war, at what level of intensity, why it begins at all. If it is a commonplace that deterrence is capability factored by will, it is just as commonly forgotten that 'will' is not simply the determination of a political elite; rather it is largely governed by the public choices available to political leaders.

> [Therefore] credibility depends not simply on a perceived balance, or imbalance, of weapons systems, but on perceptions of the nature of the society whose leaders are threatening such retaliation. Peoples who are not prepared to make the effort necessary for operational defense are even less likely to support a decision to initiate a nuclear exchange from which they will themselves suffer almost inconceivable destruction, even if that decision is taken at the lowest possible level of nuclear escalation. And if such a decision were taken over their heads, they would be unlikely to remain

sufficiently resolute and united to continue to function as a cohesive political and military entity in the aftermath.[25]

Sir Michael concludes that Western leaders are likely to find it far more difficult to initiate nuclear uses than will the Soviet Union, and surmises that the Soviet leadership appreciates this difference. Given Soviet conventional preponderance, we may infer that the pre-nuclear stages of conflict – indeed the peacetime maintenance of substantial conventional armed forces – can be decisive for *nuclear* deterrence. The credibility of the nuclear deterrent will depend on the early stages of conflict, into which modern doctrine has infiltrated nuclear options, even if those stages turn out to be non-nuclear. And these in turn will likely depend on the political context that precipitated them.

Most strategic scenarios today are based on the least probable of political circumstances – a totally unprovoked military assault by the Soviet Union, with no shadow of political justification, on Western Europe. But Providence is unlikely to provide us with anything so straightforward. Such an attack, if it occurred at all, would be likely to arise out of a political crisis in central Europe over the rights and wrongs of which Western public opinion would be deeply and perhaps justifiably divided. Soviet military objectives would probably extend no farther than the Rhine, if indeed that far. Under such conditions, the political will of the West to initiate nuclear war might have to be discounted entirely, and the defense of West Germany would depend not on our nuclear arsenals but on the operational capabilities of our armed forces, fighting as best they could and for as long as they could without recourse to nuclear weapons of any kind.

Sir Michael concludes:

But whether these initial operational decisions are then accepted as definitive by the societies concerned, will depend, . . . [on] the importance of the political objective, and the readiness of the belligerent communities to endure the sacrifices involved in prolonging the war.

These sacrifices might or might not include the experience, on whatever scale, of nuclear war, but they would certainly involve living with the day-to-day, even the hour-to-hour possibility that the war might 'go nuclear' at any moment. It is not easy to visualize a greater test of social cohesion than having to endure such a strain for a period of months, if not years, especially if no serious measures had been taken for the protection of the civil population.[26]

This test, this strain, has already begun. The emerging crisis in the public consensus supporting American nuclear strategy is the next vulnerability with which US policy must cope. Not surprisingly, there are already several proposals evoked by this crisis. Since these proposed policies are responsive to the public alienation I have described, it is to be expected that they would make little sense within the prevailing strategic paradigm. Indeed it would appear that some proposals implicitly reject the very notion of extended deterrence (from which arose the various crises posed by earlier vulnerabilities).

The most prominent of these proposals are: the resolution calling for a nuclear freeze; the zero option for LRTNF deployment; the no-first-use pledge; the deep-cuts US START position; the recently proposed mutual ballistic missile defence system. As will be seen in the next chapter, these proposals largely derive from two distinct contemporary central approaches to the repeated crises in extended deterrence, associated with the 'minimum deterrence' and 'war-fighting' strategies of the moderate left and right wings of the American polity, respectively.

NUCLEAR FREEZE

A bilateral freeze in the development and deployment of nuclear weapons was first suggested in 1979 by a graduate student at the Massachusetts Institute of Technology who had formerly worked for the Stockholm International Peace Research Institute (SIPRI). Published in a booklet[27] in April 1980, it did not at first attract much attention. The following November, however, voters in three Massachusetts state senatorial districts approved a resolution embodying the freeze idea and by July 1981 such resolutions had been adopted in 257 town meetings throughout New England, and indeed in eight state legislatures.

The most important freeze proposal is a joint resolution first presented to Congress in March 1981. It provides,

1. As an immediate strategic arms control objective, the United States and Soviet Union should:

(a) pursue a complete halt to the nuclear arms race;

(b) decide when and how to achieve a mutual and verifiable freeze on the testing, production and further deployment of nuclear warheads, missiles and other delivery systems; and

(c) give special attention to destabilizing weapons whose deployment would make such a freeze more difficult to achieve.

2. Proceeding from this freeze, the United States and the Soviet Union should pursue major, mutual and verifiable reductions in nuclear warheads, missiles and other delivery systems, through annual percentages or equally effective means, in a manner that enhances stability.[28]

The most striking aspect of this resolution is its call for a mutual 'freeze' on deployments: were this acted upon, it would ratify the Brezhnev Moratorium proposal of December 1980, since it amounts to an unqualified repudiation by the US of the decision to modernize NATO LRTNF. In light of the SS-20 deployments that Europe currently faces, the strategic consequences of which the LRTNF decision was in part designed to redress (either by parrying them or by negotiating the removal of those missiles), such a step by the US would be the sort of decoupling move that earlier strategies have striven mightily to avoid.

The effect on arms control of such a unilateral repudiation of Alliance commitments is hard to judge. Renouncing the development and deployment of cruise missiles, the MX and the Trident 2, is not necessarily incompatible with deep cuts in currently deployed systems, though it does seem to make it harder to achieve the cuts in countersilo weapons that both the Administration and the joint resolution (in clause 2) have called for.

But the most certain difficulty arising from the adoption of a freeze is a strategic one: the Countervailing Strategy depends on reducing the Soviet threat either (1) through negotiation (for which the freeze becomes a substantial additional objective), or (2) by carefully deployed threats such that no Soviet goal, however valuable, could be gained at a level of expected US retaliation acceptable to the USSR, or (3) through a combination of negotiation and deployed threats. Negotiations for a freeze do not diminish the present Soviet threat. Without such reductions in the threat, however, the current tasks of the Countervailing Strategy require force modernization; and the potentially helpful result of the freeze – to forestall new Soviet deployments – does not relieve NATO from such a requirement since it comes too late to protect NATO systems from Russian pre-emption and limited attack. Does the freeze then contemplate an entirely new strategy? One wonders how many of the proponents of the US freeze realize that it would demand a return to an Assured Destruction strategy stripped of Flexible Response, that is, shrunk to the assured destruction mission alone.

DEEP CUTS

The US administration's START proposal was announced by President Reagan on 9 May 1981 to an audience of 2000 people at the small Disciples of Christ College where the President had studied.[29] This proposal called for a common ceiling of 850 long-range missiles, a reduction from 2350 missiles for the Soviet Union and 1700 for the United States. The 850 missiles on each side would have been allowed to carry no more that 5000 nuclear warheads, down one-third from current levels of 7500. Of these 5000 missile warheads, no more than 2500 could be carried by land-based missiles. The attractiveness of this proposal lay in its responsiveness to the widespread public desire, shared by the President, for actual arms reductions rather than mere prospective limitation. The President's critics, in fact, were temporarily disarmed, as it were, by the Eureka College proposals. As a step toward implementing the Countervailing Strategy, however, it was a doubtful one, although that strategy contemplates, to be sure, an important role for arms control.

First, the proposal may, to some extent, actually worsen the problem of ICBM vulnerability. In choosing the simpler, more communicable 'numbers' approach, and delaying to a second round any ceiling on throw-weight, the Eureka College plan does not attempt to restore the crisis stability[30] and deterrence credibility that the Administration believed was undermined by the Soviet ability to neutralize the US land-based ICBM force.

At present the Soviet Union has about 5000 warheads on heavy, accurate ICBMs with an impressive hard target kill capability.[31] The US ICBM force presents 1000 targets for a Soviet countersilo attack. Thus the present ratio is about five to one. Under the START proposal, both sides are limited to 2500 warheads on their land-based ICBMs. If the US fully deploys the MX, which carries 10 warheads, this would present 250 US targets; a likelier outcome would be some mix between MX and Minuteman 3 (which carries 3 warheads), for example 200 MX and 150 MM 3 or 100 MX and 350 MM 3.[32] Regardless of the precise allocation on the Soviet side, this amounts to roughly 2500 warheads for 240, 350 or 450 targets, or 10 to 1, 7 to 1, 5 to 1 respectively, the exact ratio depending on precisely how each side chooses to allocate its allocated weapons, within the 850 ceiling. These rough ratios are no better – and some are far worse – than the currently prevailing 5 to 1 ratio.

The present calculus is that the Soviet Union would need only two highly accurate warheads to be able to target an American missile silo with over 90 per cent confidence.[33] Furthermore, as the number of targeted US silos goes from its present 1000 to perhaps a quarter of that figure, the number of Soviet launches decreases, decreasing the number of misfires, eccentric (low-probability) launch errors, and so forth. In summary, the US proposals do nothing to improve and may greatly worsen US ICBM vulnerability.

Second, the Eureka proposal was exceedingly difficult to negotiate, because the Soviet Union would have been forced to shift its warheads to the sort of sea-basing the US currently has, requiring a write-down of enormous Soviet assets. The Soviet Union has about 75 per cent of its strategic capabilities in land-based missiles, compared with about 25 per cent for the US.[34] If the Soviets now have about 2400 long range missiles and the US has 1700, to accommodate the 850 ceiling the Russians would have had to eliminate twice as many land-based missiles as the US while embarking on an ambitious submarine programme to utilize their total limit of warheads. The current technological inferiority of Soviet submarines and the lack of Soviet port facilities no doubt discouraged the acceptance of what is admittedly an asymmetrical offer.

The institutionalizing of arms control as a formal diplomatic process, over the past dozen years, has tended to obscure the fact that the essence of arms control is conditional restraint, that is, it is the benefit one side derives from the tacit collaboration of the other that guarantees the observance of the terms of collaboration by that side, and not only formal treaties.[35] Doubtless this has not been lost on an administration that, until recently, has continued to scrupulously observe the SALT 2 treaty it entered office by denouncing. But the conclusion to be drawn from the 'deep cuts' proposal is that it is a public relations success for the same reasons it is not likely to evoke conditional restraint. The Eureka proposals depend upon the anti-strategic notion that the number of weapons and not their capabilities is the source of the threat to peace, admittedly a popular notion but one that is likely to strike a responsive chord in nations whose security policies are *not* dominated by public opinion only to the extent that drastic cuts in numbers do not translate into significant strategic restraints.

ZERO OPTION

An implicit rejection of prevailing strategy is also apparent in the Reagan administration's negotiating proposal for the Geneva LRTNF talks. The NATO decision taken in 1979 adopted a 'two-track' approach to LRTNF deployment: while preparations were to go forward for ground launched missile (GLCM) and Pershing 2 deployments, the United States would approach the Russians to negotiate a reduction in their intermediate range ballistic missiles (SS 20s, -4s, -5s) and Backfire forces, 'within the framework of SALT'. It was thought that the prospect of avoiding NATO deployments would offer some incentive to the Russians to moderate their buildup. If the Russians agreed to reductions in their European nuclear forces, the NATO deployments would be correspondingly limited.

The two-track approach (negotiate while preparing to deploy) reflected an Alliance priority of politics over purely military considerations, and this is as it should be. For reasons that were mentioned in the preceding chapter, LRTNF deployment in Europe, at least under US auspices, is largely dependent on the progress, or at least the inertia, of the strategic arms limitation process. The two-track approach was an attempt to tie these parallel elements together and thereby maximize public support in Europe. Its principal shortcoming was that it *appeared* to assume that the strategic justification for US LRTNF was the Soviet deployment of the SS-20 and thus it gave the Soviet Union a marionette-string on Western public opinion: by manipulating SS-20 deployments, promising to stop them if NATO ceased its plans, moving some east of the Urals, promising to destroy some percentage of them, and so on, the Russians attempted to affect the pace and depth of NATO's deployments.

In fact the basis for NATO LRTNF was much broader than a single Soviet weapon. The Countervailing Strategy itself required that the Russians know that NATO could respond with strikes against Russian territory if an attack were made on Europe, even if US central systems were, by virtue of the stalemate of parity for example, not engaged. The vulnerability of NATO Forward-Based Systems (FBS), particularly their fixed basing (and reliance on fixed support installations) is, it is true, greatly enhanced by the very accurate SS-20. But equally threatening in this respect is the SS-22 (or for that matter, re-targeted ICBMs). Moreover, the penetration of NATO aircraft has greatly declined and in any event their range is insufficient for virtually all Russian targets. Thus, even without the SS-20s, NATO would have faced the sort of theatre imbalance (and hence the possibility of Soviet sanctuary) that parity makes significant. The Countervailing Strategy, a response to stalemate at the strategic level and the collapse of escalation dominance at the theatre level, would have required survivable weapons whose range and penetration to Russian targets could be relied upon even if NATO still faced only Soviet SS-4s and SS-5s.

The careful consultation that led to the 1979 NATO Council decision could not, however, entirely forestall adverse European reaction. The much publicized rejection of SALT 2 by the US administration, the unfortunate press treatment of President Reagan's news conference remarks regarding limited nuclear war,[36] early fumbles of the neutron bomb decision announcement within the US Cabinet,[37] the long delay in formulating a US position on strategic arms control and, principally, the impression of hostility and belligerence projected by the American administration tended to excite European concerns about their status as enhanced targets once the new NATO forces were deployed. In 1981 an anti-deployment movement swelled throughout Europe such that, by the end of the year, two governments had backed away from the NATO decision and the German chancellor had retained his party's support for this decision only by threatening to resign if that support was not forthcoming.[38] Throughout 1981 deterioration of the Alliance position accelerated with disheartening rapidity.

Then, on 18 November 1981, the President announced the US LRTNF arms control position, the 'zero' option. 'The United States' he said in an address to the National Press Club, 'is prepared to cancel its deployment of Pershing 2 and ground-launched cruise missiles if the Soviets will dismantle their SS-20, SS-4 and SS-5 missiles'.[39] Public reaction to this bold response to Soviet propaganda was highly favourable. The velocity behind the European anti-LRTNF movement, which had become increasingly an anti-American movement, faltered. Seldom has a single stroke been so immediately effective at deflating such broad-based opposition.

Yet one must feel that this was a temporary, though stunning, victory for the Administration. In time, the proposal had either to be accepted or rejected. Had it been accepted then NATO would have to forego the option of threatening to attack Soviet territory with land-based missiles in Europe. Assuming SLCMs were within the contemplated ban, NATO would have had difficulty executing intra-war LNOs without using American land-based central systems, while the Russians would have retained the ability, in SS-21, -22 and -23 systems, to attack NATO military targets and threaten European cities. François de Rose had observed,

> [An] error has led these European countries to accept, indeed to ask for negotiations which would trade Pershing IIs and cruise missiles against SS-20s and Backfire. It may well be that the famous 'Zero option' became inevitable for political reasons. But that it should have been received with applause in the capitals of the old continent merely shows that the governments involved have been unable to protect themselves and their public opinion from the manipulations of Soviet propaganda. For that proposal would eliminate most of the American weapons capable of striking the USSR from Western Europe while leaving out of such cuts several thousand Soviet aircraft, missiles and artillery with a range inferior to 1,500 kilometres but which, deployed in the satellites of the USSR, can strike at most of NATO territory on this side of the ocean.
>
> Indeed, it is as if the only menace against Europe would come from the weapons systems deployed in the Soviet Union, and as if the only problem to be attended to was to shelter the USSR from the weapons that could reach her when deployed in Europe. The truth is that the 'Zero option' presents for the allies the maximum danger of de-coupling.[40]

Beyond this asymmetry, such an outcome would be a contradiction of the Countervailing Strategy which seeks to contain conflict at the lowest level.

When the proposal was rejected, the Russians launched a renewed propaganda effort with the counter-proposal of a 'zero option' that included French and British nuclear forces, as well as US FBS. Whatever momentum the US administration had managed to arrest began to rebound. But all this posturing sounds more like the description of a transport strike negotiation than an arms control conference. Is substance to play no part?

Substance of course must play a part if only inadvertently. The zero option was very difficult for the Russians to accept because it required such a write-down of expensive assets precisely at the time that the NATO plan seemed to be stumbling. That does not mean that proposing it was cost-free to the US, and this is the point at which substance played its role. The zero option, like the freeze, rejects NATO strategy that would cordon off central systems and modulate the slope of possible exchanges that approach those systems. Because it rejects American strategic premises, it was at first successful, hardly surprisingly, with the European peace movement. Yet its long-term impact can only be to discredit the American role in European defence, making Europe appear to be caught between superpowers whose mutual deployments threaten states in about equal measure. This in turn will put pressure on NATO strategy – the substance – which is in no position to compromise with a perspective so hostile to its premises. And as the NATO deployments go forward, the US run the risk that the USSR will actually accept the proposal.

NO FIRST USE

A no-first-use pledge shares with the other proposals a certain public appeal and doctrinal contradiction. As an idea it is scarcely new, having been frequently proposed by the Russians over the years. What gives it its present prominence is its adoption, in an important article in *Foreign Affairs*,[41] 'Nuclear Weapons and the Atlantic Alliance', by McGeorge Bundy, George Kennan, Gerard Smith and Robert McNamara (joined in the UK by Field Marshal Lord Carver). These four men, who were at various times almost continuously responsible for one important part of American strategic policy or another in the postwar period, have demonstrated a profound disenchantment with present strategy by their advocacy of this idea.

There are at least two formidable strategic arguments for no-first-use. 'Nuclear Weapons and the Atlantic Alliance' makes one of these:

(1) It would be irrational to use US central systems to initiate nuclear war, since Russian retaliation against the US would be devastating;

(2) The use of any nuclear systems is unlikely to remain limited and will escalate to central systems;

(3) Theatre nuclear systems are not necessary to deter, or retaliate against, the Soviet use of nuclear weapons in Europe since central systems can perform this task;[42]

(4) Therefore, the US should renounce the first use of nuclear weapons, whether theatre or central: the first use of central systems is irrational and the first use of a theatre system is unnecessary and tantamount to using central systems.

This argument is deeply embedded in even-handed statements of concern about Germany and the need for further study, as well as a superficially non-controversial plea for a policy entailed by the argument, *viz*, a renewed effort to strengthen NATO's conventional force.

If we assume (2), that the use of nuclear weapons is not likely to remain limited and will escalate to central systems, does it follow that (4), the US should renounce first use, since it would be irrational to use US central systems to initiate nuclear war (1)? At the outset it should be observed that (2) is not necessarily incompatible with the Countervailing Strategy. Point (2) does not assume that escalation is an absolute certainty (a stronger assumption would be contradictory to a strategy of graduated response). Furthermore, one might argue that the uncertainty of (2) is precisely what contradicts the position of (3) since a theatre nuclear force may thereby serve a deterrent function well beyond its ability to damage.

This dodges rather than answers the question so ably put by the article's authors, however, since the risks imposed on Western Europe and the US of maintaining this boosted deterrence is the disproportionate escalation it drags with it if deterrence fails. Point (2) must be denied or accepted on its merits as posing a risk to the US and her allies, regardless of the risk it may impose on our adversaries. Assume then that (2) is correct. Assume also that (1) is correct. Does the risk of unlimited exchanges decline if NATO renounces its intention to initiate limited war and lives up to this renunciation? Even if (3) is also correct, we must add the premises that (a) US central systems will not be engaged *no matter what* Soviet non-nuclear action is taken in Europe, and that (b) the likelihood of Soviet first use is not increased by a NATO no-first-use pledge (positing the increased NATO conventional force entailed by that pledge). Otherwise, the chance of engaging central systems increases rather than decreases without the threat of LRTNF, first use. One must assume that lessening the requirements of extended deterrence (e.g., such that Europe would be protected by US nuclear forces from Soviet nuclear attacks only) while raising the magnitude of retaliation lessens the likelihood of employment and that that employment, if it should come, is at least as appropriate as current pledges of US support. It is not clear, however, that it is rational for the US to be willing to participate in an assuredly suicidal total exchange once Germany has been devastated by nuclear weapons but irrational to even risk such an exchange before that happens. Indeed, so much the opposite would appear to be true that such a threat might well tempt a Soviet first use against Germany. I conclude that (4) therefore is not a necessary inference from (1)–(3).

A second argument from the NATO perspective in favour of no-first-use might be parsed this way:

(1) NATO needs theatre nuclear forces (TNF) as a deterrent to Soviet first use of TNF;

(2) NATO first use of TNF, however, cannot reverse a losing course of military operations and, to the extent that it triggered a Soviet retaliation, would actually worsen the relative NATO position;

(3) NATO TNF first use is not a rational option.

This argument, insofar as it juxtaposes (2) and (1) without contradiction appears to accept that a deterrent can consist in a threat whose actual use might be irrational (and thus shares something with the argument discussed above). This may well be so, but one is inclined to think this to be such a weak deterrent that the idea of self-deterrence begins to intrude.

At any rate, this argument for no-first-use rests on the validity and significance of (2), regardless of (1). It assumes that once war has begun the only rational use of weapons is the defeat of the enemy when in fact terminating a war in Europe on terms favourable to NATO is an important objective in itself. And 'terms favourable to NATO' is not a slogan for necessarily improving NATO's pre-war position, but rather for gaining an outcome preferable to continued devastation. If we accept the intra-war deterrence of the Countervailing Strategy, then the imposition of higher costs on the Soviets by TNF strikes can make the continuation of war by the Soviet Union less rational regardless of the harm the Soviet Union is capable of inflicting. The calculus of decision from the Soviet perspective, after all, is not how much pain can be inflicted but how much pain must be endured to achieve the political objective sought. A no-first-use rule by NATO puts that cost calculation solely in the hands of the Soviets and, once they have determined upon aggression, such a rule forfeits the ability to change that calculation by NATO pre-emption. Thus if (2) is correct, it suggests that a no-first-use rule may be irrelevant (since the Soviets, relying on (2), will press their advantage in any event), but not that such a rule is an irrational course (3).

Both the first and second forms of the no-first-use argument may in fact entail no-use NATO policies. There would be little occasion for NATO strikes – first or second – in the strategic environment created by a NATO no-first-use pledge. Such a 'second' use policy means that the Russians have control over whether the US will use nuclear weapons and thus NATO strikes based on such a policy cannot give the Russians reasons to halt an offensive, since they will only occur once the Russians have decided that the benefits of their own nuclear use, discounted by the costs of NATO retaliation, justify such use. Nor is such a policy more likely to induce the US to act since the environment for acting – one in which the Soviets have already struck at a time of their own choosing – is so much less favourable. In such circumstances it is hard to concur in the conclusion of 'Nuclear Weapons and the Atlantic Alliance' that a no-first-use pledge will 'reduce the risks of conventional aggression in Europe'. That conventional strengthening of NATO forces would be likelier in the absence of a plausible nuclear use in their behalf, as claimed by the article's authors, does not seem to follow from this argument. If there is a convincing reason to support such a pledge, it is atmospheric, as is much of the argument in *Foreign Affairs*.

> [We] think a policy of no-first-use, especially if shared with the Soviet Union, would bring new hope to everyone in every country whose life is shadowed by the hideous possibility of a third great twentieth-century conflict in Europe – conventional or nuclear. It seems timely and even urgent to begin the careful study of a policy that could help to sweep this threat clean off the board of international affairs. . . . The events of last year have shown that differing perceptions of the role of nuclear weapons can lead to destructive recriminations, and when these differences are compounded by understandable disagreements on other matters such as Poland and the Middle East, the possibilities for trouble among Allies are evident. . . . A posture of no-first-use should also go far to meet the understandable anxieties that underlie much of the new interest in nuclear disarmament both in Europe and in our own country.[43]

This political judgement I, at least, am in no position to question. Attention is drawn to it only to show that, in its utter rejection of prevailing strategy and its emphasis on public reaction, it is an appeal to, and is evidence of, the public alienation from the concept of deterrence. As such it belongs with the zero option, the freeze resolution, the deep cuts proposal – championed by statesmen who appear to have little in common beyond that acute sense of public sensibilities that a democracy requires of its leaders. These proposals will accelerate as much as respond to the new crisis in vulnerability described.

The freeze proposal will put the Republican Party and the Reagan administration on the spot: if arms control negotiations show progress, the Democrats can claim that, but for the freeze campaign, the American position would have been intransigent and hence unproductive. If negotiations fail, freeze proponents can offer a fresh approach. Even sophisticated persons have confided that they support the strategically absurd proposal simply because it puts pressure on a recalcitrant Administration. The zero option puts pressure on the Russians; so does a deep cuts START proposal. These are meant to embarrass the Soviet Union and discredit their posturing as peace forces in the world community. A no-first-use gambit puts pressure on the Republicans *and* the Russians. Taken together these programmes are a sort of parody of the doctrinal innovations of earlier eras: like them, they respond to the exposure of a vulnerability that tends to exacerbate problems in extended deterrence. But unlike their cyclical predecessors, these programmes depart from, or even implicitly disavow, the principal doctrinal assumption of American strategic thought in our era because the vulnerability to which they are responding is public alienation from that assumption. Thus these various, highly politicized moves amount to a kind of pasquinade, turning Clausewitz upside down: here, politics has become the extension of strategy by other means.

Finally, we should address more recent arms control proposals by the Reagan Administration. On 22 November, 1984 it was announced that the American Secretary of State, George Shultz, would meet the Soviet Foreign Minister, Andrei Gromyko, in Geneva the following January. Then, on 20 December, a 'senior official' – the code used for a government person speaking for quotation but not attribution – told journalists that the American negotiating package would include proposed cuts in offensive systems, measures of restraint on anti-satellite systems now under development, and also the subject of US defensive systems. This last item represented a change in US policy; previously the Administration had been willing only to commit itself to 'discussions' of its long-term research plans for a defensive system against incoming missiles. 'We are hopeful that there will be a comprehensive desire to talk about all offensive and defensive systems in their entirety and completeness', said the new Chairman of the Senate Foreign Relations Committee after a closed briefing by the Secretary of State on the new US 'package'. Many commentators assumed that this development implied an increased willingness by the US to negotiate limits on US defensive systems. These reactions ought perhaps to have been muted by the senior official's remark that it was crucial to engage the Soviet Union in talks on 'what constitutes stability' for it later became apparent that limits on defensive deployments were not what the US intended to propose at all. Indeed, the truly dramatic element in the new proposals was the American willingness to depart from the deterrence assumption itself. Thus Charles Corddry reported,

> The United States will urge the development of star wars missile defense systems for both superpowers as a central part of its negotiating position when it resumes arms talks with the Soviet Union, a White House official said . . .
>
> Instead of yielding to Soviet calls for banning space weapons, the official said, the United States will argue that high technology defensive arms make possible a radical shift away from the strategy of deterring war by threat of nuclear devastation.
>
> The prospect of strategic defense against missiles is a fundamental change, the official said, and it will take time to explain the concept to the Soviets and demonstrate that it is not an effort to gain a US advantage.

This, it develops, is what was meant by 'a general goal for establishing a stable military balance between the superpowers with combinations of offensive and defensive weapons'.

Ballistic missile defence and the so-called 'Star Wars' programme that calls for a combination of non-nuclear weapons that could destroy incoming missiles as they are launched, or are in mid-course, or are over the target area, are discussed in Chapter 13. For our present purposes, it is important only to note that such an arms control proposal is responsive to the latest cycle of US vulnerability, public alienation from the programme of deterrence, and not simply a reaction to any technical development, such as ICBM vulnerability. Indeed the programme is a rebuff to those who argue that only technology drives doctrinal change; the strategic defence initiative depends on the development of technology whose feasibility is far distant.

This attempt to respond to public alienation is underscored by the 'senior official's' remark that 'the fundamental change I spoke of would be away from the surreal idea that vulnerability to missiles is a good thing.' The advocates of defensive systems for civilian protection rarely speak in strategic terms. It is not clear, in fact, that defensive systems deployed by the superpowers would be in the US interest. Rather those advocates speak directly to the public, satirizing the prevailing doctrine as 'mad' or lunatic. The brute fact of civilian vulnerability – mutual assured destruction – is ridiculed as a surreal doctrine, chosen rather than responded to. In the process, the deterrence assumption, neither doctrine nor fact of life, is dismissed. A strategic evaluation of this complex problem will be attempted in a later chapter. I close the present one simply by recording this most recent response to the cycle I have described.

The movement in Congress to restrict the President's authority to use nuclear weapons comes from a different part of the US political spectrum,[44] but it arises from a similar alienation from the deterrence assumption. In time, perhaps, there will even be demands for the Congressional approval of the SIOP. Then it will not seem as far-fetched as it may now to argue that the social element of nuclear strategy is the source of future doctrine-shaping vulnerability.

10 Alternative Nuclear Strategies

Ohmè dolente! come mi riscossi
quando mi prese dicendomi: "Forse
tu non pensavi ch' io loico fossi!"

(O wretched me! How I started when he took me, saying to me: "perhaps thou didst not think I was a logician!")

Canto XXVII, *Inferno*

The realization that the Soviet Union did not endorse strategic concepts based on the deterrence assumption has intensified the disenchantment with those concepts.[1] This realization was slow in coming, given the inferior Soviet position relative to US armaments that tended to mask Soviet intentions, a patronizing Western attitude toward Soviet military doctrine,[2] and the American optimism in foreign affairs that arises from what sometimes appears to be an invincible ethnocentricity. We are often unable *both* to take Russian security concerns seriously, from their point of view, *and* to recognize that this point of view poses a danger to the West. In the light of the tremendous US buildup in the early 1960s, it was plausible to assume that the Soviet deployments and acquisitions of the late 1960s were simply a responsive effort to defend against US pre-emption. McNamara among many others[3] predicted that a levelling off would occur once a secure, assured destruction capability was gained. They were perhaps persuaded that there were no significant implications for deterrence in the margin between this capability and full parity anyway. When the Soviet Union pressed ahead, however, and matched the US, SALT 1 attempted to codify this parity through an agreement to maintain equality in the number of launchers for central systems, proceeding on the assumption that both sides would be satisfactorily secure within a 'deterrence environment'. From our present perspective, however, it is clear that the undiminished and uninterrupted Soviet weapons deployment since SALT 1 amounts to a rejection of such an environment and instead reveals a formidable determination to acquire a decisive war-fighting capability. Benjamin Lambeth has concluded,

> Although this commitment does not mean that the Soviet Union is any less interested than her Western counterparts in the continued avoidance of nuclear war, it does suggest an underlying Soviet conception of deterrence quite unlike that which has traditionally held sway in the United States.[4]

Lambeth argues that

> The Soviet Union defines the nuclear dilemma and the force requirements she sees as dictated by it using an intellectual approach quite alien to the concepts that have largely informed the strategic policies of the United States over the past two decades. To put the point of critical difference in a nutshell, the American prospensity – running as far back as the formative works of Bernard Brodie in the late 1940's – has been to regard nuclear weapons as fundamentally different from all other forms of military fire-power because of their unique potential for inflicting truly catastrophic damage in a single blow.[5]

As we have seen, American procurement, deployment, and arms control policies all reflect fundamental assumptions that follow from this conviction about the unique qualities of nuclear vulnerability. The rejection of ballistic missile defence (and even civil defence programmes) on the grounds that they might make nuclear war-fighting more feasible, and the ongoing campaign against countersilo weapons, are examples of the repudiation of nuclear weapons as a war-fighting tool. The Soviets, by contrast, have rejected the view that their security might be entrusted to an allegedly self-sustaining system of nuclear deterrence at the central level.[6]

As John van Oudenaren has acutely observed, '[i]n the Soviet Union, as in the United States, the nuclear problem is reshaped in the image of the political system itself and the threats it perceives. It is the context of Soviet ideology that requires that the Soviet military "solve" the problem of fighting and winning a nuclear war.' Operations concepts and plans are developed that use nuclear weapons in the combat environment, not the bargaining environment.

Thus it does not necessarily follow that the Soviet rejection of the deterrence assumption requires the US to abandon it also (although it does perhaps cast doubt on those arms control tactics that depend on a shared doctrinal empathy, e.g., maintaining mutual vulnerabilities or even foregoing the development of certain destabilizing weapons). Simply because the Soviet Union has become infatuated with the aim of superiority is no reason, in itself, to mimic this behaviour. If it is true that the 'central goal of the [Russian] military investment effort of the past decade has consistently been the acquisition of an overall force posture of sufficient strength and versatility to command the initiative in any determined nuclear showdown with the West',[7] as one analyst has written, it must also be acknowledged that US doctrine has conceded that initiative. If the Countervailing Strategy is flawed on the ground that it surrenders the initiative, then it is flawed at the conception because it is a cost-imposing, reactive strategic doctrine.

The Countervailing Strategy does not purport to count the cost to the US of imposing costs on the Soviets. If one were to focus on those costs, however, one might plausibly conclude a) the costs will be so high that the US will be self-deterred in a conflict in which it actually encounters Soviet war-fighting doctrine backed up with genuine central parity and Soviet sectoral superiority,[8] or b) that Soviet rationality requires that she never attempt a political objective that would justify the United States bearing such costs, i.e., an attempt on our survival or on our truly vital interests or c) that both these scenarios co-exist in the possible reality of a limited nuclear war, *viz*, self-deterrence at the sectoral level and sanctuary at the central level.

These alternative concerns about the likely course of a nuclear war between the superpowers are reflected in the principal proposals for United States nuclear strategy. It will be immediately seen that they bear largely on extended deterrence. Indeed one might characterize these proposals in this way: war-fighting doctrines, fearing (a) above, reject the deterrence assumption and conclude that everything is extended deterrence; minimum deterrence doctrines, relying on (b) above, narrow strategies simply to the deterrence assumption itself and hold that nothing is extended deterrence; concerned with (c), countervailing strategies attempt to resolve the tension between theatres by confining the risks of extending deterrence.

WAR-FIGHTING STRATEGIES

'Victory Is Possible', by Colin Gray and Keith Payne and 'Nuclear Strategy: The Case for a Theory of Victory', by Gray, put this alternative with admirable forthrightness.[9] There are two reasons, they write, why current doctrine – to the extent that it and similar doctrines of the post–1949 period incorporate the deterrence assumption – is fundamentally inadequate. First, deterrence may break down (and the authors no doubt see that all these various doctrines have depended on intra-war deterrence) through an inability to communicate or through Soviet rejection of American signals.[10] Second, the concept of deterrence does not allow for ways in which the West can employ its strategic nuclear forces coercively, in other words, to achieve some political goal other than the mere warding off of an attack on the American homeland. Theorists who rely on the deterrence assumption 'would have nothing of interest to say to a President facing conventional defeat in the Persian Gulf or in Western Europe'.[11] Moreover, such theory has led the US defence community to endorse a posture that maximizes the prospect for self-deterrence: 'a condition of parity is incompatible with extended deterrent duties because of the self-deterrence inherent in such a strategic context'.[12]

A war-fighting strategy, in contrast to the countervailing strategy that extends deterrence into war itself, for example, is a throwback to pre-deterrence assumption thought.[13] Such a strategy tacitly accepts strategic bombing premises and, by its embrace of both deterrence by denial and deterrence by punishment, demonstrates yet again that these two concepts do not encompass 'nuclear deterrence' as defined by the deterrence assumption. A war-fighting strategy recognizes that current and previous American nuclear strategy has not been designed to defeat the Soviet Union, a fact that must be at the bottom of much of the public alienation from deterrence, both of hawks who would have us seek victory and of doves who stress the irrationality of vast armaments that don't even promise victory. A war-fighting strategy rejects the deterrence assumption and thus endorses damage limitation and defensive systems with a passionate enthusiasm. If you do not believe that your weapons' offensive capabilities protect you – by making your adversary your protector for fear of what would happen to him if harm came to you – then you had better find a way to cope with your enemy's offensive capabilities. This is its most crucial feature, for, as we shall see, without active or passive defence,[14] war-fighting strategies are simply elided into tactics.

The war-fighting school stresses its realism, but is it actually realistic? It is open to doubt whether the United States could have maintained a damage-limiting superiority no matter how large its defence budgets: this sort of superiority – including that after assured destruction capabilities are achieved but before parity – exists in a bounded field, either sectorally (as with the SS-20 in Europe) that is easily parried; or globally, with a diminished significance as the warheads and dispersed means of carrying them outstrip the vulnerabilities they can exploit. More importantly, the United States has no ballistic missile defence[15] and no effective civil defence – the principal requirements of a successful war-fighting strategy – because there is, at present, no cost-effective ballistic missile defence,[16] civil defence or pre-emptive capability sufficient to disarm the USSR. A war-fighting strategy demands these requirements because such a theory of victory would, if successful in its implementation, steadily reduce the relative costs to the adversary of destroying the US. On the other hand, the Countervailing Strategy, in recognition of US powerlessness to stop such destruction, would steadily impose costs on such a move. That the Soviet Union has been persuaded to adopt a war-fighting nuclear strategy simply imposes upon them a search for a strategic objective that could possibly justify it. Can there be such an objective *vis-à-vis* a nuclear superpower except in the circumstances in which the Soviet Union itself is likely to be defeated? And isn't, therefore, the adoption of such a strategy by the United States, virtually the surest step that could validate the Russian strategy?

If the superpowers could limit damage to themselves by means of the deterrence assumption – that is, by a sanctuary for the Russian homeland guaranteed by withholding attacks on the US homeland and *vice versa* – then war-fighting strategies become plausible within an extended theatre. This is precisely why a US war-fighting strategy is anathema to the European members of the Alliance. Whether the US achieves damage limitation by pre-emption or sanctuary or by ballistic missile defence,[17] none of these solutions necessarily protects and indeed may greatly threaten Western Europe if it makes adoption of a war-fighting strategy possible for the United States. Accordingly, a war-fighting strategy for the US represents a corollary case of the theorem. It seems most unlikely that Western Europe, who, unlike Eastern Europe, has the resources and political latitude to avoid doing so, would long acquiesce in an extended deterrence that is achieved by a war-fighting strategy.

MINIMUM DETERRENCE

The second alternative strategy, deterrence *simpliciter*, is a logical extrapolation – and not necessarily the historical or political outcome – of Brodie's original perceptions as they are now bounded by central deterrence. In his most famous passage, quoted earlier, Brodie professed himself

> not for the moment concerned about who will win the next war in which atomic bombs have been used. Thus far the chief purpose of our military establishment has been to win wars. From now on its chief purpose must be to avert them. It can have almost no other useful purpose.[18]

Minimum deterrence is also the logical outcome of the subtle, indirect yet powerful series of addresses on this subject by McGeorge Bundy. Bundy repeatedly begins his argument by asserting what war-fighting theorists deny: that nuclear weapons *are* different, are so different that they make war itself a wholly different phenomenon from that we have known. Indeed Bundy quotes Brodie as saying that,

> Perhaps the most elementary, the truistic, and yet the most important point one can make is that the kind of sudden and overwhelming calamity that one is talking about in any reference to an all-out or total war would be an utterly different and immeasurably worse phenomenon than war as we have known it in the past.[19]

These weapons are different because they are phenomenally destructive, indeed cannot be made any other way, and being so destructive, render irrelevant efforts at defence since so little successful offensive penetration is required to accomplish the most devastating missions. Bundy recognizes that the deterrence assumption – which depends upon the perception of this difference – underlay all strategic doctrine in the age begun by the coincidence of thermonuclear power and Russian acquisition of that power.

> In the largest sense, all sides in the West accepted the doctrine of deterrence. After the development of plainly survivable and deliverable Soviet thermonuclear weapons there was no one left, that I am aware of, who saw thermonuclear war as a desirable undertaking. Those who wanted more strength than either Eisenhower or Kennedy chose to supply wanted it, in the first instance, to make deterrence more effective.[20]

Bundy's crucial move, however, consists in explaining why advisors to Eisenhower or Kennedy thought more strength would enhance deterrence, that is, in giving a non-war-fighting role to superiority. Once it has been established that the deterrence assumption is crucial to doctrine, Bundy must go on and show that it is sufficient, in other words, that superiority – the unsuccessful quest for which has played such a part in alienating the public – is unnecessary and that those forces required by the deterrence assumption, and no more, are sufficient.

This involves a certain amount of reconstruction of the Kennedy–Johnson years. In a persuasive way, Bundy concedes that US superiority was often claimed to exist but undercuts the strategic significance of this fact. His argument requires close scrutiny.

> In early 1962 Secretary McNamara seemed to argue briefly for a large-scale counter-force capability, and throughout his time at the Pentagon, though decreasingly in later years, he stoutly asserted that the United States had and would retain superiority in strategic weapons. But he also believed and said that the value of such superiority would decline, and it was expected that each of the two sides could and would maintain a capacity for second-strike retaliation so great as to constitute stable mutual deterrence at the strategic level.
>
> But let me fully recognize that while this was really believed by the Kennedy and Johnson Administrations, the heavy rhetorical emphasis on continuing American superiority was misleading. We did assert that we had strategic superiority, and we did assert that having it made a difference. What we did not say so loudly was that the principal use of this numerical superiority was in its value as reassurance to the American public and as a means of warding off demands for still larger forces.[21]

Putting it this way tends to obscure the fact that superiority is an indispensable element of both Controlled Response and Assured Destruction (the latter being distinguished from an 'assured destruction capability', which does not require superiority). Recognizing that force levels far exceeded the requirements of minimum deterrence in those years, Bundy attributes this to political pressures arising from bureaucratic, Presidential and Congressional interplay. Bundy concedes that neither Kennedy nor Johnson nor McNamara made statements or took steps that would appear to accept minimum deterrence, but withdraws this concession by hinting that private perceptions differed from the public front.

> *Open* recognition that usable superiority was neither necessary nor available did not come in the McNamara years (emphasis added).[22]

To make the point, Bundy quotes an article written in 1968 by Carl Kaysen who had served on the NSC staff during the Kennedy administration:

> We cannot expect with any confidence to do more than achieve a secure second strike capacity, no matter how hard we try. This capacity is not usefully measured by counting warheads or megatons or, above some level, expected casualties. Whether the result comes about with twice as many American as Soviet delivery vehicles – as has been the case in the past – or with roughly equal numbers, or even with an adverse ratio, does not change its basic nature.[23]

Bundy follows this excerpt with the observation that 'To its credit, the Nixon administration abandoned the goal of strategic superiority, substituting "sufficiency" and, later, "parity."'[24] 'Sufficiency' the *doctrine*, however, amounted to no more than a renewal of the Assured Destruction doctrine that the new Administration had inherited in the context of the rapidly dwindling superiority on which it depended; indeed most of the remaining years of that Administration were spent seeking ways to avoid the minimum deterrence implications of a parity that the Soviets forced on the US.

Any reservations about this historical account, however, should not obscure Bundy's argument. This begins by asserting that nuclear weapons are different in a way that makes the deterrence assumption an unavoidable fact of life; and the argument ends with a treatment of the most difficult issue for minimum deterrence – extended deterrence – that by assuming that bipolarity is in the same way an unavoidable fact, and concludes that arms beyond the central deterrent (with a conventional fuse) are superfluous in a bipolar world. The European balance (other theatres are dismissed as unsuitable for nuclear deterrence) endures not because of deterrence because 'both sides prefer what now exists to a large and unpredictable change by force. . . . [It represents, at present] a balance of power in which the engagement of the American [central] deterrent is an essential element'.[25]

This passage reflects a subtle and rich gloss on the usual minimum deterrence position regarding extended deterrence. That argument, which underlies Bundy's position, is:

(1) Given the risk of escalation, no American nuclear guarantee can possibly exceed the value of the objective for which it is sought;

(2) Therefore, neither the threat (i.e., deterrence) requires, nor would war require, forces beyond US central systems so long as these are adequate for central deterrence (that is, a secure second strike, assured destruction capability) since a President would have to assume these might be engaged before he would authorize *any* nuclear use and hence he (and the Soviets) would treat conflicts and planning accordingly;

(3) Thus only those objectives which would justify engaging central systems – and risking the destruction of the American homeland – ought to be, or indeed credibly can be, the subjects of US nuclear guarantees;

(4) Western Europe is an area of vital interest to the US and the Soviets recognize this.

This reasoning greatly discounts US claims. It suggests that no matter what the advertising (or the weapons capability) the US will intervene with nuclear weapons only when the reasons for intervention would justify engaging the full retaliatory force. It also implies that the Soviets make a similar discount in reverse proportion: no probe is justified since US reaction, if it comes at all (and it cannot be discounted to zero certainly so long as 300 000 US troops are likely to be immediately engaged) will be total and obliterate the benefits of war to the Soviet Union.[26]

In light of Sir Michael Howard's celebrated 'Healey's Theorem' on the deterrent effect of even such a greatly discounted threat – 'if there is one chance in a hundred of nuclear weapons being used, the odds would be enough to deter an aggressor even if they were not enough to reassure an ally'[27] – the US central deterrent as presently constituted would appear sufficient for extended deterrence.

This argument, which Bundy has offered with low-key eloquence in several places, shares one important flaw with the war-fighting alternative. Granting Howard's witty insight, we must infer that mere central deterrent forces are *not* likely to be enough to reassure the Europeans. Although Bundy's argument states the American position with disarming frankness – 'It follows that the strategic protection of Europe is as strong or as weak as the American strategic guarantee no matter what American weapons are deployed under NATO'[28] – his concluding words of reassurance are chosen with the care of a sophisticated draftsman. 'I believe the *effectiveness* of this American guarantee', he writes, 'is likely to be just as great in the future as in the past' (emphasis added). This conclusion follows from the entire argument since the Russian discounting of exaggerated American guarantees presumably began some time ago when escalation became threatening with the achievement of a Russian assured destruction capability against the US. This period of almost twenty years has been notable for the stability of the central front.

Such a period of stability, depending as it does on the uncertainties and caution of Russian discounting, does not arrest European scepticism, and thus the strategic world is not, as Bundy asserts, ineluctably bipolar. A nuclear-armed European defence community (EDC) is also a 'logical outcome' of any drastic discounting of extended deterrence by Europeans. Germany has the resources that would support, and suffers the threat that would justify, the acquisition of a superpower's nuclear arsenal. This tendency to great power proliferation is exacerbated by a desire on the part of French governments to experiment with independent diplomatic initiatives. If an EDC were to arise we would once again have seen a development in central deterrence precipitating a crisis in extended deterrence that, in turn, stimulated innovation in doctrine with profound consequences for the central relationship. A truly multi-polar world would prove far more dangerous than a bipolar one.[29]

It is, of course, difficult to assess the likelihood of such an outcome. But we may see, in the recent crises within the Alliance provoked by the invasion of Afghanistan and the hostage-taking in Iran,[30] the sorts of reactions that would move Europe in the direction of an EDC. For example, Pierre Hassner has noted,

> Taken by itself, the TNF decision of 12 December 1979, to base, in Western Europe, American long-range missiles capable of reaching Soviet territory, should have gone a long way towards allaying this mutual fear of strategic decoupling. But as soon as the Afghanistan crisis broke M. Poniatowski, one of President Giscard d'Estaing's closest associates, rushed to confirm Henry Kissinger's suspicions by stating that Europe should get rid of NATO and build an independent nuclear force in order to stay out of the conflict.[31]

It is true that the security issue alone will not drive a successful move to an EDC. The European states' desire for greater technological and economic independence from the United States as well as for an East–West settlement is an indispensable motive for such a move. Yet one cannot help noticing that, again, it is the issues of extended deterrence – in the Gulf, in Iran and Southwest Asia – that have precipitated reassessments, on both sides of the Atlantic, of the costs and benefits of the US guarantee.

This ought to make us all realize that extended deterrence is the means of preserving a bipolar world.[32] This world, though dangerous, lives within the deterrence assumption. The emergence of a third nuclear superpower is the most obvious way by which nation-states could loosen the conditions of this axiom. It is in this way that the latest vulnerability, public alienation, threatens to propel the world unwittingly in the direction the public so greatly and rightly fears.

COUNTERVAILING DETERRENCE

Strategic thought follows political thought. Strategy cannot create a comprehending and committed public. But the public can ultimately render strategy incomprehensible such that commitment seems beside the point. This threatens to be the case with the current policy, the Countervailing Strategy, the third possible strategic regime. I argued in Chapter 8 that the Countervailing Strategy is becoming increasingly inexecutable in the European theatre, according to the 'theorem' proposed in that chapter. In the present chapter, I shall argue that the strategy is difficult to make workable for technical reasons. This difficulty arises from the extraordinary demands placed by the Countervailing Strategy on fragile command, control, communications and intelligence (C^3I) networks.

Current US strategic planning depends on C^3I endurance at least equal to the ninety days allocated to the strategic nuclear forces, plus a period in which residual strategic forces are to be regrouped.[33] The strategic forces, however, whose vulnerability has been the source of such concern, are far easier to protect than the C^3I which is essential to their use in LNOs. Radar dishes, the very low frequency (VLF) communication system on which nuclear strike submarines (SSBN) depend, and satellite ground facilities are soft targets that are easily identifiable and must be located at certain fixed points above ground. Super-hardening of command posts is unlikely to do anything more to protect underground bunkers than can be done to protect ICBMs, and it is generally acknowledged that improvements in accuracy will render further hardening a marginal contribution to survivability. Of course such command posts can be made mobile, but this only emphasizes the vulnerability of the cables and antennae, the ganglion of communication links that cannot be hardened, dispersed, or proliferated and upon which the command centres are absolutely dependent. Moreover, all communications are vulnerable to the distorting effects of nuclear detonation. Beyond these general considerations, there are specific problems.

The National Command Authorities (NCA) – the President and the Secretary of Defense or their designees – must act in a co-ordinated fashion to initiate nuclear strikes. Yet it is far from likely that a President would survive an initial surprise attack. Neither the White House nor the National Military Command Center at the Pentagon are able to withstand a direct nuclear attack, and the National Emergency Airborne Command Post (NEACP) was until recently stationed at Andrews Air Force Base, some ten minutes by helicopter from the White House, although this has now been changed. If we assume an attack originating with a Soviet submarine stationed just of US coastal waters – Yankee-class SSBNs are known to patrol routinely within close range of Washington – the warning time to the President could well be less than five minutes, or not even time to summon a helicopter; indeed, in a recent evacuation gaming, the President did not survive the trip to a rendezvous with the NEACP.[34] The US Constitution prescribes succession to the Presidency[35] (a succession that puts five persons before the Secretary of Defense, including the House Speaker and President pro tempore of the Senate) and since this list includes some persons likely to be in the White House if they are available in Washington at all (the Vice-President now maintains a West Wing Office) it is open to doubt whether, in the event of a President's death in the circumstances described, it would be possible to reconstitute the NCA with any confidence in precisely who had lawful authority.[36] Because LNO's require considerable sophistication of the decision-maker, the devolution of authority upon the Secretary of Interior, for example, must be presumed to vitiate the strategy to some degree. Moreover, even once aloft,[37] the NEACP does not have the data-processing facilities available on the ground.

Relatively recent testimony before the House Appropriations Committee disclosed that 'Airborne Command Post has a bunch of file cabinets. If they want to generate various options they have to go to the file cabinets and do things basically by hand'.[38] One assumes this has been changed. Furthermore, the intensity and variety of their radio transmissions make command-and-control aircraft particularly vulnerable to location and the interception of their signals by hostile intelligence. Desmond Ball has speculated that 'a few handfuls of weapons could destroy all aircraft in the relevant operating area' and,[39] in any event, he notes that there are only '14 ground entry points which allow the NEACP and the SAC AABNCP (Alternative Airborne National Command Post) access to ground-based communications networks',[40] and these present soft, stationary targets. The Airborne Launch Control System has no capability to retarget or indeed even to determine what ICBMs are remaining and functional.[41] Ball observes,

> There are a number of ironies in this extreme reliance on airborne C^3 systems. For example, it is at first sight curious that airborne systems which are in general considered a relatively vulnerable leg of the Triad are responsible for the back-up control of the rather more survivable submarine- and land-based missile systems. Moreover, much of the land-based systems ability to be used in controlled fashion through reliable two-way cable communications – which is, of course, one of the principal rationalizations for the silo-based ICBM – is lost when radio links via airborne systems have to be used . . . . The problematical survivability of the airborne command systems, together with their lack of flexibility, suggests that the increasing reliance on these systems actually impairs the chances for controlled escalation.[42]

These shortcomings of airborne command and control would seem to make uncontrolled escalation very difficult to avoid. This is scarcely compatible with a doctrine relying on the careful modulation of LNOs. For LNOs to succeed in the countervailing role, they must be part of a centrally commanded programme that is sensitive to what vulnerabilities are opening up as the adversary attempts to prosecute the offensive. There must be an authority, in control, to calculate the costs *to the Russians* of each US strike. If this authority has devolved to unco-ordinated commanders, the strikes can certainly take place, but the strategy can't function. For within the Countervailing Strategy, implicit costs – threats withheld that are preceded by threats that are executed – are crucial. If the process of withholding/striking cannot be interrupted, then the re-calculation by the Soviet Union cannot take place. If the process cannot be interrupted, then defeat for the US in a theatre conflict inevitably becomes vastly more threatening because pursuing the chief object of the strategy results instead in the undoing of the entire intra-war system of deterrence and the American homeland is dragged into the exchanges.

Both the United States and the Soviet Union are dependent on satellites for C^3I, indeed the 'hot line' linking the two countries, as well as the means of communicating between their respective NCAs and their national forces, use communications satellites. Satellites provide the US with the means of assessing strike damage and residual strategic capabilities, an essential task in determining the intention to move to countervalue strikes and in deciding which LNOs to employ. Yet the total number of satellites is small (about 30 in the case of the US and perhaps 80–90 Soviet),[43] and they are highly vulnerable as are the ground stations that control them and the communications that connect the two. Without dwelling further on this vulnerability – or adding to it by a consideration of the dependability and survivability of communications with submarines (since these are, in any event, less suitable for launching limited and selective strikes intra-war)[44] – it should be clear that the Countervailing Strategy places great and indispensable reliance on systems that are unlikely to survive even the initial strikes of a high-intensity nuclear conflict. Plans for launching fresh satellites once the conflict has begun, or turning on previously 'dark' satellites, recognize this problem.

Finally it must be observed that for the Countervailing Strategy to work, *not only* must there be a co-ordinated decision among allies who may not share strategic objectives matching the phased sequences of PD 59, and a survivable, sophisticated command apparatus to effectuate those decisions, and also highly accurate, re-targetable, survivable weapons.[45] The Soviet Union must to some extent also co-operate. That is, the Soviet Union must allow itself time for a re-calculation of the costs of pressing an offensive. It must be able to communicate with its commanders, and its pre-packaged plans must permit improvisation in light of changed circumstances. It must moderate its own retaliation lest the cost to NATO of massive strikes suddenly become acceptable to the West when there is little left to lose. To some extent, this can be expected. A war-fighting doctrine is well adapted to limited nuclear, as opposed to strategic, strikes. The Soviet notion of a 'limited nuclear operation', however, envisages a large-scale pre-emptive theatre-wide nuclear strike against NATO, perhaps coupled with a simultaneous countermilitary attack against the US while holding US cities as hostages with a large residual force to deter the United States from retaliating.[46]

Desmond Ball concludes that the idea that,

> once the nuclear threshold is passed it is the task of the nuclear forces to terminate the war by achieving military victory through massive, crippling strikes is deeply rooted in Soviet strategic culture, and the preferences and habits of the culture, and the preferences

> and habits of the military bureaucracy would tend to rule out any possibility of improvisation in favour of American-formulated rules of intra-war restraint.[47]

Ball concludes that for the US to prepare for controlled nuclear exchanges on the basis of this possibility is therefore likely to be a fruitless exercise, reflecting wishful thinking rather than the realities of the situation. I am less certain. Too much depends upon the circumstances under which war starts. If the Russian offensive were a general assault across the European central front, with little political warning, then it seems least likely that the Countervailing Strategy could avoid the collapse of the restraint it requires to be effective. But if the crisis does not explode but instead begins with relatively localized conflicts, any one of which then threatens to burst into general war, then it should not matter to the countervailing approach that Soviet doctrine calls for massive damage limitation. With warning, NATO assets will be able to avoid being targeted with high assurance or they will not; if they do, then they are available for LNOs and to enforce a re-calculation; if they don't, then their use in LNOs was doomed in any event. If they cannot be targeted with assurance then the decisive step to cross the nuclear threshhold will perhaps be avoided by the Soviet Union precisely because it risks an irrevocable commitment to general war.

In this chapter, I have reviewed three strategies: a war-fighting strategy, a minimal assured destruction strategy, and a countervailing strategy. I have observed that each does not in fact modify the central deterrent, supporting the inference that each is actually responsive to concerns felt in the extended context. I have argued that each differs from the others primarily in terms of the relationship between the deterrence assumption (that unique, thermonuclear deterrence of central systems) and extended threats (derived from the deterrence provided by pre-nuclear, strategic bombing strategies). Once a basis for judgement is established – the contribution to extended deterrence – the shortcomings of each approach are easily seen.

Compare, for example, these three assessments of the requirements of extended deterrence. For McGeorge Bundy, the American nuclear guarantee rests 'on two great facts: the visible deployment of major American military forces in Europe, and the very evident risk that any large-scale engagement between Soviet and American forces would rapidly and uncontrollably become general, nuclear and disastrous'.[48] Henry Kissinger, implicitly stressing damage limitation, argues that reassuring our allies requires not 'verbal reassurances', but rather that the US acquire 'a plausible war-fighting capability and [not be] forced to protect its vital interests and the vital interests of its allies by the threat of [the] war extermination of civilians'.[49] Anthony Cordesman believes that 'while [the] US will not be able to launch counterforce strikes in the sense of being able to degrade Soviet capabilities to strike at an unacceptably large number of US urban industrial complexes and other-than-military (OMT) targets, it will, nevertheless, be able to strike selectively at those Soviet strategic forces which are employed in theatre conflicts, and to strike at Soviet strategic forces as an option in conducting [LNO] strikes'.[50] These three statements are representative of the three alternative paradigms discussed in this chapter. Freedman, and perhaps others,[51] have recognized that there are fundamentally three possible nuclear regimes. What has not perhaps been appreciated is that these three regimes differ most significantly with respect to extended deterrence. This accords with the analysis in Book I.[52]

Those readers who began this chapter with the hope that I might offer a profound restructuring of the available strategic alternatives are disappointed, I fear. I have not treated options such as disarmament, guerilla and militia defence, terrorism, etc. I do not believe these are true alternatives to present nuclear strategies, because they each discount what I believe with a sad but confirmed conviction: that nuclear weapons cannot be disinvented, that their possession contributes to national power *vis-à-vis* other nations, that the organization of international life, especially now that some nations have nuclear weapons, is going to continue to be defined by national conflicts. I do not believe that, as is often urged, we can re-invent the world. Those readers who hoped this chapter would offer profound alternatives to 'deterrence dogma' will be disappointed at the paucity of options and the fact that even these are evaluated in terms of deterrence. But while it should be obvious that there is nothing inherently conflictive about US–Soviet relations, recognizing that fact does not imply that the basic nuclear threat we have known would be removed from the world even if relations were greatly improved. It has been said that 'academic strategists are so intent on facing up to the nuclear dilemmas that beset us that they tend to forget that the danger of nuclear war stems mainly from the superpowers' conflictive relationship and only incidentally from the existence of nuclear weapons. They . . . see no connection between the high level of hostility and the assumptions of Western deterrence dogma. . . . When it comes to the danger of world war, the enemy is largely ourselves.' This is true, but it is a half truth. The presence of nuclear weapons will forever structure national attitudes; they are not incidental. They pose significant constrains on political relationships and generate enduring commitments. We do not command our worlds by willing different attitudes; to say otherwise is the message of the guru perhaps, but not the strategist. There are, of course, many, many strategies. But, for the US, here and now, they can be stated as three.

11 Alternative Nuclear Weapons Technologies

Sappi che non son torri, ma giganti, e son nel pozzo intorno da la ripa da l'umbilico in giuso tutti quanti.

(Know that they are not towers, but giants, and that they are every one in the pit, round its banks, from the navel downward.)

Canto XXXI, *Inferno*

In Chapter 10, we explored the possibility that strategic innovation might, as it has in the past, compensate for the impending collapse of extended deterrence. In this chapter, we will study new technologies to determine whether they might enable the US to maintain its extended commitments in light of the strategic developments discussed in Chapter 7 and the operation of the 'theorem' introduced in Chapter 8.

Since LRTNF was designed to cure decoupling, we might conveniently start with a review of the particular objectives envisioned for the programme of NATO modernization. We might then establish as a criterion for new systems that they be able to accomplish the same tasks as the proposed LRTNF while avoiding the uncoupling phenomenon. One strategy for such avoidance is the reversal of those developments that brought uncoupling to the fore in the first place: the loss of escalation dominance, the arrival of parity in central systems, the vulnerability of land-based weapons. Therefore for each of the weapons to be studied in this chapter we shall ask: (1) does it accomplish the re-coupling objectives planned for LRTNF; (2) does it avoid uncoupling by redressing in some way those interacting phenomena that detached the American theatre of war from Europe? Three new technologies will be reviewed: the US Missile Experimental (MX); the cruise missile, particularly the air-launched (ALCM) and sea-launched (SLCM) versions; the Trident 2 SLBM armed with a new warhead (the D-5).

The political debate over LRTNF – indeed the politicizing of the military debate within the High Level Group – has largely obscured the strategic requirements of LRTNF deployments. There are three such requirements and they impose corresponding characteristics on the weapons systems.

First, LRTNF is supposed to hold Warsaw Pact forces at risk throughout the depth of their deployment, thereby forcing a dispersal of forces even beyond second echelon divisions. The difficulty for NATO has always been the length and location of the defence perimeter to be maintained in the light of the Alliance's essentially defensive posture. Indeed a Soviet offensive capability, because it can be massed, could achieve success even if overall force ratios were unfavourable. When overwhelming sectoral superiority is added to this element of initiative, it is not surprising that NATO has, from its inception, relied on nuclear weapons to compensate for a lengthy defence perimeter and conventional inferiority. This clearly emerges from the 1975 Department of Defense study, *The Theatre Nuclear Force Posture in Europe*,[1] which served as the basis for the modernization proposals made to the Nuclear Planning Group in 1976. It is an obvious enough objective, once we compare the opposing forces (110 Soviet divisions against 26 NATO)[2] at the time and in the context of a strategic offensive.

The principal weapons requirement imposed by the goal of forcing dispersal is survivability.

> It is not the absolute numbers of nuclear weapons that are significant in NATO's nuclear force requirements, but rather their survivability and effectiveness in executing certain missions. The most important mission for NATO nuclear weapons is to 'hold at risk' the vast Soviet ground forces and their supporting air armies and nuclear elements.[3]

Although atomic artillery shells and short-range rocket systems, as well as atomic demolition mines, have accounted for roughly two-thirds of the NATO nuclear inventory, the main reliance in NATO planning was placed on aircraft. Once the new generation of Russian counterforce missles was deployed, however, the viability of the NATO hold-at-risk/dispersal mission was called into doubt. Not only were the SS-20s and SS-22s so accurate that NATO airfields in every European country were vulnerable but they were supplemented by over a thousand Frog/SS-21 and Scud/SS-23 missiles. These targeted less than a hundred NATO Lance missiles and fifty-four short-range Honest Johns.[4] This vulnerability to Russian attack had the effect of reducing the scope for the dispersal mission to that conferred by artillery and mines: that is, to little more than the immediate battle area (assuming deployment one-third of range beyond the forward edge of the battlefield area). As a consequence, the first requirement of LRTNF modernization was enhanced survivability because this was necessary for the dispersal mission.

A second objective is to hold targets at risk in Russia herself. It doesn't appear to matter whether this is done by great numbers of weapons – a full-scale exchange could be executed by abundant central systems – so long as it is apparent that the Soviet Union could not be assured of a homeland sanctuary once it attacked in Europe. On the complementary objective from the Russian point of view, to *ensure* sanctuary, turns the entire debate over, indeed even the name for, 'forward based systems'. From the Russian point of view, it was terribly important that only US-based weapons be capable of attacking the Soviet Union since this offered the greatest likelihood of US self-deterrence and hence Russian sanctuary. Weapons in Europe capable of striking the Soviet Union were 'forward-based' – like aircraft carriers – and might be used by the US without the same fear of retaliation as if they were US based. For the US it is equally important to deny this view since it subordinates European risks to the security of the two superpowers. The Alliance's professed views treat the US and her Western European allies as a single unit to be protected with the same intensity of interest wherever it is attacked. Weapons in Great Britain or West Germany are no more 'forward-based' than similar weapons in Poland or East Germany or Russia that, while incapable of hitting the US, could strike her European allies (indeed; as we shall see, are significantly less threatening owing to limitations in range).

This objective – to deny sanctuary and threaten Russia directly – imposed a range requirement on LRTNF. With few exceptions, however, NATO aircraft cannot reach the USSR on nuclear missions from Europe, though a very large proportion of Soviet aircraft have the range to penetrate deeply into Western Europe from present bases.[5] Partly this is a geopolitical asymmetry: aircraft in East Germany that can strike London or Paris have a shorter distance to fly than aircraft in West Germany attempting to reach Moscow. Thus, even though a large majority of aircraft on both sides have comparable range capabilities, the 'forward based' Warsaw Pact forces can cover virtually all NATO territory. Moreover, the latest generation of Russian aircraft – the 5500 km range Backfire, 3100 km Blinder and 2900 km Badger have no NATO counterparts. Thus, putting aside the increasing problems of survivability and penetration that have cast doubt on NATO air systems, the limitation on the scope of activities imposed by range tends to enhance the possibility of Russian sanctuary. By contrast, if Russia herself could be targeted, it would be credible to maintain that an attack on Western Europe would be met by more than a retaliation against the Eastern Europe client states.

The third objective is actually a reinforcement of the second. In addressing that objective, it has no doubt occurred to the reader that the range problem might be solved simply by consigning more central systems to NATO since these, by definition, have the requisite range to threaten Russia. Why is credibility enhanced by putting the weapons in Europe since the decision to use them will still be made in Washington? The answer lies in the limited vulnerability of the proposed LRTNF and its objective of providing a countervailing threat to a Soviet offensive, conventional or nuclear. If the weapons, though survivable enough to withstand a pre-emptive attack, could be overrun by deep salients, then the attacker would have to consider the greater likelihood that they would be used rather than overrun as opposed to the likelihood that their use would be simply postponed if they were safely based in the US or at sea and thus if nothing appeared to be lost by the postponement. Thus, unlike the various central systems, a land-based LRTNF puts countervailing pressure in the hands of NATO precisely to the extent that the Soviet attack is pressed. A deep salient, or deep encirclement, would threaten the basing modes and thereby increase the fear of nuclear response.

The weapons capability demanded by this objective is accuracy. It will do no good if the European weapons can't be employed in a limited fashion. NATO would be thrown back into the dilemma of igniting a general nuclear war over a European incursion, a scenario unappealing enough to have precipitated decoupling concerns in the first place.

We have thus far established these three re-coupling objectives and their correlative systems requirements: the ability to force dispersal and deter massing; the capability to threaten targets in Russia; the credibility necessary to persuade the Soviet Union that NATO would in fact use its nuclear weapons; and the survivability, range and accuracy dictated by these objectives. In the following three sections, three new technologies will be tested against these objectives and then analyzed in terms of the uncoupling theorem.

THE MISSILE EXPERIMENTAL (Peacekeeper)

In this light let us then consider the range, accuracy and survivability of the Missile Experimental (MX). The MX has a range of 6000 miles,[6] easily adequate to target any point in the Soviet Union. Its accuracy will be discussed in terms of lethality, and the survivability of the missile in terms of its proposed basing mode. As of this writing, it is still not known what basing mode the US Congress and the President will ultimately choose for the Missile Experimental,[7] but the principal characteristics of the weapon itself are well known. It has three solid fuel booster stages and a fourth post-boost, MIRV stage, or 'bus'. The MX is 70 feet long, 92 inches in diameter and weighs 192 000 pounds. Thus the MX is approximately the same size as the Russian SS-19 (designated by SALT 2 as having the maximum size allowable for a new ICBM) but substantially smaller than the SS-18 and about two and a half times as heavy as the US Minuteman 3.

The 'bus' of the MX is designed to carry ten MIRV warheads. Each warhead will have a yield roughly equal to those atop the Minuteman 3 missiles, or about 350 kiloton (KT). This warhead in a later modification (Mod 2) can have its yield increased to about 500 KT, should this prove necessary to increase '*lethality*', a concept to be discussed.

That decision will turn on the accuracy of the new missile, and it will be readily seen that, since the warheads of the MX and the Minuteman 3 are almost identical in yield (in the initial, Mod 1 version of MX), it is enhanced accuracy that constitutes the missile's most important innovation. Greater accuracy is obtained through the use of an advanced inertial reference sphere (AIRS) guidance system, which provides precise corrections of mid-course trajectory. This is achieved by means of a carefully machined beryllium sphere, floated inside a case, permitting it to measure acceleration in three directions simultaneously.[8] This guidance system is predicted to achieve an accuracy of 300 feet c.e.p. (see p. 301 *infra*).

'Lethality' is the ability to destroy a point target. It is defined as the MTE (equivalent megatonnage) to the two-thirds power divided by the square of the c.e.p. If lethality is known, it is possible to calculate the theoretical probability,[9] disregarding fratricide, bias, unreliability, etc., of destroying a point target of known hardness. Indeed a hand-held 'Damage Probability Computer' has been developed by RAND for this purpose. In determining lethality, accuracy is the most influential factor, being equal to the cube of the yield. Thus, for example, a four-fold improvement in accuracy is equivalent to a sixty-four fold improvement in yield, as each results in a sixteen-fold increase in lethality.

Without AIRS, each MX warhead would have a 68 per cent probability of being able to destroy a Soviet ICBM silo, hardened to a blast pressure of 3000 psi (3500 pounds per square inch is thought to be the maximum hardening feasible). Using two warheads per silo would increase this probability to 90 per cent. With AIRS, the MX would have a 99 per cent kill probability with one warhead.[10] By contrast the Soviet SS-18 carries 10 warheads of enormous yields up to 1 MT but with a guidance system somewhat less accurate than the Mark 12A, or about 800 feet, resulting in a 82 per cent probability, at the present time, of destroying a Minuteman silo.[11]

Lethality is increased in three ways: by increasing accuracy (compensating for inaccuracies, actually); increasing the yield by increasing the payload either by enlarging the missile, or multiplying the number of warheads; and increasing the yield per pound through more efficient technology. The MX will have a greatly increased lethality over existing Minutemen because it is larger, and its warhead is somewhat more efficient and much more accurate.

With respect to basing, the United States Administration received a recommendation from a special committee considering,[12] among other, undisclosed options, (1) a tight pattern of hardened silos that either would depend on the fratricidal, self-destructive effect of a tightly targeted, incoming pre-emptive force or would be able to ride out the attack if the attacking force were staged in phases to avoid fratricide (Dense Pack); (2) deployment aboard a continously airborne alert aircraft, modified from the current C54/E4 (Big Bird); (3) deep underground missile basing that relies on the polar patterns of Soviet ICBM launches by burying silos on the south faces of mountains; and (4) various remedies that may threaten existing arms control treaties, such as a new ABM system, mobile launching, or the construction of hundreds of empty but deceptive silos.

This last option is an ironic one, for it is often charged that MX is a SALT-created weapon. The correctness of this statement will be analyzed in the following pages as a prelude to determining (1) what strategic functions *are* served by MX, (2) what basing mode is appropriate to these functions, and (3) to what extent decoupling is ameliorated by the MX deployment.

MX is a SALT-determined weapon. Its precise size, the number planned for deployment and the proposed basing mode – even, perhaps, its very procurement which was made the price by Kissinger and others of their support for SALT 2 ratification – were dictated by the treaty. Moreover, the demise of Congressional support for the MX parallels that for the treaty. Nevertheless, it would be an error to conclude that there is no strategic rationale for the weapon. Because this has been frequently charged by commentators making the rhetorical mistake of describing the SALT–MX link and excluding any other rationale by a kind of Occam's razor, it will perhaps be useful to review the connections between SALT and the MX. It will be seen that, although SALT may account for the precise characteristics of MX – how large, how many, and so forth – its strategic relationship to the treaty is much more subtle. Both SALT and MX represent an attempt to re-couple stable central deterrence to increasingly doubtful extended deterrence, SALT by reducing the threat (as will be discussed in the next chapter) and the MX by parrying that threat.

Article 2 of SALT 1 provides:

> The Parties undertake not to convert landbased launchers for light ICBMs, or for ICBMs of older types deployed prior to 1964, into land-based launchers for heavy ICBMs of types deployed after that time.[13]

The United States sought this provision as a means of limiting the deployment of Soviet 'heavy' ICBMs, the SS-9 and its successors. The SS-9, of which 308 were deployed by 1972 at the time of the treaty, was capable of carrying a warhead of 20 MT. Even the 'light' SS-11 was larger than the US Minuteman. Although Soviet accuracies were, at this time, distinctly inferior to those of US ICBMs, these tremendous payloads (made possible by tremendous throw-weights) were a cause of concern to those who foresaw the potential for increased lethality. The US was unable to obtain agreement on a quantitative definition of a 'heavy' missile that would limit future Soviet weapons to the SS-11 size.[14] Thus on the final day of the negotiations, the US delegation stated:

> The US Delegation regrets that the Soviet Delegation has not been willing to agree on a common definition of a heavy missile. Under these circumstances, the US Delegation believes it is necessary to state the following: The United States would consider any ICBM having a volume significantly greater than that of the largest light ICBM now operational on either side to be a heavy ICBM. The US proceeds on the premise that the Soviet side will give due account to this consideration.[15]

Despite the US declaration, the Soviet Union made clear that it did not plan to accommodate the United States on this point and shortly thereafter began the testing and the eventual deployment in 1975 of even larger payload missiles, the SS-18 replacement for the SS-9 and the SS-19 follow-on for the SS-11. These payloads gave the Soviets a much greater number of ICBM warheads with high yields than the US had. Although US guidance systems were superior to those of the USSR at the time, it could easily be foreseen that this payload advantage represented an inchoate lethality that, when multiplied by MIRVing, would create a decoupling vulnerability by US ICBM exposure to pre-emption (and thus would also give rise to an unwillingness to commit such weapons to non-central theatres).

Consequently, the US strove hard in SALT 2 to bar the 'heavies' or, failing that, at least to define them and limit them.[16] This latter effort was successful and SALT 2 contained a clear demarcation, in terms of missile launch weight and throw weight between light and heavy ICBMs. Under the treaty, both the US and the Soviet Union could develop one new ICBM of the same size as the SS-19 but no larger. This provision ultimately determined the size of the MX. In fact, a smaller design with a diameter of 83 inches (instead of 92 inches) had been proposed in the Pentagon so that the new missile would be compatible with existing submarine launch tubes. Despite this, and the endorsement of the Undersecretary of Defense for Research and Engineering, who testified that this version could be built with 'no significant degradation of performance to the MX missile',[17] there were great pressures to deploy to the very limits of the treaty. Finally, with the treaty ready for signing in eleven days, the White House announced that the largest possible version of the MX had been selected for development.[18]

The number of MXs planned for deployment was similarly derived from SALT 2. The strategic purpose for the MX was to neutralize the lethality of the SS-18s and SS-19s by posing a counter-lethality of its own. If the Soviet countersilo weapons faced targets that were themselves capable of advantageously retaliating against silos, then the Soviets could not hope to gain an advantage in long-term residual forces through pre-emption.

This was the way in which the MX proposed to close the 'window of vulnerability', a metaphor in which the US ICBM force became increasingly vulnerable as Soviet lethality increased to the theoretical capability to destroy 90 per cent of the US ICBM force (i.e., as the window opened wide) and then became less vulnerable as its own capability for hard target destruction increased in a relatively protected environment (the window closes when MX comes fully on line, with its 90 per cent lethality).

In the aftermath of a hypothetical Soviet first strike, the Pentagon estimated we would need 1000 warheads to destroy any Soviet missiles left in their launchers. The size of the MX system was therefore set at 200 missiles with 2000 warheads because calculations showed that in the event of a Soviet attack with its forces available under the SALT II Treaty, only half, or 1000 warheads, would survive, even with the proposed new invulnerable basing scheme.[19]

If, however, the Soviet Union violated the treaty limits, by using the vast payloads of the SS-18 to stack more MIRVs than the thirteen allowed (as many as thirty to forty were possible),[20] then the number of MXs decided upon was too small.[21] The actual number of MXs to be deployed was governed and even derived from SALT calculations, even if the weapon was not occasioned by SALT.

Because MX force sizing depended on a reliable knowledge of the numbers of Soviet warheads and missiles, and the strict requirement that the SALT 2 limits be verified, the US basing plan for MX had to provide a credible and accurate way for the Russians to verify US deployments. In the original basing mode for MX, the US went to very great lengths to concoct a scheme that would satisfy this requirement.

US negotiators had originally applied considerable pressure to get a ban on mobile ICBMs in SALT 1 because such a basing mode would render verification so difficult. On this matter, as with the 'heavies', the US was unsuccessful and so, here also, she fell back on a unilateral declaration that the US 'would consider the deployment of operational land-mobile ICBM launchers during the period of the Interim Agreement as inconsistent with the objectives of that agreement'.[22] Again, the Soviet Union made clear that it did not concur in this declaration and would not be bound by it.

When the Carter Administration took office, it inherited a plan for reducing ICBM vulnerability by deploying a mobile system in tunnels. This was rejected and, in a speech in February 1977, President Carter appealed to the USSR, which was then testing the SS-16, the only mobile ICBM developed at that time,[23] to exercise restraint in the deployment of mobile ICBMs.[24] A replacement for the Ford tunnel system was proposed subsequent to this speech: that a large number of vertical silos be built and a much smaller number of MX be shuttled among them. Since it was difficult to assure the other side that only one missile was in fact in each of the cluster of silos – after all, if that could be verified, the system could be defeated – and impossible to make credible declarations that stockpiles of missiles would not be kept to use all those 'empty' but fully operational silos, this plan was also rejected on verifiability grounds.

The plan finally designated on 4 September 1979 used a racetrack with twenty-three shelters per missile; all shelters could be opened at once to demonstrate to Soviet satellite reconnaissance that only one missile was shuttling among a single system of shelters. Since the Administration had successfully negotiated a launcher limit in SALT 2 (on which the force sizing of the MX could be based), it was imperative that the MX basing mode be compatible with this limit. Unlike vertical launch schemes, such as empty silos, a horizontal shelter could not be labeled a launcher. Thus even the basing scheme itself was a result of constraints imposed by SALT 2. But, it should be emphasized, those constraints were themselves imposed not by goodwill, but by the need to establish a verifiable criterion for sizing the MX force.

One consequence of this interplay between the military requirements of force sizing and the political requirements of ongoing arms control negotiations was that no criteria beyond survivability were devised by which to choose among the various basing options. Once it became clear that there was no non-mobile basing mode that could assure the survival of land based ICBMs attacked by weapons with the lethality of present Soviet weapons, the entire procurement programme was called into question. Unwilling to abandon arms control by shifting to a fully mobile system – although this may not in fact have been necessary, as we shall see – but equally unwilling to spend an initial $23 billion on a system whose principal selling point, its closure of the ICBM vulnerability issue, had now been undermined, the Congress refused to vote even procurement funds for the missile and directed the President to develop a survivable basing scheme as a prerequisite for further development of the MX. A commission was appointed to study the issue, and, as noted earlier, its report has now been presented.

All this need not have occurred if attention had been focused on the strategic objectives of a survivable basing mode and had not been mesmerized by the technologies of the modes themselves. For once it is accepted that a non-mobile scheme cannot endure a hard-target attack, a solution to the basing issue appears rather than vanishes.

The strategic objective of survivable basing is to deny the Russians the threat to pre-empt the land-based ICBM, that most time-urgent, command-sensitive, accurate arm of the triad with the greatest assurance of penetration. This objective is sought for two reasons. First, effective deterrence is to some extent diminished if the Russians have the opportunity to pin the US to non-action by either destroying the ICBM force, leaving only American assured destruction, counter-value weapons or intimidating the President into a reluctance to use a portion of the ICBM force for fear this might trigger the destruction of the remainder. Second, the Countervailing Strategy requires that the Soviet Union never contemplate a realistic option such that the ratio of weapons could be made significantly more favourable to the Russians by a pre-emptive attack on US ICBMs with the Soviet Union emerging as the only party capable of holding long-term strategic reserves.[25] Such a possibility would transform the political costs and benefits in a crisis and might make war a plausible option when, otherwise, no political calculation from the Russian point of view would justify such risks.

It is true that one way to accomplish the US objective is to develop an assured survivability through basing. And this could be attempted, within the constraints discussed above, in two ways. The US could deploy mobile ICBMs that could be photographed by satellite reconnaissance while within airbase checkpoints but that could be dispersed upon receiving (and thereby providing to the other side) strategic warning. If, at the same time, the US and the Soviet Union were to agree to modernize their forces by phasing out MIRVed weapons in favour of single warhead weapons, the issue of vulnerability would be greatly muted. Alternatively, the US could attempt to assign the MX mission to the survivable SSBN Trident 2 armed with the SLBM/D5 and develop some means of supporting the SSBNs at sea and communicating complex re-targeting data.

A more straightforward and less technically challenging way of meeting this strategic objective (and therefore one that is cheaper and with a more imminent prospect of initial operating capacity) becomes clear once we cease trying to satisfy this objective through an insistence on survivability through invulnerability. This option entails a scrutiny of Russian incentives to exploit ICBM vulnerability in the first place, given that the USSR has a larger percentage of its warheads (75 per cent compared with 24 per cent) throw-weight (70 per cent compared with 33 per cent), and launchers (56 per cent compared with 51 per cent) in land-based ICBMs than does the US.[26]

Once the SALT treaties codified parity, no improvements in the accuracy of warheads alone could have, by themselves, made counter-silo pre-emption an attractive possibility. It would always take 1+ weapons to successfully target a single silo and hence, a pre-emptive attack could only worsen the ratio of remaining weapons against the pre-emptor. It was MIRVing that made pre-emption logically attractive (even if it took a few years for developments in accuracy to make it technically possible), for once a single missile carried more than one warhead, it became plausible to plan on a missile destroying 1+silos, and increasing the favourable ratio of exchange as the attack mounted. Thus the key to pre-emptive strategies is the existence of a *reserve force* that is not committed in the initial attack. If the attacker must use all his force to pre-empt the other side, there can be little incentive to do so and if only one side has the requisite lethality to improve its relative position through pre-emption, the incentive for the other side to retaliate, once attacked, actually decreases as the attack is pressed.

It is sometimes argued that the US ought not to procure the MX since its chief distinction from the existing Minuteman is that it is a more effective countersilo weapon. There are indeed very few hard targets other than missile silos that require the yield and accuracy – the lethality – of the MX. MX is an unwise deployment, it is argued, because it jeopardizes the security of the Soviet ICBM force and thereby compels the USSR to put its ICBMs on a launch-on-warning, or launch-under-attack alert,[27] by which is meant a computer-assisted decision-making apparatus of such celerity that, should Russian ICBMs be attacked, they can be launched prior to being trapped in their silos.

What is not usually appreciated about this point is that the consequences of such a possible strategy are completely different depending on the lethality of the *targeted* weapons, not just the lethality of the attacking weapons, and whether that lethality is mutual. Without MX the weapons the US would launch on warning would either have to be wasted on ICBM silos that require more US missiles be used than the number of Soviet missiles to be destroyed or would have to be dumped on so many targets in the USSR that a general nuclear war would be unavoidable. Thus it has been asserted that the USSR has a countersilo capability of such devasting depth and magnitude that, in a partial assault – one leaving a substantial reserve force – the entire US ICBM force could be destroyed with 90 per cent confidence without the fear that the US would adopt such a computer-assisted plan of retaliation. The USSR need not expect the US to go to launch-on-attack so long as the USSR alone has an advantageous a countersilo capability. In such a situation, the US does not face the use-it-or-lose-it dilemma: what is lost, the proportionate response of which only ICBMs are assuredly capable, would be lost anyway as US ICBMs were thrown away against Soviet targets without bettering the

US position; what is accomplished by 'use' can be accomplished anyway since, if a countervalue war would be ineluctable, that is an option that could just as easily be excuted by the SLBM force. There exists, therefore, in a situation such as the perception of imminent war, an incentive for a *Russian* pre-emption in these circumstances. They have much to gain from pre-emption and little to fear since the US has more to lose through retaliation than through acquiescence.

Suppose, however, the US had its own favourable countersilo capability, deployed in the same vulnerable modes currently targeted by the USSR. Then the USSR must avoid steps that offer the US an incentive to go to launch-on-warning or launch-under-attack status. More importantly, the USSR must assume that it is their reserve force against whom the threatened US ICBMs will be launched. This means that there can be no incentive for the USSR to use its countersilo weapons in a pre-emptive attack since, at best, it will marginally worsen the ratio of systems remaining against them after the attack. This means, in turn, that the fears associated with launch-on-warning – that it might be triggered by accident – can in fact be reduced since both sides, with MIRVing, can absorb a good many strikes before retaliating against the other's reserve force. Indeed, it makes of launch-on-warning and launch-under-attack exactly what they ought to be: powerful deterrents of such little war-fighting use that neither side could nor need to do more than make them plausible.

Thus, one basing mode appropriate to the strategic functions sought by MX deployment is to put the new weapons in the old Minuteman silos. This is technically feasible, despite the fact that the MX is a much larger missile than the Minuteman, because the Minuteman silos were designed to be larger than the missile itself in order to permit the escape of exhaust gases. The MX by contrast uses compressed gas to wholly emerge from its launcher, its first-stage rockets not igniting until the missile is free of the silo (a cold-launch technique). Moreover, this basing mode would not violate the undertakings of SALT 1 and SALT 2 that the parties to those agreements promise not to start construction of additional (SALT 1)[28] or new (SALT 2)[29] ICBM silos. Finally, this analysis suggests an approach to solving the difficult issue posed by the coincidence of capabilities that are useful for time-urgent, controlled, proportionate retaliation *and* for disarming first strikes. The US need only deploy MX in a number sufficient to destroy the Soviet reserve force and not so many as would be required to disarm the entire Soviet ICBM system.

If it is correct to conclude that Minuteman vulnerability, along with the loss of strategic superiority and escalation dominance, provoked fears of decoupling, it seems obvious that MX is, to some extent, a remedy. Its enhanced accuracy does nothing, however, to upset parity (nor have the Russian 'heavies' for that matter). Nor is it plausible to maintain that the use of central strategic systems with a countersilo capacity are required for theatre roles aimed at containing escalation and restoring deterrence: just the opposite is likely to be true. Thus the MX, while a useful component in executing the Countervailing Strategy, contributes to extended deterrence only to the extent that it reduces ICBM vulnerability.

The decoupling/uncoupling predicted by the 'theorem' might be phrased, with respect to MX, in this way: does the availability of a relatively secure MX (that is, one unlikely to be pre-empted save at the cost of the adversary's own ICBM force) make the President more likely to commit that nuclear weapon, or others, to the defence of Europe? And, if this is so because he or she believes the risks to the US are marginally decreased, are they decreased because MX use makes confinement of a nuclear war to Europe more plausible? The answers are yes and no. Insofar as Minuteman vulnerability exercised a cautionary influence on the President's willingness to initiate nuclear hostilities, re-coupling is improved by MX deployment which avoids the consequences of the theorem. But since ICBM vulnerability was, as discussed in Chapter 7, the least significant factor eroding extended deterrence, this contribution must remain marginal.

Early in April 1983, the President's Commission on Strategic Forces issued its report.[30] The Commission proposed, and the following week the President endorsed, the deployment of 100 MX in existing Minuteman silos. At the same time, the Commission urged the development of a new single-warhead, mobile weapon. Because of its size, – 40 feet as opposed to MX's 71 feet, 22 000 lbs compared to MX's 192 000 lbs – it was named in the press 'Midgetman'. The Midgetman plan calls for a mobile system deployed with a checkpoint on military reservations. The checkpoint would provide a means of verification by satellite of the missile's comings and goings.

There remain formidable technological barriers to realizing this recommendation. A transporter must be designed that can withstand a nuclear blast without turning over. Most importantly, a single warhead weapon is – as we have seen the MX to be – an arms-control-designed system. Recognizing that MIRVing has created a first-strike potential despite parity, the Commission wished to move to un-MIRVed systems. The difficulty, of course, is that unless the USSR agrees to do the same, it can defeat the Midgetman deployment by simply proliferating warheads. Warheads are always cheaper to manufacture than missiles, even relatively small missiles. Former Secretary of Defense Brown, who was appointed to the Commission but later withdrew, observed that 'unless the United States can negotiate severe limits on a level of ICBM warheads, the numbers of single warhead missiles needed for a force of reasonable capability and survivability could make the system costs, and the amount of land required, prohibitively great'.[31]

One further point ought to be noted. Mobility is not crucial to Midgetman. If one accepts the argument given in the preceding chapter regarding the destabilizing ratios resulting from a 'deep cuts' proposal *and* the argument just given with respect to secure land basing, one might wish to examine the option of 'Midgetman' deployment in existing Minuteman silos as an alternative to the MX if the USSR agrees to the sort of arms control agreement proposed by the Scowcroft Commission – an increase in launchers, a drastic cut in warheads, in effect another regime to rid the superpower balance of the instability (and sectoral advantage) caused by the SS-18 and SS-19. But whatever the basing mode, would such a weapon restore extended deterrence? The contribution of the Midgetman innovation to the US strategic dilemma would be precisely the same as that offered by MX deployment. Extended deterrence is rehabilitated to the extent that ICBM vulnerability was one of the reasons for its slackening in the first place. But only to this marginal extent.

A final note: the first wing of ten MXs, renamed 'Peacekeeper', was deployed in December 1986. Congress has appropriated funds thus far for 33 weapons.

CRUISE MISSILES

In the following discussion, I shall concentrate on the potential contribution of the air-launched cruise missile (ALCM) and sea-launched cruise missile (SLCM) since the discussion of ground-launched cruise (GLCM) formed a large part of Chapter 8. Indeed, it was the peculiar significance of the ground-launching of GLCMs that made them, at once, a formidable cure for decoupling (since the Russians must assume, in planning, that GLCMs would be used rather than permitted to be overrun) and an invitation to uncoupling (since Soviet pre-emptive attacks against the GLCMs would not involve attacks on the US while GLCM accuracy and slow speed permit the tailoring of missions to avoid threatening Soviet central systems and cities).

A cruise missile is an unmanned, armed 'air breathing vehicle'[32] that relies on programmed guidance co-ordinated with periodic up-dates. The major technical distinction between cruise and ballistic missiles is that the former, being air breathing, have a substantially longer range than ballistic missiles of comparable weight since a ballistic missile must carry aboard its own oxygen (a feature augmented by the fact that, at least for ranges up to several thousand miles, the amount of energy required to propel a cruise missile is less than that required by a rocket-powered missile to reach the same range ballistically).[33] The shortcoming – if such it be – associated with this advantage is that an oxidizing, air breathing cruise cannot approach the speed of rockets and accordingly the cruise missile must fly at relatively low velocities. This means that it cannot be guided to its target inertially, since the drift of even the most accurate inertial systems – a few tenths of a mile per hour – is too great. Thus, cruise missile technology might have remained the servant of target and reconnaissance missions but for the revolution in microprocessing that made terrain-contour matching (TERCOM) and the digital scene matching area correlator (DSMAC) feasible for a lightweight, relatively small, relatively cheap weapon.

> In its simplest form TERCOM consists of a radar altimeter and a computer. Stored in the computer are digital altitude profiles of parallel strips of terrain from selected locations along the missile's intended flight path. Each set of profiles makes up a terrain contour map. As the missile – steered by a commercial-class inertial navigation system – reaches the approximate location of a map, the radar altimeter returns generate a real-time altitude profile, which the computer compares with the stored profiles to determine which stored profile the cruise missile just flew across. (Data for both course correction and location with time are needed for the system to fuse its warhead at the right time.) When a correlation is made, the INS is reset and a course correction begins. The missile continues to the next map location and so on until it reaches the target.[34]

Once near the target, the DSMAC system takes an image, performs a correlation with information in its memory (the early, analog systems simply compared a stored photo negative with a photograph taken in flight) and provides the missile with its terminal guidance.[35]

Flying at the low altitudes made possible by this system, the penetrability of the cruise missile is greatly enhanced. Ground radar that can detect aircraft flying at 5000 feet one hundred miles away will not detect the same plane until it is only twenty miles away if it is flying at an altitude of 200 feet since the earth's curvature and the clutter of buildings, forests, etc. consipire to confuse ground-based defence radar.[36] Two conclusions that are adverse to cruise missile technology may be drawn from this, however: (1) terminal defences may be effective against the missile since it will be moving slowly enough to enable a defensive response; (2) a 'look-down, shoot-down' or aerially-based radar, enhancing this terminal defense capability and allowing defenses to distinguish between incoming cruise missiles and ground clutter, will provide a formidable defensive barrier. These limitations mean that, at some time, the cruise missile will cease to be as effective as it is now. These developments, however, are still in the womb of time and for the period of the 1980s, before either MX or Trident 2 become operational, the cruise missile has offered an attractive alternative to bolster US extended deterrence.

Development of the cruise missile programme has been driven by the goal of extended deterrence and not, I think, by the appetites of the services; indeed until 1977, the Air Force and the Navy were resistant, if not hostile, to the development of long-range air-and-sea-launched cruise missiles. The former threatened the mission of the penetrating bomber; the latter, the missions of both fleet aircraft and attack submarines.[37] The ALCM and the SLCM require launching platforms, and given a finite defence budget for producing a particular number of planes and ships, use of these planes and ships as mere platforms must require a reduction in the number of them available for their usual missions. What kept cruise missile development alive was emphatically not the enthusiasm of the Navy or Air Force, but the repeated intervention of US Presidents who, under pressure from other members of the Alliance troubled by the loss of escalation dominance and responding to pressures generated by SALT-codified parity, sought a weapon that would enhance extended deterrence. Thus the ALCM/SLCM decisions that seemed so arbitrary to some commentators or which appeared to justify highly optimistic predictions of cruise missile performance in fact were dictated by the strategic developments discussed in Chapter 7.

> The cruise missile would not have proceeded as fast and as far, if indeed at all, had it not been for the intervention and support of

high-level political figures in the Pentagon, the White House, and even the US Department of State. For individuals operating at this level in the American government, the driving factors were negotiations with the Soviet Union on SALT I and II, the concern expressed by NATO's European members about the reliability of America's foreign policy and the credibility of the US nuclear umbrella over them in the era of strategic parity between the superpowers, and White House anticipation of adverse congressional action on SALT II if this new technology were not developed to its fullest.[38]

With the background provided by Book I we will be able to measure ALCM/SLCM capabilities against these strategic objectives: do they permit re-coupling? If so, do they do so at the risk of uncoupling?

The principal historian of cruise missile development has concluded that, for all practical purposes, the history of the modern strategic cruise missile began in June 1972 when Secretary of Defence Melvin R. Laird requested $20 million to start developing such a weapon.[39] Six years earlier, the Air Force in the course of studies evaluating the penetration of the B-52 bomber had noted that the Quail decoy missile was becoming obsolete. It proposed follow-on drone, described in a January 1968 statement, was modified (to the horror of the Air Force) by the Office of the Secretary of Defense (OSD) and became, in January 1969, precisely what the Air Force feared, a subsonic cruise *armed* decoy (SCAD),[40] a potential threat to the need for a new penetrating bomber. The SCAD programme demonstrated that small turbofan engines were capable of achieving ranges up to 1400 miles but in spite of, or perhaps because of this fact, Air Force opposition forced cancellation of the programme. Nevertheless, the idea of using standoff bombers with long-range missiles as an alternative to, rather than decoys, as an enhancement of, the penetrating bomber had been launched.[41]

In the interim, the Navy had been testing the Harpoon, an anti-ship cruise missile with a 70-mile range. When this testing programme was augmented by the evaluation of missiles launched from the torpedo tubes of attack submarines (SSNs), it coincided with the development of a longer range anti-ship cruise missile planned for use from vertical tubes in an entirely new class of submarine. By June 1972, however, this proposal had been replaced by an OSD effort to achieve strategic capability with SLCMs.[42]

OSD had transformed the issue for two reasons. First, the US had been unable to win Soviet agreement on restricting naval cruise missiles in SALT I. Secretary Laird testified that this would not have been the case if the US, as in the successful negotiations over ABM, ICBM and SLBM systems, had developed a counterpart weapon to those it wished to restrain in the Soviet arsenal. Second, it was thought that the SLCM could make important positive contributions to extended deterrence.[43]

The services were not as enthusiastic. Relying on Air Force criticism of the SCAD programme. Congress cut the budget request for SLCM development from $20 million to $6 million and, in fiscal year 1974, only $2.5 million was appropriated. This kept the programme alive, however, and in 1974 with the decoy issue out of the way, OSD began to press for both ALCM and SLCM development.[44]

In February 1975, the Defense Systems Acquisition Review Council (DSARC) approved the issue of contracts for SLCM prototypes, and by 1976 OSD had openly assigned the weapon to a theatre nuclear (LRTNF) role. One year later it announced:

> The primary need for the land attack cruise missile is in a theater role where its single warhead, high accuracy capability with resultant low collateral damage, penetrability and survivability make it ideal for use in limited nuclear attacks as a theater weapon. It represents one of the few new systems the US could deploy if needed to maintain theater balance in the face of growing Soviet peripheral attack capabilities that include such systems as the BACKFIRE bomber and the SS-20 mobile ground launched missile.[45]

The last stand of the Air Force against ALCMs came in the Joint Strategic Bomber Study submitted to Congress in December 1974.[46] It concluded that, at least for an ambitious set of objectives ranging across the entire target set and unsupplemented by other legs of the triad, a new penetrating bomber was cost-effective. A few months later, however, an influential Brookings study[47] was prematurely released that, by assuming a bomber role restricted to assured destruction, countervalue objectives, supported the ALCM as a substitute for bomber penetration and sharply criticized the vulnerability of the proposed B-1.

Then in January 1977, a DSARC meeting on cruise missiles took place. 'Eight years after the SCAD was initiated the Air Force was instructed to give first priority to the development of a full-range air-launched cruise missile'.[48] Air Force-Navy co-operation was formalized by the creation of a joint project office for cruise missile development, and the Navy was put in charge.[49] The Air Force nightmare had come true.

When the Russian downing of an American U-2 forced the cancellation of the B-70 by demonstrating that high-flying bombers were vulnerable to Soviet surface-to-air missiles, the Air Force had first developed penetration aids such as the Quail decoy and then pinned its hopes on the low-flying, highly maneuverable B-1. Now, by reviving the aging B-52 force as an inexpensive launcher for the ALCM, on the assumption that Soviet air defences relatively favourable to the B-1 (as opposed to the non-evasive, non-defensively armed ALCM) would not come on line until the 1990s, the technology envisioned to protect the concept of the penetrating bomber had defeated it. On 30 June 1977, President Carter announced the cancellation of the B-1 programme in favour of a large force (3400) of long-range ALCMs.[50] In five years, over internal service objections, two administrations, one Republican one Democratic, had brought the cruise missile to pre-eminence. By February 1978, Defense Secretary Harold Brown would announce that the ALCM was 'our highest national priority'.[51]

131 B-52Gs were converted to ALCM carriers by the end of 1986. Beginning in October 1985, these aircraft were fitted with launchers enabling them to carry up to twenty ALCMs.[52] Second-generation ALCMs, with ranges of 2600 nautical miles and employing various 'stealth' technologies are currently under study, with projected operating capability in 1987.[53] The first SLCMs have now been deployed.

In summary of this history, Art and Ockenden have concluded,

> The dominant group within each service – the strategic bombers in the Air Force, the carrier admirals in the Navy, and the NATO-conventional arms lobby in the Army – opposed any cruise missile variant that threatened [that service's mission]. Thus, all of the present . . . versions of the cruise missile owe their existence largely to the political incentives – born of SALT II politics, NATO alliance considerations, and the political needs of presidents – that caused high-level political appointees within the executive branch to push for their development. It was these factors that converted the technologically possible into the politically necessary.[54]

But are these two variants of the cruise missile in fact satisfactory in light of the political-strategic justifications that have driven their extraordinary development?

The Air-Launched Cruise Missile (ALCM)

The dilemma usually posed by LRTNF may be stated as follows:

> Given the reality of mutual superpower deterrence at the strategic level, some American strategists believe tactical nuclear forces offer an alternative to strategic forces if the Soviet Army begins to succeed in a conventional invasion. To many European allies, however, the only desirable role for theater nuclear forces if conventional deterrence fails is to serve as a catalyst that ensures that US strategic forces would be drawn into the engagement. Thus policy on TNF has traditionally remained muddled because of the latent contradiction between American and alllied interests.[55]

Prominent analysts have agred that it is in NATO's interest not to be explicit as to precisely what role TNF ought to play.[56]

> This ambiguity need not and perhaps should not be resolved, since uncertainty complicates Soviety military planning and buttresses NATO's political solidarity.[57]

Chapter 8 argued, however, that if LRTNF is to have any strategic recoupling significance, it cannot do so by means of serving as a powder trail to the US central deterrent. If this were so, then the calculations regarding LRTNF use could not be differentiated from those for the central systems and no additional deterrence is achieved by LRTNF deployment. It scarcely makes sense to deploy new systems in extended theatres where they must confront the twin problems of enhanced vulnerability by their (a) *not* being on the US mainland (where their location would raise the stakes of pre-emption by the Soviet Union) and (b); being *in* Europe where political consensus is required for their use and pre-emption is technologically easier.

What operational opportunities, then, does the ALCM offer for the extended Countervailing Strategy – curing decoupling, that is, by posing a theatre nuclear threat sufficient unto itself to deter or terminate hositilities at a level below central engagement – and how might this avoid the uncoupling consequences predicted by the 'theorem'?

The high accuracy of the ALCM suggests that it is a very promising weapon for the hold-at-risk function earlier noted as crucial to LRTNF re-coupling. Furthermore, because recallable bombers constitute the launching platforms for ALCMs, they may be dispatched on warning of attack. One shortcoming of cruise missiles for this mission – their slow speeds when pitted against the mobile, movable or only momentarily valuable assets of the second and third echelon – is mitigated by their being lauched from manned, airborne platforms. Moreover, the vulnerability of cruise missiles to terminal defences is also reduced when the targets are military assets on the move or held in reserve in Eastern Europe, neither hardened nor near the sites of the more sophisticated air radar/stationary surface-to-air missile systems.

A second requirement of LRTNF in a re-coupling role is the ability to hold the Soviet Union under threat.[58] Here it ought to be noted that some believe the single-warhead design of the cruise is more conducive to credible selective targeting than the 10 MIRVs of a highly accurate ICBM. More important, perhaps, is the contribution of the ALCM toward restoring the credibility of the forward-based NATO bomber. It will be recalled that it was the declining penetrability of this weapon that, with its increasing vulnerability, in part animated a decoupling reliance on central systems to fill the void. The ALCM does little to enhance survivability, an ambivalent issue in the theatre context anyway, as we shall shortly see, but to the extent that it rehabilitates the bomber threat against the Soviet Union by providing a stand-off weapon, it satisfies the requirement of what might barbarously be called 'de-sanctuarization', that is, the denial of a Russian sanctuary otherwise arising from the limits imposed by range or difficulty of penetration.

The requirement that LRTNF deployment increase the credibility of the NATO deterrent by forcing an adversary to suppress it and thus having to plan on forcing the Alliance to launch, is addressed also by the ALCM option. Air-bases are likely to be among the first targets of any Soviet offensive. The number of ALCMs that are likely to survive however, is not encouraging.

> Until the late 1980s part of the B-52 force will continue as penetrating bombers and part will serve as standoff launchers of ALCMs. In the 1990s all B-52s will be cruise missile carriers. In the first phase of ALCM deployment, 151 B-52Gs will carry 12 cruise missiles apiece, giving a force total of about 1800 missiles. These aircraft would also carry 1200 to 1500 bombs and short-range attack missiles (SRAMs), roughly 8 to 10 per bomber. If even half the aircraft were kept on altert (almost twice the current bomber alert level) and the prelaunch survivability was 80 percent, only about 700 ALCMs and 500 to 600 bombs and SRAMs would survive. Of these survivors, perhaps as many as 500 to 600 ALCMs would successfully

penetrate Soviet air defenses and denote on target – a number that does not suggest wide target coverage capabilities.[59]

Moreover, the ALCM may not really enhance the threat to the Soviet Union posed by NATO bombers, because ALCM deployment is made at the sacrifice of other nuclear weapons, notably gravity bombs. Fewer total weapons will be carried by the alert B-52G force projected for the second phase of ALCM deployment, despite the fact that the ALCM force itself will increase by 67 per cent, because the stand-off mission fulfilled by ALCMs requires weapons to carry their own propulsion and thus makes them heavier than gravity bombs.[60] One corollary of the relationship between the ALCM and its platform is that increasing the number of ALCMs does not necessarily increase the number of surviving weapons (including ALCMs) after a Soviet pre-emption. No matter how many weapons, of whatever type, are carried by the bomber, it is *its* survival that is determining.

Against this set of objectives, the customary criticisms of ALCMs seem beside the point. Critics usually complain that ALCMs cannot be used against soft countervalue targets (because the bombers on which they depend cannot be withheld for indefinite periods, as doctrine requires)[61]; but cannot be used against counterforce targets either (because these targets are time-urgent and the flight speed of a cruise missile is too slow).[62] It is also sometimes noted that ALCMs are particularly inappropriate for the intra-war deterrence contemplated by the Countervailing Strategy since they are not survivable over time (even if their bombers escape a pre-emptive strike by launch-on-warning, they can scarcely keep returning to land or remain aloft indefinitely) nor are they re-targetable.[63]

It is of course correct that the purpose of targeting countervalue, urban-industrial targets is to deter Soviet attacks on US cities by withholding the US attack. For this reason ALCMs are an inappropriate means to execute the assured destruction mission. It is also true that the slow flight time for cruise missiles make them unlikely candidates for pre-emption against missile silos and mobile ballistic missiles. (Though with respect to the former, flight time is hardly the problem; a Soviet leadership that had pre-empted US ICBMs would scarcely hesitate to put its reserve force on launch-on-warning status and thereby frustrate even a US ballistic missile countersilo attack.) But the universe of important targets is not exhausted by these two classes of objectives.

The target potential previously defined by the theorem for LRTNF is principally counterforce though not countersilo, and thus the fixed nature of roads, oil storage facilities, ports, bridges, railway depots and the force deployments shaped by natural terrain, offer a useful role for the pre-targeted ALCM.

A lack of countersilo capability actually tends to bolster US strategy in this context because it reduces US self-deterrence lest the Soviet Union fear that central systems are being attacked. The ALCM's short useful life-span (its lack of endurance, re-targeting, return and launch survivability) does mean that the NATO decision to 'go nuclear' will have to be taken early in the conflict. This enhances deterrence, for the reasons noted above with respect to the GLCM – to the extent the Soviet Union threatens an attack it virtually commands retaliation – but it jeopardizes re-coupling. The pre-programmed ALCM can deter force concentration and decrease the likelihood of Soviet sanctuary but, by itself (or with SRAMs) it does not constitute a force capable of limiting escalation by cost imposition, which depends upon intra-war deterrence and compellance.

Despite this limitation in achieving re-coupling themselves, it is useful to observe that ALCMs make a collateral, but by no means incidental, contribution to re-coupling by ameliorating ICBM vulnerability.

For ALCMs restore the need for the Soviet Union to pre-empt bombers at their bases. Since they can be launched on warning (being recallable), bombers must be targeted by Russian missiles with relatively short flight times. For this reason it is usually assumed that US air bases are targeted by Soviet SLBMs that would move close to the US (or British) shorelines. Soviet ICBMs, however, take much longer to reach their counterpart silos in the US (and only they have the lethality necessary to profitably target these silos). Accordingly,

> the Soviet Union would be faced with the choice between launching its ICBMs first so that they would arrive on target at the same time as the SLBMs and launching both types of missiles simultaneously. In the former case, the bomber (or air-launched cruise missile) would receive a much longer warning time. In the latter case, the probability of receiving unambiguous warning and confirmation of a Soviet attack would be increased.[64]

To put the point in a more generalized way: the differing flight times of weapons to targets require either different launch or differing detonation times. By rehabilitating the bomber force, ALCMs draw airbases into any pre-emptive targeting, thereby maximizing the differential already present by virtue of geography, missile speed and position, and force the USSR to give the USA's most time-urgent and accurate weapon a margin of warning.

> In the most likely case – a simultaneous launch of Soviet ICBMs and SLBMs – the United States would have about half an hour of sensor warning time before an ICBM launch became necessary, and thus would have about fifteen minutes after SLBM detonations on U.S. air bases to launch its ICBM forces before the Soviet ICBMs arrived. In this way, the launch-under-attack contingency is quite different from the typical conception of launch-on-warning with its reliance on uncertain warning information.[65]

Thus the ALCM's contribution to the solution of the contemporary problems of extended deterrence must be regarded as important, but not decisive. ALCMs do accomplish some of the re-coupling tasks, but within a too-restricted time span; they also reduce one decoupling condition, if in a somewhat roundabout way.

The Sea-Launched Cruise Missile (SLCM)

The SLCM programme has developed three distinct variants of the same prototype missile: the nuclear-armed Tomahawk land-attack missile (TLAM-N); a conventional version of this weapon (TLAM-C); and a Tomahawk antiship missile (TASSM).[66] All three can be fired from a submarine torpedo tube or surface ship launcher. Previously, a procurement figure of 1200 SLCMs was contemplated, equally divided between TLAM-N and TASM.[67] The first year purchase figure was set at 439,[68] which may also include some TLAM-Cs, a more recently conceived system that apparently has usurped the enthusiasm with which the TLAM-N was formerly embraced.

This disenchantment reflects a weapon that is fundamentally unsuited to the standard doctrinal roles for nuclear weapons at sea: if the TLAM-N is a strategic weapon, it performs tasks better allocated to the SLBM; if it is a theatre weapon, it requires naval platforms better allocated to other tasks. Although our principal concern is with the SLCM as an LRTNF weapon, it is useful to consider its avowed purpose as a strategic weapon. In 1975,

> [t]he principal rationale offered for the weapon was that it would provide a strategic nuclear reserve aboard attack submarines for use in . . . limited nuclear wars or in a third strike.[69]

The US, of course, already possessed an extensive submarine fleet armed with strategic weapons, the SSBNs with SLBMs. In the next section, we will discuss the limitations of this force regarding limited responses. It will be seen then that the principal barriers to submarine launched limited strikes do not, as is often supposed, lie in the accuracy of the warhead but in the difficulty of control of and communication with the submarine arising from the nature of the submarine itself. As with ALCMs, the flexibility of the SLBM and the SLCM depends on characteristics of the launcher.

This point regarding SSBN/SLBM accuracy was not always appreciated, however, and the great accuracy and range of the cruise missile made it seem attractive as a solution to this perceived problem. If the cruise missile's shortcomings in its air based form were lack of endurance and vulnerability, then the highly survivable SLCM basing aboard submarines must have appeared to promise a solution. Overcoming these particular obstacles, however, did not produce a weapon with a specially useful role in strategic terms. In fact, it produced a weapon with a unique combination of attractive features but that served no unique function within the countervailing strategy.

It is true that lack of endurance in the ALCM meant that it was unsuitable for countervalue, assured destruction missions. Correcting this by sea-basing did not mean that SLCM had found a purpose because its high accuracy was no advantage over the SLBM, which is also highly survivable, sufficiently accurate and more effective against these targets. Accordingly, the rationale for SLCM deployment was changed and came to be stated:

> A sea-launched cruise missile development provides a desirable augmentation of capability, a unique potential for unambiguous, controlled single-weapon response and an invulnerable reserve force.[70]

But this rationale fell foul of the terminal defence, final penetrability problems of the cruise missile. Unless aided by Pershing 2 or SRAM strikes, for example, it was unlikely that a SLCM could get to a strategic target through heavy Soviet air defences. 'A single weapon response' of the limited nuclear option variety occurs early on in the conflict, however, before air defences are degraded and is valuable, strategically, precisely at this stage. As a result, the mission conceived for the SLCM changed again. 'Rather than being targeted only against strategic targets within Russia, The TLAM will be a worldwide theater nuclear weapon'.[71]

This brings us to the LRTNF role.[72] I shall claim that, despite recent plans to deploy SLCMs aboard SSNs, this weapon does not enhance the re-coupling mission though, ironically, it has some benefits regarding uncoupling (benefits that have prompted some ministries to suggest the SLCM as an alternative to the NATO decision to deploy 464 GLCMs).

The SLCM does satisfy the first requirement of LRTNF, the hold-at-risk function. Pre-planned strikes are possible against second and third echelon targets. Against this must be counted the loss of anti-submarine capabilities entailed by the conversion of a large percentage of the SSN fleet to nuclear responsibilities (including the replacement of some technology by weapons systems). Moreover, the firing of a SLCM would generate accoustic signals that might reveal the SSN location. Since guidance alignment requires twenty minutes after missile loading into a torpedo tube, the SSN could fire only infrequent salvos and must endure a high risk of detection relative to the target coverage.[73] This casts some doubt on the ability of the SLCM to continue to hold-at-risk throughout an extended conflict (not just the protracted war of six month's duration, but even the conflict that, with pauses, may last three weeks) and brings us to the crucial reason why an SSN launched system is ill-suited to the limited, dynamic missions of theatre deterrence. SLCMs could not rely on pre-programmed target data since (in contrast to the ALCM which faces considerable re-targeting problems of its own) communications with the launcher/submarine are so limited that it would be difficult to provide enough data to enable the SLCM to re-target; yet such selectivity is crucial to intra-war deterrence based on limited nuclear options.

> The SLCM force submarines would have to come closer to Soviet shores to cover comparable targets because of the shorter range of SLCMs than of Poseidon and especially Trident missiles. And the withheld force must be capable of performing a variety of flexible missions against a variety of target types determined during a conflict. Since both execution and targeting information would have to be sent to the SLCM force, messages would have to be considerably more detailed than at present, going beyond the likely capability of the force to receive such messages, especially in a hostile environment. At the same time, the SLCM submarines, which lack reconnaissance, damage assessment, and related capabilities, could not act independently.[74]

Thus the SLCM, like the ALCM, partially – that is, initially – meets the challenge of the hold-at-risk mission and thereafter is less useful.

SLCMs do have the range to threaten Russia. But they suffer from the terminal defence problems that are characteristic of cruise missiles. Given the limitation on numbers imposed by the number of SSNs to be diverted, there will be too few SLCMs to saturate air defences. And, finally, moving the SSNs close into Soviet waters to enable targeting against interior points increases the vulnerability of the platform. Thus, on balance, SLCMs present the capability to threaten a Russian sanctuary, but in less than robust terms.

Nor do SLCMs enhance the *credibility* of this 'de-sanctuarization'. It is usually argued that basing at sea can affect a re-coupling since the US President could more readily order a nuclear attack from sea-based units than from US-based launchers.[75] This presumes that Soviet retaliation would take the form of an irrational attack on the locus of the origin of attack, an unlikely event given that re-targeting is so difficult at sea. (This same sort of thinking presumes that GLCMs are a re-coupler because the US President can be assured of Soviet retaliation against their empty launchers rather than elsewhere.) Moreover, given the numbers of cruise missiles necessary to defeat air defences, it would be difficult for the Soviet Union to correctly define an attack as limited, regardless of its origin. Finally, the very survivability of the submarine launched weapon makes it a less than assured target (while this endurance does nothing to insure the intra-war utility of its nuclear strikes).

On the other hand, a lowering of the threshold of US nuclear commitment might be brought about through the judicious selection of targets for SLCMs. For example, a threat of nuclear attack on Soviet naval elements might actually deter Soviet attack on the US since the confinement of retaliation to sea is plausible enough to suggest that the US would not be self-deterred. The use of carriers as SLCM platforms in *this* regard would appear promising and would avoid the command, control and communication problems of the SSN. This engages US nuclear forces without uncoupling the Alliance states. Whether nuclear weapons thus engaged would deter attacks on Europe is of course to some extent uncertain. Carrier based SLCMs would not have the range for deep strikes against the Soviet Union in the case of European attack and would require an unlikely pre-positioning. And, in any event, the choice of a sea-based target does not dictate a sea-based launcher.

The SLCM presents us with a paradox: if it is invulnerable (SSN-based) its communications limitations (among other facts) render it less useful for the Countervailing Strategy. If its single shot characteristics are exploited by surface ships, it exposes them to a nuclear pre-emption that, by virtue of the very fact that they are at sea, is made likelier since it is less likely to evoke a retaliation exacting unacceptable costs.

There was an understandable move on the part of some European governments to push the NATO LRTNF (and thus the targets of Soviet pre-emption) 'out to sea'. This move was anticipated by the Americans and may have contributed to the subordination of the TLAM-N to the TLAM-C in 1978.[76] At any rate, we can now appreciate the futility of such a move: while it does avoid the uncoupling of the GLCM deployments, it does little to accomplish the re-coupling that underlay the need for LRTNF. It is like taking a less bad tasting medicine that does not confer the medical benefits offered by the rejected potion.

Summary

In April 1977, the US offered a 'three-tier' proposal to the Russians in SALT. ALCMs would be limited in range to 2500 km, SLCMs and GLCMs to 600 km if deployed within a three-year period to be specified in a protocol to the main treaty. This protocol had been carefully crafted to expire at about the time it was expected that GLCMs and SLCMs would be ready for full-scale deployment. The other members of the Alliance reacted with alarm, however, when the Soviet Union accepted the proposal, offering in exchange provisions that did nothing to lessen the threat to Europe. These provisions imposed range and production limitations on the Soviet Backfire bomber only to the extent of preventing it from striking the US and excluded the SS-20 from any deployment restraints whatsoever. To European members of the Alliance.

> the United States appeared to be magnifying the long-range theater nuclear force threat to the Europeans in order to reduce the long-range strategic threat to its own territory.[77]

This concern culminated in the address before the International Institute for Strategic Studies in October of that year by the German Chancellor, Helmut Schmidt, discussed in Chapter 8. The Chancellor asserted that SALT, by the omission of restraints at the theatre level and by the open acceptance of parity at the level of central systems, had emphasized the theatre imbalance. From this concern arose the particular LRTNF plans that were ratified by the December 1979 decision by NATO. Thus the claim that SALT is responsible for cruise missile development, by not constraining it, is true only in this sense: that SALT propelled concerns about decoupling to the top of the American agenda.

The SLCM/ALCM will do little to enhance extended deterrence, however, because they cannot redress the conditions that eroded the extension of US deterrence nor compensate in ways that avoid severing the European theatre. Specifically, the original view that a relatively cheap, highly accurate long range cruise missile would overcome parity was factually and analytically wrong: factually, because the number of ALCMs is constrained by the numbers of penetrating, or stand-off bombers that are their platforms; the number of SLCMs is similarly governed by the number of SSNs or some assigned surface vessels to be diverted (disregarding the suggestion that communication-poor trawlers and the like could be usefully pressed into service; analytically, because superiority could not be regained by simply swamping air defenses, so long as the Soviet Union retained the capability to manage its own run-up of limited nuclear attacks without jeopardizing its assured destruction capability.

Nor are the SLCM/ALCM ideal for limited attacks that might restore escalation dominance.

> In its capabilities for flexible and limited attack, the cruise missile appears to have more disadvantages than advantages. On the surface, its relatively low yield and high accuracy suggest a potential for discriminating and effective limited attacks. However, most important Soviet targets are located well in the interior of the Soviet Union; a cruise missile launched at interior targets will fly over or near many other potential targets and may create confusion about its actual objective.[78]

Unlike the trajectories of ballistic missiles like the Pershing 2, the destination of a cruise missile is impossible to plot. Swamping the defence with decoys will make it difficult for the Soviet Union to determine the true scope of an attack that appears to be coming in great numbers. Thus the fact that, many hours later, the relatively discriminating damage done by the cruise missiles can be clearly determined will be of little use in persuading the USSR that the attack should have been classified 'limited' by them when it was under way.

It must also be observed that retargeting is cruical to the Countervailing Strategy,[79] but that TERCOM makes this extremely difficult for cruise missiles. This system depends on terrain maps that must be anticipated and stored, along with the relevant terminal guidance information.

> The problem of storing such maps alone would severely limit the capability to retarget an ALCM, especially once its carrier was airborne. Retargeting would also require a wealth of other information, such as defense locations, accessible air corridors, and, for ALCMs, refueling possibilities for the carrier aircraft.[80]

In summary, the cruise missile variations reviewed in this section can be seen to be responsive to the dilemma of extended deterrence. Driven by this dilemma, US Presidents and their Secretaries of Defense repeatedly rescued these weapons; the SALT process, for much the same reason, gave an additional impetus to the programme. Yet it can be seen that these systems make a limited contribution to resolving the problem.

The Submarine-Launched Ballistic Missile

Both SALT 1 and SALT 2 placed limits on the deployment of SLBMs. This reflected the characterization of these systems as central, strategic systems that could be targeted on the US–USSR homelands. American employment doctrines for the SLBM depended on three features of the weapons system: its range, relative invulnerability and its inability to execute precise, limited strikes. These characteristics uniquely suited the SLBM as the ultimate carrier of the assured destruction capability. The SLBM was secure (and therefore would allow the withholding of the assured destruction mission emphasized in Chapter 6) and it was imprecise, requiring predetermined targeting against soft, large objectives and thus posing little threat to Russian ICBMs. In both its advantages and its shortcomings, the SLBM seemed the ideal weapon for countervalue targeting.

For this reason, it is difficult to justify the dedication of three Poseidon SSBN (nuclear-powered submarines carrying SLBMs) to SACEUR (the NATO Commander) in light of the developments discussed in Chapter 8 that have tended to diminish the credibility of a countervalue attack in defence of the European theatre, except to acknowledge that this is precisely why the dedication was made by the US. In an effort to emphasize its willingness to extend deterrence, the US wished to make a gesture as if to declare that changed conditions would not affect US policy.

The possible role of the SLBM in LRTNF has been a subject of debate since the Multilateral Force. In this section we will briefly analyze whether the development of a new warhead for the latest model SLBM fits it for a mission for which, in the absence of some means of going beyond assured destruction attacks, the SLBM force is otherwise clearly unsuited.

The first deployed US SLBM, the Polaris A-1, carried a relatively small warhead (.7 MT) and could achieve only a relatively high c.e.p. (about twice as high for the inertially guided A-1 as for its radio guided contemporaries, the Atlas and Titan ICBMs, which were themselves not particularly well adapted to small targets). In other words, it was a weapon of such low lethality that it was necessarily limited to large, soft targets. In November 1964, however, the Defense Department's Special Projects Office was directed to include as a characteristic of the new B-3 SLBM (to be carried aboard a new SSBN, the Poseidon) MIRVs of improved accuracy such that some hard target, counterforce capability could be achieved.[81]

MIRVing alone – once a c.e.p. range of .25 miles is achieved – increases the probability of hard target destruction. Undersecretary of Defense David Packard testified that the MIRVed Poseidon had achieved a 6 per cent greater hard target capability compared to the un-MIRVed Polaris A-3[82] and other calculations have estimated this potential improvement as much as 11 per cent (against targets hardened to 300 p.s.i.).[83] At the same time, advances were being made in accuracy. The 1964 requirements that an inertial guidance system be developed similar to the Minuteman ICBM system were met and in 1967, OSD directed the Navy to develop a stellar inertial guidance system. This was considerably aided by progress in submarine navigation. By 1974, various systems such as

> SINs, the TRANSIT/NAVSAT Navy navigational satellite system, the VLF communications stations, Omega, and other radio and accoustic aids [meant] that overall navigational errors of about 200 feet could be continuously available, although errors of 600 to 800 feet [were] more likely.[84]

The 1975 budget allocated funds for the construction of three new Trident submarines to carry a new missile that would further enhance counterforce capabilities, the C-4. Vice-Admiral Charles H. Griffiths, then Deputy Chief of Naval Operations for Submarine Warfare, stated that:

> [B]ased on progress to date, we project that by 1982 . . . we will have the technology in hand to give the SLBM force accuracy at SLBM ranges comparable to the accuracy of longer range ICBMs.[85]

The new US Administration, in announcing its strategic package on 3 October 1981, stressed the procurement of a highly capable, counterforce SLBM. The new missile, according to Rear Admiral William A. Williams III, Director of the Navy's Strategic and Theater Nuclear Warfare Division, would be effective.

> across the entire target spectrum – from hard silos and command and control facilities to softer military and war supporting industrial targets.[86]

The effect these enhanced capabilities will have on the usefulness of the SLBM for re-coupling depends on these questions: What characteristics of the SLBM equip it for executing limited nuclear options? How are these affected by the D-5 (the name of the new missile)? Does the D-5 accomplish the re-coupling tasks discussed in this section while avoiding uncoupling?

Three remarkable characteristics differentiate SLBMs from ICBMs: their survivability, mobility and reduced flight time. The addition of high accuracy to these attributes creates a formidable counterforce weapon; but, as will be seen, the submarine's particular advantages ineluctably, not technically, affect the role of such a weapon within the Countervailing Strategy and limit that role sharply. Advances in accuracy do not change this fact.

The overwhelming advantage of the SSBN/SLBM is its security. For the foreseeable future, SSBNs are virtually invulnerable to pre-emption when on station. Partly this is a consequence of their mobility; if their locations were known the force would be substantially more vulnerable than land-based ICBMs because of its concentration of relatively large numbers of missiles on single, soft launching platforms. But primarily this is a function of their invisibility, when submerged, to photo-reconnaissance satellites and the difficulty of their detection through sound in vast oceans. This partly accounts for the otherwise counterintuitive[87] continuing increase in size from Polaris to Trident given that larger submarines are noisier and thus easier to detect: the greater range that larger boats confer can mean greater undetectability since virtually the entire ocean becomes a possible domain for the SSBN, and more weapons aboard – also a function of size – mean greater devastation if the sumbarine is not detected. This raises the detection requirement for pre-emption to virtually the entire on-station force. It is the survivability of the SLBM that has led to the overwhelming reliance on it within the triad. The SLBM force contains half the total warheads in the SIOP inventory (more than 5000) and these, by the mid-1980s, are expected to provide 5 out of every 6 warheads that would actually arive on target, discounting for assured penetration.[88]

The SLBM now shares great accuracy with the ICBM. Although inaccuracy was once regarded as the principal shortcoming of the SLBM, a relentless and imaginative compaign to reduce the c.e.p. of SLBMs has succeeded. Beginning in 1975, funding was provided for the Improved Accuracy Program (IAP), the first systematic technological effort to account for SLBM errors in accuracy, assess the potential for improvement by various means, and develop promising systems. This programme,[89] completed in 1982, resulted in the development of stellar inertial guidance by which the launched vehicle takes a star sight during the post-boost phase of flight, and then corrects its flight path. This promises to reduce c.e.p. from 1500 to 750 feet. When accompanied by a new post-boost vehicle, the reduction may go to 400 feet.[90] Two other untested technologies have also emerged from the IAP: the use of a Global Positioning System to update missile guidance by providing velocity and position information during flight before re-entry, and a system of terminal guidance. These two systems promise accuracies up to 150 and 100 feet respectively although they are also both highly vulnerable to enemy countermeasures ranging from the destruction of land-based beacons and satellites to the jamming of the electromagnetic communications used to provide navigation information (unlike stellar guidances).[91] These are very impressive figures, better even than the projected c.e.p. of the MX.

A third important feature of the SLBM is its mobility. This enables the SSBN to launch from distant waters and unpredictable azimuths, greatly complicating a terminal defence programme, as well as to launch from close in and ensure such a short flight time that warning is impossible and inaccuracies, since error is largely a product of inertial drift over time, are even further minimized.[92] A diagram[93] comparing the ranges of the Polaris A-2, Poseidon B-3 and C-4, and the proposed Trident D-5 shows a dramatic increase in range (see opposite).

To what sort of strategic role beyond the traditional assured destruction mission of the SLBM are these qualities of the SLBM/D-5

Figure 11.1 Missile submarines and national security

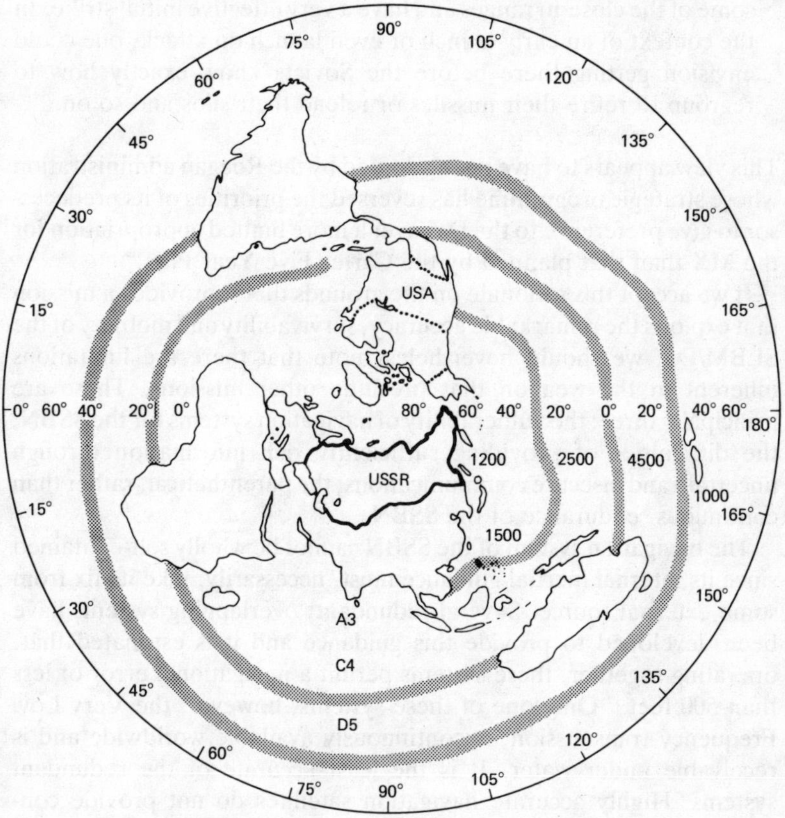

especially useful? Originally, support for a counterforce, submarine launched weapon was based on a response to the Schlesinger strategic innovations of 1974.[94] For reasons that will be discussed below, it soon became clear that the SLBM, regardless of its accuracy, was unsuitable for intra-war limited nuclear options in a protracted conflict. For a time the rationale for the SLBM/D-5 shifted to that of a counterforce reserve, supplementing land-based counterforce ICBMs. The current OSD rationale, however, emphasizes a preference for the initial use of SLBMs. According to the Deputy Undersecretary of Defense for Research and Engineering under the Carter administration,

> the one merit of the sea-based system of course is that you can have forces close in as well as far out. The close-in forces can have ultra-

> fast response and you could deliver weapons within [deleted] from some of the close-in ranges and have a very effective initial strike. In the context of an early launch or even launch on attack, one could envision getting there before the Soviets know exactly how to regroup to refire their missiles or reload their silos and so on.[95]

This view appears to have been adopted by the Reagan administration whose strategic programme has reversed the priorities of its predecessor to give preference to the D-5 over a more limited appropriation for the MX than that planned by the Carter Five Year Plan.[96]

If we accept this rationale on the grounds that it provides a mission that exploits the remarkable accuracy, survivability and mobility of the SLBM/D5, we should nevertheless note that there are limitations inherent in the weapon that preclude other missions. These are principally three: the vulnerability of navigation systems for the SSBN; the difficulties of providing sufficiently rich information through uncertain and insecure communications; the parenthetical, rather than continuous, endurance of the SSBN.

The navigation system of the SSBN cannot be wholly self-contained since its internal inertial guidance must, necessarily, take its fix from some external source. Several redundant, overlapping systems have been developed to provide this guidance and it is estimated that, operating together, these systems permit a navigational error of less than 500 feet.[97] Only one of these systems, however, the Very Low Frequency transmission, is continuously available worldwide and is receivable under water. It is the least accurate of the redundant systems. Highly accurate navigation satellites do not provide continuous coverage, and their VHF and UHF signals can only be received if the SSBN projects an antenna above the ocean surface for several minutes. Low Frequency systems which are receivable by underwater aerial, and therefore do not compromise the survivability of the submarine, provide a very limited global coverage. None of this, however, would decisively limit the role of the SLBM, given the very great accuracies attributed to it, were it not for the vulnerability of the satellites and their corresponding ground-based stations, and the similar vulnerability of the Low Frequency and Very Low Frequency ground transmitters.[98] The problem is not, therefore, that a ballistic trajectory requires a precise starting point to execute a preprogrammed strike but rather that the mobility that is an important SLBM asset is greatly compromised if, during war (that is, for other than a first-strike mission), the opportunity for precise submarine navigation becomes impossible. That would mean that, while limited strikes are not ruled out by navigational difficulties, precise counter-silo strikes probably are only possible if the SSBN has arrived at its launching point before a Soviet attack.

Considerably more problematic is the vulnerability of command, control, and communications in the SSBN/SLBM context. As with the navigations systems, communications relays, satellites and transmitters are soft and inherently vulnerable, not only to destruction but also to jamming and blackouts. This vulnerability becomes especially critical when one realizes that the backup communications systems for use in war – the airborne TACAMO VLF, low power VLF and ELF systems and the satellite replacement/mobile ground links – do not have the capacity of the huge VLF stationary communications stations to transmit the rich data, in great quantity, required for detailed targeting. 'These have only the capacity for minimal essential communications, such as those required for counter city retaliation'.[99] As Albert Langer has argued:

> For the counter-city warfare all that is really required is a single message that gives the code to unlock the firing mechanisms on the missiles (whether ICBMs or SLBMs). Even if all further communications are cut off, the local commander can then proceed to hit pre-assigned targets. It is of course preferable that more detailed command and control should be possible, but it is not absolutely essential. Moreover, for purposes of 'deterrence' it does not matter much how great a delay there can be in receiving such a message. The certainty that no matter how greatly a communications network is damaged, eventually such a message will get through, is quite sufficient (provided the missiles themselves remain effective). The many and various 'back-up' systems are adequate for this purpose. For counter-force warfare on the other hand, very much more detailed information is required. The submarine commander must be informed precisely which targets are to be attacked, on a 'real-time' basis. There is no point in hitting missile silos which are already empty or which have been destroyed by other strategic forces. All sorts of data must be supplied, continuously and rapidly.[100]

This tends to limit the counterforce effectiveness of the SLBM warhead no matter how low a c.e.p. is achieved.

Finally, even the survivability of the SSBN is vulnerable on grounds difficult to avoid since they inhere in some of the positive characteristics for which the weapon was developed. The boats carry an enormous number of warheads yet once a single missile is launched the position of the boat may be exposed, and further, authoritative command channels sufficient to exercise precise, centralized control over SSBNs may require the boat to expose itself to receive such messages. Thus, there can be a trade-off between the survivability of the submarines and the execution of limited and selective attacks. As Secretary Schlesinger perhaps overstated the difficulty, commenting on the adaptability of SLBMs to the strategic policy of limited and selective nuclear options,

> a submarine like Poseidon is hard to adapt to [the strategy] because you have so many MIRVs permissible and so many missiles per boat. As soon as you fire you expose the boat.[101]

This difficulty arises from the SSBN's parenthetical rather than continuous endurance: the SSBN is secure on station but can become less so after its first use. In the context of war, the later first use occurs, the more difficult it will be to execute limited strikes for lack of information; the earlier first use occurs, the riskier it becomes to execute a limited strike for reasons of abundance, that is, warheads that are not used are jeopardized (an ironic variant of the use-it-or-lose-it syndrome). Poseidons carry 16 SLBMs with 10–14 C-4 warheads each; when retrofitted with Trident 1 missiles, with 8 warheads each, the number of warheads per boat will fall to 128. D-5 deployment aboard Trident 2 SLBMs, however will raise the number to 192 warheads.[102] In either case, there will be intense pressures against constraining SLBM strikes to very limited numbers.

We must not overstate SSBN vulnerability following a partial launch, since such exposure is by no means necessarily fatal. If, however, substantial launches are delayed, then pre-planned targeting begins to lose its relevance:

> SLBMs have relatively little targeting flexibility. Each submarine reportedly carries targeting data for a variety of contingencies on prepared magnetic tapes, but this obviously allows only limited choice of targets, and there is evidently no capacity for improvisation.[103]

Thus in 1975, even before the enormous strides in accuracy were made, Desmond Ball had concluded,

> Essentially, the SLBM's counterforce capability is restricted to particular situations – for example, a first strike or an immediate follow-up strike where target information can be completely

coordinated in advance and the follow-up modifications can at least be transmitted with reasonable speed; or to circumstances of slow-motion controlled counterforce war-fighting in which navigation and communication systems are left intact for some period.[104]

We are now in a position to evaluate the potential contribution of the D-5 to the re-coupling/uncoupling problem.

The hold-at-risk function of LRTNF requires endurance. It is not clear that the SLBM, despite its secure basing, can actually provide the assurance that it will endure throughout a protracted conflict. The other requirement of this function, however, is accuracy and there should be little doubt that, despite the limitations of earlier SLBMs,[105] the Trident 2/D-5 can be made highly accurate. Insofar as the hold-at-risk function is discharged by highly accurate capabilities (which force dispersal) and can be executed on the basis of pre-planned target information, the SLBM is a formidable theatre weapon. It can be inferred from this, however, that there are pressures inherent in relying on the SLBM that, despite its unique survivability, push for early use.

A second LRTNF function is the ability to threaten the Soviet Union. Obviously the Trident 2/D-5, and its predecessors in advantageous locations, have the range to strike targets deep in the Soviet Union. The difficulty is one of self-deterrence. The Soviet homeland is not going to be struck in any situation, short of its assured destruction, by weapons in great numbers. Yet the SLBM, because it is so highly MIRVed, and because its firing may compromise all the other SLBMs aboard by exposing the SSBN launcher, is a multi-strike weapon. Despite the fact that there will be great pressures, tactical and political, to use the SLBM option early in the conflict, the abundance of its warheads make it particularly inappropriate for such use.

Here the relative, or parenthetical, invulnerability of the SLBM actually works against its use in a theatre role, because it foregoes the credibility enhancing role of more vulnerable weapons that must be used or be lost to the attacker. At the same time, sea basing may attract political pressure for SLBM use since retaliation against it does not take place on land. Both these points must be examined in light of the third function derived for LRTNF, the cost-imposing function.

The Countervailing Strategy seeks – to employ an algebraic metaphor – to pair a negative value with every positive formulation that an attacker might consider. For this reason, it is, as has been observed, a defensive strategy and not a war-winning strategy. For the attacker, various routes are open since he possesses the initiative. A decision to attack will be made only so long as there is one 'equation' that is positive, that is, one course of action that promises to be of greater value to him than a continuation of the status quo (or the likely status if he does nothing). The defender, in the Countervailing Strategy, must attach to any possible positive equation some sufficiently negative, necessary concomitant so that the entire value is not positive to the attacker. This is why the vulnerability of the otherwise relatively survivable GLCMs is significant: they are mobile enough to survive pre-emption (thereby lessening any positive value of such a strategy, or 'equation') but not so mobile that they would not be overrun by a deep salient and therefore could be presumed to be used in such a situation (thereby negating any possible value of *that* strategy, the equation of a rapid conventional assault). The task of the Countervailing Strategy is to provide credible (limited, non-countervalue) negative responses to every plausible, otherwise positive, strategy of the attacker so that no formulation appears to justify the attack.

The D-5 provides enormous capabilities for an initial strike: it is accurate and can be launched from near its target or from distant, unpredictable points which current radar warning systems did not anticipate, and it is capable of limited launches. This must render Soviet planning extremely doubtful since such a flexible weapon is able to impose proportionate, but very damaging costs in reply to virtually any Soviet initiative.

At the same time, sea-basing provides a powerful political incentive for first use. Quoting Gregory Treverton, I have provided an account of this point in Chapter 7.[106] Whatever the salutary effects on deterrence of such first use credibility – and they are not negligible – this political pressure merely reinforces the early strike characteristics of the weapon itself when it is deployed for purposes other than assured destruction. These limitations ill-suit the SLBM for limited nuclear operations in a protracted conflict. But that is simply another way of concluding that the SLBM, no matter how impressive its achievements in accuracy, does not resolve the dilemma of extended deterrence in the current strategic context.

CONCLUSION

These conditions led to the recent erosion of extended deterrence: the vulnerability of the US ICBM system, parity in central systems, and the loss of escalation dominance within the extended theatre. In this chapter we have observed the marginal amelioration of each of these conditions by the deployment of new weapons technologies.

The MX can, if deployed in existing silos, actually reduce the vulnerability of the ICBM leg of the triad. The ALCM can restore the usefulness of the bomber leg of the triad and thereby lessen ICBM vulnerability and rehabilitate parity, if not control, at the theatre level of conflict. The SLBM could, as part of a follow-on, pre-planned strike, threaten counterforce targets from a non-pre-emptable launcher thus greatly complicating Soviet confidence in escalation dominance. But the fundamental dilemma identified in Chapter 8 – the theorem and its predicted alternatives of decoupling or uncoupling – is neither avoided nor resolved by any of these weapons technologies.

12 Multipolarity

Chi poria mai pur con parole sciolte dicer del sangue e delle piaghe a pieno ch' i' ora vidi, per narrar più volte?

(Who could ever tell, even with words untrammelled and the tale often repeated, of all the blood and the wounds I saw now?)
Canto XXVIII, *Inferno*

In Chapter 8 I introduced a 'theorem' that postulated the uncomfortable necessity of either decoupling or 'uncoupling' the central and extended theatres. That is, the current strategic context required the President either to refuse to use nuclear weapons on behalf of Europe (or other non-US states) or confine their use *to* European (or other non-Soviet) theatres. Chapters 9, 10, and 11 explored various compensations for the undesirable politico-strategic consequences of this theorem: perhaps the resulting public alienation from deterrence could be cured by shrewdly packaged arms control proposals; perhaps as before, doctrinal innovations might be introduced to resolve the crisis; finally, perhaps a new generation of strategic weapons might be deployed that could evade the theorem. In this and the next chapter, I will discuss some consequences of simply abandoning extended deterrence in those theatres where the political culture makes the operation of the theorem strategically significant, since it is the effort to maintain extended deterrence that engages the theorem in the first place.

As early as 1963, General de Gaulle wrote,

> The Americans, our allies, our friends, had for a long time alone, a nuclear force. So long as they alone had such a force and so long as they showed the will to use it immediately if Europe was attacked – for Europe alone could then be attacked – the Americans saw to it that the question of invasion did not pose an issue and that a [Soviet] attack was improbable. Then it was a question for the Atlantic Alliance, that is to say, for the American Command, to deploy in Europe and in American tactical and strategic air power capable of delivering atomic bombs (for at that time only aircraft could do so) and thus protect Europe. It was also a question of lining up in Europe itself conventional land, naval and air forces which could assure the deployment and use of the atomic means.

One can say that during this time deterrence played its full role and that there was a practically insurmountable barrier to an invasion of Europe. I cannot overestimate the extent of the service, fortunately passive, that the Americans have thus rendered during this period to the freedom of the world.

Since then, the Soviets have acquired also their own nuclear force and this force is powerful enough to endanger the very life of America. . . .Ever since, the Americans . . . find themselves faced with the possibility of direct destruction.

Then, the immediate . . . defense of Europe, and the military concurrence of the Europeans, which were lately the fundamental basis of [American] strategy pass by force of circumstances into second place. . . . In these circumstances, no one in the world, in particular no one in America can say, if, when, when, how and to what extent, the American nuclear forces would be employed to defend Europe.[1]

There are numerous politico-strategic arrangements that are responsive to such an analysis, that is, that might result from the imperatives created by the collapse of US extended deterrence in the Euro–Japanese theatres (the Northern tier). At present, international security in this tier is dominated by a *bipolar* arrangement that includes both elements of confrontation and co-operation. This system, in theory, might yield to (a) a *unipolar* arrangement, that is, an empire or a federation; or (b) a *multipolar* system; or (c) a system without poles, either *autarkic* (with many nuclear states, each independently threatening and threatened by its adversaries) or *universal* (for example, a league of nations pledged to collective security) or (d) the system of biopolarity might be preserved despite the deep erosion of extended deterrence. (This last possibility is the subject of Chapter 13.) Of these possibilities, (a) is beyond the realm of the likely and, at any rate, well beyond the scope of this book; (c) will be briefly discussed, while the discussion of (b) will comprise the main argument of this chapter.

Universality and autarky, the two variations of (c)'s system of widespread nuclear armament among states, might be characterized as 'all for one, and one for all' and 'every man for himself' respectively.[2] These arrangements are promising only if we ignore the highly developed deterrence apparatus of the bipolar relationship already in place. For example, with regard to a universal system, two observations must be made. First, *politically*, it is unlikely that both the US and Russia could credibly pledge a nuclear guarantee to every state threatened by an aggressor (indeed the waning credibility of an even less taxing regimen is precisely the subject of this book) unless they acted in concert, in which case the collective security arrangement is not really an advance over the present system. A formal system of collective security that requires the independent consensus of the superpowers obviates the system: without their concurrence it will not work, with their agreement it is not needed. Second, it is *strategically* absurd to think that a universal system could commit the superpowers to threats from any number of nuclear regional conflicts, whatever may be the likelihood of their political agreement on the merits of those conflicts and whatever may be the nature of the systems of the powers involved. The very fact that the non-superpower, nuclearized members of such an arrangement would have insecure retaliatory capacities (*vis-à-vis* the superpowers) would make the former bipolar actors more threatened. Far from the stable relationship of bipolar symbiosis, each superpower now must face numerous 'hair trigger' threats. And because the superpowers are also more threatening, they could not lower their nuclear profiles even in a world of universal nuclear armament. Such a system, therefore, would not really be a universal system without poles, but a precarious arrangement of collective security within a weak bipolar context. The same holds for an autarkic world. The mere possession of an 'independent' deterrent does not erase the overwhelming position of the superpowers, particularly their possession of damage limiting capabilities that are probably currently effective *only* against such smaller arsenals. Accordingly, neither autarkic nor collective security models lead us away from the alliance conundrum of extended deterrence that arises from the bipolar competition.

Thus we turn to (b), the multipolar option, Precisely what political form this might take, that is, whether it be the result of multinational integration and, if so, what states might be included, is a matter of speculation. It is nevertheless probably true that unless bipolarity is maintained (either through stable confrontation or disengagement) multipolarity will replace it. What are the strategic consequences of such a development? To put this question in the terms of Book I: if the dilemma of extended deterrence is ultimately resolved through multipolarity, how will *this* strategic innovation – more radical than any earlier doctrinal changes – play back into the (formerly) central relationship?

The literature on 'multipolarity' is, largely, nothing of the sort, but instead is devoted to questions of '*n*th' power problems, that is, to the horizontal proliferation of modest nuclear weapons capabilities.[3] These events can have no *polar* consequences unless the positions of the US and Russia are fundamentally affected thereby. Horizontal proliferation does not, by itself, establish poles or eliminate them in the present context of the MIRVs, highly accurate warheads and variable yields, versatile and numerous launchers of the superpowers. The fact, in part, explains why no federation of small nuclear powers can 'add up' to a polar power. At most, this literature can provide an inferential basis for determining by contrast how a multipolar world would function. For we know, by definition, that a truly multi*polar* world will not be a world of '*n*' nuclear powers (where '*n*' is an undetermined finite integer) that essentially replicates the bipolar world across *n*/2 conflicts.[4]

Such a world is described in *The Spread of Nuclear Weapons: More May be Better*[5] by Kenneth Waltz. Waltz quite correctly perceives that horizontal proliferation to '*n*' powers does not necessarily mean multipolarity. He begins his paper by contrasting the multipolar and bipolar worlds. While 'in a multipolar world there are too many powers to permit any of them to draw clear and fixed lines between allies and adversaries',[6] there are yet so few that the action of any single power is likely to affect the security of the others. In a bipolar world, the great powers depend militarily on themselves since the roughly equal sharing of burdens among allies is no longer possible in light of the vast differences in wealth among states and the tremendous costs of defence. These two distinctive factors of bipolarity – the sure knowledge of who is an adversary and who is not, and control over the maintenance and execution of military capabilities – lower the costs of uncertainty in a bipolar context, enabling states to calculate with greater precision the exact risks of conflict. When we factor in the magnitude of costs imposed by nuclear use in war and the increasing likelihood that nuclear weapons will in fact be used when a defending nuclear nation faces conquest, the cost/benefit analysis of a campaign of conquest almost always yields a negative result, favouring the status quo. To summarize:

> Miscalculations causes wars. One side expects victory at an affordable price, while the other side hopes to avoid defeat. Here the differences between conventional multipolar and nuclear bi-polar

> worlds are fundamental. . . . Uncertainty about outcomes does not work decisively against the fighting of wars in conventional worlds. . . . Calculations about nuclear war are differently made.[7]

For the purposes of our present study, we may leave aside Waltz's conclusion that such bipolar, nuclear-related calculations as have been drawn by the superpowers and led to the prudent avoidance of war would in fact be replicated among the many 'n' and '$n+1$' states. To draw such a conclusion requires that each of the new states have but a single, nuclear armed adversary; and also that each state actually have such an adversary, since otherwise the temptation to coercion of non-nuclear states would presumably enter the otherwise stable calculus drawn by Waltz; and that the extended deterrence of the superpowers be limited to parrying threats from the opposing superpower without resulting in any fundamental change in the bipolar relationship; as well as a host of assumptions about the nature of the political cultures of the *n*th nuclear powers. However this may be, Waltz's analysis is useful in constructing the deterrence environment of the multipolar world. For whatever the clarity of calculation and certainty of retaliation in the 'n' numbered world of modest nuclear states, very great complexity and uncertainty is introduced with a truly multipolar world. As Waltz observes, the loss of knowledge of who is an adversary and the loss of control of military capabilities tend to increase the difficulty of precise, mutually ascertainable calculation. This makes deterrence difficult, for the mechanism of deterrence is calculation.

What would a multipolar, strategic environment be like? What conditions would it bring about? What effects would a change to such a world bring in the US–USSR deterrence relationship?

A genuinely multipolar environment would contain more than two states targeting each other, with each polar nation possessing weapons in such depth that each could maintain a global conflict. We currently live in a world of two poles, not the geophysical north and south, but the geopolitical east and west. Despite the fact that there are at least five nations with deliverable nuclear weapons, there are only two 'poles', for only two of these nations entertain retaliatory ambitions of world-dominating dimensions (and possess the resources to realize their ambitions). Only the US and Russia have perceived a need to maintain not only a secure, second strike retaliatory force against a superpower possessing a similar force, but also to develop nuclear weapons in very great numbers that can be used without engaging that capability.[8] Whether for conquest or pre-emption, or to enhance deterrence, only two states have entertained the global ambition to do more than simply deter attacks on their homeland. In the company of other nations, these two face the life-threatening war plans of their adversaries; but only they have found it necessary to oppose these threats with the variegated and complex array of a superpower arsenal. For the world to become tri-polar, then, another power would have to enlarge its retaliatory ambitions to require something vastly more than a mere secure second strike countervalue force, and be able to field such a force.

We are, in some respects, closer to such an environment than is usually thought. For the strategic world does not consist of neat pairs of '*n*th' power nuclear states, each performing a wary *pas-de-deux*. Nuclear targeting is instead very largely targeting against superpowers. Of the present three non-polar nuclear states, the UK targets Russia while France[9] and China[10] possibly target both the US and Russia. Nevertheless, the retaliatory ambitions mentioned above that create a strategic 'pole' have not come into being. What conditions have been missing? There must be a threat present that would justify the enormous expense and diversion of resources to nuclear development; that threat must be unparried by other means; the resources, human and material, must be available for such a re-allocation.

Of course, a threat of enormous magnitude has long been evident to those nations possessing independent nuclear deterrents. It was always clear that these deterrents originated in doubts about the vitality of the American assurance of extended deterrence and therefore, *a fortiori*, in an effort to deter Soviet attack. Thus Labour Party leader Hugh Gaitskell in 1960:

> I do not believe that when we speak of our having to have nuclear weapons of our own it is because we must make a contribution to the deterrent of the West. . . . [It arises instead] from doubts about the readiness of the United States government and its citizens to risk the destruction of their cities on behalf of Europe.[11]

And Conservative Minister of Defence Peter Thorneycroft in 1963:

> As an increasing number of more and more powerful missiles will be aimed at Washington and New York, can we be certain that a threat directed against our country would always be answered by an American counterthreat? And should we admit this certitude, would the Russians be equally persuaded? Is a deterrent under the exclusive control of America absolutely reliable?[12]

What has since developed, however, is the rapid erosion of such minimal security as the independent deterrents once gave. The fundamental move in a nuclear strategy in the mutually-thermonuclear age is the *fait accompli* by which an opponent is forced to either acquiesce or initiate hostilities at a level likely to provoke an assured destruction attack. The recent SS-20 deployments are accurate enough to suppress all but the on-station assured destruction SLBM force (and those few bombers of doubtful penetration on airborne alert) of the various independent deterrents. As a result, these states are 'pinned' as in chess, unable to use their defensive force without at the same time assuring the destruction of their societies.

Even this uncomfortable vulnerability is by no means a sufficient condition for multipolarity. Vulnerability initiates the impulse to heighten retaliatory goals but there must also be resources to achieve these goals (and the political will to mobilize these resources). Moreover, such ambitions are likely to remain unrealized, so long as such vulnerability is enveloped by the protection of a nuclear superpower. Hence the *polarity* of such ambitions, and the fact that *bi*polarity is maintained by extended deterrence.

For the purposes of this chapter, we have postulated a decline in the effectiveness of extended deterrence (owing to the political effect of the theorem discussed in Chapter 8). Then we have seen that, for an 'independent deterrent' to avoid self-deterrence and be effective against a polar state, the 'independent deterrent' must acquire the complex communications, surveillance and command facilities, the counterforce targeting and survivability of limited options, that characterize the superpower. In other words, to be effective – to avoid the consequences of what was above identified as 'the fundamental move in a nuclear strategy' – the independent deterrent replacing (rather than just supplementing) the lost extended deterrent, must be 'polar'.[13]

There remains the question of realizing such ambitions, the question of resources. Waltz writes,

> Great powers are strong not simply because they have nuclear weapons but also because their immense resources enable them to generate and maintain power of all types, military and other, at strategic and tactical levels. Entering the great-power club was easier when great powers were larger in number and smaller in size. With fewer and bigger ones, barriers to entry have risen. The club will long remain the world's most exclusive one. We need not fear

> that the spread of nuclear weapons will turn the world into a multipolar one.[14]

This is perhaps more optimistic than the facts warrant. It is not merely an unfortunate coincidence that it is in precisely those states where the political effects of the theorem are most acutely felt that the technology, technocracy and wealth exist to compensate for the effects of the theorem. Japan's GNP roughly equals that of the Soviet Union and will soon surpass it.[15] A European Defence Community with German participation could call on states whose combined GNP is twice that of the Soviet Union and roughly equal to the United States.[16] Furthermore, nuclear weapons are relatively inexpensive and, for states such as Japan, might appear to offer an option far less costly than the maintenance of conventional forces, an item that comprises the greatest part of the US defence budget.[17] Of course I concede the supremacy of the political and historical context, and I note that both Japan and the FRG are signatories of the Non-Proliferation Treaty,[18] and that the Japanese Constitution contains its famous renunciation of war and offensive weapons.[19] Yet the current political context is not immune to the calculus of strategic obligation and vulnerability. It is the purpose of this book to treat the parameters of nuclear strategy: one of these must be polarity.

If we assume that there are societies whose strategic dilemma results from the nexus of vulnerability (facing a superpower threat) and the withdrawal of previously credible protection (from a superpower), it is troubling that these are the same societies who possess the resources and know-how to acquire a superpower's arsenal. Should this acquisition occur, however unlikely this may be, multipolarity would be the result. What effect would this have on the deterrence relationship between the US and the USSR?

In Book I, I argued that the central relationship has for some time been one of great stability. Crises in vulnerability were actually felt in the extended relationship. The 'assumption of deterrence', I have further argued, was responsible for this remarkable stability. This assumption held that to any attack on the homeland of either superpower there would be a reply in kind, and that the immense devastation of nuclear weapons ensured that such retaliation would be impossible to prevent and measureless in its potential destruction. This assumption amounted to a supra-strategy, overlaid on the other relationships of extended deterrence, conventional forward defence, and so on which were dynamic (and not stalemated) variations of the classic deterrents of punishment and defence. This assumption of central deterrence tended to ensure stability. Many believe that mutual assured destruction, the inevitable consequence of the mutual possession of thermonuclear weapons, dictates this assumption and consequently this stability, but does it? Is the assumption dependent on bipolarity? The remainder of this chapter is devoted to these questions.

First, we shall see what conditions are necessary to the operation of the deterrence assumption and then determine how multipolarity affects these conditions. Second, we shall ask what conditions are peculiar to multipolarity, and from this what strategic effects might be expected from its emergence.

The deterrence assumption might be re-stated in this way: If either superpower determines that its 'vital interests' are at risk from the other superpower, it may decide to launch a society-crippling strike against the other superpower; but if that decision were to be made, there exists a secure retaliatory capacity in both superpowers such that a society-crippling retaliation would likely be the response. This responsive retaliatory superpower strike loses its deterrent effect, of course, in precisely those situations in which the first society's vital interests are life-threatened. So that to truly threaten the other superpower's vital interests, in the context described, is to ensure one's own destruction. Thus neither society can afford to permit its political or military leadership to jeopardize the other superpower's vital interests. The most obvious vital interests of the nation-state are its physical and ecological existence and, secondarily, the maintenance of the secure retaliatory capacity that undergirds the assumption (since once this is compromised there is no decisive reason for a superpower not to destroy its adversary, no matter how willing she may be to compromise, because this retaliatory capacity can, presumably, be reacquired and the threat of destruction re-imposed). Recognizing that there are many undefined terms in this very general characterization, we may nevertheless use this formulation to inquire into the conditions necessary for this 'assumption' to be well-founded.

(1) Each side must have the capacity to inflict a society-crippling destruction on the other, and this capability must be overt (recognized by both sides) and secure (able to function in any foreseeable context, including after a pre-emptive attack) and assured, that is, able to convey confidence that the mission will be executed despite defences, degraded communications, and so forth. The will to use this capability may be presumed, in the extreme conditions following the social

destruction of the attacked state, as an amalgam, perhaps, of revenge, a desire to cease further attacks, the prevention of the political domination of the postwar world by the adversary or, more simply, in the absence of all those restraints that have been destroyed in the initial attack. In the thermonuclear age, this capability has not required many weapons, although advances in delivery systems, air defences, and pre-emptive capabilities have made launcher requirements more extensive if their mission is to be assured.

(2) Each side must have enough information to be able to judge when her own vital interests are threatened by the other superpower. This is a matter of incomplete, but not imperfect, information, as the game theorists would say, for the underlying dynamics of the situation are well-understood by both sides even though the specific content of any interest may not be known. Because it is the conclusion of the deterrence assumption, described above, that each superpower must refrain from jeopardizing the vital interests of the other, there will be a certain motive for exaggerating what constitutes one's 'vital' interests (a bluff, if you will) and also for probing to determine the extent of one's freedom of action. In this grey area exist the Cuba and Berlin crises, and the chronology of the post-war intersection of US and Russian collisions. But whatever the extent of this grey area, it is assumed that the territorial integrity of the state, and the preservation of its means of protecting that integrity, are vital in the sense that the life of the state is jeopardized by their destruction. Sometimes these points are confused, even by sophisticated commentators. Thus Robert Jervis observes:

> President Kennedy was reported as saying that he thought the chances of war during the Cuban Missile crisis were one in three. If he believed this, he either placed an incredibly high value on prevailing or else did not understand probability-utility calculus. It is hard to accept the notion that Kennedy thought that the costs of war, diluted by twice the gains that would accrue if we won (i.e. the pay-off for standing firm when the odds are two to one that the Russians would back down), were anything like equal to the value of losing combined with twice the pay-off of a compromise (i.e. the pay-off for backing down when the odds are as stated).[20]

But President Kennedy's threat was not to initiate a nuclear attack on the USSR if they failed to back down in the crisis, dismantle the weapons and so on but rather:

> It shall be the policy of this nation to regard any nuclear missile launched from Cuba against any nation in the Western hemisphere as an attack by the Soviet Union on the United States requiring a full retaliatory response upon the Soviet Union.[21]

Thus he was not escalating the risk beyond the well-understood deterrence assumption; and it seems likely that, without the overwhelming conventional superiority the US enjoyed in the theatre, the US would not have been able to force the ultimate Russian withdrawal (and therefore this is not a matter, as is usually argued, of the American nuclear superiority at this time).

To put it somewhat differently, President Kennedy did not threaten to attack the USSR if nuclear weapons were not removed from Cuba. This would have amounted to a flouting of the deterrence assumption and would surely have justified Bertrand Russell's celebrated telegram.[22] Instead, the US initiated conventional preparations for invasion. This operation would have been decisive, excepting the possibility that an invasion force was met by an MRBM attack on the US from Cuba. For this reason the US declared that a nuclear attack on the US homeland would violate the deterrence assumption itself, thereby causing a nuclear retaliation *against the USSR*. Whatever President Kennedy may have believed the chances of war to be in Cuba, it is doubtful that he thought the chances of the deterrence assumption itself being violated – a nuclear attack on the US mainland – were very high, since he took such trouble to underscore that asssumption and placed such reliance on it.

Kennedy's 22 October statement, stripped of the diplomatic invocation of the Monroe Doctrine, simply said: if Cuba launches nuclear weapons against the US, the US will retaliate against Russia. In the context of an imminent US invasion this might be taken as: either remove the reason for the invasion or the US will proceed. Thus the ultimate resolution – removal plus a US guarantee of non-intervention – developed naturally (though not without great effort and skill) from the crisis.

It has often been observed that it is a shortcoming of deterrence theory that what may appear vital to one side may appear differently to the other. This is quite so. But for our purposes it is enough to say that the assumption of central deterrence is clear enough: namely, that the homeland of a superpower and the nuclear retaliatory capacity ensuring that homeland are vital interests, and are mutually recognized as such, whatever may be the perceived significance of other interests.

(3) Each side must be able to communicate its perception of its own interests to the other side. Fortunately, the very operation of a fundamental, shared 'assumption' makes much communication unnecessary. Little persuasion is required to convince an adversary that you regard your own destruction with more distaste than his or that you will be willing to endure his continued existence if it is a precondition of your own. Nevertheless, there may be 'vital' interests, the vitality of which the other side must be persuaded. Or, to put a different case, the stability of the deterrence assumption can be upset when a superpower appears to cease regarding as vital some interest hitherto protected. These situations require the art of crisis management, since it aims at a restoration of stability through convincing signalling. We have observed, in (1) and (2), that particular capabilities and information, respectively, are preconditions of the deterrence assumption. Convincing communication conveys this information.

Some messages may appear to jeopardize capabilities. Both sides must be able to avoid signalling an imminent attack (that is unintended) as well as to avoid perceiving the imminence of an attack that is apparent only. In light of the recent historical experiences of both superpowers – the June 1941 Nazi attack on Russia preceded by weeks of German reassurance and British and American warnings,[23] and the 7 December 1941 bombing of Pearl Harbor at the very hour of Japanese diplomatic exchanges[24] – it is to be expected that a certain jumpiness would prevail in their military relations even if their political relationship was not dominated by hostile suspicion. Furthermore, many so-called defensive measures are indistinguishable from the measures required by offensive or at least pre-emptive strategies. Thus ballistic missile defence (and civil defence) are shown in Chapter 10 to be integral parts of a nuclear war-fighting strategy and have as their objective the erosion of an adversary's assured destruction capacity. And, as has been frequently pointed out, the deployment of counter-silo weapons is a precondition for both second-strike proportionate response strategies *and* first-strike plans. No amount of diplomatic reassurance is likely to be effective in such contexts for it, too, is exactly what would be expected if the adversary were in fact planning a surprise attack. The irony of these double-edged preparations has led many commentators to oppose them on the ground that, whatever the intention of their proponents, they must at best send an ambivalent message, undermining the stability of the deterrence assumption in crises. Indeed the term 'crisis stability' has been invented to distinguish the contribution of this sort of communication from strategic stability generally, which may have different requirements.

Fortunately, both sides have developed national systems that reduce the need for communication (on this issue) to only those unmistakable gestures that, by their ferocity, would moot any other attempts at signalling.[25] These systems are the array of satellite reconnaissance and their associated computer-assisted interpretative means, and the satellite-assisted communication to the SLBM fleets. When one side has determined to disarm the other it will be perfectly clear and, so long as the other elements of the deterrence assumption hold, it will be a straightforward enough task to absorb such an attack and still execute the assured destruction, society-crippling mission. So long as these national features of inter- and intra-state communication hold, each side will know beyond doubt that its adversary (whatever its intentions) has launched weapons in the hundreds (or thousands) and that, without further communication, a commensurate retaliatory response can be assured.

Given these three conditions for the deterrence assumption, and the description thus offered of their operation in a bipolar world, how will they be affected by a multipolar environment?

(1) The addition of one superpower to the present powers would not seriously erode the assured destruction capabilities of the US or Russia, if it were thought necessary to maintain such a capability against this new power. In light of heightened air defences and the enhanced pre-launch vulnerability of bombers and ICBMs, this capability resides, in the final analysis, in the SLBM fleet. While the USSR maintains a larger SLBM force (950 SLBM launchers compared to 576 US SLBMs), it has chosen to put a smaller percentage of its warheads at sea (38 per cent compared to 50 percent US).[26] Hypothesizing that a withdrawal of extended deterrence would induce multipolarity and therefore that the Soviet Union would wish to acquire new targets in that country that elected to become a competing superpower, without augmenting the SLBM force (as by further MIRVing, for example) the USSR would retain numbers sufficient for an assured destruction capability *vis-à-vis* all superpowers.[27] This is equally true of the US.[28]

The difficulties for the present superpowers would occur, instead, with respect to their bomber and ICBM forces.[29] The force multiplication of MIRVing, in the context of multiple opposing superpowers, would mean that an even smaller fraction of the potentially hostile forces of the other superpowers would be exhausted in the pre-emptive destruction of a single superpower's land based arsenal, and the salutary deterrent effects of reserve force counter-silo targeting, discussed in Chapter 9, would be foregone. This need not erode the secure, second strike capabilities required by the deterrence assumption; it does mean, however, that a superpower would be more vulnerable to an exchange of counterforce attacks intended to erode the target nation's capability down to its anti-cities weapons, at which point the target state presumably would be self-deterred as to less than vital threats.

(2) Things would become somewhat more difficult for the present superpowers with respect to the information conditions of the assumption. While it may be assumed that the security of the territory of the US is a vital interest of that state, and a similar assumption holds regarding the USSR, nations may be inclined to be sceptical that the security of a third-party state is a vital interest to their adversaries. This is, of course, an element in the problem of extended deterrence in the bipolar world. Indeed were this not the case, bipolarity would probably persist. In that interim period between bipolar and multipolar worlds, this scepticism would meet its greatest test. During the transitional period from non-nuclear power to nuclear superpower, a pre-existing superpower might not credit the other superpower's guarantee to the new state and might attack that state before it can go nuclear, hoping to evade the rondeaux of retaliation. The transitional power attacked would then have to rely on the discredited protector at a moment when that nuclear guarantee is at its weakest.

In other respects the information conditions are not much changed by multipolarity. We may still assume that a state's homeland and its retaliatory capacity would be vital interests. The grey areas would become greater, no doubt, and therefore the tendency toward crisis would become greater. There would be more areas that can be plausibly maintained to be 'vital' and more opportunities for co-extensive interests.

(3) Perhaps the greatest loosening of the conditions necessary to the deterrence assumption would occur with respect to communication. It might not be possible, in a multipolar environment, to determine the national origin of the attack originating from an SLBM force or, even if this be done, then to communicate the necessary re-targeting to a strategic reserve residing in a SLBM force.

In the bipolar context, the targets for the SLBM force are preplanned; this fact, and the virtual impossibility of detection confer an assuredness to retaliation that must give even the most reckless aggressor pause. But in the multipolar environment the stealth and security of the SLBM can be a destabilizing element: an attacking

SLBM force can pre-empt ICBMs and bombers without disclosing the identity of the attacking force, which identity in any case must then be relayed to a retaliating SLBM force who can no longer simply pre-plan an attack against a single, certain adversary.

Similarly, concerns about ICBM vulnerability are greatly muted in the bipolar world by the deterrence assumption: one superpower is hardly likely to launch a pre-emptive anti-ICBM strike against the other inflicting 12–20 million ancillary deaths (ancillary, that is, to the mission of silo killing) and assume, with confidence (or even daring), that the cycle of retaliation has been avoided because the ostensible targets of the strike were weapons and not cities. But where the launch was disguised, and the targeted country could not be certain to have destroyed its adversaries (and accomplished even the most barren postwar objectives) when it used its retaliatory force, the terms of doubt begin to shift. Now the attacking country can reasonably doubt that retaliation will take place, whereas in the bipolar context it could not be reasonably confident it would not. Moreover, in a multipolar world, after a disguised SLBM counterforce attack, the third or fourth powers might be forced to complete the attack simply to avoid the possibility of mistaken retaliation, hoping – as a second best alternative – that without an available proportionate reply the state attacked would husband its SLBM retaliation.

There is even the grotesque possibility of a cycle of pre-emptive attempts in which an attacked nation – having been forced to go to a launch-on-warning posture since the presence of multiple superpowers deprived the SLBM force of a proportionate response capability – would attempt to protect itself from further attacks by responding with ICBM strikes against an 'innocent' party. This complexity is compounded by the fact that while multipolarity would force launch-on-warning or launch-under-attack programming, it would have the side-effect of masking precisely against whom the pre-attack programs ought to be directed.

While it is usually in the interests of both parties in a bipolar world to maintain communications with each other (and certainly in the interests of their clients), this might not be the case in a multipolar world. Jamming and false signals could not be interpreted as necessarily originating with a particular adversary. Moreover, the important national means of reassurance that exist in the satellite surveillance systems – on which the deterrence assumption has in part depended – might be undermined by a state wishing to introduce uncertainty. It would be in the multipolar environment that such 'blinding' would have its maximum effects. We are inclined to forget, in the stable political environment of bipolarity, that wars have been launched in earlier eras in the midst of shifting coalitions. Indeed, I would think it is obvious that the emergence of nuclear multipolarity would do much to blur the ideological lines between East and West.

It appears that the conditions of the deterrence assumption would be weakened by the arrival of multipolarity. The capabilities for assured destruction would still exist, the most fundamental vital interests would still ensure commitment, and it would remain possible – in all but the most complex situations – to communicate the information necessary to make the scheme of deterrence function. Yet there would be doubt present in a multipolar system, and this would loosen the bonds of deterrence. The deterrence assumption is, finally, a strategic *assumption*.[30] To the extent that any of its simple fundamentals is called into doubt – can they retaliate? will they retaliate? will they retaliate against us? – the stability of assured assumptions gives way to net assessments.

In the next section of this chapter, we will canvass the conditions peculiar to multipolarity. First, however, it ought to be conceded that whatever the effects of multipolarity on nuclear deterrence between the US and Russia multipolarity is likely to enhance general deterrence. There will be fewer wars in the world than there would otherwise be (although conceivably greater terrorist activity). As Beaufre has observed,

> The existence of a multilateral nuclear system produces an additional risk of instability and this restores to the nuclear level the deterrent capacity which, in the bilateral situation, tends to disappear as soon as the forces reach a certain degree of nuclear equilibrium.[31]

Beyond this 'hopeful' aspect, there are several troubling elements that would arise within the conditions that make multipolarity possible. The most obvious of these is the problem of attracting pre-emption during the acquisition period obliquely referred to by Beaufre. While it is unlikely that the renunciation of extended deterrence would give way to the complete desertion of former allies, it is probably not to be expected that substantial assistance in acquiring nuclear weapons would be forthcoming either. In the case of the US and the UK, statutes as well as treaties forbid such transfers. There is likely to be a period of transition in which the old nuclear guarantee is scarcely credible but the new capability is not on line.

Also peculiar to multipolarity is the problem of catalytic war, once discussed in the context of Sino–Soviet–American relations.[32] It is difficult to imagine a national leadership so reckless as to initiate an attack in the hope that it would be able to lure its competitors into war while itself remaining aloof, waiting only to pick up the pieces. It is perhaps not so difficult to imagine a superpower, in the multipolar context, being tempted to triangulate its ambitions by forcing a reluctant ally to join a war once begun or even attempting some disarming strike in the hope that the uncertainty of its origin (plus the pressure of other superpowers) would make retaliation less likely. Such catalytic strikes are far more plausible once war has begun.[33] Catalytic war, however, demands not simply uncertainty but positive deception; given the costs of failure, could any conceivable gain justify attempting such a deceit?

Here too belongs the question: to what degree are the chances of arms control agreements altered by the presence of more than two superpowers? One may presume that, since the US and Soviet models do not exhaust all the possibilities, that the problems of force structure asymmetry and differing strategic concepts that have bedevilled SALT[34] will be made even more complex if new superpowers are included. If, on the other hand, they are not included, it is difficult to imagine any agreement on limitation between the parties who seek it. Against this shortcoming we must balance the incentive that multipolarity is likely to give the superpowers to conclude multilateral arms control agreements, insofar as they are persuaded that the further proliferation of weapons imperils them. Moreover, without the responsibilities of extended deterrence, some considerations that may have militated against agreements in the past would be removed. It remains to be seen whether the removal of such considerations, usually thought to have been given insufficient weight, will be overmatched by the complications introduced by the addition of new national negotiating partners. Certainly the pace of technological advance will only be accelerated when three or four nations are trying to perfect a particle beam missile defence, for example, rather than merely two. At the same time there lies the quixotic possibility of inducing arms control by the threat to ally with that nation making the most forthcoming concessions.

This last notion depends on negating the rule that is believed to hold in the bipolar world, that nuclear weapons are non-additive and that alliances are, in this respect, beside the point. If this is changed in the multipolar world, it is far from a reassuring change for, as has been observed even by commentators who favour the proliferation of nuclear deterrents, the stability of the present alliance system reflects the stability of nuclear politics. To the extent nuclear weapons capabilities are additively significant at the superpower level, they lend a political significance to alliance formation that recalls the pre-nuclear period.

More troubling, however, is the prospect of competing nuclear strategies. This, in a multipolar world, is a function of overlapping extensions of deterrence. We may observe this today, even in the bipolar context, with respect to French and NATO strategy regarding Germany. While NATO contemplates the forward defence perimeter strategy of flexible response, resorting to nuclear weapons as a last resort and attempting to stabilize the central front with conventional weapons, the French strategy calls for the use of tactical nuclear weapons (the 120 km, 10 KT Pluton and the 350 km Hades) as a threshold signal, followed by rapid escalation to countercity attacks on the Soviet Union. This has the paradoxical effect of deterring West Germany (since to the extent it becomes a theatre of war it becomes the target of French nuclear weapons), while providing a sanctuary for the Soviet Union so long as her forces don't begin to threaten French territory. If this strategy were implemented, NATO strategy could be collapsed by rapid French escalation.

Extended deterrence has tended to conceal these differences in national strategies. A 1965 SRI study arrived at the comparison shown in Table 12.1.

The difficulty posed by these varying approaches is that the most highly escalatory one is likely to drag all other strategies with it. It will not be possible for Russia, for example, to determine whether the MIRVs striking her come from a US Poseidon, a US Poseidon dedicated to NATO or from an SSBN developed by a third party. This renders measured, limited response strategies like the Countervailing Strategy absurd but, in a multipolar world, it does not allow for their replacement with total response/limited commitment strategies. The result must be the least stable amalgam: the commitment of immense retaliation on behalf of interests conceded to be less than vital. And yet it is precisely those nations who wish to maintain a low nuclear threshold *and* commence homeland attacks if that threshold is violated who are the likeliest candidates for new superpower status for the very reason that the current superpowers would not maintain such risks. These new candidates for a superpower's nuclear arsenal face an immediate threat from an adversary whose campaign, if not halted,

Table 12.1 Salient features of strategic concepts for the defence of Western Europe

	United States	*Great Britain*	*France*	*Germany*
Conventional Warfare	Prolongation of conventional defence as long as possible	Short conventional defence to ascertain Soviet intentions	No conventional defence except for border incidents	Short conventional defence at border to ascertain Soviet intentions, but with a very low nuclear threshold
Tactical Nuclear Warfare	Employment of tactical weapons in a selective manner	Employment of tactical weapons in demonstration of resolve and then in conjunction with strategic forces	Immediate nuclear retaliation on Russia	Almost immediate use of battlefield nuclear weapons in zone of conflict with possible demonstration strikes on Soviet territory

Source: Amme, *Problems Posed by Conflicting Views Concerning Nuclear Weapons* (SRI, 1965), p. 34.

will be fought on their territory; so they must rely on the threat of prompt and overwhelming retaliation, not proportionate and protracted exchanges.

This brings us to the unavoidable point of specifying the candidates for new superpower status.

It is not the purpose of this book to speculate on political events but only to establish the significant strategic alternatives which events may or may not bring to life. It must be clear from the foregoing, however, that the candidates for new superpower status are not those states, as might otherwise be thought, who possess independent deterrents at the present time. These deterrents do not contribute to extended deterrence, and were not intended to. Insofar as they are reactions to the possibility of national annihilation, they are modest perhaps outmoded efforts to establish a kind of deterrence assumption, bilaterally, with the Soviet Union (or, conceivably in the case of the *force de frappe*, bring about a certain relationship between France and Germany). But none of these countries is the focal point for the resources, technology, technocracy *and* the threat that would justify the expense[35] and national diversion of energy necessary to acquire a superpower's arsenal. The possessors of the independent deterrents do not face the threat (France) or do not have the resources (China) or fulfill neither of these preconditions (UK) to mount a polar force.

The two nations who stand at this peculiar nexus[36] are the Federal Republic of Germany (FRG) and Japan, both powers who have renounced nuclear weapons and who are protected by the American nuclear 'umbrella'. Indeed it is important to draw the line connecting these two facts.

The negotiations by which the FRG renounced the production of nuclear weapons took place in London in 1954. West Germany was represented by its Chancellor, Konrad Adenauer, who clearly depended upon the vital American guarantee as a condition for West Germany's foregoing atomic arms. Adenauer wrote that after he made the declaration renouncing nuclear weapons for Germany, Dulles arose and said:

> Mr Chancellor, you have just declared that the Federal Republic of Germany renounces the production of [nuclear] weapons on its own soil. You meant this declaration, I assume, to be valid only *rebus sic stantibus* – as all declarations and obligations in international law are!

To which Adenauer replied: 'You have interpreted my declaration correctly.' Accordingly, for our own period, we also should not view German renunciation in isolation from the vitality and viability of the American extended commitment of nuclear protection.

The FRG is bound by the Paris Agreement of 23 October 1954 – the outcome of the London conference – and the Protocol on Armaments Control. This provides:

> Article 1 of the Protocol: The Federal Republic of Germany undertakes not to manufacture on its territory any atomic, biological or chemical weapons. . . .
>
> Article 3: The size of the stocks of nuclear, biological, and chemical weapons shall be decided by a majority vote of the Council of the West European Union (WEU).
>
> Annexes I to IV spell out the declaration relating to West Germany in fuller detail. They define atomic, biological and chemical weapons; they state which weapons are not to be produced in Western Germany; and they indicate which armaments are to be controlled as a matter of principle within the WEU.[37]

This treaty is not with the United States, but between the FRG and a group of nation-states who comprise the Western European Union (WEU), a body specifically constituted to limit West German rearmament. Largely moribund for thirty years, the WEU may prove to be the vehicle by means of which West Germany will finally gain access to nuclear weapons.

On 27 October 1984 the foreign and defence ministers of Britain, France, Italy, the FRG and the three Benelux countries resuscitated the WEU and thus took the first step toward the creation of a purely European defence force since the project to form a European Defence Community collapsed in 1954. The particular membership of the WEU has several advantages over NATO or the EEC for such an enterprise: it includes France (which NATO's Eurogroup, its policy-making body, does not) and excludes Greece and Denmark (whose presence in NATO has made nuclear planning more difficult) and excludes neutral Ireland whose presence in the EEC makes defence discussions within the European community troublesome. Importantly, it excludes the United States and Canada. France and West Germany have proposed that the WEU staff be delegated the task of integrating weapons production, a NATO objective thus far unachieved.

The US has pushed for the revival of the WEU, reminiscent of the Nixon reversal of Johnson's efforts to stem proliferation to Europe. One wonders, however, whether the White House fully appreciates the possibility that the WEU offers Germany a way-station in its transition to nuclear status. Nuclear weapons could be dedicated to such a group – France and Britain are already nuclear states – initially with West German collaboration in the formulation of strategy accompanied by West German financial contributions, eventually with West German production of WEU nuclear assets, finally with the devolution of those deployments on West German soil to the FRG.

A European defense force follows the analysis and proposals of the late Hedley Bull. In a series of powerful and influential papers, Professor Bull advocated 'the Europeanist alternative'. In the spring of 1983, Bull's article 'European Self-Reliance and the Reform of NATO' appeared in *Foreign Affairs*;[38] it merits serious attention. Bull attributes the recent centrifugal drives within the Alliance to many causes – including differences over trade exacerbated by the recession, European uninterest in the restoration of US pre-eminence in world affairs, and conflicts over how best to respond to the political and economic upheavals in the Third World. But 'more important than any of the above . . . are the differences over the security of Western Europe'.[39]

> [In] Western Europe . . . the security of the region is perceived to be threatened, and is in fact threatened, not only by the military power of the Soviet Union but also by the possibility of war itself, especially of nuclear war, which could begin not only as the result of failure to deter the Soviet Union, but also . . . as the consequence of decisions taken by the United States.
>
> It is true that the security of the United States also rests on a structure of understandings with the Soviet Union . . . . But the United States is not as vulnerable to the effects of decisions on matters of nuclear peace and war taken by the West European countries as the latter are to the effects of decisions taken in Washington: it is the West European countries which are dependent on the United States for a nuclear deterrent against a Soviet attack, and it is on their soil that American nuclear weapons are deployed that can bring destruction upon them but whose use they are not able to control.
>
> Underlying the peace movement in the West European countries and the wider spectrum of opinion that is uneasy about our present

> defense arrangements, there is the correct perception that the risks of alliance with the United States on present terms have grown to such an extent that they threaten to outweigh the gains. This points to the conclusion that the West European countries should seek to assume greater control of their own security, not by leaving the Atlantic Alliance but at least by seeking to change its structure.[40]

This, in a more graceful and limpid exposition, is the outcome derived from the 'theorem' in Chapter 8. It is precisely because of the decoupling/uncoupling phenomenon that the US nuclear guarantee has a 'double-edged nature' 'which on the one hand serve[s] to deter attack by an adversary but on the other hand expose[s] [Europe] to increased risks in the event of war'.[41]

The solution that Bull and others propose is a nuclear-armed European defence force. The 'countries of Western Europe need to take steps towards providing themselves with nuclear deterrent forces that will in due course assume the United States' function of neutralizing any Soviet nuclear threat'.[42] Bull recognizes, as few critics have, that European anti-nuclear sentiment does not preclude such a force – as many Americans believe – because he correctly identifies the source of that sentiment in the consequences of American extended deterrence.

> The anxieties, including the many legitimate ones, which large sections of public opinion have today about our present dependence on nuclear weapons in no way preclude this course. For these anxieties derive in part not from reluctance to recognize the role that nuclear weapons must continue to play in our security, but from the fact that the particular nuclear weapons on which we chiefly depend are controlled by an ally whose policies in the matter of security are substantially at variance with those of the West European countries. In France, of course, where there are no foreign nuclear weapons or proposals to deploy them, but rather a national nuclear force, there is a broad basis of public support for the government's approach to nuclear security. It is notable also that, in Britain, public opinion polls indicate a majority against deployment of the US-controlled cruise missiles, but also a majority for retention of a British nuclear force. This should not be put down to misguided nationalist sentiment in these two countries; it is eminently arguable that our security is better served by nuclear forces that we control than by those we do not.[43]

Bull acknowledges that a European nuclear force is not immediately attainable, and thus his initial prescription is modest.

> A first step in this direction would be the establishment of a European Nuclear Planning Committee, analogous to the NATO one, to which Britain and France would report on their policies in regard to nuclear weapons, and at which other European governments could make known their concerns. A European political authority controlling nuclear forces of its own is indeed beyond the bounds of practicability at present, but this does not preclude the taking of steps toward a European role for the Anglo–French forces, especially at a time when concern about dependence on US weapons is high in Western Europe, and a broad consensus about policy toward the East unites the West European countries.[44]

And he also recognizes that the role of the FRG is crucial to any European defence force. While such a force may begin as simply an Anglo–French force with heightened retaliatory ambitions and an expanded defense perimeter, it must soon accommodate a larger role for West Germany.

> A Europeanist policy is not possible unless a more positive role comes to be played by West Germany. Germany is the largest and richest country in Europe. It is only on the basis of West German power that a West European counterpoise to the Soviet Union can be constructed. This means that West Germany will need to play some role, even if at first a small one, in the control of European nuclear forces; that West Germany's already considerable preponderance in West European conventional land forces will increase; that the discriminatory arms control provisions applying to West Germany under the 1954 agreements must further erode, if not disappear altogether; and that West Germany must come to play a more prominent role in the taking of political and strategic decisions.[45]

It is refreshing to encounter such forthrightness regarding a subject usually characterized by a resolute refusal to grasp the nettle. It is pleasurable to find such a thoughtful and distinguished scholar whose analysis of an important problem accords with one's own. But how disturbing it is to see such analysis deployed in behalf of the 'solution' one most fears. For I cannot believe that West Germany will long acquiesce in a defence community dominated by Anglo–French interests, once the FRG has been able to use such a community to legitimate a nuclear role for herself. Professor Bull's prescriptions are a perfectly logical, almost an inevitable response to the current situation. But what situation will they in turn create? And what will *its* logic be? Even if the WEU is the initial umbrella for a European nuclear force, will it be the ultimate configuration of nuclear possessory interests in Europe? The dilemma for the West is nicely stated in Eden's remark:

> If Germany is to be neutral and disarmed, who will keep her disarmed? If she is to be neutral and armed, who will keep her neutral?[46]

Where the costs of credulity can be so high, one must move with great caution. I remain profoundly sceptical of the long-term positive contributions of a European Defence Force.

Japan has been similarly *officially* committed to a policy of no manufacture of nuclear weapons, no introduction nor acquisition of nuclear weapons. The Japan Defence Agency has issued two White Papers on this subject. In the first, it was argued that the possession of nuclear weapons would not be illegal if they did not exceed the minimum needed for defence.[47] The second White Paper reiterated that strategic nuclear weapons exclusively for defence were constitutional while at the same time declaring that, generally speaking, nuclear weapons were offensive and Japan need not have them.[48] The Japanese government continues to observe the four principles stated by Prime Minister Eisaku Sato: to develop nuclear energy for peaceful purposes only; to encourage nuclear disarmament; not to possess or produce nuclear weapons; to rely on the US nuclear umbrella to deter a nuclear attack.[49]

Yet recent polls disclose a dramatic shift in Japanese opinion regarding the acquisition of nuclear weapons by Japan. Surveys now show that a majority of Japanese businessmen, for example, believe that Japan ought to possess nuclear weapons. Other polls reveal that from 1976 to 1979 the figures measuring the number of Japanese who believed Japan would acquire nuclear weapons within ten years went from 28 percent to 40 percent.[50] Any political development that brought to the public consciousness the consequences of the 'theorem' proposed in Chapter 8 could only increase these numbers. If, for example, the Soviet Union were to transfer a substantial number of SS-20s to their Eastern districts as once contemplated by the then Soviet leader Yuri Andropov, as a countermove to the recent stationing of F-16 fighter-bombers at Misawa; if a collapse of the Philippines regime forced the US to abandon its bases there and as a consequence intensify its presence in Japan; if the Korean truce were to fail – but it is useless to speculate. It ought to be obvious that a great many events could have the effect of moving Japanese opinion in the direction of acquiring a nuclear force because the underlying strategic logic of the situation makes the US extended deterrent so politically precarious.

Of course, such developments, if they come at all, will not come instantly. Both the FRG and Japan lack suitable test sites and delivery systems. Neither has an early warning capability, sophisticated satellite warning system or remote interception sites.[51] The most suitable Soviet targets are 6000 miles away from Japan and neither West Germany nor Japan has a suitable SSBN system though both possess nuclear powered submarines,[52] and Japan – who must import 99 per cent of her energy – is a leader in the field of nuclear technology.

Without speculating on the political realities and the likelihood, however remote, of West Germany or Japan bringing about multipolarity, it is sufficient to observe that such a development will have profound effects on what is now called the 'central relationship'. Mutual assured destruction may prevail but the deterrence assumption with which it is often confused and whose stability is often attributed to it is likely to become obscured. This has been noted earlier in this chapter with respect to the hitherto stabilizing role of the SLBM; orbital weapons, for example, also achieve in a multipolar environment a destabilizing character absent in the bipolar context.

Perhaps most troubling is that, beyond the fact that multipolarity does not ensure the spread of the deterrence assumption and to some extent weakens it with respect to the present superpowers, multipolarity makes war termination, should deterrence fail, immensely more difficult. Then warring parties must calculate the costs, once their own nuclear forces have been degraded, of ceasing war in a context in which significant damage limitation may, for the first time, be available to a third party.

The Nobel laureate Steven Weinberg has observed,

> [P]hysicists generally are aware, that problems in celestial mechanics are usually very easily solved. It's very easy to predict what will happen when you have just two bodies. When you have three bodies, it gets much more difficult and, at a certain point, you get into a situation which is now technically known as chaos; that is, the

> outcome of any situation is so sensitive to the initial conditions that it is impossible to predict what will happen.[53]

This, one fears, describes the complexity introduced by superpower proliferation, that is, the acquisition by other states of nuclear force structures comparable to those today possessed only by the US and the Soviet Union.

In the next chapter, we will survey another possible compensation for the political crisis pregnant in US extended deterrence. Chapter 13 explores various means of reducing the nuclear threat to those states protected by US extended deterrence (while Chapter 12 has examined ways of parrying that threat). Among the ways to be discussed are various political accommodations, including arms control agreements and also enhanced defence capabilities.

13 Alternatives to Nuclear Deterrence

Ché dove l'argomento de la mente
s'aggiugne al mal volere ed al a possa,
nessun riparo vi può far la gente.
(for where the equipment of the mind is joined to evil will and to power men can make no defence against it.)

Canto XXXI, *Inferno*

In the preceding chapter I argued that extended deterrence might be replaced by multiplying nuclear deterrents; that actually to constitute a force that was not, in the present strategic environment, self-deterred, these new independent nuclear forces would require sophisticated surveillance, command arrangements, and selective, counterforce capability; that such forces would amount to a 'polar' rearrangement of the current system with uncertain results for nuclear deterrence.

If one argues, however, that to preserve an environment that is stable for central deterrence the US must preserve bipolarity, how can bipolarity be preserved when the means of doing so lie in preserving a credible extended deterrent and such a credible extended deterrent grows increasingly either less likely or less acceptable? Yet absent such an extended deterrent, those nations with sufficient resources, technology and technocracy and who face such threats to their security that would justify their acquisition of a 'polar' force, would by such a move rearrange the relationship of the present superpowers into a multipolar relation. This is our problem. Recalling the four great transformations in nuclear strategy that were discussed in Book I and were precipitated by four critical periods of vulnerability, we might call this problem, 'the fifth crisis'.

It might be, nevertheless, that even a greatly diminished extended deterrent would be satisfactory if the threat it is intended to parry were itself reduced. In this chapter, we explore three ways of reducing that threat: enhancing conventional deterrence, negotiating arms control agreements, deploying ballistic missile defenses.

CONVENTIONAL DEFENCE

On 16 November 1982, speaking before the Military Committee of the North Atlantic Assembly, McGeorge Bundy put the case for an enhanced conventional NATO force as an initial step toward a no-first-use policy for NATO.[1] In so doing, he emphasized the conviction of many within the Alliance, regardless of their willingness to adopt a pledge of no-first-use, that conventional re-building in NATO is overdue. Reliance on the use of nuclear weapons was increasingly becoming, in Raymond Aron's words, 'a bluff'.[2] An enhanced conventional defence, it has been argued by Michael Howard, Lawrence Freedman, and Jonathan Alford among others, would lessen this reliance and raise the nuclear threshold.[3] At the same time, it has been argued by Bernard Rogers and Henry Kissinger that the sagging credibility of the threat of first use must be bolstered by a credible conventional threat.[4]

The broad consensus among critics of Alliance strategic affairs that a greater conventional effort is required arises from two quite different convictions. Some believe the reliance on nuclear weapons must be reduced; others think that reality has already reduced such reliance, as a plausible option, and force planning must acknowledge that fact. Some commentators, like Bundy, believe both these propositions. And all rely on the unstated assumption that conventional deployments, at least in some contexts or at some levels, are fungible with nuclear systems. Accordingly, in this section, we ask whether or not extended deterrence might be replaced altogether by an enhanced conventional force.

The dilemma for the states in the extended theatre with respect to conventional deployment arises from the decoupling/uncoupling phenomenon. A relatively weak US conventional commitment would serve as a 'powder trail' to the American central deterrent, which would be an enhanced threat, to be sure, but one that invites decoupling in a period of parity in central systems; while a robust conventional force structure appears to permit the US President to choose a commitment confined to forces in Europe, preserving a homeland sanctuary for the superpowers, and uncoupling the extended nuclear deterrent. Thus if conventional forces, including US forces, were too strong they would, in the eyes of many Europeans, weaken deterrence since they would tend to weaken the nuclear link between a European battlefield and the United States. Such a defence would run the risk of inviting a protracted conventional conflict in

Europe, with all the destruction that would surely follow. So although Europeans, for the most part, have slowly come round to recognizing the vital role that conventional forces play in deterrence, they have stopped short of wanting to build up that role to such a point that the nuclear element would be markedly downgraded.[5] For this reason, among others, the Lisbon force structure goals[6] were never vigorously pursued by the European members of the Alliance, and the frank acceptance of the failure to achieve these goals provided the impetus for MC 14/2, the NATO policy decision that adopted the theatre correlatives of Massive Retaliation. Only by emphasizing the possibility of decoupling was the US able to win adoption of MC 14/3, the Kennedy Administration's proposed NATO strategic plan that required a greatly strengthened conventional commitment. Thus Robert McNamara was in the awkward position of disparaging the US extended deterrent by arguing that 'the threat of an incredible action is not an effective deterrent'[7] in an effort to win support for MC 14/3's force levels, while at the same time reassuring Europeans of the continuing American nuclear commitment. This dilemma is a predictable consequence of the 'theorem' discussed in Chapter 8[8] and it led, predictably, to conflict within the Alliance, culminating in the French withdrawal from military planning within NATO and France's acquisition of her own central deterrent. The US, however, was able to persuade the remaining members of the Alliance of the necessity of MC 14/3 and thus, as was argued in Book I, was able in an extended theatre to compensate for an erosion in effective deterrence by means of a shift in strategy.

MC 14/3 may be summarized in part as providing that:

1) In the event of a Soviet attack, NATO will initially fight a conventional battle. A figure of 'five' or 'a few' days is usually quoted for this phase.

2) NATO will eventually resort to tactical nuclear weapons when conventional defense fails.

3) Initial nuclear use will be on a limited 'demonstrational' scale.[9]

MC 14/3, like MC 14/2, is a doctrinal document that sets forth the theatre policies of the prevailing central strategic doctrine. If we assume an end to such centrally-derived theatre nuclear doctrines, what would the successor to MC 14/3 – which sets forth conventional doctrine – look like? What would, that is, a non-nuclear NATO war plan be like?

It would be governed by at least four important structural constraints: (1) that NATO is a *defensive* alliance that must prepare for a Warsaw Pact *offensive*; (2) that a forward defence is required by the geopolitical position of West Germany; (3) that the Alliance's strongest member is separated from the theatre of conventional operations by a vast ocean; (4) that the Alliance is multi-national, and therefore national tactical styles, the non-integration of forces and the absence of inter-operability of weapons systems, zones of national deployment arising from other than military considerations, and the complexities of decision making at the political level are likely to cause difficulty in executing whatever strategy is employed.

By far the most important of these constraints is the assumption of the defensive nature of the Alliance. To this it may be objected that the Soviet Union is not an offensive power. Marshall Shulman has observed, that

> it [is] by no means evident from the [Soviet] government record in foreign policy – outside its own declared sphere of interest – that its aims [are] offensive. Its policy [is] certainly opportunistic . . . but that [is] not to say that it [seeks] to *create* the opportunity for an offensive in Western Europe, the risks of which would probably be judged too high.[10]

This, however, shows the essential irrelevance of a political characterization of the Soviet Union. Whether or not the USSR is offensive in nature, its responses in Europe to opportunities or to what it perceives to be mortal threats are likely to be 'offensive' in the sense that the USSR plans to initiate hostilities, seeks strategic surprise and trains and equips its forces for offensive operations.

This is the case, setting aside political considerations, because the military advantage across the largely unfortified, smooth terrain of the central front lies with the attacker; and because the correlation of military forces is most favourable to the Warsaw Pact *before* US divisions stationed in the US can be brought to the fighting, a fact that rewards surprise and penalizes delay. Only an attacker can hope to force a settlement in the time frame of his own choosing.

> The Soviet aim in a full scale war against NATO must be to surround, destroy or otherwise neutralize NATO forces, and thereby bring about a collapse of the NATO political structure within a matter of days – during the 'initial period'. . . . The strategy

> adopted by the Soviet Union to deal with winning a war in Europe quickly *must* be seen in toto. There can be no *tactical* defeat of NATO. There can indeed be no certainty of military victory during the phase of hostilities if the preparatory phase and crisis phase have not succeeded in reducing NATO's capacity to react in time. It is *inconceivable* in present circumstances to envisage a gradual and predictable development into war, culminating in a declaration of war by the USSR, prior to an invasion of Europe. (emphasis in the original).[11]

These conditions have dictated Soviet doctrine in the European theatre and, to that extent, such doctrines may be taken as confirming the assessment of Soviet planning as 'offensive' in the qualified way in which that term is used here.

Soviet doctrine (like that of the German Army in the Second World War) depends upon initiative, surprise and mobility. Priority is put on maintaining the initiative through 'continuous operations' and efforts to achieve rapid breakthrough, assisted by second echelon forces. Accordingly, Warsaw Pact (WPO) forces

> have operational objectives strictly defined in the course of the operation as the commitment of follow-on formations to reinforce attacks, or exploit breakthroughs. The actual course of battle may require early commitment of follow-on formations, OMGs, reserves or even second echelon formations, in order to achieve the objective – to exploit a sudden unexpected successful breakthrough or to block a counter-attack. While it is tactically rigid, this system is intended to permit the operational and strategic levels to maintain its operational momentum.[12]

Mobility and speed are crucial to this tactical design. WPO forces project average rates of advance as high as 50 kilometres a day during conventional operations, and would place substantial forces behind NATO's forward defences at the end of the first day if breakthrough were achieved.

Recent studies[13] conclude that the Warsaw Pact offensive will proceed along a broad front with the aim of developing a small number – six to nine – axes of advance along which superiority is to be concentrated, masked by the generality of attacks. Each of these axial thrusts will deploy in successive waves if necessary, depending on the preparedness, depth and configuration of the defence. If strategic surprise is achieved, the front will deploy its armies in one wave, maintaining a small reserve; or if two waves are required, either a strong second echelon (with a small reserve) will be used, operating along pre-planned axes, or a much larger reserve will be kept if the attack is pressed without pre-planning. These second echelon forces are employed to exert force along an axis to achieve breakthrough. The Operational Manoeuvre Group (OMG), by contrast, is committed only to develop a breakthrough, operating as a rapid exploitation force in depth. Such highly aggressive tactics in the context of successful deception offer the best possibility, it is thought, of avoiding NATO tactical nuclear strikes by maintaining a high rate of advance and preventing the establishment of clear lines separating areas controlled by friendly and hostile troops at a very early stage of the war.[14]

> Modern conditions have introduced new factors into the equation of how to develop success: with complete mechanization, armour, and new weapons, all troops have become mobile. Consequently great possibilities have emerged for developing an operation at high speed and engaging in manoeuvre with tank and combined arms armies. In this connection there have been qualitative changes in the structure of action in the whole depth of the enemy defence. There are far greater opportunities nowadays than in the past, especially on account of the great depths to which rockets, long range artillery, aircraft and desants can be used. Even so, examples from the last war have in no way lost their relevance in theory or in practice. Rather they encourage ideas and suggest solutions to the modern problems of how to get major forces in the offensive deep into the operational depths of the defence, so as to achieve decisive aims at high speed.[15]

This brief sketch of the WPO offensive is offered as a basis for determining what is required of the NATO defence. Furthermore the offence/defence scheme has conceptual significance for any 'balance' drawn between NATO and the WPO: to take the most shop-worn example, WPO tank forces should be compared to NATO anti-tank capabilities; a mere counting up of the tanks available to each side tells us little. (But one must be careful how this is done. It is often claimed that the WPO advantage in main battle tanks, 2 : 1, is offset by a NATO superiority in anti-tank guided missiles (ATGM), 3:1. ATGMs, however, do not target other, hostile ATGMs. And the number of hostile targets is not limited to heavy tanks, but must include light tanks, armoured personnel carriers and other armoured vehicles. The actual number of such WPO targets in fact exceeds NATO ATGMs and anti-tank guns by a factor of 7.)[16] And finally, these conceptual implications are reflected in the present force structures of each side. NATO forces are organized in divisional and corps clusters deployed in depth with relatively elaborate logistical support. WPO armies are organized into smaller divisions with extensive armour and artillery support and relatively slight logistic backing. As mobile striking forces designed to carry out offensives in depth they are well-equipped, but equipped only for a war of continuous penetration and limited duration. NATO has served endurance at the expense of the combat arms, and plans to be able to maintain and supply forces in the field for 60–90 days, prolonging the conflict until its endurance advantage can be felt, and American forces stationed in the United States can be brought to bear. The comparison has been graphically represented in Figure 13.1.

These conclusions can be drawn from the offensive/defensive constraint when taken together with the political and geostrategic constraints listed above: (1) NATO combat battalions must be of sufficient strength such that, if the WPO achieves strategic surprise, there will be enough combat ready troops – before reinforcement – to stabilize a front. Given the long defensive perimeter, this places considerable demands on C^3I, transportation and sheer numbers. (2) NATO must maintain secure internal lines to be able to move troops to respond to developing axes of attack. This requires air defences and air superiority behind the front. NATO ought also to be able to interdict second echelon forces; this requires combat aircraft in sufficient numbers and of a technological capability to be able to deny air cover to a rapidly moving offensive. (3) NATO must be able to maintain open sea lanes. Even if all US troop reinforcements came by air, the use of sea transport would be required to bring munitions and heavy equipment. Less than one third of the US inventories for a central front defence are pre-positioned in Europe.[17] The sinking of early shipments would have a drastically foreshortening effect on the endurance, survivability and reinforcement of NATO forces. (4) NATO must develop a deep strike potential. The commitment to forward defence – deemed essential by the FRG – prohibits NATO from trading territory for time, exhausting the thin logistical and communication support of Soviet salients. NATO must therefore be able to interdict WPO echelons as far forward as possible given that the timing, direction and weight of the attack will be chosen by the WPO.

Figure 13.1 The balance now: conventional forces in Europe

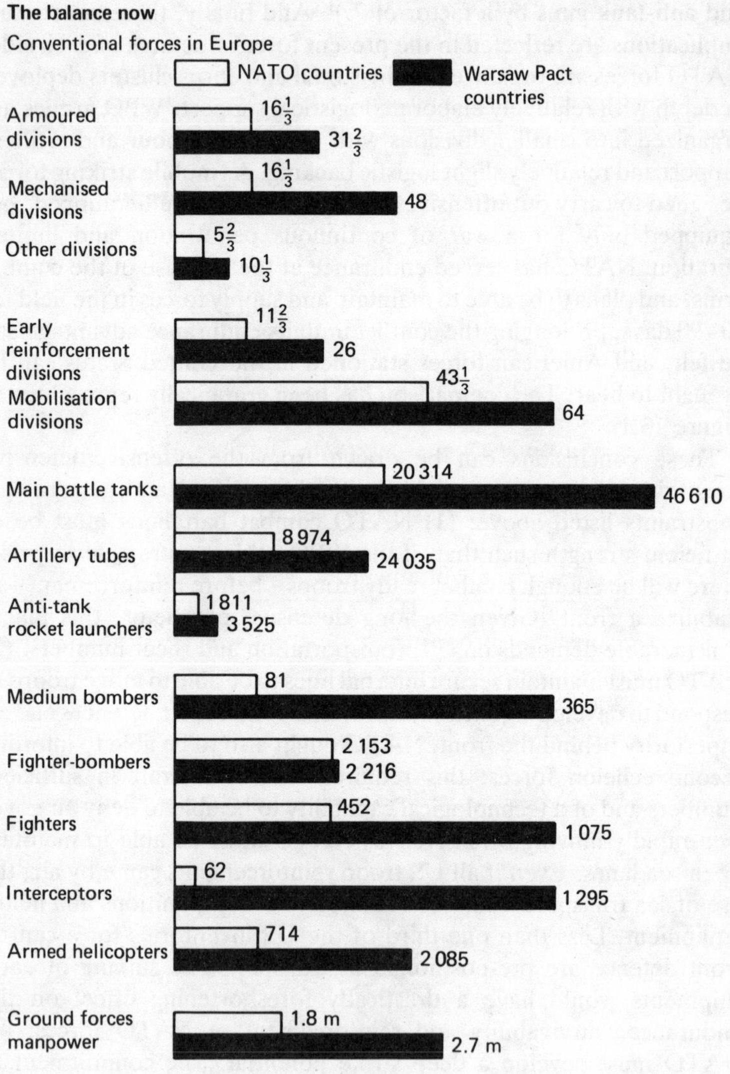

Source: Derived from *The Military Balance, 1985–1986*.

(5) Co-ordination problems inherent in executing the complex Airland Battle scheme[18] must be overcome through co-ordinated national training. Otherwise, differing national tactical plans will render the target acquisition and air defence goals of the plan impossible to execute once a WPO breakthrough has been achieved.

In the remaining pages of this section we will explore what allocations might be responsive to these demands and whether even enhanced allocations would substitute for extended deterrence. Let me emphasize that I am not attempting an assessment of NATO strategy which must, in any case, be measured against a spectrum of potential contingencies and not be driven solely by the possibility of a large-scale invasion.

It is generally asserted that, against Central Europe, the WPO could deploy 90 divisions (pre-mobilization: 30 armoured, 50 mechanized, 10 early reinforcement) and 4000 aircraft (2000 fighter-interceptors, 500 fighter-reconnaissance, 1500 fighter-ground strike). The terrain offers five main avenues of approach – the Baltic coastal line, the open plain of North Germany, the Göttingen corridor, the Fulda Gap and the Hof-Cheb corridor. These approaches are guarded by NATO with an initial defensive complement of 28 divisions (12 armoured) and 2000 aircraft (350 fighter-interceptors, 300 fighter-reconnaissance, 1350 fighter-ground strike). The US has 7⅓ divisions assigned to reinforce its forces in Europe in case of attack and, after mobilization, could perhaps field another 14⅓ divisions but in the first week or two only an additional two divisions would be available with pre-positioned supplies. In such a situation, it is easy to see why nuclear weapons – tactical to destroy second echelon forces and blunt assaults, theatre if necessary to relieve an encirclement or even central if a deep salient in force threatened a politically significant objective – are regarded as integral to Western Europe's defence. As Kenneth Hunt has noted,

> Why is there deterrence now? Briefly, because the NATO defense is of such strength that it could only be breached by a major attack, and such an attack would risk the use of nuclear weapons and nuclear escalation, with incalculable consequences. This risk appears to outweigh any possible gain that the Soviet Union could count on from making war; it is unlikely that [the Soviet Union] will do so.[19]

There are four measures that would serve, within the constraints noted above, to stiffen the NATO defence in the central front in place of the fortifying effect of nuclear systems: larger standing forces, faster reinforcement, greater use of reserves, an aggressive retaliatory threat to East European assets. In July 1982 the *Economist* published the figures shown in Table 13.1, the results of its study of what it would take to defend NATO without using nuclear weapons.

Table 13.1 How NATO needs to grow

	Increases already planned	*Increases we think are needed (including column-one increases)*
Fighting battalions (infantry, tanks, artillery)	23½	30
Support battalions	120	200
Tanks (over and above those assigned to the extra combat units)	500	800
Combat aircraft	100	300
Transport aircraft	—	200
Anti-aircraft missile launchers	400	600
Anti-aircraft missiles	10,000	14,000
Anti-tank helicopters	170	500
Anti-tank missile launcher tubes (including helicopters)	40,000	100,000
Anti-tank guided missiles	100,000	200,000
Artillery ammunition	20m rounds	40m rounds
Air-to-air missiles	—	20,000
Minesweeping ships	100	170

Source: *The Economist*, 31 July 1982, pp. 30–2.

The study concluded that:

> [n]ot enough units are assigned to the plain now, and the prospect of a conventional only war would allow the Warsaw pact to concentrate its forces for a breakthrough in a way that would be risky if NATO were likely to use nuclear weapons.[20]

Assuming that extra battalions were deployed on the North German plain, at the force levels prescribed, it was observed that:

> [i]f the Russians risked an attack even against NATO's improved forces, they might not break through to rapid victory (as the Germans did in France in 1940) but on failing to achieve that rapid victory they might settle down to a grinding battle of attrition (as happened after the first German advance in 1914). The NATO

defenders in the numbers we suggest might prevent a fast victory, but without nuclear weapons they might not prevent a long war.[21]

Additional steps would perhaps include the pre-positioning of vast inventories in conjunction with an airbridge; registration of potential draftees in the US;[22] the incorporation of reserve units into 'framework' divisions staffed by NCOs and officers in Europe. These measures would permit a longer war in which the Alliance's greater collective strength could be brought to bear. Putting to one side the enormous costs of such a regimen – the *Economist* estimates its programme could be implemented by sizeable but not crippling increases (FRG spending would go to 4.2 per cent of GNP from 3.4 per cent; France to 5 per cent from 4.2 per cent; US to 7.5 per cent from 5.8 per cent)[23] – is it plausible that an enhanced and more aggressive conventional defence could in fact defend Western Europe against a Soviet invasion without relying on the possibility of resorting to nuclear weapons?

I shall claim, in the ensuing discussion, that such a putative defence could actually result in only one of two outcomes: rapid conventional defeat for NATO or equally rapid NATO defeat caused by Soviet nuclear threats or attacks. If we assume the offensive/defensive configuration of forces and events as described, then we must also assume that the USSR has decided to accept the risks of nuclear attack on themselves or their forces before initiating hostilities. Should, however, NATO dispositions or behaviour convince the Soviet Union that, except for a central strategic attack on a nuclear armed member of NATO, the war would be prosecuted by the Alliance on a conventional basis alone, then it would appear to follow that the risk to the Soviet Union of their use of nuclear weapons plummets. They would then possess the means to end the war if the conventional phase should become too drawn out or appear to turn adverse to their offensive. While the contemplation of a no-first-use policy assumes that NATO has the initiative, a conventional-only retaliatory policy assumes the opposite, namely that NATO is self-deterred in all contexts save the homeland strike.

An argument resembling this was put forward by Bernard Brodie in a 1965 RAND paper. He asked

> How can we then assume that the Russians will be more willing to accept defeat in a battle that has remained conventional than in one that has gone nuclear? Is it not a compelling surmise that it must be just the other way around.[24]

The situation he confronted roughly anticipates the context here, an attack across the central front.

> How do we cope in advance with the conceivability of such an attack?
>
> One answer often heard is that we must anticipate it by building up our conventional forces, thus deterring the enemy from starting his fight. But the premise is essential to this argument that the opponent is either (a) prepared to fight even with nuclear weapons or (b) is utterly convinced that we will not under any circumstances use them. Otherwise, he will certainly not let himself be provoked into attacking our forces with their large nuclear capabilities. Now if he is prepared to fight with nuclear weapons, but observes from our costly efforts to build up to conventional parity with him in Europe that we are deeply unwilling to see them used, his cue, as we have already noted, is to threaten their use or actually to introduce a few. But if portion (a) of the premise above does not apply, why should we permit or even encourage the conviction described under the portion (b)? What has our conventional buildup bought us except the encouragement of that conviction.[25]

If NATO were to adopt a conventional-only policy, is it really fantastic to suggest that West Germany would wish to safeguard its homeland by the possession of nuclear weapons? And this is scarcely an idle aside, for when we ask what political event would most tempt the Soviet Union into the risks of launching an attack on the central front, the pre-emption of a West German acquisition of nuclear armament hardly provides an implausible scenario. Thus the ironic sequence might be: the erosion of extended deterrence yields enhanced conventional deployment; this yields to the development of a German nuclear force since, by itself, a conventional force on the central front actually increases the likelihood of nuclear warfare against West Germany; this attempted nuclear armament provokes a WPO conventional attack across the central front; if successfully halted, the attack must 'go nuclear'.

Moreover, this situation is not really alleviated by the currently fashionable NATO strategy of enhancing conventional retaliation by attacking Eastern Europe in the event of a WPO invasion. An understandable US desire to seize the initiative and engage the enemy by means of armoured manoeuvre ignores the fact that this strategy, in

WPO hands, depends upon a political collapse in the West that is unlikely in totalitarian states that are leashed to the Soviet Union at least as much by our strategy as by her garrisons. Indeed the political consequences of such a strategy are precisely the opposite of what was expected because the theorem, i.e., that a cure for decoupling – here, a more threatening conventional strategy – imposes greater risks on the FRG – has been ignored. Discussing the proposed heightened conventional response, a former West German defense minister commented:

> Instead of forward defence in the sense of defending the NATO area close to its borders, there is to be forward defence in the sense of advancing into enemy territory. By means of highly mobile units with strong fire power, NATO is to be able to advance rapidly into the depth of enemy territory and seek a decision there. This concept too is unacceptable in the Federal Republic. We would expose ourselves to Soviet charges that we wish to launch a conventional attack and involve its territory in a war. We Germans in particular would, in view of our invasion of the Soviet Union during the last war, find it difficult to withstand such a campaign, not least because of the Federal Armed Forces' particularly high contribution to NATO's conventional deterrent in Europe. Reflections of this kind also raise questions which might substantially change or strain East–West relations. We need more, not less, mutual confidence and understanding between East and West.[26]

Now, by contrast, we have the American reply – which, although it may strike one as uncomprehending of the European position and even somewhat ominous in its veiled threat, in fact comes from a very distinguished American commentator who is responding, creatively, to a terrible dilemma:

> One would think that German leaders would endorse a military strategy that, in comparison to the alternatives, promised to produce stronger deterrence at lower cost, to reduce the probability that nuclear weapons would be used in the territory of the Federal Republic, and to shift at least some of the fighting, if war did occur, from the Federal Republic to East Germany and Czechoslovakia. It is hard to see why it might be good politics in West Germany to oppose such a move. If, after the normal debate necessary for policy innovation in any democratic country, the West German govern-

ment was unwilling to support such a change, the United States would clearly have to reconsider its commitment of forces to a strategy and posture that is doomed to be found wanting.[27]

Whatever the merits of the 'scenario with enhanced conventional arms' in the context of a committed extended US nuclear deterrent – and I think the conflicting arguments are usually overlooked – it has decisive and negative implications for plans that would erase the extended deterrent completely and substitute a heightened conventional defence. But consider the recent report of the Alternative Defence Commission which concludes with the recommendation that:

> Britain should seek to initiate a process of nuclear disarmament in Europe by staying in the Alliance subject to the condition that NATO does move decisively towards abandoning any reliance on a nuclear strategy. The goal of de-nuclearising NATO strategy implies the following steps:
>
> (1) Acceptance by NATO of a policy of no-first-use of nuclear weapons.
>
> (2) Withdrawal of short-range, 'battlefield', nuclear weapons.
>
> (3) Withdrawal of 'theatre' nuclear weapons.
>
> (4) The decoupling of the US strategic nuclear deterrent from NATO by ending reliance on US nuclear weapons as an element in NATO strategy.[28]

Such a programme would require the US to commit 200 000 troops (more, on some of the alternatives proposed by the Commission) on the understanding that if these troops were about to be destroyed – even by Russian nuclear attacks – the US could not use nuclear weapons or even threaten such use to prevent her army's destruction. The same thing is, of course, also true of France. The report at one point observes, hopefully, that:

> [Without the US], maintaining NATO conventional forces at their existing level would not be impossible, but a great deal would depend on the attitude of the French both in terms of their willingness to adopt a non-nuclear strategy and to commit more troops to West Germany. Without French co-operation, an integrated multinational European conventional force in Germany, and an orthodox conventional defence strategy, would be very difficult to sustain. It would however be possible without French involve-

ment to mount some form of in-depth defence of West Germany, drawing on British, Belgian and Dutch contingents but relying heavily on the existing German forces. This approach could allow for British support for air defence and a naval role in a European defence body.[29]

It is obtuse, however, to offer such a proposition without showing why, of all the nations involved, the FRG would plan to permit itself to be overrun in such a way – an 'in-depth defence' – particularly in light of French theatre nuclear capabilities that could prove almost as devastating for Germany as an invasion itself.

My analysis also has implications for proposals that would substitute advanced conventional *technologies* for nuclear weapons. Why, it is sometimes asked, could not modern conventional weapons – Assault Breakers, conventionally armed cruise and ballistic missiles, and SKEET are most frequently mentioned – be used in those counter-force roles now assigned to nuclear weapons?[30] And then why cannot these conventional weapons be interposed in the gap created by receding extended deterrence? Given the high accuracies of the new weapons and increasingly efficient ordnance, it ought to be possible not only to blunt tank attacks and force dispersal (a role hitherto assigned to battlefield nuclear weapons) but also to destroy Soviet tactical and theatre ballistic missile sites, bridges and railyards, fuel and ammunition storage facilities, and command and communication centers within 800 km of the border. Once it is realized that such substitution, *in the absence of extended nuclear deterrence*, renders the troops who rely on it vulnerable to nuclear attack if their reliance is justified, and marginally worse off conventionally if their reliance is misplaced, it becomes clear that such substitutions are feasible only within the context of a robust extended deterrence. Indeed, in the absence of effective extended deterrence, battlefield nuclear weapons themselves offer little gain in defensive security.[31]

Conclusion

The conventional balance in Europe changed significantly in the 1970s as NATO's qualitative superiority was offset, and then overcome, by both the comprehensive modernization of Soviet forces and their relative quantitative increase. Moreover, the

> [n]umerical advantages of the Warsaw Pact over NATO are much more pronounced in key equipment categories such as main battle

tanks, tube artillery, and infantry combat vehicles than in manpower. The Warsaw Pact enjoys a superiority of 3:1 in tanks and 2:1 in artillery in Central Europe. There also took place a large increase in the number of artillery tubes available to both motorized and tank divisions during the decade of the 1970s. Similar significant improvements took place in Soviet Frontal Aviation amounting to a fourfold increase in payload and a 2½ fold increase in range. In the early sixties a forward deployment of the Soviet Frontal Aviation was necessary to provide combat support aircraft to one third of West Germany with the Soviet forces based in East Germany. Today Frontal Aviation aircraft operating from deep bases cover all of NATO's airfields.

FLOGGER (MIG-23/27) and FENCER (SU-19) can deliver nuclear or conventional ordnance to all NATO bases even when flying at low altitudes. Soviet Frontal Aviation in Central Europe alone is equal to the total number of available NATO aircraft.[32]

In light of these changes it was to be expected that NATO, after some procrastination, would respond with an enhanced conventional posture. The Long Term Defence Programme (LTDP) and the LRTNF decisions taken in 1979 were such a response. Given the two track nature of the LRTNF decision, it was perhaps also to be expected that there would be calls in some quarters for the replacement of the nuclear counterweight with a more ambitious LTDP. Such calls might be interpreted as recognizing that the balance of *nuclear* confrontation in the Central Front had shifted also in the 1970s, rendering NATO strategy more and more of a bluff.

During the 1970s the relative advantages in [nuclear systems] numbers underwent some significant changes. With respect to short range (100km) systems FROG deployments increased by some 50% during the 1970s, and a new generation missile (SS-21) with increased accuracy, longer range and improved response time is under deployment. LANCE has replaced HONEST JOHN on the NATO side. However, there has emerged a 5:1 Warsaw Pact advantage in short range missiles.

With respect to medium range missiles (100km) the number of Soviet systems have increased almost threefold. Successor systems to the SCALEBOARD and SCUD missiles (SS-22 and SS-23) have been developed. NATO has 180 PERSHING-1s with a range of 600 km. The NATO dual capable aircraft include F-104, F-4, BUCCANEER and JAGUAR. [But the] number of nuclear capable aircraft has doubled on the Soviet side, resulting in a combined medium range numerical advantage for the Warsaw Pact of about 3:1[33]

Thus, the realistic demand for less reliance on nuclear weapons by NATO may well have played into the demand for a de-nuclearized NATO.

For if the requirements of extended deterrence could be met by an enhanced conventional posture, the unfortunate implications of the decoupling/uncoupling theorem could be avoided. This, however, is not the case. Enhanced conventional defence – with or without an extended deterrent – simply replicates the dilemma: it renders US nuclear retaliation less likely and thereby threatens to decouple the theatres (as, for example, by a no-first-use pledge); or it does *not* make US nuclear use less likely in which case the operation of the 'theorem' takes over and the US President can recouple the deterrent to the theatre only by 'uncoupling' the two theatres, and confining war to the extended theatre. This permits the USSR to take the conventional initiative as far as *it* chooses, and then resort to deep strikes in Europe to coerce a rapid settlement. Such a scenario is even more disturbing when we contemplate the dynamics of a multi-national alliance in crisis. The Soviet Union, to achieve surprise, might well move after a crisis had appeared to peak (as was the case with Czechoslovakia in 1968). NATO, by contrast, would be reluctant to mobilize or even reinforce its positions for fear of committing a provocation and forcing a Soviet attempt at pre-emption, the one plan for which WPO forces are configured. In such a context, even greatly enhanced conventional forces would be sorely tested by an initial assault on the forward defence line. NATO defence might stabilize once the WPO salients had been identified and had outrun their material support. At that hour, without nuclear weapons, what course could NATO countries in Europe agree upon?

A US threat of nuclear strikes against the Soviet Union? Against the European theatre, itself? These two possibilities simply repeat the two options posed by the theorem. To the extent that the removal of the nuclear threat from NATO's options ensures a firmer, less revocable self-deterrence with even the present uncertainties removed from the calculation of Soviet planners, it takes the present situation in Europe and makes it worse. The risks of war borne by the USSR go down and thus the objectives for which war can be waged become more numerous. The willingness to war goes up, correspondingly, and the most exposed nations must react accordingly.

ARMS CONTROL

If an effective extended deterrent is necessary to preserve the stability of the present deterrence environment – the conclusion of Chapter 12 – and yet it appears increasingly difficult for the US to restore or replace an increasingly troubling system of extended deterrence, then one alternative remedy might lie in the pursuit of arms control to reduce the threat that is sought to be deterred. In this section that possibility will be discussed.

Initially it ought to be said that the possibility of *theatre* arms control will be the primary subject of our examination and this must be explained, for this course is by no means obvious. Extended deterrence has waxed and waned as the threat to the United States, not simply the threat in extended theatres such as Europe, has decreased or increased. Accordingly, one might think that one alternative means of enhancing extended deterrence lies in reducing the central threat, that is, the threat to the US homeland. This is in fact so – as will be seen in the subsequent discussion of ballistic missile defence – but it is not likely to be achievable through arms control, because parity in central systems, codified by both SALT 1 and SALT 2 and accepted by both sides as at least a nominal requirement for START, is one of the principal causes of the decline of extended deterrence, as was discussed in Chapter 8. It is most improbable that the Soviet Union would acquiesce in a treaty that sought to reduce greatly US vulnerability without corresponding protections for the Soviet Union. Nevertheless, the US Administration has made an effort that would enhance extended deterrence by reducing the central threat through the so-called 'Phase Two' portion of its original START proposals.

In his Eureka College speech of May 1982,[34] President Reagan emphasized the US's goal of significantly reducing the 'most destabilizing systems, intercontinental ballistic missiles, the number of warheads they carry and their overall destructive potential.' MIRVed ICBMs with heavy payloads are the 'most destabilizing systems' only from the point of view of ICBM vulnerability,[35] however. Otherwise they provide more limited collateral damage, more secure communications and more reliable penetration than other systems. ICBM vulnerability is principally an issue, as was shown in Chapter 7, for US extended deterrence and thus the Reagan proposal does, to some extent, endeavour to treat the problem of the extended theatre through arms control. The Reagan START proposals are designed to reduce the land-based systems of both sides and, in the second phase, the countersilo capacity of the remaining systems. Given differing force structures, the greater changes would be those required of the Soviet Union.

> In phase one, each side would be limited to 5000 warheads on no more than 850 intercontinental land-based and sea-based missiles. Because the Administration maintains that each side has nearly 7500 warheads, the cuts would be equal. But because the Soviet Union deploys more missiles (about 2400) than the United States (1700), the Soviet Union could have to cut twice as many missiles.
>
> The ceiling of 2500 land-based warheads will also affect them more seriously since the Soviet Union has 5500 warheads or 70% of its total, on land-based missiles, compared with 2152 or 20% for the United States. It is expected that these reductions would take place over a five to ten-year period.
>
> The US also proposed a sublimit of 210 on Soviet MIRVed ICBMs (SS-17s, -18s, and -19s) and a further sublimit of 110 on Soviet heavy ICBMs (SS-18s).
>
> In the second phase, both sides would reduce their payload or throw weight to 4 million pounds which would mean Soviet reductions of 7 million pounds.[36]

The changed emphasis to warheads (from launchers) and, in the second phase, the focus on throw-weight underscores the US objective of reducing ICBM vulnerability through START.

The Soviet reaction to these proposals reflects an evident awareness of US strategic objectives. First, in a speech to the Young Communist League (Komsomol) in Moscow, President Brezhnev announced Soviet conditions for a START agreement.[37] The agreement must preserve parity; the talks should pay due regard for each side's equal security; the earlier results of SALT 1 and SALT 2 should serve as the basis for further progress. These conditions confirm the strategic significance of parity in central systems for extended deterrence since they are joined to the deceptively bland Russian requirement of 'equal security', which, roughly, translates into the demand for a US guarantee on a limitation on all anti-Soviet systems in the extended theatre such that they do not exceed Soviet central deployments. This sensitivity to the implications of START for extended deterrence is perhaps more sophisticated, in this respect, than the public statements of the US appear to be.

Second, the Soviet Union denounced the US START approach as attempting to upset the strategic parity to which it believes both sides are committed by SALT 1 and 2. In the Russian view, the US proposal to reduce each side's ballistic missile forces to equal numbers while postponing to some later stage reductions in bombers and cruise missiles, in which the US enjoys an advantage, is simply an effort to force unilateral reduction of Soviet strategic strength and to restore strategic superiority to the West. (The US has now agreed to discuss these systems as part of the recently convened Geneva talks.) The following excerpt appeared in a comprehensive arms control editorial in *Pravda* on 2 January 1983:

> The incompatibility of the American selective approach with the principle of equality and identical security particularly clearly manifests itself in how the American side would wish to dispose of the Soviet IBMs. An analysis has shown that if the whole package of American proposals had been accepted, the Soviet side would have to dismantle more than 90% of all of its IBMs, which are known to make the basis of the USSR's strategic defense might. This proves to be the aim of the American plan – ensure by hook or by crook a unilateral weakening of the USSR's defense potential, while the United States would at the same time, owing to the same unilaterally drawn up proposals, get an opportunity to increase considerably the number of the warheads in its intercontinental ballistic missiles and carry on the implementation of its programs already drawn up for building up the strategic means.
>
> Thus, the American approach . . . is not a way to reaching a mutually acceptable agreement, but a plan for a unilateral disarmament of the USSR camouflaged as a proposal on 'reductions', and thus ensuring for the United States the superiority it once had in the strategic field.[38]

Third, the Soviets have now actually made the proposal suggested in Chapter 8[39] that would effectively link the INF and START negotiations by offering to accept deep cuts in central systems in return for a US commitments to forego the deployment of LRTNF and to accept stringent restrictions on future cruise missile deployment. Such a proposal reflects an acute awareness of the importance of the extended theatre. It need not be re-emphasized that its acceptance by the US would be highly compromising to Alliance interests. Rather, I mention the offer here simply because the Soviet tabling of such proposals does not offer grounds for hope that in negotiation over central systems the USSR will be careless enough to permit some mending of the unravelling US role in extended deterrence.

Again, the *Pravda* editorial, describing the Russian proposal:

> What is the essence of our proposals? The USSR proposes to reduce stage-by-stage by the year 1990 the aggregate number of ICBM launchers, SLBM launchers, as well as of heavy bombers down to 1000 units for each of the sides – that is, to lower by 25% the initial ceilings for these means, which was fixed under the SALT II treaty.
>
> The number of nuclear charges in these carriers would also be reduced to equal agreed levels.[40]

This Soviet proposal was made conditional on a US agreement not to increase its forward-based systems near the Soviet Union:

> In putting forward the above-mentioned proposals, the Soviet Union considers the fact that the United States has at its disposal forward-based nuclear means deployed in close proximity to the borders of the USSR and its allies. These weapons are strategic in character for the USSR insofar as they are not balanced by anything on our side. (We do not have such means close to US territory.) If there were a reduction in ICBMs, in submarines and heavy bombers, the proportion of the American forward-based nuclear means would steadily increase in the strategic balance of the sides.
>
> Therefore, the Soviet proposals presuppose that in a mutual reduction in strategic nuclear forces, the United States, will, at least, not build up its other nuclear forces, which are capable of reaching objectives in the Soviet Union's territory, failing which the United States would receive a channel for by-passing and, as a matter of fact, undermining the very fundamentals of a future agreement.[41]

This Soviet demand amounts to a linkage of the START negotiations to the US–USSR intermediate-range nuclear force (INF) negotiations. The implication is that, were the United States to go ahead with the planned deployment of cruise and Pershing 2 missiles in Europe, the Soviet Union would wish to withdraw or modify its START proposal. In fact, the INF talks did not produce a negotiated solution, NATO did commence deployment and, to the expressed surprise of many, the USSR did walk out of both talks, START and INF. In the following pages, I will attempt to explain this link.

As with so much else, the public debate on INF has been largely devoid of discussion of the strategic context. It is the purpose of this book to provide one layer of that context and nowhere is this more needed than with respect to theatre arms control. For such a context will help explain the differing positions of the USSR and the US and thereby offer an account for their quite different claims regarding existing theatre nuclear deployments (on some basis other than mere venality) as well as provide some rational basis for public decision (on some basis other than whether a 'balance' exists).

The strategic context of the INF talks is set by the problem of extended deterrence, and the clash of opposing US–Soviet political paradigms. Very briefly, it can be said that the US wishes to treat Western Europe as part of its homeland (NATO having arisen in the period when there was only central deterrence, as argued in Chapter 2) but must recognize the reality of the end of deterrence identity between the US and Europe and the consequent incentives to negotiate a protocol that differentiates between the US and European homelands. At the same time, the USSR wishes to treat Western Europe as a mere launching platform for the US, not as a superpower in itself and not as a part of a superpower's homeland (since a threat against it is manifestly not as forceful as a threat against the US homeland). Unwilling to concede the identity of security interests between the US and Europe, the USSR cannot, however, insist on wholly separate treatment either since to do so would jeopardize the Russian requirement that its position as superpower entitles it to parity with 'the other half', the rest of the developed world, largely arrayed against it. This explains the constant Russian pressure on Western Europe to identify itself as distinct from US interests, coupled with the complete refusal to treat Western European security concerns as on a par with those of the US and the USSR. These paradigms were reflected in the superpowers' SALT positions; they account for the compromises struck there; they are reflected in their respective START proposals; they determined the course – including the breakdown – of the ongoing INF negotiations, and they even determined US/Soviet positions in the Vienna negotiations over conventional force levels in MBFR/CSCE.[42]

One might state the comparison this way. For the Soviet Union, a superpower is entitled to pose threats (deployments) equal to the threats it faces; a *balance* exists when each superpower faces equivalent threats. For the United States, a superpower is entitled to pose threats equal to the threats posed by the other superpower; a *balance* exists when each superpower faces threats equal to those it poses. These paradigms are derived directly from the respective superpower relationships to Western Europe, one threatening, as it must if its empire in Eastern Europe is ever to be truly secure, the other protecting, as it must if its political and philosophical position is not to be isolated in the world.

The USSR SALT position was: a superpower is entitled to the sanctuary of parity – a standoff with regard to nuclear weapons from the opposing camp. Given the geopolitical asymmetry of the two superpowers, this would have meant a decoupling of US and European interests since ballistic missiles and bombers going west into Europe would have been unregulated while those going east would have been rigidly limited.

The US SALT position, similarly derived from its extended security paradigm was: a superpower is indeed entitled to the sanctuary of parity, but the US sanctuary includes Western Europe. This would have recognized the US–West European relationship, a legitimization that would contradict the USSR's goal of decoupling that relationship.

The compromise that resulted depended on SALT's being regarded as a kind of 'Step I'. An initial agreement was negotiated that was compatible with subsequent steps in opposing directions. The conceptual breakthrough in the talks was to focus on *range* as the criterion for inclusion since limiting only long range systems was compatible with both paradigms. Thus began the US fixation on equality in numbers with respect to classes defined by range. (The resulting detachment from strategic reality – and indeed any apparent awareness of the objectives of arms control – reached its apogee, one hopes, in the 1980 Democratic and Republican demands for a freeze on and deep cuts in nuclear weapons, respectively.) So, for example, the Poseidon SLBMs assigned to SACEUR and the European theatre are counted in SALT as are Russian SLBMs in the Baltic actually targeted on Western Europe. 'Step 2' appeared differently to the two parties: the USSR would press for the inclusion of what, in light of its paradigm it quite properly called 'forward based systems,' i.e., those weapons theoretically capable of targeting the USSR from an American launching pad beyond the American homeland (an aircraft carrier or a base on the territory of an ally), while resisting the inclusion of WPO/Soviet weapons that could strike Western Europe but not the US. To the US, 'Step 2' would be movement toward the protection of Europe and Japan by a limitation on the weapons that could theoretically target them in exchange for a limitation on those weapons of less than intercontinental range that could strike the Soviet Union and WPO countries. In other words, if one side believed Western Europe was part of the US vital interests – on a par with the United States's own national survival – then that side would treat weapons threatening Western Europe as equivalent to those threatening the Soviet Union. If the other side disbelieved this – either as a proposition reflecting political realities or as an ideological and geopolitical objective – then that side would not consent to such equivalence. Indeed in its treaty proposals *that* side would press for the inclusion of threats launched from Western Europe against the superpowers but ruthlessly exclude from limitation threats posed solely against European targets.

These 'Step 2s' were, in fact, the opening positions of both powers when talks began in Geneva in October 1980. The Russian perspective offered Western Europe a subordinate parity: it was entitled to whatever relative sanctuary it derived from a limitation on weapons that could strike the other superpower, whereas the superpower was entitled to sanctuary from whatever source. From the Russian point of view, this amounted to little more than equality with the position that the other superpower, by virtue of its geopolitical situation, already enjoyed.

The US INF position reiterated its initial SALT programme and reflected these fundamental paradigms. The US argued that the Alliance was entitled to relative sanctuary to the same extent that it offered relative sanctuary. Thus the extended theatres were to limit their weapons precisely to the extent that their vulnerability was limited. The continuation of the US SALT position from central to extended theatres was phrased by the US Administration as: LRTNF arms control will be negotiated 'within the SALT framework'.

This time there was no ready compromise at hand. The 1981 US proposal – the zero option – however strategically unsound was perfectly compatible with the US paradigm: vulnerabilities were to be reciprocally reduced, the Western European states were regarded as on equal footing with the USSR.

The Brezhnev moratorium[43] – each side to cease further deployments as of December 1981, that is, before the initial operating capability (IOC) of the GLCMs and Pershing 2s – when added to the threat to deploy new weapons against the US should the LRTNF deployments go forward, simply reiterated the category distinction between superpower and extended theatre that was the basis for Russian policy. To some observers it seemed absurd for the USSR to complain about the ten minutes it will take a Pershing 2 to reach Moscow; after all, an SS-20 travelling from the opposite direction will take precisely the same time, a fact seldom mentioned in the popular commentary. In light of Russian geopolitical objectives, however, such one-sided sensitivity is not hypocrisy at all, and is quite explicable in terms other than the simple seeking of marginal tactical advantage, which is often the only analytical perspective journalists and commentators attribute to the USSR.

There has been an unfortunate tendency to ignore the political paradigms drawn above. As a result, the public debate has focused on whether, in fact, a 'balance' exists. NATO has submitted its figures. The USSR has submitted its own figures. One distinguished commentator has even pointed out that the Russian figures appear to reflect the application of different rules of counting to NATO forces than to WPO forces.[44]

But of course they do, and it ought to be clear now why this is so. The tendency to treat both sides as motivated solely by efforts to achieve marginal tactical advantage has been enervating to real analysis. Such a focus cannot explain why a 'balance' – the idea of equality – is important in the first place;[45] nor why the Russians have resolutely refused to accept the zero option proposal that, as was shown in Chapter 9, is clearly to their tactical advantage; nor how to decide between the two sets of figures. In the following pages, I will give the competing sets of numbers and relate their differences to the conflicting political paradigms described above. Then I will evaluate theatre arms control as a means of reducing the threat to Western Europe.

Table 13.2 is derived from data submitted by the US and the USSR to the Geneva INF Talks.[46] The data are arranged in this way, as opposed to the customary manner of presenting the US view of the balance followed by the Soviet view, to emphasize the strategic sources of the differing estimates. As has been argued, the important insight arises from the political paradigms from which the counting rules derive, and not from the Soviet and US conclusions that there is, or is not, a present 'balance'.

We shall work our way through these charts presently, but the first observation to be made is the striking congruence in the US and Soviet figures, an agreement that is obvious when the data are presented in the configuration in Table 13.2. The difference in the two sides' estimates of NATO aircraft, for example, are almost wholly a matter of the strategic objectives discussed above (which account for the Russian inclusion of non-NATO assigned UK and French forces, as well as the enlargement of the carrier-based figure from those aircraft in Europe to those anywhere that could be brought to bear against Soviet territory). For the Soviet Union, a superpower is entitled to pose threats equal to the threats it faces; thus every potential threat

Table 13.2 The nuclear balance: US and Soviet figures

	United States Figures	*Russian Figures*
Missile Launchers		
NATO		
Land-based	0 (US)	0 (US)
		18 (S2/S3 Fr.)
Submarine-based	0	0 (US)
(US Poseidon counted in SALT)		80 (M20 Fr.)
		64 (Polaris A3 UK)
Total NATO missile launchers	0 (US Est.)	162 (USSR Est.)
USSR		
Land-based	250 (SS20 USSR)	243 (SS20 USSR)
	350 (SS4/5 USSR)	253 (SS4/5 USSR)
	100 (SS/12/22 USSR)	
Submarine-based	30 (SSN5 USSR)	18 (SSN5 USSR)
Total USSR missile launchers	730 (US Est.)	514 (USSR Est.)
Aircraft		
NATO		
in Europe:		
Medium bombers	164 (F111 US)	172 (F111 US)
		46 (Mirage 4 Fr.)
		55 (Vulcan UK)
Strike aircraft	265 (F4 US)	246 (F4 US)
on carriers:	68 (A6/A7 US)	240 (A6/A7 US)
in US:	63 (FB111 US)	65 (FB111 US)
Total NATO nuclear armed aircraft	560 (US Est.)	824 (USSR Est.)
in Soviet Union:		
Medium bombers	45 (Backfire B. Tu22M)	114 (Backfire Tu22m)
	65 (Blinder Tu22)	65 (Blinder Tu22)
	285 (Badger Tu16)	282 (Badger Tu16)
	325 (Fencer Su19/24)	
Forward-based strike aircraft	1600 (Flogger MIG23/27)	
	775 (Fitter C Su17)	
	100 (Fitter A Su7)	
Total USSR nuclear aircraft	3195 (US Est.)	461 (USSR Est.)

must be counted. For the Americans, a superpower is entitled to pose threats equal to those posed by the other superpower; hence threats posed by independent allies are not counted.

The differences between the US and USSR estimates for the F111 (63 or 65) or the F111 (164 or 172) or the F4 (265 or 246) are trivial. The same observation may be made for the remaining three tables. There is agreement on what counts; disagreement on what to count.

Taken as a whole, two counting rules determine 98 per cent of the difference in the US and Soviet totals. The US claims for itself and the Alliance a total of 560 systems; the Soviets charge this figure is in fact 986. Of the difference, however – 426 systems – 263 are French and British systems, while the remainder is actually exceeded once we add in the non-Europe based US carrier air systems (172). This amounts to a mere repetition of the original USSR position: a superpower is entitled to sanctuary from nuclear weapons, whatever their origin. Similarly, the US claims that Soviet systems total 3925, against the USSR's own count of 975. Of the difference – 2950 – 2900 systems can be accounted for by noting that these weapons are launched from Soviet bases in Eastern Europe (accepting *arguendo* the implausible Soviet claim that the Fencer range is less than 1000 km).[47] Western Europe is thus not treated as part of the US superpower – that would entitle her to a set-off from all threats she faced – but instead is merely a subordinate entity in the superpower world. Against her weapons must be offset all the threats the superpower (the USSR) faces; against the weapons she faces, only the threats posed by the Soviet Union require offsetting. The Russian rule of counting is derived from the consistent Soviet strategic paradigm, a paradigm that, like its American counterpart, is structured by political objectives. At stake is not, then, the marginal haggling of two bargaining partners, but two competing geopolitical paradigms that largely dictate the counting rules.

Excellent work has been done by Freedman, noted above, to expose the mendacity of Soviet counting: that if the Soviet range rules by which the F4 is counted were to apply equally to the Soviet Union, the Fencer would be brought in, and that the age limits on SSBN counting proposed by the USSR in fact exclude the British and French systems. Other commentators – notably Neuman[48] – have made similar points with respect to the exclusion of the Flogger in contrast to the inclusion of the F4, while Garthoff has attempted to perform the same function regarding US aggressive-competitive counting.[49] Though helpful, these papers do not address the political and strategic wellsprings of the two positions.

Given such contrasting perspectives, why was LRTNF arms control pursued so ardently by the West prior to deployment? I shall argue that it was the tacit operation of the theorem introduced in Chapter 8 that drove the Alliance to attempt a simultaneous arms control/deployment initiative. For it was apparent as early as the autumn of 1978 to several NATO governments that the 'hardware' solution to the extended deterrence problem would be difficult to sustain in the face of the public opposition it was foreseen to arouse. This is the consequence predicted in Chapter 8 and discussed in Chapter 9. For this reason – to demonstrate that the US was in search of progress toward reducing the threat to Europe and would deploy weapons there only as a last resort – NATO established the Special Group (the SG later to become the Special Consultative Group, SCG) in April 1979 to contrive an arms control approach that would respond to the political upheaval generated by the LRTNF deployment plan.[50]

This history ought not to be taken to suggest that the SG was disingenuous in its efforts. It quickly established a number of realistic guidelines: the deliberations of the High Level Group (HLG) were to govern SCG proposals; an LRTNF modernization plan, which was the Alliance response to the HLG decision discussed in Chapter 11, was to be agreed upon before any arms control talks began; the LRTNF talks would be conducted 'within the framework of SALT 2'. By the fall of 1979, the outlines of the two-track approach were clear: NATO LRTNF modernization would proceed simultaneously with negotiations to remove the advancing SS-20 deployments. To the precise extent that these weapons were written down and the pre-existing SS-4s and SS-5s retired, NATO LRTNF would be withheld. The extent of the deployment sought was 'the lowest possible level'.[51] Meanwhile, preparations for deployment would proceed and adverse public opinion would be forestalled by the ongoing, parallel negotiations. Following the Russian invasion of Afghanistan in November, the Alliance publicly announced on 12 December 1979 that a decision had been made to deploy a modernized LRTNF, consisting of 572 launchers – 464 GLCMs and 108 Pershing 2s – in five European countries. This amounted to a rejection of a 6 October offer by President Brezhnev to negotiate on LRTNF provided the modernization decision was not taken. Partly as a result of the Afghanistan invasion, SALT 2 was shelved by the US Senate after consultation with the President. At that point Soviet officials announced that the

December NATO decision removed any basis for LRTNF negotiation and declared that SALT 2 ratification would henceforth be a precondition for LRTNF talks.

The US role in these events amounted to a serious misreading of the implications of the theorem and the important function it holds for arms control negotiation. Contrary to one's intuitions, exaggerating, or heightening the awareness of, the Soviet threat to Europe does not build a constituency for NATO nuclear modernization. European publics will fear that the new weapons, targets for Russian pre-emption, either will not be used by the Americans to protect Europe or, conceivably worse, will be used. Rather it is by linking deployments to reduced threats that public opposition is avoided. This meant that SALT 2 had a positive role in LRTNF deployment that was lost when the treaty was withdrawn. The connection between LRTNF deployment and SALT 2 ratification was presumably not clear in the US, however, and for a while it appeared that the two-track offer would go forward without Soviet exploitation of the offer's obvious vulnerability to manipulation of the public. For six months the USSR was intransigent and support for the NATO decision in the West appeared firm. Then in June 1980, following Chancellor Schmidt's visit to Moscow, the USSR announced it was dropping its precondition that SALT 2 be ratified and the LRTNF decision be rescinded. The USSR publicly indicated its willingness to enter into preliminary discussions. These were begun in October 1980.[52]

These negotiations were terminated pending a reassessment of the American position by the newly elected Reagan Administration. In May 1981 the US Secretary of State, Alexander Haig, announced that the US would begin negotiations before the end of the year.[53] This statement was welcomed within the Alliance but the new Administration had by that time gone a long way to undermine its own credibility regarding the negotiations. This has proved costly since, as was argued in Chapter 8, the principal audience for INF arms control, in light of the decoupling-uncoupling theorem, is the European public. Statements from the new President regarding a limited nuclear war in Europe played into this vortex. The discrediting of SALT 2 by the Republican campaign served to undermine the most convenient ameliorative available to the US. At this time, the North Atlantic Assembly concluded:

> European observers and officials alike expressed the almost unanimous view that the non-ratification of SALT II had had a profound

effect on public opinion in Europe. It had been a major factor in the growth of opposition to the NATO decision and the rise of the anti-nuclear movements. European public opinion had found it difficult to understand that a treaty that had been evolved under four administrations could suddenly be dismissed as fatally flawed and contrary to the interests of the Alliance. American interest and willingness to negotiate arms control is considered an essential to Alliance security and specifically to the implementation of the NATO LRTNF decision.[54]

It is a pity that the US, who obeyed anyway the requirements of SALT 2 for the period, and beyond, of its five-year term, cast away the advantages of ratification (and indeed subjected itself to criticism for ceasing to observe SALT 2 limits that would have expired had the treaty been ratified).

In November, 1981, President Reagan announced the US endorsement the 'zero option.'

The US stuck to this position throughout 1982 during which the Soviets countered with a number of proposals culminating in December 1982 with the offer of a ceiling on Soviet missiles equal to the total of British and French weapons. US rejection of this proposal was followed by an American announcement that the US was willing to accept an agreement at some level of mutual deployment other than zero. The USSR was invited to pick a ceiling level between zero and 572. Press stories revealed than an earlier 'walk in the woods' by the US and Russian negotiators had yielded one such compromise proposal. This encouraged many serious commentators to speculate that some level of deployment on both sides would eventually be agreed upon. Indeed, right up to the Russian walkout and suspension of the negotiations – timed to coincide with a Bundestag vote on LRTNF – the Americans and Russians were exchanging proposals. Some Russian proposals included British and French forces; some focused on central systems. But all would have had the effect of producing the same net result for NATO LRTNF: none.[55]

Thus one of the bizarre incidents emerging from the negotiations occurred only a few days before the walkout. Soviet negotiator Yuli Kvitsinsky approached the American negotiator Paul Nitze in mid-November 1983 saying that he had been instructed to invite the US to propose equal reductions of 572 warheads or missiles in the European theatre. (This would have required the Russians to dismantle all their SS-4, and SS-5 missiles, while reducing the number of SS-20s aimed at

Europe to 120.) The USSR appeared willing to drop its insistence that British and French forces be included in the 'balance' so long as the total reduction happened to coincide with the exact total projected for the NATO force – 572.

Then, on 17 November Russian ambassadors delivered notes to several NATO governments claiming that the Americans had in fact made such a proposal. Analysts for the IISS professed to find this behaviour 'difficult to fathom'[56] but it does not seem hard to explain. The Soviet Union presented a proposal it wished the US to make and then its ambassadors fanned out across Europe claiming the US *had* made such a proposal because the goal of the entire enterprise was not to get an agreement but to impress the Soviet view of European status on the negotiations, and on the Europeans themselves. The Russians wished to make it appear that, at the least, the negotiations – if not a resulting treaty – would legitimate the view, with American acquiescence, that NATO was not entitled to deploy weapons capable of striking the Soviet Union on a par with Soviet weapons incapable of striking the US. It was only the consistent and relentless refusal by analysts and political commentators to listen to the Soviet position and interpret it on its own terms rather than dissolve it as a mere negotiating tactic en route to a marginally advantageous agreement that made Russian motives seem complex and obscure. The Soviet Union was always unwilling to legitimate NATO deployments based on an agreement that contradicted the fundamental Soviet views of superpower relations in Europe and thereby signalled *Soviet* acquiescence in the US view of European security.

The INF talks were broken off by the Russians on 23 November with the statement by Yuri Andropov that further Soviet participation 'would only serve as a cover for the actions of the United States and . . . other NATO countries directed at undermining European and international security'. Senior American officials were predicting, right up to the hour of the walkout, that the threat to leave the talks was only a bluff. This line reflects not so much optimism as a failure to understand the political and strategic basis for Soviet negotiating.

But for the zero option proposal it is unlikely that an INF agreement will emerge, even though the Soviet Union has been lured back to the table with the US promise to discuss space-based weapons. So long as the INF agreement is not linked to trade-offs in some other arena, there is simply no intersection of interests that would provide the basis for an agreement. *Regardless of the numbers*, it would seem improbable that the USSR would legitimate the role of US-European joint security by permanently agreeing to so much as 50 weapons systems. And we must hope that the US, having responded creatively and unfailingly to the challenges of extended deterrence for thirty years, will not lose its way owing to conceptual murkiness and cast away all it has sought to protect by accepting proposals that remove all NATO modernized LRTNF while leaving Russian weapons capable of striking the extended theatres. Only the political context created by the zero option could bring this about.[57]

Does this mean that arms control has nothing to offer the United States by way of an alternative to the present strategic impasse? By no means. Rather I am urging that any set of objectives for arms control negotiations must be grounded in (1) a thorough political understanding of the strategic relationships involved and (2) a complementary relationship between strategic objectives and arms control objectives. In both cases there is room for substantial intersection between the interests of the US and the Soviet Union, and between that of the arms control lobby and strategic planners. Aims for an agreement, like the agreement itself, will elude all parties when such recognition is not forthcoming. This is one reason why the focus of the arms control lobby on the technological impetus behind the arms race has not yielded, and is unlikely to yield any recent agreements on arms control.

What implications does this analysis hold for the talks recently convened in Geneva? Specifically, how and to what extent does the triangulation of issues – the combination, in concurrently held negotiations, of talks over strategic offensive weapons, defensive systems, and intermediate weapons – play into the clash of paradigms that brought the earlier talks to an impasse?

First, the triangulation tends to mask the problem. By blurring the focus which was previously on the INF talks and which, therefore, brought the contrast in US and Soviet approaches into high relief, the tripartite arrangement may permit observers to ignore the Russian walkout last winter. Insofar as the recent past is relevant, it will be easier to claim that the walkout was merely petulance or a negotiating tactic. Indeed one can expect this from some of the quarters that expressed absolute confidence that the threatened walkout was only a threat. This triangulation simply puts off the day when we are forced to recognize the substance of Russian concerns; its very success in bringing the parties back to the table suggests that the departure was never really substantive after all.

For this reason it is well to remember precisely why the Russians came back to the table. American diplomatic virtuosity consisted in triangulating two stalled sets of negotiations – START and INF – with the one subject as to which Russian security concerns were keenest, SDI (the American programme on ballistic missile defence). It is interesting to pause for a moment and ask why this is so, in light of the virtually universal scepticism in the US that President Reagan's ambitious agenda – to make nuclear weapons 'impotent and obsolete' – is in fact even a realistic possibility, and the oft-reported ambivalence or in some cases hostility within the Alliance to an American SDI programme. If the Americans don't think it will work, and the Europeans don't think it would help if it did work, and everyone agrees it will be hideously expensive, why should SDI disturb the Russians?

Partly this is a matter of perspective and there is at work an asymmetry that always appears when risk is assessed by a nation-state that is the target of a hostile political initiative. For the target states, even a slight likelihood of the initiative's success is intolerable if the consequence of that success is potentially catastrophic; for the targeting state a slender chance of success usually means wasted resources. Partly also this may be a function of the offence/defence phenomenon: as Walter Slocombe has pointed out, it seems to be in the nature of defences that they appear differently to those who have them than to those whose must overcome them.[58] But partly also Western reaction has been premature and, as in other instances, largely indifferent to Russian concerns. It is not obvious that SDI research will not yield effective defensive systems based on principles as yet undefined, to say nothing of technologies as yet unexplored. From the Russian point of view, having launched the first satellites and then watched the US far surpass them in surveillance technology, having developed the first ICBM and then been forced to witness the dramatic US manned space programme while Russian exploration is still confined to low-orbit procedures – from this background, a healthy scepticism is the by-product, even if it seems to be directed against scepticism. More importantly, the Russians recognize how crucial American vulnerability is to the Soviet role in Europe. Without such vulnerability there would be no stalemate at the level of strategic weapons and the entire postwar campaign to separate US security from that of Europe would collapse. The 'equality' of superpowers, the fruits of detente, the spectre of decoupling would ebb as quickly or as slowly as the defensive systems were deployed.

In coming to the negotiating table to discuss SDI, despite the confirmation of its misgivings in the INF talks, the Soviet Union found itself in a position similar to that of the US at the ABM talks. Despite American recognition that MIRVing would ultimately render fixed ICBMs obsolete, the US was forced to dispense with a MIRV ban because only the possibility of MIRVed weapons made ABM unfeasible, since even the most optimistic ABM supporters conceded that it was cheaper to build MIRVs that could swamp ABM systems than to multiply ABMs to cope with them. The US was compelled to choose: a ban on MIRVs or ABMs? And since the latter potentially threatened the vitality of all legs of the triad, the choice was clear. Here, from the Russian perspective, a system has appeared that threatens to compromise the security of the Russian homeland as well as re-coupling the Alliance states. Facing such a prospect it is hardly surprising that the Russians would be willing to drop their demands for the complete withdrawal of US GLCMs and Pershing 2s as a precondition for an INF agreement which, even if successful from their perspective, could not undo the potential damage that the SDI threatens.

Does that mean, then, that triangulation will serve some other purpose than simply getting the Russians to the table; that it might permit trade-offs between the systems in different negotiations?

The US Administration has made clear that it will not negotiate away SDI research for *any* trade-off, presumably including an INF agreement. But the US might move beyond its somewhat patronizing objective of educating the Russians about the benefits of defensive systems (with which the Russians have had more experience and to which, even after SDI, they continue to devote more resources), and relax its self-imposed restraint to the extent necessary to permit a limited ASAT treaty, for example. This is certainly in the interests of both sides and, if confined to particular ranges, need not compromise SDI research. I am most pessimistic that such an offer, so far from the SDI lure that brought the Russians to Geneva, could possibly serve as the incentive for Russian concurrence in an INF agreement that permits LRTNF modernization. It is, I believe, only the intense Soviet interest in SDI that has obscured what, by now, ought to be the unmistakable hostility of the Soviet Union to any legitimation of US forces in Europe capable of striking the Soviet Union with nuclear weapons.

So we have this situation: the United States will not move the negotiations by abandoning SDI and the Russians will not alter their position regarding INF. There is therefore little chance that either side will get the agreement it sought by amalgamation of the talks. The US will not give up SDI simply to legitimize its INF deployment. The

USSR will not acquiesce in SDI (by treaty) in exchange for the cessation and removal of the new NATO LRTNF, the GLCMs and Pershing 2s. Indeed, SDI enhances the pressure on the Soviet Union in Europe because, precisely to the extent that it reduces the vulnerability of the American homeland, it restores deterrence identity in the West. Thus the purpose of *Soviet* LRTNF modernization – to permit Russian limited nuclear strikes against European targets while reducing, through the mobility and accuracy of the SS-20, the risk of preemption and counterstrikes – is undermined by the potential of SDI to re-couple the Alliance states.

All this means that pressure will be brought to bear on the third set of talks, that dealing with strategic (offensive) weapons. There will be intense interest in using this aspect of triangulation to break the logjam created by the interaction of the other two sets of issues, SDI and INF. Here there is a potential deal, although one that would be very costly to the US.

The USSR has proposed deep cuts in offensive systems – 50 per cent, for example – in exchange for a US repudiation of LRTNF modernization. This is very tempting for the Administration. Such an agreement would please many sectors of European opinion since it would lead to the withdrawal of what otherwise will be a constant source of fear and a focus for political criticism and demonstrations, the GLCMs and the Pershing 2 deployments. At the same time it would demonstrate American sincerity in pursuing the two-track agenda, a sincerity that was in doubt in the first years of the Reagan administration, and it would accomplish this at no great cost to the Pentagon which has largely disfavored the deployments from the start. Most significantly, US domestic opinion would be enraptured as it was when Nixon delivered SALT 1 and for much the same reason: once again a conservative, staunchly anticommunist President, who promised that confrontation would inevitably lead to co-operation, had been vindicated. Only this time, the situation is even more exaggerated, for the President can justly claim that such an agreement would reduce stockpiles, a feat no earlier agreement even attempted. The American President would thereby appeal to that constituency, by no means confined to the right, that is alienated from deterrence and in part tempted by SDI. Reductions in the present, invulnerability – and 'defensive' at that – in the future: surely this coup surpasses those achieved by Nixon and could conceivably unite, if only for a time, an American consensus around the essentially benign character of American purposes and the futility of offensive arms deployment.

Of course acceptance of such a proposal would also shatter the US strategic paradigm discussed earlier; this, presumably, is why it was proposed by the Russians in the first place. The US cannot seek agreements that do nothing to reduce the vulnerability of Europe – or indeed enhance that exposure – in exchange for cuts in intercontinental systems alone. This amounts to unilateral decoupling and it cannot be long, no matter what the initial public relations reactions, before there is irresistible pressure in Europe to manage their own nuclear arsenals, and conduct their own 'negotiations from strength'. Here too, SDI plays a wild card role: because Soviet deployment of defensive systems will, it is feared, largely negate the European independent nuclear deterrents, we can expect the European demand for a variegated, counterforce nuclear arsenal to replace that of the countervalue deterrent. Such a polar force would, I fear, have incalculable consequences for the stability of the US–Soviet relationship. Then, of course, the cheering will stop; but this may be too far in the future to affect the plans of today's politicians.

Here, however, the triangulation actually works against such a trade-off of INF/START objectives. SDI will presumably make it much harder for the Russians to agree to deep cuts in offensive systems since the cheapest way to defeat defensive technologies is usually to proliferate warheads (or warhead decoys which, if they are to work in wartime, are probably ambiguous or at least unverifiably benign in peace as well). This means that all angles of the triangle must be brought into play and suggests that, apart from the public success in having talks at all, triangulation has not meant a greater likelihood of agreements truly acceptable to the long-term strategic interests of both sides.

As if in recognition of this stalemate, the new Russian leader Mikhail Gorbachev unveiled a dramatic arms control proposal on 19 January 1986. It claimed as its objective the total elimination of all nuclear weapons by the year 2000. This would be accomplished in three stages.

Stage 1. (5–8 years) Each side will reduce by 50 per cent the nuclear arms that can reach the other's territory. Neither side will retain more than 6000 warheads on the remaining delivery vehicles. The initial proposal stated that a major part of Stage 1 would be the renouncement of 'the development, testing and deployment of space strike weapons.' Later the Soviets stepped back from their original position that any space-based defense system would halt negotiations. The US and USSR will completely eliminate all intermediate-range missiles, both ballistic and cruise missiles, from the 'European Zone'.

Britain and France will pledge not to build up their existing nuclear forces, and the United States will agree not to transfer medium- and long-range missiles to other countries.

Nuclear explosions (testing) shall be immediately halted by both sides.

Stage 2. (8 years) Beginning in 1990 and lasting 5–7 years. The 'other nuclear powers' will begin to disarm. A 'freeze' will be in effect, and no transfer of weapons will be permitted. The USA and USSR will continue reductions, eliminating medium-range missiles and freezing tactical nuclear weapons. After such reductions, all countries will eliminate tactical nuclear arms with a range of up to 1000 km. Major industrial powers will make the ban on space strike weapons multilateral. All nuclear tests will stop. Non-nuclear weapons with great destructive capacity will be banned.

Stage 3. (14 years) Total Elimination by 2000. Beginning no later than 1995, all remaining nuclear weapons will be eliminated. Verification will be carried out by on-site inspection as well as 'national technical means'. Special procedures for the destruction of the weapons will be worked out.

These proposals – despite their dramatic billing of 'nuclear disarmament by the year 2000' – in some ways resembled proposals previously discussed in this chapter. Like all Russian proposals for INF, they required the complete removal of NATO missiles from Europe. Like earlier SALT successes, the proposals focused on classes of weapons by range, thus presenting the US in this context, however, with a difficult problem: how to resist the appealing call for mutually eliminating the same 'class of weapon' (intermediate range launchers) in light of the asymmetrical impact on Europe and Japan, who would remain subject to nuclear pre-emption *from* the Soviet Union after NATO gives up its ability to pre-empt selectively *against* the Soviet Union. And, like the nuclear free zone proposal, the Gorbachev version of the 'zero option' has its principal impact on the self-deterrence of the FRG.

On 23 February 1986 President Reagan responded with a US counterproposal. This plan focused directly on INF arms control and offered the Russians two options, with the goal of eliminating medium range nuclear armed missiles altogether in three years.

The Soviet Union currently has deployed 441 SS-20 MIRVed missiles, 270 within range of Europe, and 162 in the Far East and 9 in Central Asia. The Americans are about halfway through their proposed deployment of 572 single warhead weapons.

The Reagan proposals, also contained in a letter to the opposing head of state but briefed to the press, were reminiscent of earlier proposals, discussed in Chapter 9. One option called for both sides to reduce their intermediate range forces by 80 per cent. The USSR would be permitted to retain 90 SS-20s with 270 warheads, to be restricted to two bases in Soviet Central Asia, out of range of Japan and most of Europe. The US would withdraw all its INF missiles from Europe, with the right to store 270 weapons in the continental US. This amounts to a slow-motion 'zero option'.

The alternative option proposed in the US letter reiterated a November 1985 US offer that would allow the Russians 140 SS-20s in the Far East. In return the US would simply halt further INF deployments. The goal of this proposal, also, was the complete elimination of medium range missiles in three years.

Would such an offer, if accepted by the Russians, reduce the threat to countries in the extended theatre? Alas, the answer is No. Even if the US is careful to remove – rather than just move, say to Central Asia – all SS-20s, 21s and 22s from the Soviet arsenal, the USSR would still have the capability to pre-empt NATO nuclear assets selectively, while NATO could do the same only by relying on US strategic systems striking the Soviet homeland. Although it is commendable that the US is finally attempting to respond to Japanese fears that an INF agreement between the superpowers in Europe would simply shift Soviet forces to the East, and the White House has responded quickly to the Russian public relations challenge of the Gorbachev letter, such measures do not offer the prospect of evading the theorem.

The White House professed to be surprised that the Germans, British and Japanese all expressed misgivings about the American proposal. In Tokyo, Japan's foreign minister warned of 'tremendous political problems' if the US accepted an agreement eliminating SS-20s in Europe while leaving some in place against East Asia. The West German Chancellor Helmut Kohl wrote directly to President Reagan warning that Europe would still be threatened by the Russians' shorter range SS-21 and SS-23 missiles but would lack a commensurate reply, if the proposed agreement was accepted. The British are reported to have told the American envoy briefing them that such an agreement would leave Europe even more vulnerable to WPO conventional forces.

It is understandable that Washington might expect a more enthusiastic audience for a reiteration of what, after all, were the very successful US proposals of 1982. The difference is that now, with the Gorbachev letter, it appears that the US proposals might actually be accepted and this prospect exposes the fact that the US offers of 1982 were public relations successes only. As strategy, they did nothing to alleviate and, in some permutations, did much to worsen the fundamental problem of extended deterrence to which the NATO INF deployments were a response.

Equally understandable, but far more regrettable, is the reaction in some US quarters that would exploit European and Japanese distress at the Reagan reply to the Gorbachev letter. To demonstrate this unfortunate reaction, and to show how fundamental the 'theorem' is both to an understanding of European concerns for Soviet–American relations and of the consequences of American misunderstanding, I offer the following passage from a former senior official of the Reagan Administration.

> Mikhail Gorbachev's proposal to remove US and Soviet missiles from Europe has already provoked some unfamiliar reactions among America's allies. Usually our allies position themselves as the 'peace party' and hope aloud that the United States will be more forthcoming. This time our allies seem worried that the United States might be too forthcoming. To forestall any such possibility, strong negative reactions to virtually all aspects of the latest Soviet proposal are being expressed.
>
> An agreement to eliminate US and Soviet missiles (which have been deployed in Europe only since 1980) would not violate America's legal or moral commitments to our European allies. It just might stimulate Western European countries to assume a greater responsibility for their own defense. That, of course, would be a good in itself. The nations of Western Europe are populous, strong, technologically advanced and, in principle, quite capable of self-defense against a Soviet threat. So is Japan.
>
> It is refreshing to have them worry that the United States may be too eager for arms reductions.
>
> Now it is our turn to be the 'peace party' in the Western alliance.[59]

This quotation amply shows the results of a failure to appreciate the strategic significance of extended deterrence and the difficult problems it poses for the future of the Alliance, indeed the future of the world. The desire to achieve a public relations coup through arms control is apparently a temptation that is irresistible to the right as well as the left.

Is there, then, some other proposal that might use arms control as a means of reducing the threat in the extended theatre and thereby compensating for the deployments discussed in Chapter 8? The balance of this chapter is devoted to one plausible regimen, the proposal for a nuclear free zone.

The Soviet bloc has frequently put forward such a proposal. The Rapacki Plan proposed in 1957 by the Polish Foreign Minister would have forbidden the manufacture, maintenance, or installation of nuclear weapons within Poland, the DDR, FRG, and Czechoslovakia. This was, and was perceived as, an attempt to pre-empt a December 1957 North Atlantic Council decision. That decision adopted the 'nuclear shield' concept in recognition of the Alliance's failure to reach the Lisbon force structure goals that were to check Soviet conventional superiority. Since that time, similar proposals have been tabled, in November 1958 and March 1962. There have also been various non-central front, regional zones proposed: the Balkans and the Adriatic area were the subject of these, as was the Scandinavian/Nordic region, first suggested by Khrushchev in 1959.[60]

In June 1982, the Independent Commission on Disarmament and Security Issues published its final report,[61] calling for a nuclear-free zone of 150 km in width across the central front. Assuming that neither side would wish to deploy LRTNF within 75 km of the front, the proposal amounts to a tactical-nuclear-weapons free zone. Debate on the proposal has taken the usual, unprofitable channels:[62] does a nuclear tripwire enhance deterrence by a coupling to higher systems or does it increase the likelihood of deterrence failing by its very presence so near the front? Would the removal of these weapons pacify the peace community, allowing the more important LRTNF deployments to go forward, or would it merely whet the appetite of unilateralists and focus all attention on the remaining weapons? Would negotiations lend momentum to detente (since the proposal has been endorsed by Soviet commentators) or prove unnegotiable[63] (since the proposal calls for an accompanying MBFR agreement as a pre-condition, the negotiation of which has eluded the superpowers for eleven years)? Such questions are of little analytical value since they are at once as complex as but less politically central than the issue of policy to whose resolution they are meant to contribute. With the clearer idea of the problem that a developed view of the conditions of extended deterrence offers, and with the operation of the 'theorem' to avoid, we can perhaps ask more tractable questions.

Obviously the proposal for a nuclear-free zone does not involve strategic systems; thus parity and ICBM vulnerability are not affected. What effect would it have on escalation dominance? This probably depends on the outcome of conventional commitments that must be mutually adjusted to reassure both sides, but, let us assume that such adjustments are satisfactorily made. What of the 'theorem'?

By introducing a zone wider than the ranges of NATO's principal tactical nuclear weapons – Lance (115 km), Honest John (38 km), the M-109 155 mm gun (18 km), the M-110 203 mm gun (16 km) and France's Pluton (120 km)[64] – the scheme virtually guarantees that if any tactical nuclear weapons are used by NATO they will be used on FRG soil. Far from enhancing extended deterrence, the proposal gives momentum to the centrifugal development of multipolarity since it amounts to a self-deterrent of German forward defence. Since a nuclear-free zone is not enforceable against an offensive once begun, one may see that such a plan resembles no-first-use proposals in that it provides a guarantee rendered absurd by the very event it has made, if only marginally, more likely.

There *are* arms control proposals that offer theoretically satisfying options to reduce the threat extended deterrence seeks to parry. The likelihood of such options becoming reality, however, is diminished by the fact that, insofar as they do aid in re-coupling, they require Soviet assistance toward an outcome incompatible with their postwar European policy. The most recently tabled arms control option outside the INF/START discussions, the proposal for a nuclear free zone, does not offer one of the possibly satisfactory options. The Outer Space Treaty of 1967 prohibits the development, in space, of nuclear weapons and 'other weapons of mass destruction'. This does not touch, however, most anti-satellite systems; indeed in 1977 the Soviet testing of such a system prompted the United States to initiate negotiations on this subject. At the negotiations the US proposed a ban on the testing of anti-satellite weaponry. This foundered on Soviet insistence that the US space shuttle, then planned but not yet operational, was potentially, an anti-satellite system. This is exemplary, I fear, of the difficulty in concluding such a treaty: many systems that are necessary to space exploration or the defence of earth-sited objectives would also be useful as anti-satellite technology. A comprehensive ban of all potential anti-satellite deployments in space

– without qualification – would jeopardize the US ballistic missile defence programme, for example.

This does not mean, however, that there are no available treaty provisions that preserve US options regarding benign or defensive space technologies. Article 12 of the ABM Treaty of 1972 contains a prohibition on the interference with each side's 'national technical means of verification', (the euphemism for photo-reconnaissance satellites). This prohibition might be extended to all satellites and space vehicles. Hans Mark, former Secretary of the Air Force, has proposed that a treaty,

> write some 'rules of the road' for the operation of space systems and space vehicles in peacetime. These might require that, as a safety measure, satellites operated by each side would be placed in orbits that would not approach other satellites closer than some prescribed distance. Another portion of the 'rules of the road' treaty might deal with the substantial amount of 'space junk' now in earth orbit – the debris from launch vehicles, shrouds, fuel tanks and satellites no longer in use. The North American Air Defense Command now keeps track of about ten thousand pieces of space junk and the space shuttles have been struck by such debris on several missions. Though this is not yet a dangerous situation, it will be in about ten years, if Soviet and American operations in space continue without some operational changes. A 'rules of the road' treaty might contain provisions for limiting the space junk that can be left behind in any given launch operation and ultimately for cleaning it up. These 'rules of the road' might be based on certain applicable precedents in international maritime law.

The real security to surveillance systems, however, probably lies on the ground and not in space. A system of serial launches into space of new satellites and decoys in a crisis, coupled with the ability to 'turn-on' hitherto dark satellites, may well provide the best protection for a society whose strategy is so dependent on accurate and timely information. Arms control agreements that restricted this option would not serve the ultimate goals of arms control – stability and the reduction of destruction if stability collapses.

Nor are there helpful agreements that focus solely on cutting numbers of central systems. Indeed agreements on central system numbers without limits on intermediate and short-range weapons and conventional forces – or worse, in exchange for limits on NATO only – will exacerbate the problem of extended deterrence.

BALLISTIC MISSILE DEFENCE[65]

Roughly, there are two types of ballistic missile defence: *area* defence (of cities and industries) and *point* defence (of hardened silos, command and communication centres). For reasons that have as much to do with the re-definition of the BMD mission as with technological progress, BMD research and development has become an issue of intense public interest. It is the cornerstone of President Reagan's Strategic Defense Initiative (SDI) and the source of a heated debate about the desirability of complying with the Anti-Ballistic Missile (ABM) Treaty. Recalling the discussion in Chapter 7 of the relationships between MIRVs and ABM, it should be noted that only when advances in technology made it realistically conceivable to intercept attacking ballistic missiles in their boost and post-boost phases – before the separation of the multiple RVs – did this relationship change significantly enough to cast doubt in some quarters on the desirability of the treaty. In this section we will assess the potential significance of BMD for extended deterrence. It is beyond the scope of this book (and the expertise of its author) to predict whether such research and development is likely to be fruitful.

Point defence

The *1981–1982 Strategic Survey* concluded:

> The most promising advances in ABM technology since 1972 are thought to have been made in the area of short-range or low-altitude systems – those which seek to intercept and destroy incoming nuclear warheads or re-entry vehicles within the atmosphere (endoatmospherically), at altitudes below about 50 000 ft.[66]

This remains true of technology that could be deployed by the year 2000. American defence research has hitherto concentrated on a layered defence system that attempts to co-ordinate the endo-atmospheric Low Altitude Defence System (LOADS) with an exoatmospheric tier, at one time provisionally called the Homing Overlay Experiment (HOE). Such a layered system attempts to eliminate some re-entry vehicles (RVs) by means of long-range missiles carrying multiple, possibly non-nuclear homing warheads (the development of which may be several years further away), with a backup array of LOADS – using low power radars and small, nuclear-tipped missiles – to catch any warheads that have made it into the atmosphere and are directed toward the protected target. HOE consists of single missiles with multiple 'killer vehicles', protecting a large area by attacking weapons before they are widely dispersed, while LOADS launches a single warhead against a single, incoming and narrowly vectored RV at a quite minimal altitude, depriving the offense of effective decoy tactics.

Such a terminal hard-point defence – defending, for example, ICBM silos – relies on technology currently available, and thus potentially operational in ten to fifteen years. This includes interceptors like the Spartan missile for targeting RVs outside the atmosphere and shorter range weapons, like the Sprint, for endoatmospheric interception; the present design of these missiles requires nuclear warheads.

It would be a significant advance, even for the more modest objectives of point defence and an indispensable one for area defence, if a technology could be developed that intercepted attacking missiles during their boost phase, i.e., before the RVs (and decoys) have separated from the rocket. As regards point defence, it appears feasible to develop a system using space-based kinetic-energy weapons. The most immediately available technology uses chemically propelled rockets that destroy the offensive missile either by impact or nearby detonation.

Thus, soon after the year 2000 there could be deployed by the US a space-based kinetic system in co-ordination with high altitude and low altitude defensive systems. These three layers would be able to achieve modest kill probabilities in each layer, resulting in a high overall success rate.

The task of terminal defence is rendered more manageable as point defence has become a matter of concentrating protection on a given set of selected, changing targets. In collaboration, for example, with the MPS (multiple protective shelter) basing mode for MX, such a system might have performed the significant service of multiplying, beyond any sensible utility, the required number of Soviet warheads for pre-emption, thus effectively solving the ICBM vulnerability problem despite an admitted inability to constitute a 'leak-proof' defence.

> Specifically, if a shelter-warhead kill ratio of unity is assumed (and also unrealistically – no reliability problem), the Soviet Union can be certain of 'killing' one MX for every 23 warheads dispatched to saturate a particular 'linear track'. However, if a minimal LOADS deployment (one interceptor per 'linear track') is added (at an

estimated FY 1980 cost of $11–12 billion), Soviet targeteers – not knowing which shelter contained the MX missile – would have to double their warhead allocation, since the interceptor missile could be defending any of the 23 shelters.[67]

The important point to be emphasized is that terminal defences gain effectiveness from the nature of the deceptive basing that allows point defence to become selective. This makes the scheme highly relevant to new, single warhead or other mobile ICBMs but no less helpful for fixed command installations (or silos) since these can be hardened.

Assuming that such selective point defence could be made practicable, what effect would this have on extended deterrence? It would rehabilitate it precisely to the extent that ICBM vulnerability diminished it in the first place. That extent, I argued in Chapter 8, is not very great and thus, in Chapter 11, I concluded that the benefits to extended deterrence of a secure MX basing mode were marginal.

Area defence

Exoatmospheric non-nuclear interception is a much less proven technology. For point defence, both layers are expected to operate synergistically, with the HOE systems compensating for LOADS vulnerability to radar blackout, and LOADS compensating for the infra-red homing system difficulties in discriminating between the various payloads a ballistic missile can carry. The real promise of exoatmospheric systems, however, lies in their potential to intercept attacking missiles during their boost and post-boost phase within the atmosphere.

The boost phase (about 3 to 5 minutes) is the period during which the ballistic missile rockets operate to bring it to (or near) its peak velocity. At this stage, the missile has all its warheads aboard, its initial location is known, it is moving relatively slowly, and the heat from its engines allows tracking. In the post-boost phase (about 3 to 6 minutes) the warheads (and decoys) are released from the last stage of the missile. It is followed by the mid-course phase outside of the atmosphere, the lengthiest part of the trajectory (about 20 minutes). The terminal phase is the period from shortly before re-entry into the atmosphere until detonation (about 1 minute).

The attraction of attacking a missile throughout its trajectory is that it allows a multi-layered defense, each of which can be less than

> perfect. [I]f each layer disabled 85% of the remaining warheads, a five layered system would allow less than one warhead in 10,000 . . . [although] a respectable 50% rate would allow through over 300 warheads.

Several technologies are being explored to attack the incoming missile during the first three stages. (1) The LASER (Light Amplification by Stimulated Emission of Radiation) requires a perfectly aligned beam of light that can disable its target; (2) particle beams are streams of subatomic particles that disrupt the structure of missiles. Each system has its shortcomings: particle beams tend to lose focus in the vacuum of outer space, while laser beams disseminate within the atmosphere, owing to clouds, dust, and water vapour.

A *chemical laser* uses the energy stimulated by chemical reactions – for example, the combination of hydrogen and flourine – to create an intense, focused beam of light, directed by a mirror. It is estimated that such a technology could be deployed in the decade following the year 2000. Chemical lasers – based in space because their wavelengths will not penetrate the atmosphere – are probably more useful as anti-satellite weapons, however, since elementary ICBM countermeasures, such as rotating missile boosters or decreasing the propulsion period critically reduce the time allowed the laser to concentrate on a single point. It may be that new developments in optics such as phased arrays and phase conjugation – efforts to increase brightness and coherence – will prove successful. At the current period, even a most optimistic commentator conceded:

> US laser research and development programs are, at the time of this writing, at a technical crossroads. No laser weapon, of any size or character has been demonstrated in space, and important engineering, though not fundamental scientific, issues await resolution and demonstration in the areas of the ancillary technologies of optics (mirrors for laser beam control), of target acquisition, tracking and precision pointing, and of control mechanisms to marry the aiming mirror to the sensors. Therefore, any predictions concerning the strategic promise of laser weapons in space in the late 1990s must be phrased cautiously.[68]

Ground-based lasers can be used with mirrors in space for boost-phase interceptions. Two such technologies are the excimer laser, employing higher-energy ('excited') states of molecules to produce the

Figure 13.2 A ballistic missile trajectory

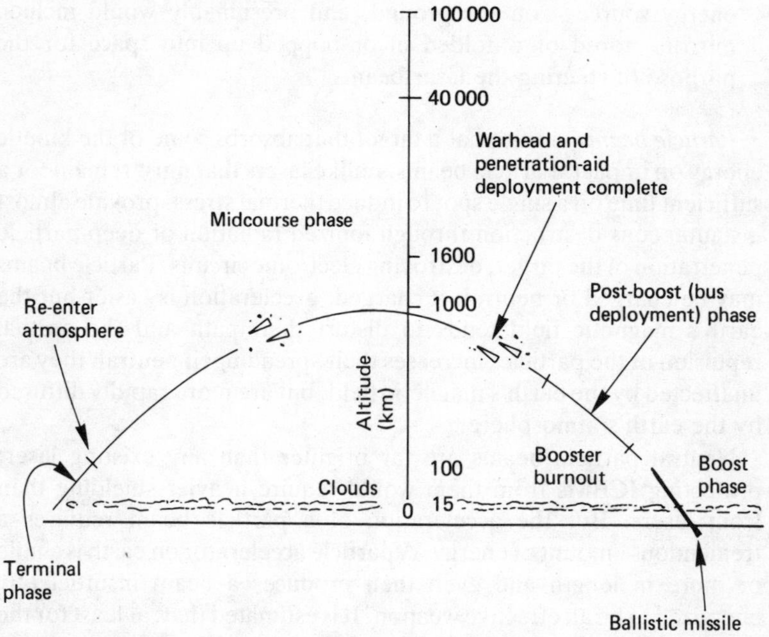

beam and the free electron laser (FEL) which uses the effect of oscillating electromagnetic fields on electron beams to stimulate radiation. Unlike chemical lasers, the wavelengths of these technologies allow penetration of the atmosphere. Both are thought to be at least 20–25 years away from deployment and neither has demonstrated anything approaching the required lethality to destroy ICBMs.

Farther away are X-ray lasers, powered by nuclear explosions, which would have wider beam angles and higher power than optical lasers. At least as distant as X-ray lasers are rail guns, which electromagnetically accelerate objects to speeds above 15 kilometres per second.

> Finally it should be noted that all laser systems would be vulnerable to other lasers. In general, the rules of the competition are that ground-based lasers will defeat space-based ones, larger ones will defeat smaller ones, and bomb-driven X-ray lasers looking up through the fringes of the atmosphere will defeat the same sort of X-ray lasers looking down into the fringes of the atmosphere. Vulnerabilities will also differ as between ground-based and space-

> based lasers. The former would have the weapons – or at least their energy source – on the ground, and presumably would include mirrors stored or unfolded in or popped up into space for the purpose of steering the laser beams.[69]

Particle beams are fired at a target that absorbs some of the kinetic energy on impact. Particle beams, unlike lasers that must remain for a sufficient time on a single spot to induce thermal stress, provide almost instantaneous destruction through ionized radiation or deep particle penetration of the target, destroying electronic circuits. Particle beams may be charged or neutral: if charged, acceleration is easier but the earth's magnetic field tends to distort their path and the mutual repulsion of the particles increases their spreading; if neutral, they are unaffected by the earth's magnetic field, but are more rapidly diffused by the earth's atmosphere.

Neutral particle beams are far brighter than any existing laser; protecting ICBMs from them would require heavier shielding than from lasers. But the acceleration of a particle beam requires a tremendous amount of energy. A particle accelerator on earth is a mile or more in length and even then produces a beam insufficiently energized to be an effective weapon. It is estimated that, at least for the next decade, we will be unable to develop a technology capable of putting more than 10 per cent of the primary energy generated by an accelerator into the particle beam itself. Such large energy plants might be assembled in space, or new technology might obviate the need for such large plants; in any event, this probably means a nuclear energy source would have to be developed to compensate for low efficiency. Even if this were accomplished, and energy output greatly increased, particle beam weapons would still face the hurdle of overcoming jamming, decoys, and space mines.

> Before an operational beam weapon becomes a reality, major problems will also have to be overcome in the development of power generation equipment to meet such a system's enormous energy demands, in the miniaturization of beam formation equipment, and in beam pointing, tracking and attack assessment.
>
> Optimistic estimates see operational laser weapons being as much as 10–15 years away, and particle-beam weapons 20 years away.[70]

Even if the technological problems of space-based BMD were mastered, these systems would have to be protected from killer satellites, mines, and opposing beam-originating systems.

Through all of these considerations is entwined a serious problem for space-based ABMs: however effective space-based systems may be against ballistic missiles, they would appear to be more effective in suppressing defenses. And direct-ascent antisatellite systems or ground-based lasers may be still more effective than space-based systems in this latter role.[71]

Assuming for the purposes of this discussion, however, that these obstacles could be overcome, what would be the strategic significance of such a development? Specifically (1) would it restore effective extended deterrence and (2) would it undermine the deterrence assumption? Based on the analysis of Book I, it ought to be clear that such a development – to the extent that it reduced the vulnerability of the US homeland alone – would, precisely to that extent, re-credit extended deterrence and re-couple the two theatres. This would surely justify President Reagan's dramatic proposal for a Strategic Defense Initiative even though it would scarcely render nuclear weapons 'impotent and obsolete'. The fact that BMD might not be deployed in favour of protecting the European or Japanese theatre itself is largely irrelevant. (It is a failure to grasp this point that underlies the observation that American allies in Europe are supposed to be dismayed by the prospect of BMD because 'it has nothing in it for them'.) It would become possible for the US to plausibly threaten that an attack on European states would be treated as an attack on the US homeland. Deterrence identity within the Alliance would be restored. At the same time, it must be conceded that such BMD technology, in the protected, effective mode assumed for the sake of this analysis, would also have profound effects on extended deterrence were it in the hands of the Soviet Union alone.

Suppose then that both superpowers were to deploy defensive systems that protected their national homelands. What effect would this have on the extended theatre? *Mutual* BMD does not restore US deterrence identity with Europe. Rather it purchases extended deterrence by making a sanctuary of the US and the USSR and confining conflict to Europe. In other words, the uncoupling implication of the theorem returns – in a heightened form to be sure – with the consequence that proliferation to European states, including France and Great Britain, would have to be polar to be significant.

Would such technology, if successfully deployed by the US, weaken the deterrence assumption? It will be recalled that, in Book I, the relationship of central deterrence was characterized as highly stable, yielding the relative invulnerability of the vital interests of each state from an assault on those interests by the other. Only if these vital interests appear to be compromised would either side be willing to risk them further by a nuclear attack that invites nuclear retaliation. What if one side could prevent that exposure; wouldn't that upset the stable calculus of central deterrence? If BMD were to render the US homeland – the physical and ecological protection of which may be taken to be the United States's most vital interest – invulnerable to Russian missiles, we might see a more aggressive US attitude toward the vital interests of the USSR. (Although this was not appreciably the case before the US became vulnerable to Soviet nuclear weapons.) One need not speculate on the precise geopolitical events, in Eastern Europe, or in China, that this would precipitate to acknowledge that such freedom of action is denied to both superpowers at present. The argument that, because the Soviet Union does not rely on an assured destruction strategy, she would therefore be indifferent to, or 'might actually be reassured to see' US BMD deployment is absurd. Soviet nuclear strategy, which might appropriately be classified as a 'war-fighting' strategy, depends on an assured destruction element[72] (indeed the Soviet SLBMs, SS-4s and -5s are good for little else). It would be a serious limitation of such a strategy that central theatre capabilities against the US were nullified.

For the very reason that BMD is crucial to war-fighting strategies, as argued in Chapter 10, we may expect an aggressive Soviet pursuit of such technology, regardless of American research and planning. Since the arguments of the previous paragraph are symmetrical with respect to the superpowers, it would therefore appear to be unavoidable – at least within the confines of the ABM Treaty that do not prohibit BMD research – that the US pursue the possibilities of a BMD programme. Thus the usual questions about BMD policy – would BMD be technologically effective; would BMD development encourage an arms race or a competition in what are usually, and misleadingly (in light of their contribution to war-fighting strategies) called 'defensive' systems[73] – are not likely to have much impact on whether such programmes will be explored. The answers to such questions, if we could know them, would not respond to the dynamics of deterrence that drive BMD research.

There is one more point to be made regarding BMD and the deterrence assumption. According to this assumption, there is no decisive advantage to striking first, indeed there is a substantial penalty – assured retaliation – to doing so. Suppose, however, that both superpowers deployed effective 'defensive' systems, for example, in space. Then that society that struck first, *at the defensive systems*, would gain a decisive advantage if it would emerge with its own defensive systems intact. Obviously this would have a profound and malignant effect on the continued vitality of the deterrence assumption.

This brief section attempted to acquaint the reader with the basic technologies and doctrinal significance of BMD deployment. Its very brevity suggests that the assumption of feasibility is one made for the purposes of evaluating argument and does not imply any judgement regarding the practicability of what is, for the present, a highly uncertain weapons system with respect to its most crucial element, the boost phase interception. Despite the visionary television address by President Reagan on the subject,[74] the official US position on BMD development – and the Strategic Defense Initiative that has been launched to pursue research – remains that of the Department of Defense's five point programme referred to Congress, which concluded that BMD today

> is not at the technological stage where it could provide an adequate defense against Soviet missiles. For the future, we are not yet sure how well ballistic missile defenses will work; what they will cost; how Soviet ballistic missile defenses – which would almost certainly be deployed in response to an US missile defense system – would affect US and allied offense capabilities; and what would be the political ramifications of altering the ABM Treaty.[75]

One must simply say that while BMD technology may be at a turning point, it is uncertain where the paths that have opened up will take us. For the foreseeable future, BMD offers the most realistic possibility of providing point defence particularly if it is accompanied by negotiated cuts in those systems most threatening to hardened targets and deceptive basing for those targets. In light of Soviet doctrine, one must ask whether a US BMD programme is likely to increase or decrease the willingness of the Soviet Union to make significant cuts in her largest, most accurate ICBMs. Finally, we should recall from Chapter 12 that superpower deployment of defensive systems virtually requires that any proliferation in the absence of extended deterrence be polar.

CONCLUSION

One alternative to maintaining an extended deterrent in any particular theatre is to obviate the need for such a deterrent by reducing the threat sought to be deterred. In this chapter we have evaluated three possible means of doing this in the European theatre: through an enhanced conventional defense, through theatre arms control, by deploying ballistic missile defence. For different reasons, none of these approaches in isolation appears wholly satisfactory at the present time. Conventional forces do not reduce the nuclear threat since they are not really fungible with NATO nuclear deployments. Arms control will not reduce the Soviet threat, which is to say negotiated agreements are unlikely to remove those deployments that, by threatening the theatre, require a deterrent. Ballistic missile defence cannot reduce the threat (beyond the not insignificant, but not decisive, contribution to ICBM security) for at least the foreseeable future since it is unable to do more than promise a remote possibility of reshaping the nuclear strategic map so thoroughly that deterrence identity between the US and Europe would reappear.

14 Conclusion

Di nova pena mi conven far versi. . . io era già disposto tutto quanto a riguardar ne lo scoperto fondo. . . .

(Of new pain I must make verses . . . I was now wholly set on looking into the bottom disclosed there. . . .)

Canto XX, *Inferno*

What policies a society should adopt for its nuclear weapons is a profoundly *moral* question. But it is not the same sort of moral question that confronts an individual who must make particular choices in the decisions in his daily life. What is right and wrong for a society constitutes a different inquiry from the questions of right and wrong for the individual. Few of us deny that to preserve its national security in a war, a society may legitimately destroy enemy targets in the course of which it will kill unarmed persons; indeed that society may authorize individuals to do the killing who, were they acting simply on their own behalf, it would try for murder. In a democracy, the citizen faces two questions: what ought I authorize my society to do on its behalf (which includes, but is scarcely limited to, its responsibility to protect me)? What ought I to do – or refuse to do – to discharge my own responsibilities (which are not limited to considerations on my own behalf but which include my duty to protect my society)? What these questions have in common in any particular instance is that they demand that we understand the factual context of such choices. For there is no moral question of any significance that is not fact-drenched and no 'facts' of any importance that are not inextricably embedded in particular ways of looking at the world. Accordingly, I believe that the citizens of democracies require of themselves that they be informed of the salient facts about nuclear weapons policy and that the assumptions that organize these facts be exposed. This I have endeavored to do in Book I: to inform the reader by describing the history of US nuclear strategy and to expose the strategic context that structured that development. I have not tried to explain that history, merely to describe it from a strategic point of view. Thus I have described not so much what men thought but how they thought. I have avoided saying – because I do not know – why they thought so. This has not been done in the service of a particular political agenda. The arguments made in the preceding chapters might well serve programmes with which the author has little sympathy.

Book I followed this theme: crises in vulnerability did not directly perturb the stable *central* relationship between the US and the Soviet Union, a relationship structured by the 'deterrence assumption', but were felt in the realm of *extended* deterrence; when these tensions in the extended theatre were resolved by innovations in strategic doctrine, these innovations then played back into the central relationship, changing *that* relationship. With this hypothesis it was possible to account for the stability of the central relationship despite significant change in strategic doctrine, and to give an account of the cyclical nature of doctrinal change.

To note briefly in recapitulation some aspects of the doctrinal changes: How was Controlled Response different from its predecessor, Massive Retaliation? It targeted counterforce objectives in a phased sequence, requiring a new Single Integrated Operations Plan (SIOP) and rejecting the Optimum Target Mix. Was Assured Destruction different from Controlled Response since no new SIOP was required? Certainly; it rejected a dependence on damage limitation, relying instead on Flexible Response by NATO in the theatre to perform the run-up to a withheld counter-city mission. How is the Essential Equivalence/Countervailing Strategy different from its predecessor, Assured Destruction, retaining as it does an assured destruction mission? It rearranges the counterforce element of phased attack into much smaller packages and now confines the run-up to command and control, nuclear assets and war reserves, and forces in the theatre.

And all of these changes, revolutions between total and graduated responses with the wheel not quite returning to the same place when the cycle was completed, can be described in terms of the increasingly difficult demands of extended deterrence; that is, the desire to project the nuclear threat beyonds the confines of the deterrence assumption in the context of the declining margin of US advantage that was the result of increased US vulnerability. By extricating the recurring patterns of central deterrence from the developing pattern of extended deterrence, one could observe a direction to this change, as a bicycle wheel might be observed going down a slope. And by approaching the problem from a strategic perspective we were able to draw the connection between nuclear deterrence and proliferation, subjects which, unfortunately, are usually discussed separately.

The concepts of central and extended deterrence and the relationships between them are absolutely indispensable to a strategic grasp of the facts of nuclear strategy. The failure to master such concepts and relationships is maddening to strategic commentators. Edward Luttwak, for example, writes:

> It has been reported that on the eve of his assumption of office President Carter asked the Joint Chiefs of Staff to supply him with an estimate of the minimum number of strategic nuclear weapons that would suffice for deterrence; the Chiefs were specifically invited to consider the possibility that 200 ICBMs might be enough.
>
> Even without knowing the exact form of words employed by the President, it is a fair speculation that the 'deterrence' he had in mind could only have been simple, strike-back-only deterrence – that is, deterrence for the self-protection of the United States *strictu sensu*. It will be recalled that during that same period President Carter was insistent on expressing his devotion to the North Atlantic Alliance.
>
> Subsequent events show that it would be wrong to attribute sinister motives to the conjunction of the presidential enthusiasms; no conscious intent to decouple European security from stategic nuclear deterrence is to be imputed. One is not dealing with holy selfishness, nor indeed with strategic logic of any kind. It is rather a case of unstrategical pragmatism, apt to pass virtually unobserved in a political culture itself profoundly unstrategical. For the President NATO is one subject and strategic nuclear policy quite another; why confuse matters by connecting the two?[1]

Yet even when specialists attend to these matters and develop an acute and sensitive appreciation of ideas within the strategic context, they may fail to appreciate the assumptions that provide that context. For example, Earl C. Ravenal, in a recent article for *International Security*,[2] clearly recognizes the *paradoxical* – not contradictory – requirements created by extended deterrence within the context of central deterrence as structured by the deterrence assumption, and recognizes also that this paradox has driven the evolution of nuclear strategy. He does not go further, however, and recognize also the mutually affecting quality of the two regimes; thus his call for an abandonment of extended deterrence, based on his correct perception that it threatens the otherwise stable central relationship, ignores the possibility that the rescission of extended deterrence would yield multipolarity with its profound and malignant effects on central stability. Ravenal has simply assumed the stable context of mutually assured destruction, within which concepts of deterrence operate, to be ineluctable and thus has inadvertently been led to propose a tactical cure that would be a strategic catastrophe.

Book I draws connections between deterrence and the development of strategy in an effort to cultivate in the reader some appreciation for the morphology of nuclear strategy. At each turn in the cycle of doctrinal change, it was a development in strategic vulnerability – operational, logistical or technological – that threatened the viability of the prevailing strategy. At present, the source of the latest vulnerability – the fifth discontinuity – arises not from technological or operational developments but from the growing social alienation of the democratic publics from the policy of nuclear deterrence.

Both experts and the laity appear to recognize this. A recent Adelphi Paper, whose topic is scarcely one of widespread popular interest,[3] begins 'with the simple proposition that the defense policies and strategies of democratic states will not remain viable if a majority (or even a substantial, vocal and influential minority) of their populations hold these policies to be undesirable'. Reporting on the IISS Conference in the Hague in 1982, Flora Lewis wrote for the *New York Times*:

> [E]xperts acknowledge that democratic countries cannot successfully plan for their security without broad public support, and that such support can no longer be taken for granted.
>
> Whether a consensus existed and was lost, or whether public indifference was mistakenly read as endorsement of intricate plans, can be argued. What is clear is that a big gap has opened between people who thought they knew best and people who didn't really know what the others were up to.[4]

Yet the strategic problem that gives rise to those aspects of nuclear deterrence from which European and American publics are alienated – the constant demand for new weapons, the necessary overtness and brutality of the threat to fight a nuclear war in Europe, the modesty of our arms control objectives, and the apparently reasonable intransigence of the Soviet Union – has not been resolved. The problem of extended deterrence is still very much a problem because, (1) as before, the Russians pose a frightful threat to European and Far Eastern security and, (2) in a new development, superpower proliferation has become a realistic possibility. Large parts, I should think most, of public and expert opinion would deny the first and second of these propositions, respectively, because both groups have become accustomed to a world that is itself accustomed to nuclear deterrence.

But there is nothing inevitable about our present security. One purpose of the present work is to shatter this complacency lest it inadvertently lead to that catastrophe with the fears of which it currently co-exists in the public mind.

It is true that the Soviet Union poses little immediate threat to the states of Western Europe or China. For many reasons it is appropriate to describe the USSR as a conservative rather than adventuristic world power, decidedly risk averse and perpetually willing to put off the universal triumph of socialism if the immediate pursuit of that objective appears to commit her to ineffectual allies (Somalia) or superpower conflict (*vide* the Cuban missile crisis, the 1973 Arab–Israeli war). At the same time, she can be described as shrewd (Somalia, again), duplicitous (the 1973 Egyptian surprise attack, the Cuban missile crisis, again) and willing to use force when the odds are overwhelmingly favourable (Czechoslovakia, Hungary, Afghanistan). But the fact that the Soviet Union is such a power does not mean that the Russians are incapable of dreaming of a Russian empire that has neutralized its adversaries in Central Europe and whose vision is as faithfully repeated in Paris and London as it is now in Berlin and Sofia. It simply means that extended deterrence has been an overwhelming success in shaping not only our expectations of the Soviet state but the Russians' expectations of themselves. Were Europe the weak and disorganized area that China once appeared to the Soviet Union, incapable of responding credibly to a nuclear threat or attack, I have little doubt that Western Europe would begin to appear differently to Russians with about the same rapidity that the Soviet Union would appear differently to the West. Then the popular essays would stress Russian historic expansionism just as they once stressed Russia's historic vulnerability to foreign invasion. As it is with the economist explaining yesterday's stock-market events, there will always be plausible narratives that purport to find in national histories the prologues to the story about to be told.

Much the same thing is true of our expectations regarding nuclear proliferation to Germany and Japan. Thus far, US extended deterrence has functioned so thoroughly that we see these states, and they see themselves, as that policy has shaped them. But there is nothing inevitable about this, and those who most strongly urge that the US abandon the demanding role imposed by extended deterrence would do well to contemplate the multipolar world that would come in the wake of such an abandonment. For those who merely urge that the US relinquish those programmes and policies that constitute the extended deterrent but who seem unaware of why those policies were undertaken in the first place, there lies the danger that they will move the US all the more forcefully down that path to whose terminus they have given so little thought.

The requirement that a credible nuclear threat in the extended relationship must be a variegated, potentially selective counterforce threat has consequences for all relationships. Hitherto, the national 'independent deterrents' of non-superpower nations, e.g., the UK and France, did not disturb the central relationship. And precisely because they were not capable of modulated attacks, they were unlikely to be used as a trigger for another nation's forces. The events that eroded extended deterrence in the 1970s and 1980s, however, also made the acquisition of a sufficient nuclear deterrent in the extended theatre that much more difficult. The barriers to truly effective entry to the relationships of nuclear deterrence were raised and the sufficiency of the independent deterrents confined to a remote possibility that was in any event unavailable to nations without a geographical buffer to invasion. This has had the effect of ensuring that such entry, if it were successfully accomplished, would prove that much more lethal to the deterrence assumption whereby central stability has been maintained.

Something like the 'deterrence assumption' is meant by those statesmen who speak of mutual assured destruction as a part of the world, or a fact of life. They wish to distinguish this notion from a strategic policy and are right to do so. But this admirable programme is carried too far if it is assumed that such a stalemate is *necessarily* a part of the strategic environment. Indeed one implication of the view adopted in this book is that Japan and the Federal Republic of Germany are not some sort of 'dependent variable, waiting passively for the evolution of new trends in the superpower relationship. On the contrary, the relationship itself will depend in no small degree on the effects of'[5] Germany's and Japan's policies and actions.

To avoid this common error, I have chosen to introduce the term 'deterrence assumption' to demark uniquely thermonuclear deterrence from the classical deterrence strategies of defence and punishment and to distinguish that strategy from the condition of mutually assured destruction. To recapitulate: Mutual Assured Destruction is neither a doctrine nor a strategy; it is therefore to be distinguished from Assured Destruction (the strategic doctrine of the United States from roughly 1963–73) and also from an assured destruction capability (the secure forces able to destroy with high confidence a third to a half of the population and half to two-thirds of the industrial capacity of the targeted nation). An assured destruction capability is one of the missions composing the present US strategy. The mutual possession by the superpowers of such a capability is a necessary, but not a sufficient condition for the deterrence assumption to function. Thus those critics, usually on the right, who decry MAD as a strategy are off the mark; but those commentators, usually of the left, who assure us that the condition of MAD is an unshakeable fact of international life are also being misled.[6]

We have seen arise a new idea in deterrence, a peculiarly nuclear phenomenon, that would restructure threats so as to make homelands inviolable at the very hour of their greatest vulnerability. Extended deterrence thereafter arose as an anomaly, a preservation of the theory of strategic bombing in a new context, resulting in the evolution described in Book I. The result, in every doctrinal era since the deterrence assumption arose, was a managed response controlled by a single decider. These doctrines could not have developed in the absence of a *single* integrated operations plan, even if, as has been shown, every new doctrine did not require a new SIOP. Nor could they be managed in the absence of a single decision maker, or in the presence of multiple deciders any one of whom might precipitate what otherwise would have been a withheld threat.

If such remarks are directed to students of this subject, this book as a whole is directed to the public. The logic of its argument is, after all, that vulnerabilities have been cyclical and that the next cycle of vulnerability lies in the public itself. For it is the public that is asking the wrong questions and ignoring the crucial ones. So long as debate focuses on US–Soviet central deterrence which is secure, as the left argues, and which is increasingly less stable, as we hear from the right, we will be unable to achieve the social consensus upon which strategy in a democracy must depend.

Indeed I fear a genuine crisis of authority in the West as governments appear, to their publics, more and more in the grip of a mindless and deadly bureaucratic dynamic while opposition parties exploit this alienation, *as they should*. Unless governments are willing to educate their publics, they ought to fail and, in this field, education by leaders must be preceded by the understanding of experts, not simply the facile manipulation of concepts within a system sealed off from any political reality. Who has not felt this disturbing sense of unreality, as described by Sir Michael Howard?

> When I read the flood of scenarios in strategic journals about first-strike capabilities, counterforce or countervailing strategies, flexible response, escalation dominance and the rest of the postu-

lates of nuclear theology, I ask myself in bewilderment: this war they are describing, *what is it about*? The defense of Western Europe? Access to the Gulf? The protection of Japan? If so, why is this goal not mentioned, and why is the strategy not related to the progress of conflict in these regions? But if it is not related to this kind of specific object, what are we talking about? Has not the bulk of American thinking been exactly what Clausewitz described – something that, because it is divorced from any political context, is 'pointless and devoid of sense'?

It is precisely to restore this 'political context' for strategy that I have relied on the concepts of centrality and extension. It is beyond the scope of this book to determine why these concepts should provide such helpful analytical perspectives. One may speculate, however, that this is the case because these ideas relate deterrence to the underlying *political* commitments of self-protection and self-assertion, to vulnerability and to competition, that is, to the political realities from which so much deterrence theory seems itself to be 'decoupled'.

Why then was strategic innovation repeatedly resorted to as the means of coping with crises in extension? Again, for a political, not a military reason: the deterrence assumption was sufficient to create a strategic fact, but it only partly served the political purpose for US forces. The American political culture required something more than simply a morally desolate fortress, shared alone with our most implacable adversary. This commitment to protect democratic societies because they are thought somehow necessary to the US purpose in the world may be difficult to convey to older cultures accustomed to greater cynicism in alliance making. Yet, this American commitment, more than any military fact, accounts for the continuing refusal of the US to decouple her security from that of her allies by designating SIOP targets for European priority, that is for use only in behalf of Europe rather than in retaliation for an attack on the US herself.

The public must become aware that stability in central deterrence does not assure stability in extended deterrence. This awareness will not be promoted by politicians who claim to have no idea why the US should have more than the relatively few weapons required to effectively destroy Soviet society. Moreover, the public must also come to appreciate that instability in the extended context can play back into central stability. One sometimes feels that such an appreciation is lacking in US administration officials whose calculated belligerence toward the USSR has such debilitating effects on relations with our allies.

But most necessary is an appreciation, by publics and officials alike, of the political basis for strategy. Consider the following excerpt from a generally hostile notice in the *New York Times Book Review* of *Missile Envy* by Helen Caldicott.

> Dr Caldicott is convincing in her criticism of the American deployment in Europe of the mobile, highly accurate Pershing missiles – some 10 minutes' flight time from obliterating the computer command structure with which the Russians control their arsenal. The Reagan Administration defends the Pershings on the ground that Russian missiles could destroy European targets in the same 10 minutes, but Dr Caldicott points out that the Russians are much more threatened by the loss of their own command system than we are by the loss of lives in Europe.
>
> Within the logic of nuclear warfare, Dr Caldicott is generally skillful in showing how we ask the Russians to assume risks that we would never tolerate if our national positions were reversed. We demand parity with, or superiority over, the Soviet arsenal one-to-one, ignoring the fact that all other nations with strategic nuclear weapons are allies to us but enemies to the Soviet Union. In strategic matters, we see what we want to see, quietly pressing our advantages while howling loudly to rectify our disadvantages. This is all too human.

A more accurate description would be: in strategic matters 'we' seldom see anything at all, and thus tend simply to extrapolate from our domestic and personal lives. The fact that the Soviet Union must face 'all other nations with strategic nuclear weapons [because they] are allies to us' is scarcely a reason for the US to agree to deploy a significantly inferior force than the Soviet Union's. The US is not behind the fact that other nations have nuclear weapons or that they are targeted on the Soviet Union. It is rather because these nations perceive a realistic threat to their security that they have become 'enemies' to the USSR. Yet the view that there are no such threats, that the broad stability of central deterrence is the norm among nations, the commonplace rule for other states, is so pervasive in America that it sometimes appears that, to Americans, all international conflict is simply a ghastly mistake.

From a view of one person addressing another, it is perhaps unfair to 'ask the Russians to assume risks we would never tolerate if our national positions were reversed' but from a *strategic* point of view that is precisely what must be done. Such risks are not assumed by the Russians as the result of a polite acquiescence in our requests but are imposed by the US because they do give the USSR less freedom of action. If, in treaty negotiations, a US proposal asks the Russians to assume certain risks we must not expect that such a proposal will be accepted unless the outcome is relatively less costly to the USSR, that is, imposes fewer risks, than other courses of action within American power. Snide (or self-serving) characterizations of such proposals may bear on our sincerity, or our optimism or our cynicism but they do not bear on the fairness of such proposals because the objective of the negotiations is not to achieve equivalent force structures, but to achieve stable ones and not only stable as to each other, but enhancing stability among all nuclear and potentially nuclear states. Unfortunately, equivalence is about the only standard some commentators can bring to a judgment of the matter. As I endeavoured to show in the preceding chapter, even this simple concept is strategically laden and its use as a standard is vacuous rather than determinative in the absence of some grasp of the strategic consequences of the point of view of the observer.

This is perhaps why Dr Caldicott and her reviewer find themselves in agreement that the loss of European lives is less significant to the US than the risk to the Soviet Union of the loss of her command centres (leaving aside the point that the range of the Pershing 2 is insufficient to strike most Russian command centres and that the far more numerous SS-20s to which the review obliquely refers are themselves not targeted on European cities, but on NATO bomber fields, warhead inventories and command centres all of which are easily within their range).

From a point of view empty of any basis for strategy, of course European publics are extinguishable at less cost to the US than Russian military centres to the USSR. They don't 'count' by such rules any more than the hyper-technical calculations of first-strike vulnerabilities count the emotional impact of the loss of millions of 'collateral' casualties. What follows from this may not, however, be quite what the two authors had in mind; if Pershing 2 deployments truly impose a greater threat than the threat opposed to them, then they are an excellent means of protecting European publics. Whether this is a justified inference depends upon many other matters, discussed in Chapter 8.

Book II introduced a 'theorem' that, broadly stated, proposed that attempts to cure decoupling must either fail, since they would fail to alter the calculus of risk for the US, or succeed, and if succeed, do so by uncoupling the central and extended theatres. By 'uncoupling' was simply meant a policy of altering the risk to the central homeland by attempts to confine nuclear strikes to the extended theatre. The long-range theatre nuclear force (LRTNF) was explained in these terms. Threatening the Soviet Union through its increased range and penetrability, LRTNF promised to recouple the strategic and extended deterrents. Yet by its accuracy and survivability it also offered the option of limiting US retaliation such that, with the withheld option of an attack on the Soviet homeland from theatre weapons, the likelihood of Russian retaliation against the US might be reduced. The consequences of the theorem implied an increasingly alienated public opinion in some theatres of US nuclear extension. As Stanley Hoffmann has observed,

> Clearly the present debate is but the latest manifestation of the permanent West European fear of becoming a war zone. If the United States, by refusing to risk its homeland in the event of a Soviet attack on Western Europe, 'decouples' because of its loss of nuclear superiority or for any other reason such as NATO's present inability to strike the western part of the Soviet Union, Western Europe would be left to the mercy of the Soviets, or destroyed in a conventional or limited nuclear war. . . . It is awareness – dim or blinding – of these points which explains the psychological contradictions and contortions of the European protest movement. People who are in an impossible position . . . tend to react with a mix of illusions, resentments, and inconsistencies because the grammar of emotions has nothing to do with the logic of the mind.[7]

The US, though often concerned about European fears, has seldom determined what Europeans actually fear. If the theorem is correct, it is the United States that the Europeans, and the Japanese, will come to fear.

Having set forth the theorem and sketched the strategic vulnerability that might be inferred from its operation, I devoted the remainder of Book II to ways of mitigating or avoiding this result. A canvass of various measures that might rehabilitate extended deterrence did not disclose any decisively promising options either in the deployment of new nuclear strategies or new nuclear technologies. The possibility of replacing the extended deterrent with new national central deterrents appeared to weaken the very structure of nuclear deterrence itself. Finally, I assessed programmes to accommodate an eroded extended deterrent by obviating the need for such a deterrent and concluded that such programmes were unlikely to prove helpful or, in the case of missile defence, to be of more than marginal assistance in the foreseeable future.

Of course it does not therefore follow from this melancholy review that the Soviet Union has ceased or will cease to be deterred from an attack on a theatre hitherto regarded as enjoying the protection of the US nuclear force. First, we may go on as before, in a strategic environment that appears to have decoupled the US deterrent. Given the necessary uncertainty surrounding such a development and the devastating costs of miscalculation, we can expect that the USSR would exploit the opportunities conferred by this situation with great caution. Even if it has become, in some theoretical way, irrational for the US to act out of the pretension that decoupling has not occurred, it is not irrational to maintain the pretence. And what adversary can be wholly confident that the US is only pretending? Robert Jervis has noted that

> [a] state can credibly threaten to initiate risky action when it could not credibly threaten to actually start a war. And the former threat could be enough to deter . . . [T]here is an irreducible chance that a Russian conventional attack would lead the US to use its tactical nuclear weapons, an irreducible chance that, no matter what doctrine each side professes, such use would lead to strategic nuclear war.[8]

Second, we might face up to the uncoupling predicted by the theorem and through a variety of political means attempt to cope with its consequences. Deterrence has the inertial weight of accepted dogma. The alternatives, with an exception discussed below, will appear manifestly implausible from the point of view of the accepted perspective. There are procedural means, such as the High Level Group (HLG), that might be used to assuage fears of US provocation in a crisis. Ultimately, and fundamentally, the interests of strategic solidarity among the industrialized democracies, whatever those interests may be, will be determined by cultural and economic competitions only marginally related to strategic concerns. If these nations understand such solidarity to be an imperative then they will perhaps be able to persuade themselves that certain risks simply must be borne and US leadership will self-consciously minimize those risks. This demands an extraordinary educational effort by leaders to bring understanding to their publics; and, equally, a creative effort by experts to break the gridlock of the current, highly politicized debate. Such understanding might well be the outcome of the twofold recognition that the extension of deterrence is ultimately the necessary means of securing the stability of central deterrence by avoiding polar proliferation and that in any case a nuclear war limited to the scope of an extended theatre will remain a US option. For my own part, I should favour an institutionalized form of decision-sharing at a much higher level than the HLG, such that all deterrent forces beyond those few absolutely indispensable for central deterrence be under collaborative control.

To the extent that neither of these possibilities proves feasible, the likelihood of a third or fourth superpower, drawn from the previously extended theatres, increases. Yet it may be that such a development, masked in a larger confederation, could avoid tempting pre-emption in its early stages and, through co-ordinated planning avoid also some of the destabilizing effects discussed in Chapter 12. It need only be added that these consequences represent another generation in the evolutionary hypothesis of Book I. The emergence of another polar nuclear power will have fateful and I fear extremely dangerous consequences for the world. We will all bear responsibility for these consequences if we go on as we are now, pre-occupied by a largely irrelevant debate conducted with half-truths and impatient repetition.

No effective American policy can be either pacifist or militaristic: for the US must pursue an accommodation with the Russians in which we do not wholly believe, and at the same time arm to prevent a conflict in which we do not truly wish to participate. Alliances commit the United States to parallel approaches in international affairs. While she must maintain a modernized and effective deterrent within a changing military environment, the US must also pursue a more stable political relationship with the Soviet Union for *strategic* reasons. Arms control, among other intersections of mutual interest, can contribute to this relationship, but whether it does or not the sincere and tireless search for such improvement is indispensable to the maintenance of the deterrent, its parallel approach. As Johan Jorgen Holst has concluded,

> Societies will support the required military effort only when it is associated with an alternative vision of a more cooperative arrangement than an open-ended military competition.

This is not merely a matter of public relations, as though arms control talks were, for example, a sort of opiate for the democratic publics. It is a matter of what we are, what kind of society our 'national security policies' are trying to make secure. At the present juncture it must be observed that the necessity for this parallel approach has not always been evident to the leaders of the democracies, in and out of power, who have at times spoken as though one approach would bring the other as a consequence, or instead, even obviate it. It is, I suspect, characteristically American to want to 'solve' the problem of nuclear threats, once and for all. But it was a characteristic American who reminded us that the problems of international affairs are not like the problems of a toothache that can be dealt with conclusively; instead, they are like 'the problem of making a living' with which we must cope each morning.

We will not cope successfully if we ignore the social and political dimensions of strategy in favour of the technological or operational. The introduction of the LRTNF ground launched cruise missiles and Pershing 2s into Europe under sole US control is an unfortunate example of inattention to this aspect of strategy. The United States should not have agreed to deploy nuclear weapons on foreign soil under its exclusive control as this can only divide the US from the publics of her allies and put in jeopardy the hard-won technological and operational successes of the deployments. It is not too late, even now, for the US to insist on dual-key control for the GLCMs and P2s as it has always insisted in the past regarding nuclear weapons in Europe. What is needed is an understanding of the political basis of strategy so that superficial successes do not lead to fundamental failures.

There are encouraging signs that this is already taking place. The recent International Institute for Strategic Studies Annual Conference Papers[9] are devoted to the subject of the loss of consensus regarding nuclear defence and thus to the domestic aspects of Western security. A number of these papers recognize that nuclear deterrence no longer takes place over the heads of the publics involved and that public consent must be won if nuclear strategies are to be executable and therefore credible anywhere outside the simulations room. This recognition is a necessary first step in the education of senior officials and their publics.

Sometimes, watching a television discussion of these matters or sitting in the audience of a debate, one is struck by the confusion of the participants. Each is like a man in a room who wants to get out but doesn't know how. He tries the window but it is too high. He tries the chimney but it is too narrow. And if one enters the room behind such a man and tries to turn him around to the door through which one has come, he shakes the assistance off, and rushes instead back to the locked doors and inaccessible windows he has tried before. Yet I believe that our confusions can be cleared up and, once we have a perspicuous view of the sources of such confusion, we can avoid the more dangerous and costly policies. Then, with a wider appreciation of the facts of our circumstances, the public can actually make moral decisions on this most fateful issue. Among many others, one potent source of confusion has shaped public understanding: we think MAD to be a strategy (which would be witless) or a permanent condition (which would not require tending) or a desirable goal (which no sensible national public would voluntarily seek). We have been transfixed by it.

It has long been fashionable to concede, even to laconically assert, that nuclear weapons have doomed the earth. Sometimes such assertions are accompanied by a pseudo-logic that masquerades as 'scientific', such as the famous clock of *The Bulletin of the Atomic Scientists* that was moved forward from seven minutes to four minutes before midnight in 1981. In an address to the American Association for the Advancement of Science in 1960, C. P. Snow said,

> We know with the certainty of statistical truth that if enough of these weapons are made – by enough different states – some of them are going to blow up. Through accident, madness or folly – but the motives do not matter. What does matter is the nature of the statistical fact . . . [This] is not a risk but a certainty. . . . Within at most ten years some of these bombs are going off.

But there is no reason, statistical or otherwise, why this need be so. Indeed it may be that we can see more clearly now the requisite conditions for strategic stability than at any time since the thermonuclear era began. The American extended deterrent can be maintained through the conjunction of the various systemic alternatives canvassed in Book II. The latest vulnerability in nuclear deterrence can be compensated for by investments in the understanding and knowledge of our people.

It must be obvious that this is a faith the author shares. For who would undertake *nel mezzo del cammin di vita* such a singularly gratuitous form of failure as to attempt an analysis of a history that has doomed us, doomed analysis, doomed even history? This faith echoes in a haunting passage from Justice Holmes, written in 1913:

> It was evening. I was walking homeward on Pennsylvania Avenue near the Treasury, and as I looked beyond Sherman's Statue to the west the sky was aflame with scarlet and crimson from the setting sun. But, like the note of downfall in Wagner's opera, below the sky line there came from little globes the pallid discord of the electric lights. And I thought to myself the Götterdammerung will end, and from those globes clustered like evil eggs will come the new masters of the sky. It is like the time in which we live. But then I remembered the faith that I partly have expressed, faith in a universe not measured by our fears, a universe that has thought and more than thought inside of it, and as I gazed, after the sunset and above the electric lights there shone the stars.

The fate of the world does not hang on whether the US and USSR reduce their weapons or on whether they freeze their technologies. Indeed it should now be easy to see that were either goal pursued too single-mindedly, there would result a much more dangerous world as other powers entered the nuclear field, approaching parity with the superpowers. Rather, our situation will be determined by whether Euro–Japanese security is enhanced, from their perspective, by our strategies, military and diplomatic; whether the public can be made to understand and support such steps as do enhance the extended commitment when it has been told more or less constantly that it is the number of weapons and the advance of technology that causes (or cures) the problem; and whether democratic governments can consciously unite these elements – public and expert – that are already but unhappily linked.

For the crisis in nuclear strategy – the unusual ferment and the acerbity of the debate – arises from these connected causes: the alienation of the public to whom strategy has been made to appear ludicrous; and the deadlock among strategic thinkers for whom no dialectical progress is possible. But how can these be connected, since the public has little say in such matters? And how can the expert dilemma be related to it?

The answer arises from the origin of nuclear strategy in the prevailing concepts of the theory of strategic bombing. Precisely because nuclear strategy has not arisen from actual conflict, with the fresh recurrence to (and re-evaluation of) first principles that war precipitates, it has become ideological, and is unable to cure itself. Because it has lost its connection to strategic reality, it is in fact not disengaged from but at the mercy of public opinion. The dawning recognition of this fact has lent a peculiar hysteria to both groups, public and elite.

It is but another station in our fate and, although this development has had perturbing effects on the stability of deterrence, it need not take us deeper into our dilemma but can instead begin our departure from the circularity of the debate. The insistent role of publics can force us to pay attention to them and thus to the political basis for strategy. If the publics of the democracies can be brought to understand the restraints within which strategic options exist, and the restraints which national choices generate, it is possible to resolve the decoupling problem. It is, after all, not in Europe's ultimate interest to undermine US–Soviet central stability if she can be assured that that relationship is not inevitably leading to her sacrifice. It is, after all, not in the interest of the US to propel the world into multipolarity through a self-absorbed and single-minded pursuit of her own near term security, as structured solely by her relationship with the Soviet Union. This will be a difficult task, requiring thought and faith. But some day we shall see the world from another perspective that our patience and care have made possible.

> *Lo duca e io per quel cammino ascoso intrammo a ritornar nel chiaro mondo; e sanza cura aver d'alcun riposo salimmo su, el primo e io secondo, tanto chi'i' vidi delle cose belle che porta 'l ciel, per un pertugio tondo; e quindi uscimmo a riveder le stelle.*
>
> (The [Poet] and I entered on that hidden road to return into the bright world, and without caring to have any rest we climbed up, he first and I second, so far that I saw through a round opening some of the fair things that Heaven bears; and thence we came forth to see again the stars.)
>
> Canto XXXIV, *Inferno*

Notes and References

1 The Ideologies of Nuclear Deterrence

1. 'Countervalue' strikes are those targeted on urban-industrial centres.
2. 'Counterforce' targets are military targets and include, but are not limited to, the enemy's nuclear weapons.
3. C. Gray, *Strategic Studies: A Critical Assessment* (Westport: Greenwood Press, 1982), p. 159.
4. 'Central deterrence' is the nuclear relationship between national powers that protects a national homeland by targeting an adversary's homeland.
5. 'Extended deterrence' is the nuclear threat by which non-homeland theatres and other interests are protected.
6. 'Re-coupling' is the term of art used to describe a situation whereby the US nuclear deterrent is restored in its credibility to attack the Soviet Union in defence of the extended theatre.
7. Declaratory policy is the announced intention of the US regarding its nuclear plans if attacked; employment policy is the actual targeting plans. This distinction may have originated in Paul Nitze, 'Atoms, Strategy and Policy', *Foreign Affairs* 34 (January 1956), pp. 187–98.
8. A warhead that can be launched with other warheads on a single missile but directed to a separate target.
9. A proposed nuclear surface fleet manned by personnel from the NATO nations.
10. The current condition of domination of nuclear conflict by the two superpowers, the United States and Russia.
11. Hedley Bull, 'The Future Conditions of Strategic Deterrence', in *The Future of Strategic Deterrence*, Papers from the 21st Annual Conference of the International Institute for Strategic Studies, Adelphi Paper no. 160 (London: The International Institute for Strategic Studies, 1980), p. 13.

2 Some Concepts in the Theory of Deterrence

1. R. Jervis, *Deterrence Theory Revisited*, ACIS Working Paper no. 14 (Los Angeles: Center for Arms Control and International Security, 1978), p. 16.
2. George and R. Smoke, *Deterrence in American Foreign Policy: Theory and Practice* (New York: Columbia University Press, 1974) p. 48.
3. And to a more sophisticated but equally misleading retrospective that accepts this caricature but confines it to the declaratory aspect of policy by concluding that no real strategic planning can be identified with this policy.'George F. Kennan, 'Cease This Madness', *The Atlantic Monthly* no. 247 (January 1981), pp. 25–28; see, e.g., D. Ball, *Targeting for Strategic Deterrence*, Adelphi Paper no. 185 (London: The International Institute for Strategic Studies, 1983), p. 41.

4. A. E. Wessell, *Some Implications of Strategic Concepts for Western European Nuclear Weapons*, RAND Paper no. P-2904 (Santa Monica: The RAND Corporation, 1964), p. 3.
5. C. Bertram, *The Future of Strategic Deterrence: Papers from the IISS 21st Annual Conference*, Adelphi Paper no. 160 (London: The International Institute for Strategic Studies, 1980), pp. i, 1. This definition is preferable to accounts that do not implicitly accept that refraining from acting or responding can be a means of deterring, see A. Beaufre, *Deterrence and Strategy* (New York: Praeger, 1966), p. 24; see also G. Snyder, *Deterrence and Defense: Toward A Theory of National Security* (Princeton: Princeton University Press, 1961), pp. 9, 12.
6. R. Rosencrance, *Strategic Deterrence Reconsidered*, Adelphi Paper no. 116 (London: The International Institute for Strategic Studies, 1975), p. 3.
7. W. Kaufmann, *The Requirements of Deterrence*, Memorandum no. 27, (Princeton: Center of International Studies, Princeton University, 1954), p. 8.
8. Fritz Ermarth, 'Contrasts in American and Strategic Thought', *International Security* no. 3 (1978), p. 138.
9. Each side now possesses more than ten thousand nuclear bombs and warheads.
10. This is the ability to retaliate, having absorbed a pre-emptive first strike, with a surviving force still capable of executing its assigned mission.
11. Phil Williams, 'Deterrence' in J. Baylis, K. Booth, J. Garnett and P. Williams, (eds), *Contemporary Strategy* (London: Croom Helm, 1975), pp. 79–82.
12. 'Damage limitation' here refers to one's attacks on an adversary's offensive weapons, thereby achieving the effect of limiting his ability to inflict further damage on oneself.
13. Snyder, *Deterrence and Defense*, p. 3.
14. *Contra*, Richard Rosencrance, 'Deterrence in Dyadic and Multipolar Environments' in R. Rosencrance, (ed.), *The Future of the International System* (San Francisco: Chandler, 1972), p. 125.
15. For a discussion of the theory of strategic bombing, see the next chapter. For now, the reader need only follow the assertion that while atomic war plans – and thus 'deterrence' – initially derived from such theories, the advent of mutually thermonuclear adversaries altered political objectives and replaced classical deterrence with nuclear deterrence.
16. See, e.g., A. Cordesman, *Deterrence in the 1980s: Part I: American Strategic Forces and Extended Deterrence*, Adelphi Paper no. 175 (London: The International Institute for Strategic Studies, 1982).
17. *NATO – Facts and Figures* (Brussels: NATO Information Series, 1976), p. 301.
18. United States Secretary of State at the time of the treaty's ratification. This construction of the term 'collective force' is taken from the context of Acheson's remarks to the NATO Council.
19. D. Acheson, *Present at the Creation* (New York: Norton, 1969), pp. 398–99; see also *A Review of North Atlantic Problems For the Future* (The Acheson Report), March 1961, National Security File, Box 220, John F.

Kennedy Library (declassified 28/1/81) which speaks of the US 'obligation' to launch a retaliatory nuclear strike if Europe, but not the US were attacked, p. 40.

20. See A. J. Wohlstetter, F. S. Hoffman, R. J. Lutz, and H. S. Rowan, *Selection and Use of Strategic Air Bases*, R-266 (Santa Monica: The RAND Coporation, 1954).
21. See Lawrence Freedman, *The Evolution of Nuclear Strategy* (London: Macmillan, 1981) p. xvi, Freedman observes, of the evolution of US nuclear strategy that 'If there is an underlying theme, it is the attempt to develop a convincing strategy for extended deterrence, to make the United States' nuclear guarantee to Europe intellectually credible rather than just an act of faith'.
22. Compare McGeorge Bundy, 'The Bishops and the Bomb', *The New York Review of Books* 30 (16 June 1983), p. 6: 'The deterrence the bishops conditionally approve is deterrence only of nuclear war. They do not believe in what is called "extended deterrence", the threat to use these weapons to resist or deter conventional aggression' with Edward Luttwak, 'The Problems of Extending Deterrence', in *America's Security in the 1980s: Papers from the IISS 23rd Annual Conference*, Adelphi Paper no. 173, I (London: The International Institute for Strategic Studies, 1982) (a discussion of 'extending deterrence to negate Soviet nuclear threats'), pp. 34–35.

3 Prologue: The Theory of Strategic Bombing and the Coming of Nuclear Weapons

1. R. Aron, 'The Evolution of Modern Strategic Thought', in *Problems of Modern Strategy*, Adelphi Paper no. 54, 1 (London: The Institute for Strategic Studies, 1969), p. 7.
2. D. D. Eisenhower, *Crusade in Europe* (New York: Doubleday, 1948), p. 259.
3. Orders to proceed with the development of a Soviet atomic bomb were issued by Stalin in June 1942, possibly as a result of information relayed by Klaus Fuchs concerning the Manhattan Project, on which he was working at Los Alamos, *Bulletin of the Atomic Scientists*, no. 23 (December 1967), p. 15. D. D. Eisenhower, *Mandate for Change* (New York: Doubleday, 1963), p. 82, n. 5; David Holloway, Research Note: Soviet Thermonuclear Development, *International Security* 4 (1979–80), pp. 192–97.
4. G. Douhet, *The Command of the Air*, trans. D. Ferrari (New York: Coward McCann, 1942); see Edward Warner, 'Douhet, Mitchell, Seversky: Theories of Air Warfare', in E. M. Earle, (ed.), *Makers of Modern Strategy*, pp. 485–503. An earlier translation was done by the US Army.
5. Nat S. Finney, 'How FDR Planned to Use the A-Bomb,' *Look*, 14 (14 March 1950), pp. 23–27; J. MacGeorge Burns, *Roosevelt: The Soldier of Freedom* (New York: Harcourt Brace Jovanovich, 1970), pp. 455–59.
6. H. S. Hansell, *The Air Plan That Defeated Hitler* (Atlanta: Higgins – McArthur/Longino & Porta, 1973) p. 168.
7. H. Stimson and McGeorge Bundy, *On Active Service in Peace and War*

(New York: Harper, 1948), p. 613; L. Groves, *Now It Can Be Told: The Story of the Manhattan Project* (New York: Harper, 1962), p. 265.

8. 'Aide-Memoire of Conversation between the President and Prime Minister at Hyde Park', 18 September 1944; Barton J. Bernstein, 'The Uneasy Alliance: Roosevelt, Churchill and the Atomic Bomb, 140–45', *Western Political Quarterly* 29 (1976); see also W. D. Leahy, *I Was There: the Personal Story of the Chief of Staff to Presidents Roosevelt and Truman based on his notes and diaries made at the time* (New York: Whittlesey, 1950), pp. 265–66.
9. Barton J. Bernstein, 'The Atomic Bomb and American Foreign Policy 1941–45: An Historiographical Controversy,' *Peace and Change* 2 (1974) pp. 1–16; see Barton Bernstein, 'Roosevelt, Truman and the A-Bomb 1941–45: A Reinterpretation,' *Political Science Quarterley* 90 (Spring 1975), pp. 23–69.
10. F. G. Klotz, 'The US President and the Control of Strategic Nuclear Weapons' (Oxford University Ph.D Thesis 1980), pp. 92–103.
11. '[T]he final decision of when and where to drop the bomb was up to me. Let there be no mistake about it.' H. Truman, *Memoirs*, I (New York: Signet, 1965), p. 462.
12. L. Giovannitti and F. Freed, *The Decision to Drop the Bomb* (New York: Coward-McCann, 1963), pp. 145–53; see also F. G. Klotz, 'Control of Strategic Nuclear Weapons', pp. 112–18.
13. L. Groves, *Now It Can Be Told*, p. 265.
14. Marginalia by George Marshall, Groves to Marshall, 10 August 1945, Top Secret Manhattan Project File, Records of the Mahattan Engineering District, Record Group 77, National Archives Building, Washington, DC.
15. This was Bernstein.
16. Anthony Cave Brown, (ed.), *Operation World War III: The Secret American Plan 'Dropshot' for War with the Soviet Union* (London: Arms & Armour, 1978), p. 3.
17. David Alan Rosenberg, 'US Nuclear Stockpile, 1945 to 1960', *The Bulletin of the Atomic Scientists* 38, (May 1982), p. 28.
18. Earl E. Partridge to secretary general of the Air Board, 7 June 1946, Hugh Knerr File, Box 276, Carl Spaatz Papers (Library of Congress), quoted in David Alan Rosenberg, 'American Atomic Strategy and the Hydrogen Bomb Decision,' *The Journal of American History*, 66 (June 1979), p. 65.
19. David Alan Rosenberg, 'The Origins of Overkill: Nuclear Weapons and American Strategy, 1945–1960,' *International Security* 7 (1983), p. 39.
20. JCS 1844/4, Brief of War Plan 'HALFMOON', 6 May 1948, and Decision on JCS 1844/4, 19 May 1948, CCS 381 USSR (3–2–46), section 12, Papers of the United States Joint Chiefs of Staff, US National Archives, quoted in Rosenberg, 'American Atomic Strategy', p. 68.
21. *Ibid.*; HALFMOON is reprinted in T. H. Etzold and J. L. Gaddis, (eds), *Containment: Documents on American Policy and Strategy*, 1945–1960 (New York: Columbia University Press, 1978), pp. 315–23.
22. See discussion in G. Herken, *The Winning Weapon* (New York: Knopf, 1980), pp. 246–266.
23. Rosenberg, 'The Hydrogen Bomb Decision,' p. 69; NSC-30, 'United

States Policy on Atomic Warfare,' Department of State, *Foreign Relations of the United States: 1948*, I (Washington: United States Government Printing Office, 1976), pp. 624–28; W. Millis and E. Duffield, (eds), *The Forrestal Diaries* (New York: Viking, 1951), p. 487.

24. D. Rosenberg, 'The Hydrogen Bomb Decision' pp. 70–71; for a fuller discussion of TROJAN, see A. Cave Brown, *Operation World War III*, p. 28; for a discussion of BROILER and a contemporary alternative, BUSHWACKER, see F. Klotz, 'Control of Strategic Nuclear Weapons', pp. 158, 160.
25. D. Rosenberg, 'The Hydrogen Bomb Decision' p. 71.
26. A. Cave Brown, *Operation World War III*, p. 202.
27. J. SPC 877/59, 26 May 1949, *Records of the Joint Chiefs of Staff*, Modern Military Records Branch, National Archives, Washington, DC.
28. Analyzing the results of Allied saturation bombing of Germany, Soviet generals concluded that it was largely a wasted effort. Sokolovskii cites figures showing that German production of war material rose throughout the war until the fall of 1944 and concludes: 'It was not so much the economic struggle and economic exhaustion [i.e., countervalue bombing] that were the causes for the defeat of Hitler's Germany, but rather the armed conflict and the defeat of its armed forces [i.e., the counterforce strategy pursued by the Red Army].' V. D. Sokolovskii, *Soviet Military Strategy* (Santa Monica: The RAND Corporation, 1963), p. 21.
29. See *US Strategic Bombing Survey (European) and (Pacific)*, (New York: Garland, 1976); the quotation is from Brian Duchin, 'The Atomic Bomb and American Strategic Thought' (unpublished paper, 1981), p. 36.
30. Henry Rowen, 'The Evolution of Nuclear Strategic Doctrine,' in L. Martin (ed.), *Strategic Thought in the Nuclear Age* (Baltimore: Johns Hopkins University Press, 1979), p. 137.
31. Louis Ridenour, 'The Hydrogen Bomb,' *Arms Control* (San Francisco: Freeman, 1974) pp. 51–55; this article first appeared in *Scientific American* 182 (March 1950), pp. 11–15.
32. Which can be replaced by a laser trigger, Freeman J. Dyson, 'The Future Development of Nuclear Weapons', *Foreign Affairs* 38 (April 1960), pp. 457–464.
33. *Hansard* (Commons), 5th series, vol. 537, col. 1899 (1 March 1955).
34. It is true that atomic bombs might have a profound *tactical* effect, in a reversal, as it were, of strategic bombing theory. Ignoring the society waging war, one might focus on the armies in the field. As these are likely to be within Allied territory this poses a troubling prospect, and a further difficulty is that, facing a vastly superior conventional force in partial occupation of one's territory with its own tactical atomic weapons, the advantage would appear not to be neutralized but actually to shift to the aggressor.
35. NSC-68, 'United States Objectives and Programs for National Security', Dept. of State, *Foreign Relations of the United States: 1950*, I (Washington: GPO, 1976) p. 244; on the origins of NSC-68, see Paul Y. Hammond's account in W. Schilling, P. Hammond and G. Snyder, *Strategy, Politics, and Defense Budgets*, pp. 267–330; and Samuel Wells, Jr., 'Sounding the Tocsin: NSC 68 and the Soviet Threat', *International Security* 4 (Fall,

1979), pp. 116–38. Note the lawyerly tone of the excerpted passage.
36. J. L. Gaddis, *Strategies of Containment: A Critical Reappraisal of Postwar American National Security Policy* (New York: Oxford University Press, 1982) pp. 101–2.
37. *Ibid*.
38. G. Calabresi and P. Bobbitt, *Tragic Choices* (New York: Norton, 1978), pp. 195–199.

4 Massive Retaliation

1. Henry S. Rowen, 'Formulating Strategic Doctrine', in *Report of the Commission on the Organization of the Government for the Conduct of Foreign Policy*, 4, Appendix K: Adequacy of Current Organization: Defense and Arms Control (Washington: GPO, June 1975), p. 222.
2. R. F. Futrell, *Ideas, Concepts, Doctrine: A History of Basic Thinking in the United States Air Force 1907–1964*, 2 (Maxwell Air Force Base: Aerospace Studies Institute, June 1971), 551; Aaron Friedberg, 'A History of the U.S. Strategic "Doctrine" – 1945–1980,' *The Journal of Strategic Studies*, 3 (December 1980), pp. 40–1.
3. Lieutenant General H. R. Harmon, *Evaluation of Effect on Soviet War Effort Resulting from the Strategic Air Offensive* (Washington: GPO, 11 May 1949); Etzold and Gaddis, *Containment: Documents*, p. 360.
4. Friedberg, 'US Strategic Doctrine', p. 47.
5. Bernard Brodie, *The Absolute Weapon: Atomic Power and World Order* (New York: Harcourt Brace, 1946).
6. Jacob Viner, 'The Implications of The Atomic Bomb for International Relations,' *Proceedings of the American Philosophical Society* 90 (January 1946), pp. 53–4.
7. Brodie, *The Absolute Weapon*, p. 37.
8. *Ibid*., p. 40.
9. *Ibid*., pp. 76–77.
10. *Ibid*., pp. 80–81.
11. *Ibid*., pp. 91.
12. H. Baldwin, *The Price of Power* (New York: Harper & Bros, 1947). Continuing a series of articles in the *New York Times* after Bikini on the impact of the atomic bomb on American defense, Baldwin published on 16 August 1946, 'The Atomic Bomb's Scope'. Here he presented an analysis of how the atomic bomb might affect warfare in the immediate as well as the distant future, now that it was known to be a finite weapon.

    > It is true therefore, that a large nation like the US or USSR, reasonably well prepared for atomic war – its industries and its military installations rather well dispersed and with atomic bombs of its own – cannot be conquered by a few atomic bombs unless its nerves fail. The atomic bombs of the present type . . . will certainly not destroy a large nation's capacity to resist, and probably not its will to resist.

    New York Times (16 August 1946) p. 6. See also *US Naval Institute Proceedings*, 72 (April 1946), pp. 489–503.

13. B. Brodie, *Strategy in the Missile Age* (Princeton: Princeton University Press, 1959), p. 153.
14. Gaddis, *Strategies of Containment*, p. 148. Gaddis notes the celebrated press conference statement by Truman that the use of the atomic bomb was always under consideration, a statement that brought Prime Minister Atlee to Washington and yielded a 'clarifying' statement almost immediately.
15. Named for the third floor, circular sun-room at the White House where the initial organizational meeting took place. A fourth group later convened to evaluate the option 'Negotiation'.
16. This group was chaired by George Kennan whose present well-known views on the subject of nuclear strategy show a remarkable continuity with those held at this time. The 'containment' option refers to the doctrine of NSC-68, not to be confused with the vital interests limitations of its namesake, the famous Long Telegram by Kennan when he was serving in Moscow.
17. Glenn Snyder, 'The "New Look" of 1953'. in Schilling, et al., *Strategy, Politics and Defense Budgets*, pp. 379–524.
18. President Eisenhower estimated that the program required by NSC-141 (the Truman Administration's parting security recommendations) would have created a $44 billion deficit over five years. Gaddis, *Strategies of Containment*, p. 167.
19. NSC 5501 at p. 11, Jan. 7, 1955; this statement is repeated in NSC 5602, Feb. 8, 1956 at p. 6 and in NSC 5707/8, Jan. 3, 1957 at 6, Basic National Security Policy Folder, NSC Series, Policy Paper Subseries.
20. NSC 5501, p. 12.
21. B. Brodie, *Strategy in the Missile Age*, pp. 252–53.
22. At its February 1952 ministerial meeting in Lisbon, NATO agreed to a goal of 96 standing divisions by 1954.
23. *Ibid.*, pp. 341–2.
24. D. Ball, *Politics and Force Levels: The Strategic Missile Program of the Kennedy Administration 1961–63* (Berkeley: Univ. of California Press, 1980), p. 180.
25. John Foster Dulles, 'Policy for Security and Peace,' *Foreign Affairs* 32 (April 1954), p. 353.
26. Indeed West Germany was admitted to NATO on the strength of this ambiguity despite the foundering of the European Defense Community (EDC) plan.
27. Cordesman, *Deterrence in the 1980s*, pp. 6–7; see also Desmond Ball, *Targeting for Strategic Deterrence*, Adelphi Paper no. 175 (London: The International Institute for Strategic Studies, 1983).
28. K. Ward, 'Evolution of US Strategic Targeting Doctrine' (Oxford University, M.Phil. thesis 1981).
29. Albert Wohlstetter, 'Is There a Strategic Arms Race?' *Foreign Policy* 15 (Summer 1974), p. 5; see also 'Rivals But No Race,' *Foreign Policy* 16 (Fall 1974), pp. 60–1, by the same author.
30. Friedberg, 'US Strategic Doctrine', p. 60.

5 Controlled Response

1. Later to be called the Single Integrated Operational Plan.
2. MC 14/2 (a modification of the 'sword and shield' doctrine of MC 14/1) adopted the principle of forward defense. Fifty-four divisions were assigned to determine the nature and scope of a Soviet attack, after which a counter-offensive, supported by massive nuclear strikes, could be initiated. MC 14/2, 'Overall Strategies Concepte for the NATO Area' (March 1957); Rowen, 'Evolution of Nuclear Strategic Doctrine', p. 143.
3. Eisenhower off-the-record statement to senior military officers, Quantico, Virginia, Hagerty diary, 19 June 1954, Hagerty Papers, Box 1, D. D. Eisenhower Library; quoted in Gaddis, *Strategies of Containment*, p. 135.
4. Bernard Brodie, *War and Politics*.
5. Brodie, *Strategy in the Missile Age*, p. 309.
6. *Ibid*.
7. A. J. Wohlstetter, F. S. Hoffman, R. S. Lutz, and H. S. Rowan, *Selection and Use of Strategic Bases*, R-266 (Santa Monica: The RAND Corporation, April 1954).
8. Albert Wohlstetter, 'The Delicate Balance of Terror,' *Foreign Affairs* 37 (January 1959), p. 211.
9. L. D. Freedman, *The Evolution of Nuclear Strategy* (London: Macmillan, 1981), pp. 236–7 (summarizing the views of Wohlstetter and RAND analyst Andrew Marshall).
10. H. A. Kissinger, *Nuclear Weapons and Foreign Policy* (New York: Marper, 1957).
11. Eisenhower to Herter, 31 July 1957, Eisenhower Papers, Ann Whitman File, Box 14, Eisenhower Library, quoted in Gaddis, *Strategies of Containment*, p. 167.
12. Eisenhower remarks to USIA Staff, 10 November 1953, *Public Papers of the President: Dwight D. Eisenhower: 1953* (Washington: GPO, 195), p. 754.
13. L. D. Freedman, *US Intelligence and The Soviet Strategic Threat* (London: Macmillan, 1977); see also Cordesman, *Deterrence in the 1980s*, pp. 6–7.
14. H. Kahn, *On Thermonuclear War* (Princeton: Princeton University Press, 1960), pp. 559–60.
15. B. Brodie, *Strategy in The Missile Age*, pp. 293, 296.
16. Freedman, *US Intelligence and The Soviet Strategic Threat*.
17. Cordesman, *Deterrence in the 1980s*, p. 7.
18. 'McNamara was introduced to counterforce and no-cities strategies in a formal briefing by Kaufmann within a week of taking office, and was immediately impressed,' Desmond Ball, *Deja Vu: The Return to Counterforce in the Nixon Administration* (Los Angeles: California Seminar on Arms Control and Foreign Policy, December 1974), p. 11; Freidberg, 'History of US Strategic Doctrine', pp. 47–48. The White House was similarly interested. See 'Memorandum to the President,' 30 January 1961 from McG. Bundy ('The most urgent need is for a review of basic military policy') National Security File, Box 313, J. F. Kennedy Library; see also 'Memorandum re Defense Message', 13 March 1961 from McG. Bundy, ('That in the terrible event of a general atomic war, we retain the

capability to act rationally to advance the national interest by exerting pressure and offering choices to the enemy'), National Security File, Box 273, J. F. Kennedy Library.

19. Systems analysis is an approach to the study of physical and social systems which enable complex and dynamic situations to be understood in broad outline. By aid of the computer, the efficiency of various allocations can be analyzed in terms of the objectives of the 'system'. A system is identified by distinguishing its boundaries and purposes. One of the discoveries of the systems approach is the extent to which attempts to improve the performance of a subsystem by its own criteria (suboptimization) may act to the detriment of the total system and even to the defeat of its objectives. *The Harper Dictionary of Modern Thought*, Alan Bullock and Oliver Stallybrass, eds. (1977), p. 621.
20. 'Self-deterrence' refers to the unilateral refusal to initiate nuclear strikes at high levels for fear of commensurate retaliation.
21. Initial work on the SIOP revision was done by Daniel Ellsberg and Frank Trinkle under the supervision of Alain Enthoven; all were former RAND analysts. Ball, *Deja Vu*, p. 12; before becoming Secretary of Defense, James Schlesinger, himself a RAND analyst, observed, 'The McNamara Strategy embodied the basic ideas of the Air Force and RAND Corporation in ferment since the mid-fifties,' i.e., since the Wohlstetter Report. James R. Schlesinger, 'The Changing Environment for Systems Analysis', in S. Enke (ed.) *Defense Management* (Englewood Cliffs: Prentice-Hall, 1967), p. 105.
22. W. W. Kaufmann, *The McNamara Strategy* (New York: Harper & Row, 1964), pp. 44–75.
23. Robert S. McNamara, 'Defense Arrangements and the North Atlantic Community', Address given at the University of Michigan, 16 June 1962, *Dept of State Bulletin* 47 (9 July 1962) pp. 67–8.
24. Notice thus how both graduated response and total response schemes reject the premise of the theory of strategic bombing that war should be waged by attacking cities.
25. Friedberg, 'History of US Strategic Doctrine', pp. 48–9.
26. See, e.g., P. Pringle and W. Arkin, *SIOP: Nuclear War from the Inside* (London: Sphere, 1983), p. 89.
27. McNamara, 'Defense Arrangements and the North Atlantic Community', pp. 66–7.
28. Leonard Beaton, *The Western Alliance and the McNamara Doctrine*, Adelphi Paper no. 11 (London: The Institute for Strategic Studies, August 1964), p. 6.
29. Beaton, *The Western Alliance and the McNamara Doctrine*, p. 5.
30. This emerges even more clearly from Secretary McNamara's Top Secret NATO speech in Athens. R. S. McNamara, 'Remarks delivered at a restricted session of the NATO Ministerial Meeting, 5 May 1962. Released under the Freedom of Information Act, 17 August 1979.
31. David N. Schwartz, *NATO's Nuclear Dilemmas* (Washington: Brookings, 1983), p. 80.
32. Alastair Buchan, *The Multilateral Force: An Historical Perspective*, Adelphi Paper no. 13 (London: The Institute for Strategic Studies,

October 1964) p. 4. Compare Alastair Buchan, 'The Coming Crisis on the MLF', Confidential Memo, 23 June 1964 declassified 1979, National Security File, Box 23, Lyndon B. Johnson Library; see also 'Early History of the MLF,' which gives a detailed, chronology of Presidential decisions on MLF in three Administrations declassified 1977, National Security File, Box 23, Lyndon B. Johnson Library.

33. See Schwartz, *NATO's Nuclear Dilemmas*, Chapter 5.
34. George Ball, Speech to NATO Parliamentarian's Conference in Paris, 16 November 1962; for further confirmation of the argument that Controlled Response implied the MLF, see Cable 03840, Circular 927, 16 November 1962. Dept. of State, National Security File, Box 218, J. F. Kennedy Library (directing background to the Ball address, 'Speech was essentially a reaffirmation of . . . McNamara Ann Arbor'); for discussion of Ball role, see G. Ball, *The Past Has Another Pattern: Memoirs* (New York: Norton, 1982), p. 274.
35. Buchan, *The Multilateral Force*, pp. 4–5.
36. This motivation clearly emerges from the sequence of memoranda that ultimately led to the abandonment of the MLF project: 'Memorandum to the National Security Advisor', 10 October 1964, 'The MLF,' National Security File, Box 23, Lyndon B. Johnson Library; 'Memorandum to Secretary Rusk, Secretary McNamara, Secretary Ball, 25 November 1964, 'The Future of the MLF,' National Security File, Box 2, McGeorge Bundy Memos for the President, Lyndon B. Johnson Library; 'Memorandum for the President, 6 December 1964, 'Meeting on Multilateral Force,' National Security File, Box 1, McGeorge Bundy Memos for the President, Lyndon B. Johnson Library.
37. 'The first three years of the 1960s can thus be described as the zenith of extended deterrence – at least in the sense that the US could have put the SIOP and NATO Nuclear Strike Plan into operation to defend Europe with near impunity.' Cordesman, *Deterrence in the 1980s*, p. 7.
38. Kaufmann, *The McNamara Strategy*, p. 148.
39. Beaton, *The Western Alliance and the McNamara Strategy*, p. 5.
40. *Ibid.*
41. Such a strategy does force a Russian attack up to a high level of aggression, preventing a merely limited European probe.
42. T. C. Schelling, *The Strategy of Conflict* (New York: Oxford University Press, 1960), p. 207.

6 Assured Destruction and Strategic Sufficiency

1. For the view that the strategic concepts underlying Assured Destruction originated with the work of Warren Amster, see Freedman, *The Evolution of Nuclear Strategy*, pp. 191–3. See W. Amster, *A Theory for the Design of a Deterrent Air Weapon System* (San Diego: Convair Corporation, 1955) and C. W. Sherwin, 'Security Peace through Military Technology', *Bulletin of the Atomic Scientists* (May 1956), p. 12, to which is appended a short piece by Amster, 'Design for deterrence.'
2. See, *e.g.*, C. Gray, *Strategic Studies and Public Policy* (Lexington: University Press of Kentucky, 1982), p. 148.

3. T. C. Schelling, *Controlled Response and Strategic Warfare*, Adelphi Paper no. 19 (London, The Institute for Strategic Studies, June 1965), later a chapter in *Arms & Influence*.
4. Schelling, *Controlled Response and Strategic Warfare*, p. 4.
5. *Ibid.*, p. 5.
6. *Ibid.*, p. 6.
7. *Ibid.*, p. 7.
8. *Ibid.*, p. 7.
9. The literature arising from this event is considerable. Standard accounts include R. F. Kennedy, *Thirteen Days: A Memoir of the Cuban Missile Crisis* (New York: Norton, 1969); E. Abel, *The Missile Crisis* (Philadelphia: Lippincott, 1966); G. T. Allison, *Essence of Decision: Explaining the Cuban Missile Crisis* (Boston: Little, Brown, 1971); A. Chayes, *The Cuban Missile Crisis: International Crises and the Role of Law* (New York: Oxford University Press, 1974).
10. T. C. Schelling, *Arms and Influence* (New Haven: Yale University Press, 1966), p. 82, n. 22.
11. Cordesman, *Deterrence in the 1980s*, p. 7.
12. A re-entry vehicle (RV) carries one warhead.
13. Such a loss means simply that it takes more missiles to destroy targeted missiles than are destroyed by them.
14. Walter Slocombe, *The Political Implications of Strategic Parity*, Adelphi Paper no. 77 (London: The Institute for Strategic Studies, May 1971), p. 20.
15. Albert Wohlstetter, 'Is There a Strategic Arms Race?' collected in *A Decade of Foreign Policy*, pp. 21–6. IRBM stands for intermediate range ballistic missile; MRBM for medium range ballistic missile.
16. Cordesman, *Deterrence in the 1980s*, p. 8.
17. *Ibid.*, p. 8.
18. MC 14/3 commits NATO to: 'meet initially any aggression short of war with a direct defense at the level chosen by the aggressor; conduct a deliberate escalation if aggression cannot be contained and the situation restored by direct defense; and initiate an appropriate general nuclear response to a major nuclear attack.' MC 14/3 (Military Committee document), Senate Foreign Relations Committee, *US Security Issues in Europe: Burden Sharing and Offset, MBFR and Nuclear Weapons* (Washington: GPO, 1973), p. 19; Communique, *Ministerial Meeting of North Atlantic Council*, 14 December 1967.
19. John Newhouse, *Cold Dawn: The Story of SALT* (New York: Holt, Rinehart & Winston, 1973), p. 67. This overstates somewhat the countervalue elements in the new strategy.
20. Variously defined as the secure weapons necessary to inflict damage with high confidence such that ¼–⅓ of the population and ½–⅔ of the industrial capacity of the targeted nation would be destroyed.
21. Secretary of Defense R. S. McNamara, *Fiscal Years 1964 to 1968 Defense Program and Defense Budget for Fiscal Year 1964* (Washington: GPO, 1963), p. 30.
22. *Ibid.*, p. 29; see also R. S. McNamara, 'Testimony Before the Committee on Appropriations,' US House of Representatives, *Department of De-*

fense Appropriations for Fiscal Year 1964, 88th Congress, 1st Session, Part 1, 30 January 1963, pp. 111–12; compare R. S. McNamara, 'Testimony Before the House Armed Services Committee,' *Military Posture and HR9637 Hearings*, 88th Congress, 2nd Session, January 1964, pp. 6919–21.

23. Secretary of Defense R. S. McNamara, *Annual Defense Department Report, Fiscal Year 1965* (Washington: GPO, 1967), p. 12.
24. Secretary of Defense R. S. McNamara, *Fiscal Years 1966 to 1970 Defense Program and Defense Budget for Fiscal Year 1966* (Washington: GPO, 1965), p. 39.
25. Secretary of Defense R. S. McNamara, *Fiscal Years 1968 to 1972 Defense Program and Defense Budget for Fiscal Year 1968* (Washington: GPO, 1967), p. 38–9.
26. *Ibid.*, p. 39.
27. Secretary of Defense R. S. McNamara, *Fiscal Year 1968 to 1973 Defense Program and Defense Budget for Fiscal Year 1969* (Washington: GPO, 1968), p. 47.
28. Schelling, *Controlled Response and Strategic Warfare*, p. 7.
29. *Ibid.*
30. Cordesman, *Deterrence in the 1980s*, p. 10.
31. Much mischief is done be the ubiquitous confusion of (a) Assured Destruction (the doctrine); (b) the assured destruction capability (a mission within several different doctrines); (c) mutual assured destruction (the present geostrategic context regarding the superpowers).
32. Schelling, *Controlled Response and Strategic Warfare*, p. 9.
33. T. C. Schelling, *The Strategy of Conflict* (New York: Oxford University Press, 1960).
34. With the publication of Ronald Coase's 'The Problem of Social Cost' in 1960 the Pareto standards of modern welfare economics were applied to the problem of liability rules in what proved to be a highly fruitful way. The Pareto standards hypothesized that a decision that improved the lot of one person whilst making no other person worse off was a superior decision to one that did not satisfy this criterion, and that an optimal arrangement would be one in which no one could be made better off without making some person worse off. By assuming no transaction costs (that is, assuming a world of perfect information and rational, sovereign decision makers whose acquisition of this information and use in bargaining required no expenditure), Coase attempted to show that resources would be allocated precisely as efficiently – i.e., applying the Pareto standards to determine 'efficiency' – regardless of which party in a tort claim bore the liability. In such a world, a series of bribes would be struck between injurors and the injured, polluter and those whose environment was polluted, the farmer and cow-man, and so forth, until a Pareto-optimal allocation had been achieved. Ronald Coase, 'The Problem of Social Cost,' *Journal of Law and Economics* vol. 3 (1960).
35. Freedman, *Evolution of Nuclear Strategy*, p. 191–5.
36. T. C. Schelling and M. Halperin, *Strategy and Arms Control* (New York: Twentieth Century Fund, 1961).
37. There is a vast literature on the shortcomings of microeconomic techni-

ques as applied to strategic problems. For a particularly distinguished contribution, see Hedley Bull, 'Strategic Studies and Its Critics', *World Politics* XX (July 1968); see also S. Maxwell, *Rationality in Deterrence*, Adelphi Paper no. 50 (London, The Institute for Strategic Studies, August 1968). With the latter, cf. M. Howard, 'The Classical Strategists', *Problems of Modern Strategy: Part I* (London, The Institute for Strategic Studies, February 1969), pp. 18–32.

38. Wohlstetter, 'Is There a Strategic Arms Race?'
39. In that decade, Soviet procurement of strategic forces was about two and a half times that of the US. In 1970 the Soviet procurement level was about twice that of the US; by 1979, it was almost three times. Statement of William J. Perry, Undersecretary of Defense for Research and Engineering, *Fiscal Year 1981 Department of Defense Program for Research, Development and Acquisition* (Washington: GPO, 1980), pp. vi–11, 16–7; see also Charles Sorrels, 'Limiting Strategic Forces', in R. Burt (ed.) *Arms Control and Defense Postures in the 1980s* (Boulder: Westview, 1982), pp. 170–3; But see the work of F. D. Holzman for a contrary view focusing not on strategic forces but on overall defense expenditure. Franklyn D. Holzman, 'Are the Soviets Really Outspending the US on Defense?' *International Security* 4 (Spring 1980), pp. 86–105; Franklyn D. Holzman, 'Is There a Soviet–US Military Spending Gap?' *Challenge* (September/October 1980), pp. 3–9; Franklyn D. Holzman, 'Dollars or Rubles: The CIA's Military Estimates', *Bulletin of the Atomic Scientists* (June 1980), pp. 23–7.
40. See D. Ball, *Can Nuclear War be Controlled?*, Adelphi Paper no. 169 (London: The International Institute for Strategic Studies, 1981).
41. T. C. Schelling, 'Micro-motives and Macro-behavior', in *Analytical Methods and the Ethics of Policy*, Discussion Paper no. 792 (Harvard Institute of Economics Research: Harvard University, 1980).
42. B. Brodie, *War and Politics* (New York: Macmillan, 1973).
43. Schelling, *Strategy of Conflict*, pp. 41–2.
44. D. Ball, *Targeting for Strategic Deterrence*, Adelphi Paper no. 185 (London: The International Institute for Strategic Studies, 1983), p. 9.
45. D. N. Schwartz, *NATO's Nuclear Dilemmas* (Washington, Brookings, 1983), pp. 174–5.
46. Henry S. Rowen, 'Formulating Strategic Doctrine,' in *Commission on the Organization of the Government for the Conduct of Foreign Policy, Appendix K: Adequacy of Current Organization: Defense and Arms Control* IV (Washington: GPO, June 1975), p. 220.

7 Essential Equivalence and the Countervailing Strategy

1. Press Conference, 27 January 1969, in *Public Papers of the President: Richard M. Nixon: 1969*, (Washington: GPO, 1970), p. 19; see also R. M. Nixon, *RN: Memoirs* (New York: Grosset and Dunlap, 1978), p. 415. The formal announcement actually came 18 September 1969.
2. The Nixon administration's initial perception of trends in strategic capabilities may even have strengthened its commitment to arms negotiation.

3. The capability for damage limitation is usually measured in the formula for *lethality* or 'counter-military potential':

$$\text{CMP} = \frac{\text{Yield}^{2/3}}{(\text{CEP})^2}$$

   CEP (circular error probable) is the radius of a circle within which half of the warheads are expected to fall. Since CMP varies inversely with the square of CEP, CMP is highly sensitive to improvements in accuracy. Since destructive power does not grow proportionately with a simple increase in yield, the 'equivalent megatonnage' of a warhead is usually expressed as $Y^{2/3}$. But even this figure must be divided by the expected accuracy squared since mere increases in megatonnage do little to bring more force to bear on a particular point. *The Military Balance 1982–1983* (London: The International Institute for Strategic Studies, 1982), pp. 138–9; Ian Smart, *Advanced Strategic Missiles: A Short Guide*, Adelphi Paper no. 63 (London: The Institute for Strategic Studies, 1969); for a further discussion of lethality, see Chapter 11, below.
4. Cordesman, *Deterrence in the 1980s*, pp. 12–13.
5. *The Military Balance 1977–1978* (London: The International Institute for Strategic Studies, 1977), pp. 80, 90.
6. The prevailing doctrine put a premium on the assuredness of city-destruction; the SLBMs were absolutely secure (because they were underwater and mobile) and since the targeted large, soft objectives, did not require the accuracy of land-based weapons.
7. Henry Rowen, 'Formulating Strategic Doctrine', p. 221.
8. By 1967 the total number of US ICBMs equalled 1054, that is, the original complement of 1000 planned for Minuteman plus 54 Titans. This number has remained unchanged. *Ibid.*, p. 80.
9. T. Greenwood, *Making the MIRV: A Study in Defense Decisionmaking* (Cambridge, Mass.: Ballinger, 1975) pp. 70–1; E. Luttwak, *Strategic Power: Military Capabilities and Political Utility* (Beverly Hills: Sage, 1976), p. 22.
10. R. M. Nixon, *A Report to the Congress: US Foreign Policy for the 1970s, A New Strategy for Peace*, 18 February 1970 (Washington: GPO, 1970), p. 122.
11. 'I must not be – and my successors must not be – limited to the indiscriminate mass destruction of civilians as the sole possible response to challenges.' R. M. Nixon, *A Report to the Congress: US Foreign Policy for the 1970s, Building for Peace*, 25 February 1971 (Washington: GPO, 1971), p. 170.
12. Friedberg, 'A History of the US Strategic Doctrine', p. 54. US countersilo strikes would weaken the US more than the USSR since a single successful strike (destroying one Russian launcher) would require at least two and probably three US launchers.
13. That is, by the Russian acquisition of a secure, second-strike capability.
14. That is, 'parity'.
15. W. Slocombe, *The Political Implications of Strategic Parity*, Adelphi Paper no. 77 (London: The Institute for Strategic Studies, 1971), p. 9.

16. Ballistic-missile-carrying nuclear powered submarines.
17. For a somewhat different argument supporting this conclusion, see Edward N. Luttwak, 'The Nuclear Alternatives', in K. A. Myers (ed.), *NATO: The Next Thirty Years* (Boulder, Col.: Westview, 1980), pp. 97–9. Luttwak argues that strategic superiority provided the material basis for Assured Destruction (i.e., for extended deterrence beyond the assured destruction capability):

    First, some ICBMs could be fired in small numbers, selectively, and without prejudice to the rest of the ICBM force since the Soviet Union had only a slight counterforce capability against all the ICBM silo launchers. In the same vein, the small and technically backward Soviet SLBM force of the 1960s did not effectively threaten the SAC bomber bases, thus again allowing a selective use of some bombers without prejudice to the rest of the force. Overall, the relative magnitude of the force involved allowed an extensive allocation of weapons to the tasks of extended deterrence (for attack against all Soviet targets except cities) while still [maintaining] the *ultimissima ratio* of simple, strike-back deterrence in protection of American soil. Second, even with immunity lost, the United States had a very great advantage in the balance of relative vulnerabilities that, other things being equal, assured it of a dominant position in any possible escalation. (*Ibid.*, p. 98.)

18. See sources referred to in Wohlstetter, 'Is There a Strategic Arms Race', p. 26. Carl Kaysen concluded that 'None of the evidence on the Soviet build-up points beyond an effort to move close to a crude equality with us in numbers of offensive missiles', 'Keeping the Strategic Balance,' in G. H. Quester (ed.), *Power, Action and Interaction: Readings on International Politics* (Boston: Little, Brown, 1971), p. 550.
19. W. Slocombe, *The Political Implications of Strategic Parity*, p. 7.
20. Cordesman, *Deterrence in the 1980s*, p. 19; see Secretary of Defense Donald H. Rumsfeld, *Annual Defense Department Report, Fiscal Year 1978* (Washington: GPO, 17 January 1977).
21. In September 1974, the US Department of Defense stated that it had,

    some information that the Soviets have achieved or will soon achieve, accuracies of 500 to 700 meters with their ICBMs. These figures may be a little optimistic, but that would represent about a fourth to a third of a nautical mile.

    Senate Foreign Relations Committee, *Briefing in Counterforce Attacks* (Hearing, 11 September 1974; partly declassified and released 10 January 1975), p. 10. But by November 1977, the Soviet Union had flight-tested guidance systems on two of the ICBMs referred to (the SS 18/19) with CEPs of .1 nautical mile or 600 feet. Clarence A. Robinson, 'Soviets Boost ICBM Accuracy', *Aviation Week and Space Technology*, 3 April 1978, pp. 42–16.
22. See sources cited in Albert Wohlstetter, 'The Case for Strategic Force Defense', in J. Holst and W. Schneider Jr. (eds) *Why ABM?* (New York: Pergamon Press, 1969), p. 130; see Testimony of George Rathjens, in *Authorization for Military Procurement, Fiscal Year 1970*, Part 2

(Washington: GPO, 1969), p. 1246. Ralph Lapp concluded that 75 per cent of the US ICBM force would remain invulnerable. See Ralph Lapp, 'From Nike to Safeguard: A Biography of the ABM', *New York Times Magazine* (4 May 1969), pp. 29–31.

Desmond Ball predicted that, 'In an all-out attack the Soviets could destroy the Minuteman force, but at the cost of their own ICBM force . . . There would be no loss of equivalence in this capacity.' D. Ball, *Developmens in US Strategic Nuclear Policy Under the Carter Administration*, ACIS Working Paper no. 21 (Los Angeles: Center for International and Strategic Affairs, February 1980), p. 4; by 1982 he concluded, 'Fixed-based ICBMs, then, are now obsolescent; by the mid-1980s both the US [assuming MX is deployed] and the Soviet Union, will have the capability using only a part of their ICBM forces to destroy a very substantial portion of the ICBMs of the other.' D. Ball, 'The Future of The Strategic Balance', in L. S. Hagen, (ed.) *The Crisis In Western Security* (London: Croom Helm, 1982), p. 127.

23. Colin S. Gray, *The Future of Land-Based Missile Forces*, Adelphi Paper no. 140 (London: The International Institute for Strategic Studies, 1977).
24. By 'advantageous capability' I mean one that, at least theoretically, would better the relative position of the attacker if used. Of course, the US at present has a hard-target, counter-silo capability in the Minuteman force. Its use, however, would be disadvantageous to the US.
25. Secretary of Defense Harold Brown, *Department of Defense Appropriations for 1981*, Hearings before a Subcommittee of the Committee on Appropriations, House of Representatives, 96th Congress, Second Session, Part 1 (Washington: GPO, 1980), p. 135. In April 1979 the Commander-in-Chief of Strategic Air Command, Gen. R. H. Ellis, wrote to Secretary of Defense Harold Brown that the survivability of the US ICBM silos was declining and 'is now under 40 per cent.' During 1980 both William Perry, Assistant Secretary of Defense, and Harold Brown testified that a Soviet attack in the early 1980s could theoretically destroy more than 90 per cent of US ICBM. 'This has commonly been regarded as the most important national security problem facing the US at the outset of the 1980s.' 'Trends in Strategic Forces', *The Military Balance 1980–1981* (London: The International Institute for Strategic Studies, 1981), p. 14. But see, John D. Steinbruner and Thomas M. Garwin, 'Strategic Vulnerability: The Balance Between Prudence and Paranoia,' *International Security* 1 (Summer 1976), pp. 138–181, and William H. Kincade, 'Missile Vulnerability Reconsidered,' *Arms Control Today* 11 (May 1981), pp. 1–8.
26. Gregory Treverton, *Nuclear Weapons in Europe*, Adelphi Paper no. 168, (London: The International Institute for Strategic Studies, 1981), p. 3.
27. See the arguments in Chapter 11, below.
28. Furthermore the size of the warhead and mobility of the launcher introduce a threat to Europe that Soviet central systems do not pose.
29. Luttwak, 'The Problems of Extending Deterrence,' p. 35.
30. Jeff McCausland, 'The SS-20: Military *and* Political Threat,' *The Fletcher Forum* 6 (Winter 1982) p. 13. *Military Balance 1981–1982* (London: The International Institute for Strategic Studies, 1982), p. 127.

31. The SLBMs of the Poseidon force are strategic, central systems as reflected by their inclusion in SALT.
32. *Military Balance 1981–1982*, p. 123.
33. *Ibid.*
34. G. F. Treverton, *Nuclear Weapons in Europe*, Adelphi Paper no. 168 (London: The International Institute for Strategic Studies, 1981), p. 11. On the increasing incredibility of Flexible Response, see Lawrence Freedman, 'NATO Myths', *Foreign Policy* 45 (Winter 1981–2), pp. 48–68.
35. Lynn Davis, 'Extended Deterrence in the 1980s and 1990s', p. 4; see also *Department of Defense Annual Report, Fiscal Year 1982* (Washington: GPO, 1981), pp. 52–9.
36. US Congress, Office of Technology Assessment, 'Case 3: A Counterforce Attack against the United States?' *The Effects of Nuclear War* (Washington: GPO, May 1979), pp. 81–90.
37. Laurence Martin, 'Changes in American Strategic Doctrine: An Initial Interpretation,' *Survival* (July–August 1974), pp. 58–64.
38. But not, I think, as a complete description. The Americans were not in a position of vulnerability equivalent to that of the Russians at the earlier period.
39. L. E. Davis, *Limited Nuclear Options: Deterrence and the New American Doctrine*, Adelphi Paper no. 121 (London, The International Institute for Strategic Studies, 1975), p. 5.
40. Kissinger, *White House Years* I, p. 216.
41. D. Ball, *Targeting for Strategic Deterrence*, Adelphi Paper no. 185 (London: The International Institute for Strategic Studies, 1983), p. 18; for other accounts, see Davis, *Limited Nuclear Options*, pp. 3–4, 17–8; and Cordesman, *Deterrence in the 1980s*, p. 14.
42. Senate Armed Services Committee, *Department of Defense Authorization for Fiscal Year 1979* (Washington: GPO, 1978), part 8, p. 6280.
43. Earlier Schlesinger had appeared before Congress to explain the difference in the two strategies, Assured Destruction and Essential Equivalence. Testimony of J. R. Schlesinger, *Briefing on Counterforce Attacks*, September 1974 (Washington: GPO, 1974), p. 37.
44. James Schlesinger interviewed by Laurence Martin, BBC Radio 4 'Analysis', 24 October 1974.
45. Secretary of Defense James R. Schlesinger, *Annual Defense Department Report, Fiscal Year 1976*, 5 February 1975, 2 (Washington: GPO, 1975), p. 4.
46. Schlesinger, *Briefing on Counterforce Attacks*, p. 41; Testimony before the Subcommittee on Arms Control, International Law and Organizations of the US Senate, 93rd Congress, 2nd Session, 11 September 1977.
47. Secretary of Defense James R. Schlesinger, *Annual Defense Department Report, Fiscal Year 1975*, 4 March 1974, (Washington: GPO, 1974), p. 5.
48. Senate Armed Services Committee, *Fiscal Year 1977 Authorization for Military Procurement, Research & Development & Active Duty, Selected Reserve & Civilian Personnel Strengths* 2 (Washington: GPO, 1976) p. 6422; see also House Appropriations Committee, *Department of Defense Appropriations for 1977* (Washington: GPO, 1976) part 8, p. 30.

49. Rumsfeld, *Annual Defense Department Report, Fiscal Year 1978*, p. 68.
50. Lawrence J. Korb, 'National Security Organization and Process in the Carter Administration', in S. C. Sarkesian, (ed.), *Defense Policy and the Presidency: Carter's First Years* (Boulder: Westview, 1979), Chapter 11.
51. House Armed Services Committee, *Hearings on Military Posture & H. R. 1872*, (1979) Book 1 of Part 3, p. 437.
52. Senate Foreign Relations Committee, *Nuclear War Strategy* (Washington: GPO, 1981), p. 16.
53. Harold Brown, Address at Newport, 20 August 1980; see also Harold Brown, 'The Objective of US Strategic Forces', Address to the Naval War College, Washington, 22 August 1980, News Release. Putting it this way tends to exaggerate the continuity, however, since it skips over the total response programmes of the later McNamara and Schlesinger's predecessors.
54. *Ibid.*
55. Ball, *Targeting for Strategic Deterrence.*
56. See Ball, *Targeting for Strategic Deterrence*, pp. 22–3.
57. See Treverton, *Nuclear Weapons in Europe*, p. 3.
58. A time-urgent weapon is one that can be told, quickly, when to go; a command-responsive weapon must be able to be told, quickly, where to go.
59. Comptroller General, *Report to the Congress: Countervailing Strategy Demands Revision of Strategic Force Acquisition Plans* (Washington: GAO, August 1981), pp. 27–33.
60. I am indebted to Lynn Davis for this argument.
61. Cordesman, *Deterrence in the 1980s*, pp. 17, 18, 22.
62. This is the conclusion, put most optimistically, of Ball, *Can Nuclear War Be Controlled?*
63. A review of targeting policy was begun almost immediately by the Reagan Administration upon taking office. In October 1981 this resulted in National Security Decision Directive (NSDD) 13 (the successor to PD 59) and the most recent NUWEP. Present indications are that the fundamental strategic programme of NSDM 242 has been preserved. See, Secretary of Defense Caspar Weinberger, 'The Reagan Administration's Strategic Program', Testimony to the US Senate Armed Forces Committee, 5 October 1981 ('The specific objectives of President Reagan's programme are to regain and to maintain the strategic balance with the Soviet Union, where balance is the key to deterring any attack by them against ourselves or our allies'), reprinted in *Survival* 24 (January/February 1982) p. 28; Secretary of Defense Caspar Weinberger, Report to the Congress, Fiscal Year 1983 (8 February 1982) reprinted in *Survival* 24 (May/June 1982) p. 133; Caspar Weinberger, 'Statement to the Senate', 14 December 1982:

> Today, deterrence remains – as it has for the past thirty-seven years – the cornerstone of our strategic nuclear policy, and, indeed, of our entire national security posture. Our strategy is a defensive one, designed to prevent attack – particularly nuclear attack – against us or our allies. To deter successfully, we must be able – and must be seen to be able – to retaliate against any potential aggressor in such a manner

> that the costs we will exact will substantially exceed any gains he might hope to achieve through aggression. We, for our part, are under no illusion about the consequences of a nuclear war; we believe there would be no winners in such a war . . . We must make sure that the Soviet leadership, in calculating the risks of aggression, recognizes that because of our retaliatory capability, there can be no circumstance where the initiation of a nuclear war at any level or of any duration would make sense.

Survival 25 (March/April 1983) p. 85.

64. Christopher Makins, 'TNF Modernization and the Countervailing Strategy', *Survival* 23 (July/August 1981), pp. 157–164.
65. The 1977 Alastair Buchan Memorial Lecture, 28 October 1977, is reprinted in *Survival* (January/February 1978), p. 4.
66. Schmidt, 'The 1977 Alastair Buchan Memorial Lecture', p. 4.

8 Introduction of the Theorem

1. L. E. Davis, *Extended Deterrence in The 1980s/1990s*, forthcoming Adelphi Paper (London: The International Institute for Strategic Studies); D. Ball, 'Soviet ICBM Deployment', *Survival* 22 (July/August 1980), pp. 167–70. (For this reason it was argued earlier that the competition for warheads problem associated with extended deterrence by Treverton was illusory.)
2. Pierre Lellouche, *Foreign Affairs* 59 (Spring 1981), p. 816.
3. Compare Secretary of Defense, 'Memorandum for the President, Theater Nuclear Forces', 1965 ('I recommend (1) The US continues to urge the improvement of a NATO non-nuclear capability on the primary defense against non-nuclear aggression in Europe', p. 1) with Secretary of Defense, 'Memorandum for the President, Theater Nuclear Forces' 6 January 1967 ('Nuclear weapons are a necessary complement to non-nuclear forces . . . they can be used to support our forces if we fail to contain a large scale non-nuclear aggression', p. 1) and Secretary of Defense, 'Memorandum for the President, Theater Nuclear Forces', 11 January 1968 ('We need to improve our capabilities for fighting a controlled and limited theatre nuclear war. In particular, we need to improve our capabilities for the selective use of nuclear weapons during the initial stages of such a war, p. 1) and Secretary of Defense, 'Memorandum for the President, Theater Nuclear Forces', 15 January 1969. All these documents have been sanitized, i.e. partially redacted and declassified.
4. Walter Slocombe, 'PD59 and The Countervailing Strategy', *International Security* 5 (Spring 1981), pp. 18–24; for a subtle argument that this sort of strategy actually weakens NATO's position when faced with a limited Soviet attack, see Pauli Jarvenpaa, *Flexible Nuclear Options: New Myths and Old Realities*, Peace Studies Program Occasional Paper no. 7 (Ithaca: Cornell University, September 1976), pp. 24–36.
5. Lloyd Cutler and Philip Bobbitt, 'Economic Sanctions', forthcoming article.

6. For a variant of this argument, see Robert Jervis, 'Deterrence and Perception', *International Security* 7 (Winter 1982–3), p. 7.
7. See Walter B. Slocombe, IISS Conference Papers: Nuclear Forces in Europe, 'Effects of Possible Arms Control Outcomes on US and Alliance TNF Deployments and Doctrine', pp. 1–3.
8. David C. Elliot, *Decision at Brussels: The Politics of Nuclear Forces*, California Seminar Discussion Paper no. 97 (Santa Monica, 1981).
9. D. R. Cotter, J. H. Hansen, and K. McConnell, *The Nuclear Balance in Europe: Status, Trends, Implications*, USSI Report 83–1 (Washington, United States Strategic Institute, 1983), p. 27.
10. North Atlantic Assembly, *Draft Interim Report of the Special Committee on Nuclear Weapons in Europe* (1982), pp. 14–15.
11. NATO Press Service, Press Communiqué M2 (79)22, 12 December 1979.
12. Henry Kissinger, 'The Future of NATO', *Washington Quarterly* 2 (1979), pp. 3, 5.
13. Henry Kissinger, 'Strategy and The Atlantic Alliance,' *Survival* 24 (September/October 1982), pp. 196–7; see also Henry Kissinger, 'The International Context for US Security', in *America's Security in the 1980s*, Papers from the 23rd Annual IISS Conference, Adelphi Paper no. 174 (London: The International Institute for Strategic Studies, 1981), pp. 5–6.

9 The Social Dimension of Nuclear Strategy

1. 'Secretary of Defense McNamara's annual posture statements certainly contributed to this' Friedberg, *A History of US Strategic "Doctrine" – 1945 to 1980*, n. 3, p. 67.
2. See Richard M. Nixon. A Report to the Congress, *US Foreign Policy for the 1970s, A New Strategy for Peace*, 18 February 1970 (Washington: GPO, 1970) Doc. Pr. 37.2: F 76), p. 122, repeated the following year, 25 February 1971, Richard M. Nixon, *A Report to the Congress, US Foreign Policy for the 1970s, Building for Peace* (Washington: GPO, 1971) Doc. Pr. 37.2: F 76/971), pp. 170–1. Lynn Davis states that at 'the time this report was issued, officials in the Defense Department were puzzled and irritated because the drafters of the Presidential message knew . . . that existing war plans did not confront the President with such choices,' i.e., either 'ordering the mass destruction of enemy civilians' or nothing. Davis, *Limited Nuclear Options*, p. 3.
3. Congressman Ronald Dellums recently stated that the principle of mutual assured destruction, the targeting of 'populations and industrial bases . . . has been our historical targeting approach.' *Hearings on Military Posture and HR 1872 and HR 2575 before the Committee on Armed Services, House of Representatives*, part 1 (Washington: GPO, 1979), p. 547.
4. Freeman Dyson's eloquent 1981 Tanner Lectures at Oxford, for example, appeared to be based on this notion.
5. James Kelly, 'Thinking About the Unthinkable,' *Time* 119 (29 March 1982), p. 10.

6. *Ibid.*
7. J. Schell, *The Fate of the Earth* (New York: Knopf, 1982).
8. *Ibid.*, p. 33.
9. *Ibid.*, pp. 56–57.
10. *Ibid.*, p. 55.
11. *Ibid.*, pp. 201–2.
12. Theodore Draper, 'How Not to Think About Nuclear War', *The New York Review of Books* 29 (15 July 1982), p. 36.
13. Schell, *The Fate of the Earth*, p. 197.
14. Assembly of Western European Union, 'The Problem of Nuclear Weapons in Europe', Proceedings, 28th Ordinary Session June 1982, vol. 1, Document 918 (Paris, WEV, June 1982), pp. 287–99.
15. 'The Newsweek Poll,' *Newsweek 101* (31 January 1983) p. 14. The poll was conducted by the Gallup organization.
16. *Le Monde*, 27 October 1981.
17. *International Herald Tribune*, 12 October 1981.
18. *Le Monde*, 27 October 1981.
19. Assembly of Western European Union, *The Problem of Nuclear Weapons in Europe*, Document 918, 19 May 1982, p. 291.
20. Stephen Szabo, 'European Opinion After the Missiles', *Survival* 27 (November/December 1985), p. 265, relying on a series of published and unpublished surveys conducted by various West European firms from 1979 to the end of 1984.
21. *Ibid.*, p. 269.
22. *Ibid.*, pp. 270–1.
23. Peter Paret, 'Clausewitz and the Nineteenth Century', *Theory and Practice of War* (London: Cassell, 1965) pp. 21–41, argues that Clausewitz recognized that war had become a matter for the people as a whole. See also Bernard Brodie, 'On Clausewitz: A Passion for War', *World Politics* 25 (January 1973), pp. 288–308.
24. Michael Howard, 'The Forgotten Dimensions of Strategy', *Foreign Affairs* 57 (Summer 1979), p. 982.
25. *Ibid.*, p. 983.
26. *Ibid.*, pp. 984–985.
27. Kelly, *Thinking About the Unthinkable*, p. 12.
28. A slightly different resolution passed the House of Representatives, see *Washington Post*, 24 April 1983, p. A4. It had been defeated the previous year in a narrow vote (202 to 204) on 5 August 1982. This resolution was defeated in the Senate in September 1983.
29. President Reagan's Commencement Address, 9 May 1982, *Survival* 24 (September/October 1982), p. 229; also, *New York Times*, 10 May 1982, pp. A1, A14 (text).
30. Crisis stability denotes a state of affairs such that neither side is tempted to strike first in a political crisis. It differs, of course, from arms stability, which refers to a level of weaponry that is adequate to maintain a strategic balance but is not redundant, and is therefore maximally cost efficient.
31. *Strategic Survey 1980–1981* (London: The International Institute for Strategic Studies, 1981) p. 15; see also Leslie Gelb, 'Reagan Arms Plan', *New York Times*, 15 May 1981.

32. Regardless of MX deployment, the US is unlikely to change the ratio of SLBM/ICBM currently deployed, since the severe warhead limit means that fewer than eight Tridents could be fully deployed if the mix were changed to present more than 450 land-based US missiles, even if the ICBMs were uniformly reduced to a single warhead.
33. Brown, *Department of Defense Appropriations for 1981*, p. 135.
34. *Ibid.*, p. 138.
35. I am indebted to Thomas Schelling for this reminder.
36. 'Brezhnev and Reagan on Atom War', *New York Times*, 21 October 1981, p. A5; 'Statement by Reagan on War', *New York Times*, 22 October 1981, p. A9; 'Excerpts from the President's Press Conference,' *New York Times*, 11 November 1981, p. A24; 'Soviet Says US Statements on Nuclear War Are a "Serious" Danger', *New York Times*, 7 November 1981, p. A6.
37. 'Haig Is Disputed by Weinberger on A-Blast Plan', *New York Times*, 6 November 1981, pp. A1, A13.
38. *International Herald Tribune*, 6–7 February 1982.
39. Ronald Reagan, 'US Program for Peace and Arms Control,' *US Department of State Current Policy* no. 346, 18 November 1981, p. 3.
40. Francois de Rose, Letter to the Editor, *Survival* 24 (May/June 1982), p. 143.
41. McGeorge Bundy, George F. Kennan, Robert S. McNamara, and Gerard Smith, 'Nuclear Weapons and the Atlantic Alliance', *Foreign Affairs* 60 (Spring 1982), p. 753. Bundy is a former Special Assistant for National Security Affairs to Presidents Kennedy and Johnson; Kennan is a former US Ambassador to Moscow, author of the celebrated Long Telegram, and subsequently Director for Policy Planning, US Department of State; Gerard Smith is former Chief of the US Delegation to the SALT from 1969–72; and McNamara is a former US Secretary of Defense.
42. Note that this premise assumes the ambiguity of US retaliation entailed by the 'theorem'; the authors seem to be saying that if the US will retaliate on behalf of Europe it will do so with central systems; if not, the provision of additional systems is redundant.
43. Bundy *et al.*, 'Nuclear Weapons and the Atlantic Alliance', pp. 767, 765–66, 764.
44. See Jeremy Stone, 'Presidential First Use is Unlawful', *Foreign Policy* 56 (Fall 1984), pp. 94–112.

10 Alternative Nuclear Strategies

1. John Erickson, 'The Soviet View of Deterrence: A General Survey,' *Survival* 24 (November/December 1982), pp. 242–9 argues for the view that the Soviet Union, while adopting the deterrence assumption as an unavoidable fact in the central relationship, has not confined its strategy to reliance on this assumption, and has not perceived the US as doing so either. Benjamin S. Lambeth, *The Elements of Soviet Strategic Policy*, RAND Paper No. p–6389; Dimitri Simes, 'Deterrence and Coercion in Soviet Policy, *International Security* 5 (Winter, 1980), pp. 80–103; L. Goure, F. D. Kohler and M. L. Harvey (eds), *The Role of Nuclear Forces*

in Current Soviet Strategy (Miami: Center for Advanced International Studies, 1974).

2. When Paul Warnke, then the recently appointed head of ACDA, was asked how the US ought to react to indications that the Soviet leadership was preparing in order to fight and win a nuclear war, he is reported to have replied 'In my view this kind of thinking is on a level of abstraction which is unrealistic. It seems to me that instead of talking in those terms, which would indulge what I regard as the primitive aspects of Soviet nuclear doctrine, we ought to be trying to educate them into the real world of strategic nuclear weapons, which is that nobody could possibly win.' 'The Real Paul Warnke,' *New Republic* 176 (26 March 1977), p. 23.
3. See, e.g., Carl Kaysen, 'Keeping the Strategic Balance', *Foreign Affairs* 46 (July 1968).
4. Benjamin S. Lambeth, *Soviet Strategic Conduct and the Prospects for Stability*, RAND Paper R-2579-AF (Santa Monica: The RAND Corporation, 1980) reprinted as 'What Deters: An Assessment of the Soviet View', in J. F. Reichart and S. R. Strum (eds) *American Defense Policy* (Baltimore: Johns Hopkins University Press, 1981) p. 188; Benjamin S. Lambeth, 'Selective Nuclear Options and Soviet Strategy', in J. Holst and Uwe Nerlich (eds) *Beyond Nuclear Deterrence: New Aims, New Arms* (New York: Crane-Russak, 1977); Benjamin Lambeth, 'The Elements of Soviet Strategic Policy'; see also Fritz Ermath, 'Contrasts in American and Soviet Strategic Thought', *International Security* 3 (Fall 1978), p. 138.
5. Lambeth, 'What Deters: An Assessment of the Soviet View', p. 189.
6. *Ibid*.
7. *Ibid*, p. 191.
8. Superiority, that is, either geographically – in a particular theatre – or with respect to a crucial class of weapons.
9. Colin S. Gray, and Keith B. Payne, 'Victory Is Possible,' *Foreign Policy* 39 (Summer 1980), p. 14; Colin S. Gray, 'Nuclear Strategy: A Case for a Theory of Victory', *International Security* 4 (Summer 1979), p. 84. See also, K. B. Payne, *Nuclear Deterrence in US–Soviet Relations* (Boulder: Westview, 1982).
10. Gray and Payne, 'Victory Is Possible', p. 14.
11. *Ibid*., p. 15.
12. *Ibid*., p. 16. This glosses over the distinction between parity in central systems and complete parity throughout the opposing force structures.
13. This point is clearly recognized by Payne, who refers to the preferred war-fighting doctrine as a 'classical strategy' and is careful to distinguish it from the countervailing strategy which, he notes, presumes 'mutual vulnerability'. Payne, *Nuclear Deterrence*, Chapter 8. Somewhat less careful is Thomas Powers, *Choosing a Strategy for World War III* (New York: Knopf, 1983), who fails to note the distinction and, for that reason, undercuts the thesis of his work that weapons capabilities have driven doctrinal change.
14. T. Powers, *World War Three* (New York: Random House, 1983) overlooks this distinction and thus confuses war-fighting and countervailing strategies.
15. Deployment of a ballistic missile defense would abrogate the ABM

Treaty. For an evaluation of this step, see Michael Nacht, 'ABM ABCs', *Foreign Policy* 46 (Spring 1982), pp. 155–174.

16. By 'cost-effective' I simply mean a system that permits the US to defend a target at a relative cost to itself that is lower than the expenditure to the attacker of a successful strike, given the potential gains to the attacker. When this is not so, e.g., when warheads or decoys can swamp the defensive system, an adversary will deploy them if this cost ratio is favourable, and if there is some political goal to be achieved by such hostility. Thus Switzerland can have a successful civil defence because no one targets them. But the US will have great difficulty in deploying even a successful *missile* defence.
17. Perhaps this aspect of war-fighting doctrine, rather than patronizing assumptions about the recklessness of our military personnel, gives plausibility to the claims that such doctrines predispose decisionmakers to approach nuclear war with less terror and revulsion. Cf. Spurgeon Keeny, Jr. and Wolfgang K. H. Panofsky, 'MAD versus NUTS: Can Doctrine of Weaponry Remedy the Mutual Hostage Relationship of the Superpowers?', *Foreign Affairs* 60 (Winter 1981–2), p. 290.
18. B. Brodie, (ed.) *The Absolute Weapon* (New York: Harcourt, Brace, 1946), p. 76.
19. B. Brodie, *Strategy in the Missile Age* (Princeton: Princeton University Press, 1959), p. 391.
20. McGeorge Bundy, 'Strategic Deterrence Thirty Years Later: What has Changed', *The Future of Strategic Deterrence, Papers from the 21st Annual Conference of the IISS*, Adelphi Papers no. 160 (London: The International Institute for Strategic Studies, 1980), p. 8. See also McGeorge Bundy, 'America in the 80s: Reframing Our Relations with Our Friends and Among Our Allies', *Remarks at the New York University Sesquicentennial Conference* (16 October 1981).
21. *Ibid.*
22. *Ibid.*, p. 9.
23. *Ibid.*
24. *Ibid.*
25. *Ibid.*, p. 10, citing the excellent essay, A. W. DePorte, *Europe between the Superpowers* (New Haven: Yale University Press, 1979) that argues that a divided Europe will be maintained indefinitely by the US and the USSR.
26. A no-first-use policy appears to follow from this position since a first use would, on this reasoning, ultimately engage the full Soviet retaliatory force. See Chapter 9. See also Bundy, 'America in the 80s'.

    In fact, each of the three alternative strategic doctrines discussed has its theatre corollary. For the theatre doctrine accompanying a war-fighting strategy, see J. P. Rose, *Evolution of US Army Nuclear Doctrine 1945–1980* (Boulder: Westview, 1980). Richard Garwin has proposed dedicating US central systems to European states, in his version of the deterrence assumption *simpliciter*, see Richard L. Garwin, 'Reducing Dependence on Nuclear Weapons: A Second Nuclear Regime', in D. C. Gompert, M. Mardlebaum, R. L. Garwin and J. H. Barton, *Nuclear Weapons and World Politics* (New York: McGraw Hill, 1977), pp. 106–7; but see Bernard Brodie, 'The Development of Nuclear Strategy,' *International*

Security 2 (Spring 1978), p. 65 who asserted that battlefield tactical nuclear weapons need not violate the 'firebreak' and necessarily escalate, p. 76. For a comparison of theatre options corresponding to two of the principal strategic alternatives, see W. Heisenberg, *The Alliance and Europe: Part I: Crisis Stability in Europe and Theatre Nuclear Weapons*, Adelphi, Paper no. 96 (London, The International Institute for Strategic Studies, 1973), pp. 15–28.

27. Michael Howard, 'The Relevance of Traditional Strategy', *Foreign Affairs* 51 (January 1973), p. 262.
28. Bundy, 'Strategic Deterrence Thirty Years Later,' pp. 10–11.
29. This is the subject of Chapter 12.
30. See William G. Hyland, 'The Atlantic Crisis,' *Foreign Affairs* 40 (World Issue, 1981) for a lucid account of this issue.
31. Pierre Hassner, 'Who is Decoupling from Whom? *or* This Time the Wolf is Here', in L. Hager (ed.). *The Crisis in Western Security* (London, Croom Helm, 1982), pp. 174–5.
32. See Hedley Bull, 'The Future Condition of Deterrence', *The Future of Strategic Deterrence, Papers from the 21st Annual Conference of the IISS*, Adelphi Paper no. 160 (London: The International Institute for Strategic Studies, 1980).
33. On US strategic C^3I, see D. Ball, *Can Nuclear War be Controlled?*, Adelphi Paper no. 45 (London: The International Institute for Strategic Studies, 1981); John D. Steinbruner, 'Nuclear Decapitation', *Foreign Policy* 45 (Winter 1981–82), pp. 16–29; and Congressional Budget Office, *Strategic Command, Control and Communications: Alternative Approaches for Modernization* (Washington: CBO, 1981). See also, Comptroller General, *Report to the Congress: Countervailing Strategy Demands Revision of Strategic Force Acquisition Plans* (Washington: GAO, August 1981), pp. 16–26.
34. Ball, *Can Nuclear War Be Controlled?*, p. 14.
35. US Constitution, Article 2, Section 1.
36. Department of Defense Directive 5100.30, 2 December 1971 prescribes the succession of authority from the Secretary of Defense. At the level of Assistant Secretary of Defense and below, rank is ordered by length of service. Admiral Miller, former Deputy Director of the Joint Strategic Target Planning Staff conceded in testimony that the US might have considerable difficulty in reconstituting legitimate authority in the event of the death of the President. House Committee on International Relations, *First Use of Nuclear Weapons: Preserving Responsible Control*, (March 1976), pp. 47, 71.
37. The aircraft itself, according to Congressional testimony, 'would be a rather high priority target in case of Soviet attack.' House Appropriations Committee, *Department of Defense Appropriation for 1980*, part 6 (April 1979), p. 186. William Perry, Director of Defense Research and Engineering, concluded that the 'availability of [the NEACP] aircraft cannot be unconditionally guaranteed.' *Ibid.*, part 3 (March 1979), p. 119.
38. *Ibid.*, part 6 (April 1979) testimony of Dr Dineen, pp. 192–4.
39. Ball, *Can Nuclear War Be Controlled?*, p. 17.
40. Senate Armed Services Committee, Department of Defense Appropri-

ation for 1980, part 1 (January–February 1979), p. 390.
41. *Ibid.*, part 3 (March 1979), p. 112.
42. Ball, *Can Nuclear War Be Controlled?*, pp. 17–8.
43. *Ibid.*, p. 19.
44. See Chapter 11, below.
45. Comptroller General, *Countervailing Strategy Demands Revision of Strategic Force Acquisition Plans* (1981).
46. Lambeth, 'Selective Nuclear Options and Soviet Strategy', p. 101.
47. Ball *Can Nuclear War Be Controlled?*, pp. 34–5; see also Jack L. Snyder, *The Soviet Strategic Culture: Implications for Limited Nuclear Operations*, RAND paper no. R-2154-AF (Santa Monica: The RAND Corporation, Sept. 1977).
48. Bundy, *Strategic Deterrence Thirty Years Later*, p. 11.
49. Henry Kissinger, 'The Future of NATO', in K. A. Myers, (ed.) *NATO: The Next Thirty Years* (Boulder: Westview, 1980).
50. Cordesman, *Deterrence in the 1980s*, p. 42.
51. Freedman, *The Evolution of Nuclear Doctrine*, pp. 396–8; Gompert, *et al.*, *Nuclear Weapons and World Politics: Alternatives for the Future*.
52. I propose to treat more radical strategic alternatives such as disarmament (mutual or unilateral), guerilla and territorial defence, pacifist resistance, terrorism, etc. in another book, *A Nuclear Strategy Primer*. This book explicitly builds on the deterrence assumption that each of the more radical alternative regimes discards. I, in fact, hold various political assumptions about the nature of international conflict that are incompatible with such regimes. These assumptions are: that the ability to develop, deploy and deliver thermonuclear weapons cannot be eradicated; that such an ability is of enormous political consequence to its possessor in at least some significant contexts; that this power contributes to the national means of exercising influence in world affairs and thus will be sought by at least some nations. For the links between these assumptions and the deterrence assumption, I refer the reader to *A Nuclear Strategy Primer*.

11 Alternative Nuclear Weapons Technologies

1. J. R. Schlesinger, *The Theatre Nuclear Force Posture in Europe*, A Report to the United States Congress in Compliance with Public Law 93–365, 1 July 1975; see also James A. Thomson, 'Nuclear Weapons in Europe: Planning for NATO's Nuclear Deterrent in the 1980s and 1990s', *Survival* 25 (May–June 1983), pp. 101–2.
2. North Atlantic Treaty Organization, *NATO and the Warsaw Pact – Force Comparisons*, July 1982.
3. D. R. Cotter, J. H. Hansen and K. McConnell, *The Nuclear Balance in Europe: Status, Trends and Implications*, USSI Report 83–1 (Washington: United States Strategic Institute, 1983), p. 29.
4. *Ibid.*, p. 13, 'Comparison of Existing NATO/Warsaw Pact Land-based, Surface-to-Surface Missile Launchers in Europe'.
5. *Ibid.*, pp. 22–3.
6. N. Polmar, *Strategic Weapons: An Introduction* (New York: Crane, Russak, 1982) pp. 97–101; H. Scoville, Jr, *MX: Prescription for Disaster*

(Cambridge: MIT Press, 1981), p. 14; other accounts have estimated the range to be as great as 8000 miles, Leslie Gelb, 'As a Bargaining Chip, MX May Be No Bargain For the Soviets', *New York Times*, 24 April 1983, p. E1.

7. Basing in existing Minutemen silos was endorsed by the US Senate, following a similar approval by the US House of Representatives one week earlier, on 26 July 1983. 'Senate vote OKs MX construction, despite criticism', *Daily Texan*, 27 July 1983, p. 1; see also, US Congress, Congressional Budget Office, *The MX Missile and Multiple Protective Structure Basing – Long Term Budgetary Implications* (Washington: GPO, June 1979). Congress has appropriated funds for 50 MX with the proviso that no further funds will be forthcoming unless a more secure basing mode is used.
8. R. Jeffrey Smith, 'Another In a Series of Counterforce Weapons,' *Science* 216 (7 May 1982) p. 598; see also R. C. Aldridge, *The Counterforce Syndrome: A Guide to US Nuclear Weapons and Strategic Doctrine* (Washington: Institute for Policy Studies, 1978), p. 38.
9. Robert Sherman, 'A Manual of Missile Capability', AIR FORCE, February 1977, pp. 37–8; Lynn E. Davis and Warner Schilling, 'All you ever wanted to know about MIRV and ICBM calculations, but were not cleared to ask', *Journal of Conflict Resolution* 17 (June 1973).
10. Scoville, *MX: Prescription for Disaster*, pp. 14–15.
11. *Ibid.* The mark 12A is the latest Minuteman warhead.
12. Report of the President's Commission on Strategic Forces, 11 April 1983 printed in *Congressional Record*, 10 August 1983, and excerpted in *Survival* 25 (July/August 1983), pp. 177–85.
13. G. Smith, *Doubletalk, The Story of SALT I* (New York: Doubleday, 1980), p. 504.
14. US Department of State, Bureau of Public Affairs, 'Compliance with SALT I Agreements', Special Report no. 55, July 1979.
15. *Ibid.*; see also, G. Smith, *Doubletalk: The Story of SALT I*, p. 531.
16. See the excellent account in S. Talbot, *Endgame: The Inside Story of SALT II* (New York: Harper & Row, 1979).
17. Quoted in Scoville, *MX: Prescription for Disaster*, p. 102.
18. *Ibid.*, p. 104.
19. *Ibid.*, p. 15.
20. Michael Getler and Robert Kaiser, 'Intelligence Estimate Said To Show Need for SALT', *Washington Post*, 31 January 1980, p. 1, reporting on the 1979 US National Intelligence Estimates, NIE 11-8-79, *Soviet Strategic Offensive Forces*.
21. Cf. Testimony of Harold Brown, *Department of Defense Appropriations for 1981*, p. 510 ('If the Soviets do not observe the SALT II limits – we don't know whether they will or not – if they do not we are going to have to build more aim points to keep the mobile MX system relatively invulnerable.')
22. Department of State, 'Compliance with SALT I Agreements'.
23. The SS-24 and SS-25 are now at the deployment stage.
24. Scoville, *MX: Prescription for Disaster*, p. 107.
25. Victor Utgoff, 'In Defense of Counterforce', *International Security* 6

(Spring 1982), p. 51. The bomber force obviously has very short endurance; even the submarine force, however, does not have indefinite endurance and must return to port at some point in a protracted conflict.

26. Department of Defense Annual report, Fiscal Year 1981, p. 89; see discussion in *Challenges For US National Security*, A Preliminary Report Prepared by the Staff of the Carnegie Panel on US Security and the Future of Arms Control (Washington: Carnegie Endowment for International Peace, 1981), pp. 58–62.
27. See e.g., Christopher Paine, 'Running in Circles with the MX' *The Bulletin of the Atomic Scientists* 37 (December 1981), p. 5; Herbert Scoville 'First Strike', *New York Times*, 8 October 1981, p. A27; Stephen S. Rosenfeld, 'The Other Half of the MX Debate', *Washington Post*, 9 October 1981, p. A31.
28. Interim Agreement Between the United States of America and the Union of Soviet Socialist Republics on Certain Measures with Respect to the Limitation of Strategic Offensive Arms, signed at Moscow, 26 May 1972, 23 UST 3462, TIAS 7504; Treaty Between the United States of America and the Union of Soviet Socialist Republics on the Limitation of Anti-Ballistic Missile Silo terms, signed at Moscow, 26 May 1972, 23 UST 3435, TIAS 7503.
29. Treaty Between the United States of America and the Union of Soviet Socialist Republics on the Limitation of Strategic Offensive Arms, done at Vienna on 18 June 1979, Department of State Bulletin, July 1979, pp. 23–43.
30. The report quickly became known as the Scowcroft Report after its chairman, Brent Scowcroft, former National Security Adviser to President Ford.
31. Quoted in Gelb, 'As a Bargaining Chip, MX May Be No Bargain for the Soviets' *New York Times* 24 April 1983, p. 1E.
32. 'Air-breathing' is the sense that an aeroplane or automobile takes in the air in order to oxidize fuel.
33. John C. Toomay, 'Technical Characteristics', in *Cruise Missiles: Technology, Strategy and Politics*, R. K. Betts (ed.), (Washington: Brookings, 1981), pp. 31–5. Subsequent references to articles drawn from this collection will be referred to as Betts (ed.), *Cruise Missiles*. For a good, general summary of cruise missile technology see Kosta Tsipis, 'Cruise Missiles' in B. M. Russett and B. G. Blair (eds) *Progress in Arms Control?* (San Francisco: W. H. Freeman, 1979), pp. 171–80.
34. Toomay, 'Technical Characteristics', in Betts (ed.), *Cruise Missiles*, p. 37.
35. *Ibid.*, pp. 39–40.
36. *Ibid.*, pp. 40, 42.
37. Robert J. Art and Stephen E. Ockenden, 'The Domestic Politics of Cruise Missile Development, 1970–1980,' in Betts (ed.), *Cruise Missiles*, p. 393.
38. *Ibid.*, p. 360.
39. Ron Huisken, 'The History of Modern Cruise Missile Programs' in Betts (ed.), *Cruise Missiles*, p. 83; see also R. Huisken, *The Origin of the Strategic Cruise Missile* (New York: Praeger, 1981). The account offered

here is drawn principally from these sources.
40. *Fiscal Year 1974 Authorization for Military Procurement, Research and Development, Construction Authorization for the Safeguard ABM, and Active Duty and Selected Reserve Strengths*, Hearings before the Senate Committee on Armed Service, 93rd Congress, 1st Session (Washington: GPO, 1973), part 2, pp. 1026, 1171–2; see also Henry D. Levine, 'Some Things to All Men: The Politics of Cruise Missile Development', *Public Policy* 5 (Winter 1977), pp. 117–68.
41. For a discussion of the standoff and penetrating bomber alternatives, see G. K. Burke, 'A Case for the Manned Penetrating Bomber,' *Air University Review* 28 (July/August 1977), pp. 15–26.
42. Huisken, *The Origin of the Strategic Cruise Missile*, pp. 29–30. OSD considered SLCMs operating in four modes under consideration. The Navy was able to press successfully for a fifth, a combined strategic/tactical weapon compatible with existing launchers.
43. As stressed in testimony by John Foster, Jr., the Director of Defense Research and Engineering; Huisken, 'The History of Cruise Missiles', in Betts (ed.), *Cruise Missiles*, p. 86.
44. A. A. Tinajero, 'Cruise Missiles (subsonic): US Programs', IB 76018 (Washington: Congressional Research Service, 1976), p. 19.
45. *Department of Defense Appropriations for 1978, Hearings before a subcommittee of the House Appropriations Committee*, 95th Congress 1st session (Washington: GPO, 1977), part 2, p. 235.
46. Department of Defense, Office of Director, Defense Research and Engineering, *Joint Strategic Bomber Study*.
47. A. H. Quanbeck and A. L. Wood, *Modernizing The Strategic Bomber Force: Why and How* (Washington: Brookings, 1976).
48. Huisken, 'The History of the Cruise Missile', in Betts (ed.), *Cruise Missiles*, p. 94.
49. Huisken, *The Origin of the Strategic Cruise Missile*, p. 78.
50. *Ibid.*
51. Department of Defense Annual Report, Fiscal Year 1979 (Washington: GPO, 1978), p. 119.
52. Huisken, 'The History of the Cruise Missile,' in Betts (ed.), *Cruise Missiles*, p. 98.
53. *Ibid.*
54. Art and Ockenden, 'The Domestic Politics of Cruise Missile Development, 1970–1980', in Betts (ed.), *Cruise Missiles*, p. 406.
55. Richard K. Betts, 'Innovation, Assessment and Decision', in Betts (ed.), *Cruise Missiles*, p. 20.
56. *Ibid.*; see also Gregory F. Treverton, NATO Military Considerations 'Managing NATO's Nuclear Dilemma', *International Security* 7 (Spring 1983) pp. 93–115; the *Department of Defense Annual Report*, Fiscal Year 1981, coyly notes that LRTNF are capable of making strikes within the theatre to contain escalation as well as beyond the theatre, to deny a Soviet sanctuary; *Department of Defense Annual Report* FY 81 (Washington: GPO, 1980), pp. 91–2.
57. Betts, 'Innovation, Assessment and Decision'.
58. See Bruce Bennett and James Foster, 'Strategic Retaliation Against the

Soviet Homeland', in Betts (ed.), *Cruise Missiles*.
59. Bennet and Foster, p. 143.
60. *Ibid.*
61. *Ibid.*, p. 164.
62. *Ibid.*, p. 167.
63. *Ibid.*
64. *Ibid.*, p. 140.
65. *Ibid.*
66. *Department of Defense Appropriations for 1980*, Hearings before a Subcommittee of the House Appropriations Committee, 96th Congress 1st session (Washington: GPO, 1979), part 3, p. 711.
67. John Rhea, 'Tomahawk and ALCM: Cruise Missile Decision Pending', *Sea Power* (December 1976), p. 26.
68. *Hearings on Military Posture and H. R. 6495*, Department of Defense Authorization for Appropriations for Fiscal Year 1981, Hearings Before the House Armed Services Committee (Washington: GPO, 1980), part 4, book 2, pp. 1497–98.
69. Art and Ockenden, 'The Domestic Politics of Cruise Missile Development, 1970–1980', in Betts (ed.), *Cruise Missiles*, p. 390.
70. *Department of Defense Annual Report, Fiscal Year 1976 and Fiscal Year 1977*, part 2 (Washington: GPO, 1975), p. 39.
71. Art and Ockenden, 'Domestic Politics', p. 392, n. 69.
72. With the rationale offered in Chapter 8, compare Office of Secretary of Defense, 'Modernization and Arms Control for Long-Range Theatre Nuclear Forces', US Rationale Paper, 16 October 1979.
73. This is an inescapable dilemma of the SSN launched weapon: if SLCMs, they are so limited in target coverage that they expose the launcher; if SLBMs, the warheads are so numerous that they may undermine the strategy.
74. Bennett and Foster, 'Retaliation Against the Soviet Homeland', in Betts (ed.), *Cruise Missiles*, p. 169.
75. Stanley Hoffmann, 'NATO and Nuclear Weapons: Reasons and Unreason', *Foreign Affairs* 60 (Winter 1981–2), p. 336.
76. Art and Ockenden, 'Domestic Politics', in Betts (ed.), *Cruise Missiles*, p. 412.
77. *Ibid.*, p. 400.
78. Bennett and Foster, 'Retaliation Against the Soviet Homeland', in Betts (ed.), *Cruise Missiles*, pp. 166–7.
79. The seriatim treatment of weapons systems in these chapters tends to magnify their shortcomings; acting coordinately, the various systems can re-inforce each other, e.g., the ICBMs can be assigned those tasks that require retargeting while ALCMs are reserved for targets like airbases, port facilities, and so forth.
80. Bennett and Foster, 'Retaliation Against the Soviet Homeland', in Betts (ed.), *Cruise Missiles*, p. 167.
81. See N. Polmar, *Strategic Weapons: An Introduction*, pp. 101–7; Herbert Scoville, 'Missile Submarines and National Security' in Russett and Blair (eds), *Progress in Arms Control?*, Chapter 6.
82. Cited in Newhouse, *Cold Dawn*, p. 20; Ball, *Deja Vu: The Return to*

Counterforce in the Nixon Administration, p. 21.

83. Ball, *Deja Vu: The Return to Counterforce in the Nixon Administration*, p. 40.
84. *Ibid.*, p. 42.
85. US Congress, House of Representatives, Committee on Armed Services, *Hearings on Military Posture and H. R. 6495 for Fiscal Year 1981*, part 3, 96th Cong., 2nd sess. (Washington: GPO, 1980), p. 226.
86. Statement of Rear Admiral William A. Williams III, Director, Strategic and Theatre Nuclear Warfare Division, Office of the Chief of Naval Operations, before the Subcommittee on Strategic and Theatre Nuclear Forces, Senate Armed Services Committee 3 October 1981, quoted in Joel S. Wit, 'American SLBM: Counterforce Options and Strategic Implications,' *Survival* 24 (July/August 1982), p. 163.
87. 'Counterintuitive' because increasing the size of the submarine makes it noisier and thus easier to detect; and increasing the percentage of the total SLBM warhead force aboard a single SSBN increases the consequences of loss if the SSBN is detected.
88. US Congress, House of Representatives Comm. on Armed Services, H. R. 8390 *Supplemental Authorization for Appropriations for Fiscal Year 1978 and Review of the State of US Strategic Forces* (Washington: GPO, 1977), p. 160.
89. US Congress, Senate Committee on Armed Services, *Department of Defense Authorization for Appropriations for Fiscal Year 1981*, part 6, Research and Development (Washington: GPO, 1980), p. 3514.
90. See Wit, 'American SLBM: Counterforce Options and Strategic Implications', p. 165.
91. *Department of Defense Authorization*, pp. 3730–31.
92. See Ball, *Deja Vu: The Return to Counterforce in the Nixon Administration*, who extrapolates from this fact that SLBMs are more accurate than ICBMs, pp. 41–2.
93. Scoville, 'Missile Submarines and National Security', p. 72.
94. Wit, 'American SLBM: Counterforce Options and Strategic Implications', p. 163.
95. US Congress, Senate Committee on Armed Services, *Department of Defense Authorization for Appropriation for Fiscal Year 1982*, part 7, 97th Cong., 1st sess. (Washington: GPO, 1981), p. 4026.
96. 'Transcript of Remarks by the President on Weapons Programs', *New York Times*, 3 October 1981, p. 12.
97. Desmond Ball, 'US Strategic Forces: How Would They Be Used?,' *International Security* 7 (Winter 1982–3), pp. 48–9.
98. *Ibid.*, p. 49.
99. Albert Langer, *Omega, Poseidon and the Arms Race*, AICD Occasional Paper no. 5 (Sydney: AICD, 1974), p. 15, cited in Ball, *Deja Vu: The Return to Counterforce in the Nixon Administration*, p. 44.
100. *Ibid.*
101. J. R. Schlesinger, US Congress, Senate Committee on Foreign Relations, *US–USSR Strategic Policies* (Washington: GPO, 1974), p. 37.
102. Ball, 'US Strategic Forces', p. 48.
103. *Ibid.*

104. Ball, *Deja Vu: The Return to Counterforce in the Nixon Administration*, p. 45.
105. See Polmar, *Strategic Weapons*, pp. 63–6; for the history of British policymaking regarding its strategic forces and the rationale behind a reliance on SLBMs, see L. Freedman, *Britain and Nuclear Weapons* (London: Macmillan, 1980), and Lawrence Freedman, 'The Rationale for Medium-Sized Deterrence Forces', in *The Future of Strategic Deterrence*, p. 50.
106. Despite NATO doctrines, the use of tactical nuclear weapons could not be easily approved by a German Chancellor since they go off on German territory and destroy German populations while theatre, land-based forces are equally unlikely to be authorized to strike a Soviet sanctuary since this invites retaliation against the basing country. Rather NATO joint approval is likeliest to come for an SLBM strike. Treverton, *Nuclear Weapons in Europe*, p. 12.

12 Multipolarity

1. Reported in *Le Monde*, 16 January 1963, quoted in C. H. Amme, Jr. (ed.), *Problems Posed by Conflicting Views Concerning Nuclear Weapons: Conflicting Views of Major NATO Nations on the Control and Use of Nuclear Weapons*, TR-5104-2 (Menlo Park: Stanford Research Institute, 1965), p. 14.
2. P. Hassner, *Change and Security in Europe, Part 2: In Search of a System*, Adelphi Paper no. 49 (London: The Institute for Strategic Studies, 1968), p. 7.
3. See, e.g., Richard Rosencrance, 'Deterrence in Dyadic and Multipolar Environments', in R. Rosencrance (ed.), *The Future of the International Strategic System* (San Francisco: Chandler, 1972); Ciro Elliott Zoppo, 'Nuclear Technology, Multipolarity and International Stability', *World Politics*, vol. 18, no. 4, 1966, John J. Weltman, 'Managing Nuclear Multipolarity', *International Security* 6 (Winter 1981–2), pp. 182–194.
4. See, e.g., J. Gruca, *French Contributions to Strategic Theory in the Nuclear Age: Strategic Theories of Beanfre, Gallois, Aron, and Ailleret*, Memorandum no. DRAE M44 (Ottowa: Defence Research Analysis Establishment, 1973). We have had considerable experience, after all, with a multipolar international environment. This was the configuration from the Treaty of Utrecht, with brief exception, until World War I.
5. K. N. Waltz, *The Spread of Nuclear Weapons: More May be Better*, Adelphi Paper no. 171 (London: The International Institute for Strategic Studies, 1981).
6. *Ibid.*, p. 2.
7. *Ibid.*, p. 6.
8. I take the bomber forces of the secondary nuclear powers and short-range weapons like the French Pluton and its successor, Hades, to be too few in number and too limited in range to contradict this statement.
9. Chief of Staff General Ailleret stated this policy, '"Directed" Defense or "Defense in All Directions"', *The Review of National Defense* (December

1967), subsequently confirmed by President de Gaulle, *New York Times*, 30 January 1968, quoted in M. W. Hoag, *Superpower Strategic Postures for a Multilateral World*, P-4201 (Santa Monica: The RAND Corporation 1969), p. 4.
10. *Ibid.*, Hoag, *Superpower Strategic Postures for a Multilateral World*, p. 4.
11. Hansard, 1 March 1960, col. 1136–8.
12. Quoted in Pierre Gallois, 'US Strategy and the Defense of Europe,' *Orbis* 8 (Summer 1963), pp. 248–9.
13. See Andrew Pierre, 'Can Europe's Security Be 'Decoupled from America', in C. Kemp, R. L. Pfaltzgraff and U. Ra'anan (eds), *The Superpowers in a Multinuclear World* (Lexington: D. C. Heath & Co., 1974), pp. 45–62: See also *The Changing US–Soviet Strategic Balance: Implications for Nuclear Multipolarity*, which concludes that a European deterrent force would have to approximate the American strategic forces. Moreover, the deployment of defensive systems by the US and the USSR would ensure such a requirement.
14. Waltz, *The Spread of Nuclear Weapons: More May be Better*, p. 3.
15. Japan's actual defence outlays in fiscal year 1981 already ranked eighth in the world, although her GNP ratio of .9 per cent devoted to defense expenditure is one of the lowest. Yukio Satoh, *The Evolution of Japanese Security Policy*, Adelphi Paper no. 178 (London: The International Institute for Strategic Studies, 1982), p. 24.
16. *The World Factbook*, 1983, Central Intelligence Agency, CR83–11300, (Washington: GPO, 1983).
17. Richard K. Betts, 'Conventional Forces: What Price Readiness?' *Survival* 25 (January/February 1983), pp. 25–34; see also William Kaufmann, 'The Defense Budget' in J. A. Pechman (ed.), *Setting National Priorities: The 1983 Budget* (Washington: Brookings, 1982).
18. Although it should be noted that Japanese ratification of the Treaty did not come quickly and finally occurred only after the Japanese foreign minister obtained reaffirmation of the US security guarantee. J. Yaeger, (ed.), *Nonproliferation and US Foreign Policy* (Washington: Brookings, 1980) p. 26.
19. Article 9 of the Japanese Constitution provides:

> Aspiring sincerely to an international peace based on justice and order, the Japanese people forever renounce war as a sovereign right of the nation and the threat or use of force as a means of settling international disputes.

It should be noted, however, that the argument has been made in the Japanese Diet that nuclear deterrence is defensive in nature and therefore does not violate this provision. No less a jurist than the former Chief Justice of the Supreme Court of Japan has in fact argued that Japan should develop a nuclear weapons capability. T. Tsurutani, *Japanese Policy and East Asian Security* (New York: Praeger, 1981), p. 95.
20. R. Jervis, *Deterrence Theory Revisited*, ACIS Working Paper no. 14 (Los Angeles: Center for Arms Control and National Security, 1978), p. 45.
21. Quoted in Chapter 6, p. 60, above.
22. 'Your action desperate Threat to human survival. No conceivable

justification. Civilized man condemns it. We will not have mass murder. Ultimatum means war. I do not speak for power but plead for civilized man. End this madness.' quoted in A. E. Wessel, *Some Implications of Strategic Concepts for Western European Nuclear Weapons*, P-2904 (Santa Monica: The RAND Corporation, 1964), p. 11.

23. R. K. Betts, *Surprise Attack* (Washington: Brookings, 1982), Chapter 2.
24. *Ibid.*
25. See G. Quester, *Nuclear Diplomacy: The First Twenty-five Years* (New York: Dunellen, 1970) for numerous examples, such as President Kennedy's siting of B-47s on civilian airfields during the Cuban missile crisis, also noted by Freedman, *Evolution of Nuclear Strategy*, p. 244.
26. *The Military Balance 1982–1983*, p. 140.
27. Assuming a 400 equivalent megatonnage (EMT) requirement for assured destruction mission.
28. *Ibid.* At most, only a third of the SLBM force, however, can be expected to be on-station at any one time. The IISS estimates 785 EMT in the US SLBM force; 1150 EMT for the Soviet SLBM force. *Ibid.*, p. 141.
29. As noted earlier, an attacker has two options: he can fire his SLBMs and ICBMs simultaneously or he can phase their launches so that they arrive at their targets simultaneously. There are reasons to choose each of the options: simultaneous launches enable the maximum destruction of soft command and political centres and bombers, since attacking SLBM's can move close to their targets and strike with a minimum of warning time; non-simultaneous launches enable the maximum destruction of hardened targets like missile silos since they allow the shortest unambiguous period for a defender to launch on warning. But both options have shortcomings that, so long as the triad is maintained, reinforce deterrence in the bipolar world. In the bipolar world, if the first option is chosen, the arriving barrage from the close-in SLBMs will definitively warn the attacked nation that a full-scale attack is under way, permitting the unattacked weapons of the triad to be launched against the obvious attacker before the attacker's ICBMs arrive at their targets. If the second option is chosen, the plumes of the ICBMs will alert the attacked nation through its reconnaissance satellites in time to launch both bombers and ICBMs. Thus the incentive to the attacker to pre-empt is negated. In the multipolar world, however, an early, disguised SLBM launch would not definitively identify the attacking nation; and thus the early warning would not allow the attacked nation to respond with confidence that it was retaliating against the proper adversary; and thus the deterring force to pre-emption provided by the triad is diminished.
30. This is one reason why I have used the term 'deterrence assumption' in many contexts in which others customarily use the phrase 'mutual assured destruction'. For the latter is a condition whose political and strategic consequences are by no means invariant or unchangeable even if the condition persists.
31. A. Beaufre, *Deterrence and Strategy* (London: Faber, 1965), p. 100.
32. See, e.g., Donald G. Brennan, 'Some Remarks on Multipolar Nuclear Strategy', in R. Rosencrance, (ed.), *The Future of The International Strategic System*, pp. 20–1.

33. What may be more likely is a catalytic diplomacy, by which the superpowers are put against one another by third powers seeking to prevent condominium, but the significance of this lies in the diplomatic realm.
34. See U. Nerlich, *The Alliance and Europe: Part V Nuclear Weapons and East–West Negotiation*, Adelphi Paper no. 120 (London: The International Institute for Strategic Studies, 1975–6), pp. 1–11.
35. 'The cost of developing a capability which would seriously disturb the superpowers (as opposed to one's unarmed neighbor) is staggering.' J. R. Schlesinger, *The Strategic Consequences of Nuclear Proliferation*, P-3393 (Santa Monica: The RAND Corporation, 1966), p. 9.
36. 'West Germany is the premier example of a nation where the dominant disincentive to go nuclear has been security guarantees.' T. A. Halsted, *Nuclear Proliferation: How to Retard It, Manage It, Live With It* (Princeton: Aspen Institute Program in International Affairs, 1977), p. 7. 'According to Dr Kosaka [a Japanese specialist in strategic affairs] a principal factor militating against the development of nuclear weapons is the US [nuclear] guarantee.' R. L. Pfaltzgraff, *The Changing US–Soviet Strategies Balance: Implications for Nuclear Multipolarity*, p. 172.
37. Amme, *Problems Posed by Conflicting Views Concerning Nuclear Weapons*, p. 92.
38. Bull, 'European Self-Reliance and the Reform of NATO', *Foreign Affairs* 61 (Spring 1983), p. 874.
39. *Ibid.*, p. 876.
40. *Ibid.*
41. *Ibid.*
42. Bull, 'A New Course for Britain and Western Europe', *SAIS Review* 41 (Summer 1983), p. 47; see also B. Burrows and G. Edwards, *The Defence of Western Europe* (Guildford: Butterworth Scientific, 1982).
43. Bull, 'European Self-Reliance'.
44. *Ibid.*
45. *Ibid.*
46. *Ibid.*
47. R. M. Lawrence, W. R. Van Cleave, and S. E. Young, *Summary Report: Implications of Indian and/or Japanese Nuclear Proliferation for US Defense Policy Planning*, SSC-TN-1933-1 (Menlo Park: Stanford Research Institute, 1973), p. 31.
48. *Ibid.*, p. 32.
49. Yaeger, (ed.), *Nonproliferation and US Foreign Policy*, p. 25.
50. On the issue of public opinion regarding Japanese acquisition, see Robinson, 'Japan's Growing Strategic Role: Public Attitude Shift Spurs Major Military Improvement', *Aviation Week and Space Technology*, 14 January 1980, pp., 46–7. A 1980 survey of Japanese Chamber of Commerce members showed a majority thought Japan ought to possess nuclear weapons. Taketsugu Tsurutani, 'Old Habits, New Times: Challenges to Japanese–American Security Relations', *International Security* 7 (1982), pp. 175, 183–4. Shapiro reports that from 1976 to 1979 poll figures measuring the number of Japanese who believed Japan would acquire nuclear weapons within ten years went from 28 per cent to 40 per

cent. Isaac Shapiro, 'The Risen Sun', *Foreign Policy* 41 (1980–1), p. 31. Regarding the FRG, see P. Windsor, *Germany and the Western Alliance: Lessons from the 1980 Crises*, Adelphi Paper no. 170 (London: The International Institute for Strategic Studies, 1981).

51. Robinson, 'Japan's Growing Strategic Role: Japan Pushes Toward Space Launcher Development', *Aviation Week and Space Technology*, 28 January 1980, p. 51.
52. *Military Balance, 1982–1983*, pp. 34–7.
53. Unpublished remarks of Prof. Steven Weinberg, at the Conference on Reducing the Risks of Accidental Nuclear War, University of Texas, 1983, transcript, pp. 79–80; see also R. Rosencrance, *Strategic Deterrence Reconsidered*, Adelphi Paper no. 116 (London: The International Institute for Strategic Studies, 1975), pp. 27–33.

13 Alternatives to Nuclear Deterrence

1. 'Remarks of McGeorge Bundy', Military Committee of The North Atlantic Assembly, 16 November 1982, pp. 4–5.
2. *Ibid*, p. 1.
3. Michael Howard, Letter to the Editor of *The Times*, 3 November 1981, p. 13; see also Michael Howard, 'Reassurance and Deterrence: Western Defense in The 1980s', *Foreign Affairs* 61 (Winter 1982–3), pp. 309–24. Lawrence Freedman, 'NATO Myths', *Foreign Policy* 45 (Winter 1981–2), pp. 48–68. Jonathan Alford, NATO's Conventional Forces and The Soviet Mobilization Potential', *NATO Review* 28 (June 1980), pp. 18–22.
4. Bernard Rogers, 'The Atlantic Alliance: Prescriptions for a Difficult Decade', *Foreign Affairs*, 60 (Summer 1982), pp. 1145–6. Henry A. Kissinger, 'The Future of NATO', in K. A. Myers (ed.), *NATO: The Next Thirty Years* (Boulder: Westview Press, 1980), pp. 9–10.
5. Kenneth Hunt, 'Alternative Conventional Force Postures', in K. A. Myers (ed.) *NATO: The Next Thirty Years*, p. 134.
6. The Lisbon goals called for roughly 96 divisions and 9000 aircraft, the equivalent of a Normandy invasion force. The compromise force – 26 divisions (of which 12 are Bundeswehr) and 1400 aircraft for the Central Region – is essentially what NATO fields today. Donald Cotter, 'Potential Future Roles for Conventional and Nuclear Forces in Defense of Western Europe', in C. L. Wilson (dir.) *European Security Study* 2 (American Academy of Arts and Sciences, 1983), p. 10.
7. See Chapter 5 above.
8. Thus the US, in an effort to win Alliance support for its uncoupling strategies (e.g. Flexible Response), must emphasize the unreliability of its own nuclear commitment to Europe (i.e., the imminence of decoupling).
9. C. N. Donnelly, 'The Soviet Threat During the 1980's', in C. L. Wilson (dir.), *European Security Study*, American Academy of Arts and Sciences, 1983, p. 30. Hereinafter this unpublished study will be referred to as *ESECS*.
10. Marshall Shulman, Remarks, Workshop 1, 'The Soviet Threat in the 1980s, *European Security Study*, p. 7.

11. Donnelly, 'The Soviet Threat During the 1980s', in *ESECS*, pp. 21, 22; see also Nathan Leites, 'The Soviet Style of War' in D. Leebaert (ed.), *Soviet Military Thinking* (London: Allen & Unwin, 1981) Chapter 7.
12. Final Report Workshop 1, 'The Soviet Threat in the 1980's,' *ESECS*, p. 19. 'OMG' refers to the Operational Manoeuvre Group, the modern incarnation of the WW2 mobile group, a divisional size armoured or mechanical force, allocated maximum air and artillery support.
13. *Ibid*, p. 23.
14. For a through treatment see Christopher Jones, 'Soviet Military Doctrine and Warsaw Pact Exercises', in Leebaert, *Soviet Military Thinking*, pp. 225–47.
15. *Ibid*., pp. 34–5, quoting General Krupchenko writing in the *Soviet Military Historical Journal* in July 1981.
16. *Military Balance, 1982–1983*, pp. 132–3; Johan Jorgen Holst, 'Deterrence and Stability in the NATO–Warsaw Pact Relationship', R. O'Neill and D. M. Horner (eds), *New Directions in Strategic Thinking* (London: Allen & Unwin, 1981), p. 97.
17. See the study, commissioned by *The Economist*, on what it is estimated a satisfactory NATO conventional defence would cost, 'Do You Sincerely Want to be Non-Nuclear?' *The Economist*, 31 July 1982, pp. 30–2.
18. *US Army Operational Concepts: The Airland Battle and Corps 86*, Tradoc Pamphlet 525–5 (Fort Monroe: Department of the Army, 1981).
19. Kenneth Hunt, 'Alternative Conventional Force Postures', K. A. Myers (ed.), *NATO: The Next Thirty Years*, p. 135.
20. *Ibid*., p. 31.
21. *Ibid*., p. 32.
22. A measure currently being done, over substantial protest.
23. *Ibid*., p. 31.
24. B. Brodie, *Escalation and The Nuclear Option*, RM-4544-PR (Santa Monica: The RAND Corporation, 1965), p. 83.
25. *Ibid*., p. 84.
26. Hans E. Apel, in *Challenges to the Western Alliance*, (ed.) Joseph Godson (London: Times Books, 1984), p. 47.
27. Samuel P. Huntington, in *Military Strategy in Transition*, Keith A. Dunn and William O. Staudenmaier (eds) (Boulder: Westview, 1984), p. 38.
28. *Defence Without The Bomb: The Report of The Alternative Defense Commission* (London: Taylor & Francis, 1983), p. 8.
29. *Ibid*., p. 177.
30. See, e.g., 'NATO: Can The Alliance Be Saved?', *Report of Senator Sam Nunn to the Committee on Armed Services*, United States Senate, (Washington: GPO, 1982), p. 6; see also N. F. Wikner, 'Interdicting Fixed Targets with Conventional Weapons', *Armed Forces Journal International* (March 1983), pp. 77–90; N. F. Wikner, 'Conventional Weapon Destruction of Hardened Targets', *Armed Forces Journal International*, (March 1983), pp. 91–5.
31. 'Emerging technology' will perhaps replace battlefield nuclear systems and greatly enhance the NATO position. The cost effectiveness of these technologies is a matter for technicians. My point is not to deny the potential contributions of advances in conventional arms but simply to say

they cannot replace nuclear weapons at all levels in Europe.

32. Holst, 'The NATO–Warsaw Pact Relationship', in O'Neill and Horner (eds), *New Directions in Strategic Thinking*, p. 96.
33. *Ibid.*, p. 93.
34. See the discussion of these proposals in Chapter 9. The Eureka College speech is excerpted in *Survival* 24 (September/October 1982), pp. 229–30. There have been at least three proposed modified plans since then.
35. And, as regards a first strike, there is no reason why MIRVed SLBMs might not constitute a similar threat to the land-based ICBM.
36. *Survival* 24, p. 230.
37. President Brezhnev's Address to the 19th Komsomol Congress, 18 May 1982, excerpted in *Survival* 24 (September/October 1982), p. 231.
38. FBIS, Soviet Union, 3 January 1983, p. AA3.
39. And predicted in a paper in February 1982, Philip Bobbitt, 'Nuclear Weapons and Europe,' in A. Neidle, *Nuclear Negotiations: Reassessing Arms Control Goals in US–Soviet Relations*, (Austin: Lyndon B. Johnson School of Public Affairs, 1982), p. 43.
40. FBIS, Soviet Union, 3 January 1983, p. AA2.
41. *Ibid.*
42. Johann Holst has noted that:

    > Soviet negotiators have attempted to structure the geographical parameters for arms control regimes in Europe in a manner which will preserve for Soviet territory that privileged status of being exterior to the regime in question. The definition of the reduction zone in MBFR [mutual balanced force reductions] and the refusal to include anything more than a narrow zone of 250 km of the Soviet Union in the CSCE/CBM [Conference on Security in Europe/Confidence Building Measures] regime, indicate the way in which Moscow approaches arms control as a means for structuring the broader context of the political order.

    Holst, 'The NATO–Warsaw Pact Relationship?, in O'Neill and Horner (eds), *New Directions in Strategic Thinking*, p. 93.
43. The Soviet Union had stated that British and French nuclear forces should be considered in SALT rather than the INF negotiations. For the Soviet proposals see *Survival* (January/February 1980), pp. 28–30; *Survival*, (September/October 1980), pp. 224–5; *Survival* (May/June 1981), pp. 134–7. Thus the switch to an insistence that these forces be counted in the INF talks should not be taken as compromising the Russian security paradigm discussed in the text; either inclusion is compatible with that point of view. Rather it is simply one more way of counting the 'balance' so that NATO ends up with no new weapons to deploy in Europe against the USSR.
44. Lawrence Freedman, 'The great missile gap-between Andropov and his generals', *The Times*, 19 March 1983, p. 8.
45. Such ideas do not arise from philosophical traditions that treat the ethical problems of the individual; and indeed how could they, since the philosophical bases for our moral intuitions are so cultural in origin while nation-states define themselves by their cultural differences. Rather, in

the inter-state context, ideas like 'equality' arise from geostrategic and political conflicts unique to states.

46. Robert S. Nurick, 'Memorandum: Brezhnev and Reagan figures for LRTNF', 25 November 1981, takes Soviet estimates of Western Systems from The Brezhnev *Der Spiegel* interview November 1981, no. 45, and of Soviet systems as presented in Bonn, as reported in *The Times*, 25 November 1981; US estimates from a State Department Clarification of a speech by President Reagan to the National Press Club, reported in the *International Herald Tribune*, 23 November 1981; and correlates this with the *Military Balance* estimates then current. A useful comparison is also provided in H. J. Neuman, *Nuclear Forces in Europe* (London: International Institute for Strategic Studies, 1982), pp. 9–13.
47. Cf. 'Long-and Medium-range Nuclear Systems for the European Theatre', *Military Balance: 1982–1983*, p. 136.
48. Neumann, *Nuclear Forces in Europe*, p. 11.
49. Raymond L. Garthoff, 'Brezhnev's Opening: The TNF Tangle', *Foreign Policy* 41 (Winter 1980–1) p. 86.
50. Cartwright and Critchley (rapporteurs), *Report on Nuclear Weapons in Europe*, pp. 23–2.
51. The NATO position is described in 'The Modernization of NATO's Long-Range Theaters Nuclear Forces, *Report of The Foreign Affairs and National Defense Division*, Congressional Research Service (Washington, Library of Congress, 1980).
52. Lynn E. Davis, 'A Proposal for TNF Arms Control', *Survival* 23 (November–December 1981), p. 242.
53. Cartwright and Critchley (rapporteurs), *Report on Nuclear Weapons in Europe*, p. 24.
54. *Ibid.*, p. 25.
55. See S. Talbott, *Deadly Gambits*, (New York: Knopf, 1984).
56. *Strategic Survey 1983–1984*, International Institute for Strategic Studies (London: The International Institute for Strategic Studies, 1984), p. 31.
57. On 'gray area' arms control problems, see Lothar Ruehl, 'The "Grey Area" Problem', C. Bertram (ed.), *The Future of Arms Control: Part I: Beyond SALT II*, Adelphi Paper no. 141 (London: The International Institute for Strategic Studies, 1978); M. W. Hoag, *Forward-Based Nuclear Systems in Historical Perspective: Lessons for SALT III*, P-6426 (Santa Monica, The RAND Corp., 1980); and Michael Higgins and Christopher Makins, 'Theater Nuclear Forces and "Grey Area" Arms Control', in R. Burt (ed.), *Arms Control and Defense Postures in The 1980s* (Boulder: Westview, 1982), pp. 75–96.
58. A similar phenomenon is responsible for the ban on hard target point defense in the ABM Treaty, a ban that, in light of recent advances in accuracy, hardly appears to serve the objectives of that treaty. It is only the fear that the technology used to protect missile silos and C^3I facilities would prove the basis for a more comprehensive coverage that could have justified such a ban. And it is open to proponents of SDI research to claim, legitimately, that not all contemplated BMD necessarily undercuts the ABM Treaty.
59. Jeane Kirkpatrick, *The Washington Post*, 23 February 1986, p. F8.

60. This account of the precursors of the current call for a nuclear-free zone in Europe is drawn from Barry M. Blechman and Mark R. Moore, 'A Nuclear-Weapon-Free Zone in Europe' *Scientific American* 248 (1983), pp. 37–43; A. Gosser, *The Western Alliance* (London: Macmillan, 1980), pp. 162–8.
61. Independent Commission on Disarmament and Security Issues, *Common Security: A Blueprint for Survival* (New York: Simon & Schuster, 1982).
62. One exception, which focuses instead on the political ramifications of such a proposal, is Lawrence Freedman, 'Europe between the Superpowers', in J. Segal, E. Moreton, L. Freedman and J. Baylis, *Nuclear War & Nuclear Peace* (London: Macmillan, 1983), pp. 113–5.
63. We may leave to one side the increasing disutility of battlefield nuclear weapons, discussed above in Chapter 8. Since this disutility is not symmetrical, it makes mutual concessions difficult to achieve. After all, if it is not in NATO's interest to deploy such weapons, why would the Soviets trade anything of advantage to them to persuade NATO to adopt a more efficient course? This issue, however, belongs to the different question of negotiability.
64. *Military Balance 1982–1982*, p. 116.
65. My cursory discussion of the technology of BMD is drawn from R. Banks, *The Technology of Military Space Systems*, Information Document, North Atlantic Assembly, October 1982; and Brown, 'Is SDI Technically Feasible?' *Foreign Affairs* 64, (1986) p. 435.
66. 'Ballistic Missile Defense', *Strategic Survey: 1981–1982* (London: The International Institute for Strategic Studies, 1982) p. 13.
67. Colin S. Gray, 'A New Debate on Ballistic Missile Defense', in J. F. Reichart and S. R. Strum (eds.), *American Defense Policy* (Baltimore: Johns Hopkins University Press, 1982), p. 485.
68. C. S. Gray, Discussant's Paper, IISS Barnett Hill Conference on Weapons and Space, 1982, p. 19.
69. Brown, 'Is SDI Technically Feasible?' *Foreign Affairs* 64, p. 442.
70. 'Ballistic Missile Defense', *Strategic Survey: 1981–1982*, p. 15.
71. Brown, 'Is SDI Technically Feasible?' p. 442.
72. Gray, 'A New Debate on Ballistic Missile Defense', p. 488.
73. A point not lost on the USSR:

> On the face of it, laymen may find it even attractive as the President speaks about what seem to be defensive measures. But this may seem to be so only on the face of it and only to those who are not conversant with these matters. In fact the strategic offensive forces of the United States will continue to be developed and upgraded at full tilt and along quite a definite line at that, namely that of acquiring a first nuclear strike capability. Under these conditions the intention to secure itself the possibility of destroying, with the help of the ABM defenses, the corresponding strategic systems of the other side, that is of rendering it unable of dealing a retaliatory strike, is a bid to disarm the Soviet Union in the face of the US nuclear threat. One must see this clearly in order to appraise correctly the true purport of this 'new conception'.
>
> When the U.S.S.R. and the U.S. began discussing the problem of

strategic arms, they argeed that there is an inseparable interrelationship between strategic offensive and defensive weapons. And it was not by chance that the treaty on limiting ABM systems and the first agreement on limiting strategic offensive arms were signed simultaneously between our countries in 1972.

General Secretary Andropov's Replies to *Pravda* Correspondent following President Reagan's 'Ballistic Missile Defense' Address, (Excerpts) 26 March 1983, *Survival* 25 (May/June 1983), pp. 130–1.

74. 'Ballistic Missile Defense', President Reagan's Speech to the Nation (Excerpts) 25 March 1983, *Survival* 25 (May/June 1983), pp. 129–30.
75. Quoted in 'Ballistic Missile Defense', *Strategic Survey: 1981–1982*, pp. 15–6.

14 Conclusion

1. Edward Luttwak, 'The Problems of Extending Deterrence', *The Future of Strategic Deterrence*, p. 31.
2. Earl C. Ravenal, 'Counterforce and Alliance: The Ultimate Connection,' *International Security* 6 (Spring 1982), pp. 26–43.
3. D. J. Alberts, *The Role of Conventional Air Power*, Adelphi Paper no. 193 (London: The International Institute for Strategic Studies, 1984), p. 1.
4. Flora Lewis, 'Strategy Analysts and The Common Man,' *International Herald Tribune*, 15 September 1982.
5. P. Windsor, *Germany and the Western Alliance*, p. 24.
6. As David Boelzner has observed, these positions appear to switch on the level of popular opinion.
7. Stanley Hoffmann, 'NATO and Nuclear Weapons: Reasons and Unreason,' *Foreign Affairs* 60 (Winter 1981–2), pp. 333–4.
8. R. Jervis, *Deterrence Theory Revisited*, pp. 10–11.
9. *Defence and Consensus, Papers of the 24th Annual Conference of the IISS*, Adelphi Papers nos. 183–185 (London: The International Institute for Strategic Studies, 1983).

Appendix: Reykjavik

As the present book went to press, the United States President and the Soviet General Secretary met for two days in Iceland to discuss nuclear issues. Owing to the manifest relevance of the events at that meeting, I have prepared a brief appendix.

I. WHAT HAPPENED

President Reagan and General Secretary Gorbachev met 11 and 12 October, 1986 in Reykjavik, Iceland. This followed an earlier meeting in Geneva in November 1985, and was thought to be the precedent for a subsequent meeting.

After Geneva it was unclear whether a second summit would come about. It was reported that the Soviet leadership was dissatisfied with the Geneva meeting, from which no concrete proposals had emerged, and that Moscow had insisted on some prior guarantee of specific agreements before it would be willing to participate in a superpower meeting of heads of state. Such meetings were felt to deflate domestic pressure on the US Administration and to rehabilitate the American President's image abroad; furthermore the US Administration appeared to be pressing for a meeting before the November election. For such benefits, it was felt in Moscow, the US had to show it was willing to take risks. It should not be permitted a 'free ride' as in Geneva. Soviet spokesmen indicated that the White House proposal of 'a second meeting in June 1986 and in any case no later than September' was unacceptable; June was much too soon for the complex preparation that would be necessary if the meeting were to ratify previously agreed upon proposals; indeed October was too soon unless the substantive agreements were immediately forthcoming. At the same time, the USSR launched a public relations offensive on behalf of a specific arms control agenda, an unpromising background to negotiations if such were the objective. Indeed, as Talbot and Mandelbaum reported,

> Even as they seemed to be stalling on a second summit, the Soviets stepped up their propaganda on behalf of a moratorium on all nuclear testing and a phased reduction of nuclear weapons that

would lead to the elimination of both sides' arsenals by the end of the century. These proposals were designed for maximum appeal to international public opinion.

Then on 19 September the Soviet Foreign Ministrer, Eduard Shevardnadze, delivered a letter to President Reagan from General Secretary Gorbachev. In it Gorbachev proposed an immediate mid-October meeting in Iceland as a way of accelerating preparation for a summit in Washington.

The White House was greatly attracted to the idea: its timing (just before the American election), its lack of substantive preconditions, its appeal to the personality and authority of the President, all seemed ideal. It promised to be a bonus to a Washington meeting that, only weeks before, had itself appeared to be in doubt. Gorbachev's letter was kept secret until 30 September – it doubtless had an impact on the US willingness to bargain for an American journalist who had been arrested by the Russians and whose continued confinement would have been incompatible with the summit meeting but whose release required the US to release a *bona fide* Soviet clandestine agent – and then the letter was made public. The President's immediate acceptance stunned the public with an announcement that he would go to Iceland in ten days.

At the first day's meeting, to the surprise of the US, according to its account, the Soviet leader brushed aside the subject of an INF agreement (which Russian diplomats had been hinting would be a relatively easy agreement to make and that White House officials believed could be signed at the Washington summit) and immediately went to the subject of strategic central systrems. He reaffirmed the Geneva principle to seek 50 per cent reductions in these weapons and proposed that an immediate timetable be set; at the same time he modified the Russian demand that the two sides covenant not to withdraw from the ABM treaty for fifteen years to a proposal for a ten-year commitment instead. All the Russian secretary asked was that a working group prepare materials on these topics for the next day.

That evening an arms control group met and worked through the night. According to briefings conducted by the US at the time, the two sides agreed to establish limits of 1600 on strategic offensive launchers – called strategic nuclear delivery vehicles (SNDVs) by the negotiators – and 6000 on strategic nuclear warheads (ICBM, SLBM, and ALCM warheads). Astonishingly, the Russians abandoned their position that each nuclear bomb or SRAM (short-range attack missile) on a long-range bomber be counted against the overall ceiling on nuclear weapons, and accepted a US proposal that each bomber would only count as one warhead whether it carried one bomb or ten. Equally dramatically, the USSR then agreed to exclude SLCMs (sea-launched cruise missiles) from the limit on launchers. Both these concessions were significant in light of the US lead in bombers and cruise missile technology. Finally the USSR said it was prepared to make 'significant cuts' in its SS-18s, the 'heavies' that threaten US ICBMs, but deferred precise limits until the next day.

In the working group on INF the two sides immediately agreed to eliminate all intermediate range missiles from Europe; if the US had any misgivings about this idea in light of Soviet intermediate range deployments outside Europe (the SS-20, once re-deployed in Asia, threatened Japan and China) they were put off until the next morning's session between the two leaders. Regarding verification of the agreement (since the SS-20 is a mobile weapon) the US pressed for an exchange of data, on-site observation and the establishment of a monitoring system to which the Russians immediately agreed, noting only that 'hard work' lay ahead working out the details.

When the working group addressed the problem of nuclear testing, the Soviet Union agreed to drop its proposal for a comprehensive test ban treaty – which would have prevented the development of the nuclear-driven X-ray laser, that some scientists think is the most promising technology for space-based defences – and agreed to a US plan to reduce the number and yield of nuclear tests gradually. After concluding this all-night session, the working group turned matters over to the heads of state and their foreign ministers.

On Sunday morning, presented with the achievements of the working group, the Secretary General almost immediately agreed to cut Soviet INF warheads to 100 in Asia. Secretary of State Schulz described this concession as 'breathtaking'. According to Gorbachev 'an agreement could be signed'.

The two leaders had agreed on 50 per cent cuts to be completed in five years and a ten-year renewed adherence to the ABM treaty. This latter term represented a significant concession by the Soviet Union, which had earlier sought a term of 15–20 years and to which Reagan had responded, in a letter to Gorbachev in July 1986, with a 7½-year counterproposal. Ten years was now thought to be about the earliest an ABM system could be deployed by the US in any event.

But, perhaps emboldened by the Russian concession, the US President now proposed that all ballistic missiles be eliminated within ten years as a precondition for the US to continue its adherence to the ABM treaty beyond five years. If the Russians eliminated their weapons on schedule the US would abide by the treaty for the full ten years.

The Soviet leader agreed to this, also. Indeed he countered with a variation that would have eliminated all nuclear weapons within ten years to which the President apparently replied: 'That suits me fine.' When informed that these included ballistic missiles, bombers and cruise missiles, the President, according to Russian notes since made public, reportedly told the General Secretary 'Apparently we misunderstood you. But if that is what you want, all right.' This position was reiterated by the President in his briefing to Congressional leaders and by the Secretary of State in his post-summit press conference. It was a unilateral concession of some significance – it abandoned the US advantage in cruise missiles and bombers – and ultimately was withdrawn by the US. It is likely that the President did not appreciate the inclusiveness of the term 'strategic offensive weapons' and did not really intend to make the concession, but this developed later.

At the time there appeared to be a general agreement of historic proportions. The two leaders had agreed on a ten-year elimination of 'strategic nuclear arsenals', 50 per cent in the first five years; the elimination of intermediate range weapons in Europe and their drastic reduction by the USSR in Asia; unprecedented verification measures; and the continued adherence to the ABM treaty for ten years – a treaty that was of unlimited duration anyway, for a time period shorter than that required by the US deployments the USSR sought to prevent. It is little wonder that the US participants described their feelings as heady and exhilarated.

There remained only one matter. There had previously been a dispute, occasioned by a white paper by the US Administration in concert with its efforts at funding for SDI, over whether the ABM treaty permitted the testing of technologies not available at the time of the treaty. The text of the treaty, and the current legal adviser's opinion of that text, appeared to permit the development (though not the deployment) of such systems; the intent of the US negotiators, as they now recall it, was to restrict development. According to Gerard Smith, the chief American negotiator of the ABM treaty, 'there could be testing, outside the laboratory of some new technologies and devices, as long as they were not components of a deployable system'. On the other hand, according to Judge Sofaer, the legal adviser to the Department of State, 'the Treaty, while prohibiting the *deployment* of future systems, permits their *creation*'.

What, precisely then did 'adherence to the treaty' mean? Unexpectedly, the Soviet leader insisted that all testing of the elements of anti-ballistic defence be confined to laboratories. This position is not really an 'interpretation' of the treaty since it adds a significant element to the treaty's provisions however they may be plausibly interpreted. At first the US had insisted on retaining the option of a less restrictive interpretation of the treaty. Its initial proposal had read:

> Both sides would agree to confine itself to research, development and testing which is permitted by the ABM treaty.

The US was probably prepared to abandon its position regarding the two interpretations of the treaty; it now submitted a draft attempting to accommodate the Soviet view. This read:

> The USSR and the United States undertake for 10 years not to exercise their existing right of withdrawal from the ABM Treaty, which is of unlimited duration, *and during that period strictly to observe all its provisions* while continuing research, development and testing, which are permitted by the ABM treaty. Within the first five years of the 10-year period (and thus through 1991), the strategic offensive arms of the two sides shall be reduced by 50 percent. During the following five years of that period, all remaining offensive ballistic missiles of the two sides shall be reduced. Thus, by the end of 1996, all offensive ballistic missiles of the USSR and the United States will have been totally eliminated. At the end of the 10-year period, either side could deploy defenses if it so chose unless the parties agree otherwise.

But the Russians were unmoved. Now they announced there was a further problem. After ten years, the US and the USSR must meet to 'negotiate mutually acceptable measures'. This implied that the language of the treaty – which explicitly permits renunciation by the announced intention of a party to deploy a defensive system – was being modified. But what was the point of agreeing on a ten-year adherence without renunciation if, after ten years, the agreement did not revert to the original treaty language without the non-renunciation codicil? And what could 'strict adherence to the treaty' mean if its provisions could be so substantially modified by the very promise to abide by them?

And now it appeared there was one further issue. At this point the Soviet Union made clear that agreement on INF, testing and the reduction of offensive systems were all contingent on resolution of the disputes over the Treaty.

At this point the President balked and eventually left the negotiations. The Secretary of State, appearing before a press corps who were now expecting historic revelations, appeared 'exhausted, dejected and defeated'. The White House Chief of Staff said, 'there will not be another summit in the near future as far as I can see'. On 14 October the Soviet leader made public the Russian proposals. On 22 October he released notes of meetings, including direct quotations from the President.

II. WHY THE RUSSIANS DID IT

At Reykjavik the Russians continued to pursue the geopolitical goal of isolating the US from her allies. They sought this objective through two subsidiary objectives which they hoped, perhaps, would mutually contribute to each other. At the present juncture it can be said that they very largely succeeded; why the Americans allowed them to do this is a subject I will treat in the next section.

The Russian negotiating strategy was never aimed at a specific written agreement. Russian caution about such agreements, and her usual careful preparation, should have alerted the US to this. Instead, the Soviet Union sought an *event* that would either (a) discredit the US with allied leaders by demonstrating that the US was unwilling to protect them with the US nuclear umbrella, and indeed was willing to provide an example of direct negotiations with the Russians to reduce the threat to oneself by disavowing the means to protect others, or (b) alienate Allied publics by forcing the US to appear as though, despite unprecedented Russian concessions, the US had dashed an historic arms control agreement that would have led to nuclear disarmament. The Soviet Union could scarcely have hoped that both these objectives could be accomplished, yet its 'negotiating' strategy aimed for this. Newspaper editorials in every Allied capital, public opinion polls and the statements of opposition leaders in the days after Reykjavik confirm how immediately successful the Russian strategy was at achieving its goal in terms of the public. But only recently has it emerged that Allied governments were even more horrified than their publics, albeit for diametrically opposed reasons, and that the very foundations of the Alliance were shaken. Western and Pacific allies were stunned to learn that the US had *agreed* to withdraw nuclear protection from them over a ten-year period without so much as a hint previously. There can scarcely be a responsible government that has not since commissioned its defence ministry to submit plans that would allow such a withdrawal of US protection during a similar time period, should the US again appear to be on the verge of announcing such an agreement. But if the US takes care to avoid such appearances, what of the world's publics? To them it must seem that only the US President's obstinate attachment to an apparently fanciful technology – which would, in any case, not protect them if US weapons were abolished also – had thwarted what he himself had called an historic chance for world peace and the abolition of nuclear arms.

If Geneva was a US public relations success, Reykjavik was a US strategic debacle. It would have been a more serious defeat had it not merely confirmed what many European ministries already knew to be the case.

II. WHY DID THE AMERICANS DO IT?

It should be clear now that what broke up the talks at Reykjavik – or rather what caused the President to break them off – was the dawning recognition that the US had been made the victim in an elaborate 'confidence' game. The 'small matter' on late Sunday that appeared to stall the otherwise breathtaking progress of the previous twenty-four hours was not in fact the reinterpretation of language in the ABM treaty. Gerard Smith is certainly right when he writes,

> Defining components may be a key element in the ongoing negotiation, but in the gray area between the Soviets' current laboratory definition of permissible research and the Administration's claim that anything goes, there should be a way of accommodating Gorbachev's fear and Reagan's dream . . .

but the conclusion he draws is wrong. The dispute over this interpretation, as the Americans discovered, was largely a pretext. Indeed the problem with getting an agreement was not even American unwillingness to give up SDI, as the White House was uncomfortably forced to portray it. Of course the Russians could count on the President not abandoning SDI; but even if he had, the Soviet Union would scarcely have been willing to rely – would we in the US? – on a mere agreement expressing such intensions. The technology for an effective system is still too far in the future; the developments that will determine that technology are diverse, diffused within the scientific and high tech community and to a large extent outside the control of the bureaucracy; and any treaty can be renounced by a party. If the effective elements of a system were developed – and no treaty can halt altogether such progress in a society as decentralized as the US – what Russian leader could rely on the fact that, for ten or fifteen or twenty years no President would be elected to the White House having campaigned on the platform that the earlier Administration had been duped, that the treaty was fatally flawed and should be renounced?

There was really very little the Americans could do once they had gone so far into the game by late Sunday. The only course was to cut their losses as quickly as possible. And this explains why the US did not, as some very experienced and thoughtful observers have suggested, simply table the proposals and promise to review them. Talbot and Mandelbaum wrote:

> Why did he not simply say to Gorbachev, in effect, 'This is very interesting, a lot is on the table; we'll have to study it carefully, and we'll get back to you'?

But this, of course, would only have made things worse. Then weeks would have gone by during which the Russians would have been able to bring public pressure to bear on the US to sign an agreement while watching with enthusiasm as American allies confronted the actualities of such an agreement. President Reagan's instincts did not fail him when he finally walked out of the Reykjavik talks. But it was very late; most of what the Russians sought they had got. Why did the Americans play along?

In the winsome masterpiece, *The Gentle Grafter*, O. Henry collects the stories of an American confidence man, Jefferson Peters, and his partner, the narrator. Their adventures are many and varied as they traverse the continent preying on self-confident Wall Street tycoons and smug Midwestern boosters. Peters' character particularly is shrewed and inventive, and acutely sensitive, one might add, to the media of the day in setting the proper context for promoting his scams; his partner, in the way of all narrators, is slightly obtuse yet admiring and throughout faithfully moral, even moralistic. For O. Henry's characters do not overpower and steal from their victims; instead they require the active collaboration, even the eager importuning of persons anxious to get in on a good deal.

The Americans at Reykjavik were, like the 'marks' in O. Henry's stories, a little arrogant, assuming that a President who had handled his adversary so effortlessly at Geneva did not require any extensive preparation for an encore; a little self-intoxicated, eagerly accepting the ruse that the USSR would, for *them*, make unprecedented concessions without requiring unprecedented retreats; but mainly, more than a little ignorant, never really understanding the strategic role of American nuclear weapons or bothering to study the history of their deployment, which distinguishes between the political purposes served by such weapons and their raw numbers. For if Reykjavik had never happened, and if this Appendix were the account of a hypothetical Russian proposal, no conscientious reader could have failed the test. It is precisely what this book has warned about: the abandonment of extended deterrence, the 'fifth discontinuity' – accelerating public alienation from deterrence – the failure to take the Soviet Union's security perspective seriously, the pursuit of arms control for its own sake, of numbers for their own sake, of legal documents in place of structural and mutual incentives.

But the current US Administration has not always been sensitive to the conditions I have abstracted as a 'theorem', though, one might say, the 'theorem' has been interested in it. For, like its predecessors, this Administration has attempted to restore extended deterrence through an innovation in strategy and that mixture of technologies (SDI, Stealth, the D5, the ALCM) and arms-control approaches that the strategy implied; yet unlike them, it has been unable to arrest the centrifugal dissolution of the political cohesion of the Alliance. In part this may have been the result of a failure to diagnose the fundamental forces driving this alienation. In any event, the Russian proposals can only have seemed inviting to minds utterly innocent of any sensibility alive to the theorem and its consequences, i.e. to the instability that would result from the American attempt to enhance Western security by giving a sanctuary to the superpowers. For such minds the Russian proposals must have seemed a wonderful breakthrough: low numbers, deep cuts, ongoing testing, the zero option, the eventual destruction of any nuclear weapon capable of reaching the United States.

Indeed the Russian proposals were so tailored to this Administration's particular approaches that it is astonishing that no senior official with long experience in these matters questioned the purpose of such offers. It recalls the famous scene in *Guys and Dolls* when the feckless protagonist attempts to persuade the wiser and cannier gambler to accept what appears to be a not unfavourable, even arbitary, wager. The gambler replies,

> When I was a young man about to go out into the world, my father says to me a very valuable thing. He says to me like this: 'Son,' the

> old guy says, 'I am sorry that I am not able to bankroll you to a very large start, but . . . I am going to stake you to some very valuable advice. One of these days in your travels a guy is going to come to you and show you a nice brand-new deck of cards on which the seal is not yet broken, and this guy is going to offer to bet you that he can make the Jack of Spades jump out of the deck and squirt cider in your ear. But, son, do not bet this man, for as sure as you stand there you are going to wind up with an earful of cider.'

Perhaps we will discover, when the full record is made public, that there were voices of caution at Reykjavik whose counsel was ignored in the decision to brief the press on Saturday night, accept the Russian proposals for across-the-board cuts, and so on. Perhaps some were aware that SDI contributes to European security precisely to the extent that it enables the US to credibly give nuclear protection against the Red Army and thus that to bargain away US nuclear weapons, even in exchange for an agreement that permitted SDI, would have catastrophic consequences for the West. At any rate, we would be well-served if, presented with such 'breath-taking' concessions again, we not simply think, 'Well, of course; that's us; we're lucky; we're not so bad at this!', and wonder instead whether our adversaries have abandoned their political goals, goals which rational proposals must serve and which are largely a product of history and geography and ideology and thus can be altered only with great difficulty.

Annotated Index

ABM 74–6, 80–1, 156
ABM Treaty 268–9
The agreement between the US and the USSR to limit anti-ballistic systems. Negotiations began in 1969 as part of SALT I. The agreement was signed and ratified in 1972. A 1974 Protocol limited deployment of antiballistic missile systems to one for each side.
Absolute Weapon, The, by Bernard Brodie 31
Acheson, Dean 12, 19
Adenauer, Konrad 211
Advanced inertial reference sphere guidance system 155–6
AIRS provides precise corrections of mid-course trajectory.
Air-launched cruise missile (ALCM) 148, 165, 171–5
A cruise missile designed to be launched from an aircraft.
AIRS (Advanced Inertial Reference Sphere) 155–6
ALCM compared with SLCM 176–78
Alford, Jonathan 220
Alternative Defence Commission 232–3
Andropov, Yuri 249
Ann Arbor Speech (McNamara) 48–52, 54, 55, 56
Antiballistic missile system – ABM 74–6, 80–1, 156
A system to counter strategic ballistic missiles or their elements in flight trajectory, including interceptor missiles, launchers, and ABM radars.
Antisatellite system-ASAT
A weapon for destroying satellites in orbit.
Area defence (BMD) 261, 263–9
Arms control 5, 68, 236–60
The control of nuclear and conventional arms proliferation and development. Includes any arrangement relying upon explicit or implicit international agreement, governing any aspect of the following: the numbers, types and performance characteristics of weapon systems (including their command and control, logistics support arrangements, and any related intelligence gathering mechanisms); and the numerical strength, organization, equipment, deployment or employment of the armed forces retained by the parties.
Aron, Raymond 220
Assured destruction 5, 51, 56–74, 77, 83–4, 86–9, 94, 101, 111, 140–1, 272, 276
The strategic doctrine of the US from 1963 to 1973, it depended upon the element of city withholding combined with flexible response at the theatre level.
Assured destruction capability
Condition in which secure forces are able to destroy with high confidence ⅓ to ½ of the population and ½ to ⅔ of the industrial capacity of the targeted nation.
Assured destruction mission 86, 88, 90, 94

Backfire bomber 169, 179
Soviet variable-wing supersonic bomber, which emerged in 1974. During the SALT II negotiations it was debated whether its unfuelled range classified it as intermediate or intercontinental.
Baldwin, Hanson 34
Ball, Desmond 89, 145–6, 147–8, 185–6, 188–9
Ball, George 52–3
Ballistic missile
Any missile which does not rely on aerodynamic surfaces to produce lift and consequently follows a ballistic trajectory when thrust is terminated.

Holst, Johan Jorgen 283–4
Holmes, Oliver Wendell, Jr 285–6
Homing Overlay Experiment
Consists of single missiles with multiple killer-vehicles protecting a large area by attacking weapons before they are widely dispersed.
Hotline 146
Howard, Sir Michael 117–20, 142, 220, 277–8
Hunt, Kenneth 227
Hydrogen Bomb 19, 25–6, 34
Nuclear weapon in which part of the explosive energy is obtained from nuclear fusion (or thermonuclear) reaction.

ICBM
Intercontinental ballistic missile.
ICBM vulnerability 81, 88, 123, 132, 156–65
Independent Commission on Disarmament and Security Issues 258
Inertial guidance system
A guidance system designed to project a missile to a predetermined point on the earth's surface by measures of acceleration.
INF (Intermediate range nuclear forces) 116–17, 238–40
Nuclear weapons designed for use within a specified theatre of operations such as Europe; typically range will be greater than 600 kilometres.
Intercontinental ballistic missile (ICBM)
A land-based, rocket-propelled vehicle capable of delivering a warhead to intercontinental ranges (ranges in excess of about 3000 nautical miles).
Intermediate Range Ballistic Missile (IRBM)
A ballistic missile with a range capability of from about 1500 to 3000 nautical miles. The US has no IRBMs; the SS-20 is a Soviet IRBM.

Jackson, Thomas 20
Jervis, Robert 201, 282
Johnson, Lyndon B. 68–9, 71–2, 75, 111, 140, 213

Kennan, George 28, 127
Kennedy, John F. 46–7, 52, 60, 68, 139–41, 201–2, 221
Kissinger, Henry 43, 77, 89, 105, 148, 220
Kohl, Helmut 256

Laird, Melvin 76, 168
Lambeth, Benjamin 134–5
LASER (light amplification by stimulated emission of radiation) 264–6
Launch-on-warning 62, 162–3
The launch of ballistic missiles when a missile attack against them is detected and before the attacking warheads reach their targets.
Launch weight
The weight of the fully loaded missile itself at the time of launch. Would include the aggregate post-boost vehicle (PBV) and the payload.
Lee, Robert E. 20
Lellouche, Pierre 101
Lethality 155, 158, 162
The ability to destroy a point target. Is defined as the MTE (equivalent megatonnage) to the two-thirds power divided by the square of the CEP.
Limited nuclear options (LNOS) 88–91, 93–6, 108, 126, 144–9
Limited nuclear war
A concept that assumes full-scale nuclear exchanges can be avoided, usually by targeting military and command centres rather than cities or by sanctuarizing an opponent's homeland.
Lisbon force structure goals 37, 221, 258
LNOS *see* Limited nuclear options
LOADS *see* Low altitude defence system
Long-range theatre nuclear force (LRTNF) 94–5, 103–4, 108, 116, 124–5, 128, 151–4, 169, 171–2, 175, 177, 179–80, 182, 246–8, 281, 284

Scowcroft Commission 164–5
SDI *see* Strategic Defense Initiative ('Star Wars')
Sea-launched cruise missile (SLCM) 151, 175–9
A cruise missile capable of being launched from a submerged or surfaced submarine or from a surface ship.
Second-strike capability 42, 53–6, 80, 130
The ability to retaliate, having absorbed a pre-emptive first strike, with a surviving force still capable of executing its assigned mission.
Self-deterrence 86, 136, 219
The unilateral refusal to initiate nuclear strikes for fear of retaliation.
Sherman, William T. 20
Shulman, Marshall 222
Shultz, George 131
Silo
Hardened underground facility for a fixed site ballistic missile and its crew, designed to provide pre-launch protection and to serve as a launch platform.
Single integrated operations plan (SIOP) 31, 40, 46–7, 49–50, 73, 76, 78, 89, 91–2, 94–6, 100, 133, 272, 277
The US contingency plan, promulgated in 1960, for strategic retaliatory strikes in the event of a nuclear war. It is a plan for the assignment of nuclear weapons to targets in a manner that corresponds to the strategic priority of the target and avoids duplication of attack.
SIOP *see* Single integrated operations plan
SLBM
Submarine-launched ballistic missile.
SLCM
Sea-launched cruise missile.
Slocombe, Walter 61, 78–9, 81
Smith, Gerard 127
Snow, C. P. 285
Soviet nuclear strategy 134–6
Spread of Nuclear Weapons, The, by Kenneth Waltz 195
Sputnik 44
SS-4, SS-5
Medium- and intermediate-range Soviet missiles, exempt from SALT limitations.
SS-11
Liquid-fuelled Soviet ICBM which, at the time of SALT I Accords, was the most numerous ballistic missile in the Soviet arsenal.
SS-13
First Soviet solid-fuelled ICBM. Roughly equivalent to US Minuteman I.
SS-16
Fourth-generation Soviet ICBM, solid-fuelled, capable of being deployed either in the mobile mode or in silos, with or without MIRV. Successor to the SS-13.
SS-17
Fourth-generation Soviet ICBM, follow-on to the SS-11, deployable with or without MIRV. Operational in 1974.
SS-18
Fourth-generation Soviet ICBM, follow-on to the SS-11, but with a throw weight four to five times greater; capable of being deployed with or without MIRV. Operational in 1974.
Stalin, Josef 20
SSBN
Nuclear-powered ballistic missile submarine.
SSM
Surface-to-surface missile.
Standing Consultative Commission
A permanent US–Soviet commission established in accordance with the provisions of the ABM Treaty. Its purpose is 'to promote the objectives and implementation of the provisions' of the Treaty and the Interim Agreement.
START
Strategic Arms Reduction Talks
Stimson, Henry 20–1
Strategic
Relates to a nation's military, economic and/or political power and its ability to control the

Thermonuclear weapons – *continued*
hydrogen isotopes with the accompanying release of energy. The high temperatures required are obtained by means of an atomic (fission) explosion.
Thorneycroft, Peter 197
Throw weight
Ballistic missile throw weight is the maximum useful weight which has been flight tested on the boost stages of the missile. The useful weight includes weight of re-entry vehicles, penetration aids, dispensing and release mechanisms, re-entry shrouds, buses, propulsion devices, covers and propellants (but not the final boost stages) which are present at the end of the boost phase.
TNF
Theatre nuclear forces.
TNW
Tactical nuclear weapons.
Total response (*see also* Graduated response) 8, 28, 53
TOTALITY 22
Treverton, Gregory 82–3, 85
TRIAD
The three-part US strategic retaliatory force, comprising land-based ICBMs, the bombers of the Strategic Air Command (SAC) and the SSBN/SLBM system.
Trident 151, 161, 188
A US nuclear-powered submarine and SLBM system of greater size and range than the Polaris/ Poseidon system.
TROJAN 23
Truman, Harry S. 21–2

Uncoupling (*see discussion of* 'Theorem') 105, 106, 164
A policy of altering the risk to the central homeland by attempts to confine nuclear strikes to the extended theatre.

Vandenberg, Hoyt 23
Verification
The process of determining the degrees to which parties to an agreement are complying with provisions of the agreement.
Vietnam 69–72
Viner, Jacob 31–3
VLF
Very low frequency.

Waltz, Kenneth 195, 198–9
War-fighting strategy 34, 135–8, 268
Warhead
That part of a missile, projectile or torpedo that contains the explosive intended to inflict damage.
Warsaw Pact offensive 222–5
Weinberg, Steven 217–8
Western European Union (WEU) 212
The political framework for FRG arms treaties.
Window of vulnerability 81, 86, 158
Period predicted between the early 1980s, when the USSR would possess the capability to destroy 90 per cent of all US ICBMs in a first strike, using only a slight fraction of her own ICBMs, and the mid-1980s when the US would acquire a similar capability with the deployment of the MX.
Wohlstetter, Albert 42, 47

Yield (nuclear)
The energy released in the detonation of a nuclear weapon, measured in terms of the kilotons (kt) or megatons (mt) of TNT required to produce the same energy release.

Zero option 124–7, 131, 242, 255
The US LRTNF arms control position announced by President Reagan on 18 November 1981, wherein the US offered to cancel its deployment of Pershing II and ground-launched cruise missiles if the Soviets would dismantle their SS-20, SS-4 and SS-5 missiles.